CHILE: LAND AND SOCIETY

AMERICAN GEOGRAPHICAL SOCIETY
RESEARCH SERIES NO. 19
Edited by J. K. WRIGHT

CHILE: LAND AND SOCIETY

BY

GEORGE McCUTCHEN McBRIDE

WITH A FOREWORD

BY

DON CARLOS DAVILA
Former President of the Republic of Chile

1971

OCTAGON BOOKS
New York

Reprinted 1971

by special arrangement with The American Geographical Society

OCTAGON BOOKS
A DIVISION OF FARRAR, STRAUS & GIROUX, INC.
19 Union Square West
New York, N. Y. 10003

LIBRARY OF CONGRESS CATALOG CARD NUMBER: 71-154618

ISBN-0-374-95429-1

Printed in U.S.A. by
NOBLE OFFSET PRINTERS, INC.
NEW YORK 3, N. Y.

TO
MY WIFE

CONTENTS

LIST OF ILLUSTRATIONS

FOREWORD

In " Chile: Land and Society," Dr. McBride has surpassed his classic study of the land systems of Mexico. To say that this is the most complete work that has thus far been written on the subject would be to give but little recognition to the penetrating analysis, scientific research, personal erudition, and sympathetic and novel approach of the author.

What has been said about a popular expounder of economic problems in the United States might well be applied to Dr. McBride in Chile: he plunges into the dark waters of a pond of murky economic information and comes out with a tiny brilliant fish that we can all see and admire.

It is obvious that Dr. McBride is exploring a subject in which he has more than a casual or academic interest. It is equally apparent that he has a deep and understanding affection for Chile and its people. He is thoroughly familiar with their problems, some of which he has seen come to a crisis, and his desire to aid in their solution is urgent and sincere. Although he unerringly notes our shortcomings, there are times when it seems as if he were reluctant to accept the essential reforms that must necessarily alter many of the absurd aspects of our social and economic structure, lest such reforms destroy some intangible quality of enchantment in our country.

His Tolstoian conception of Don Fulano and Zutano, of " Master and Man," as a factor that for a time has stabilized the country but in itself holds the seeds of weakness in our social and political position impels him to sound a note of warning rather than accept a pessimistic conclusion. Beneath the written word we divine a not-yet-lost confidence that our upper class will eventually meet the present situation with intelligence, decision, and equity.

There may be some difference of opinion regarding Dr. McBride's interpretation of the steps that in the last few years have led the nation to an almost inevitable readjustment. The gravity of the social problem depicted by the author with the greatest clarity and realism would seem to demand a less casual appreciation of the revolutionary phenomena. More than a mere assertion of the middle class or a reshifting of the political strata, these phenomena emphasize the birth of a national will that aspires to dominate the environment. Although such aspiration may not have been thus formulated, in it lies, from a socio-philosophical point of view, the significance of the recent revolutions and the fundamental distinction between these and the previous political movements. The latter, whatever their designation, always ended by adjusting themselves to the established environment rather than by imposing themselves on it. In this way all of them, no matter what lip service was paid to progress, served merely to consolidate the existing social order.

Don Fulano and Zutano symbolize the ethical and social constant, and every political regime has shown its incapacity to alter this relationship. The people are now striving toward a mature reformulation and redetermination of the social architecture, which cannot be contained in the frame of Master and Man. It is a process of organic reorganization that has assumed the form of insurrection against the environment.

Dr. McBride quotes a Chilean author to confirm his view that there is no country in the world where the monopoly of the land is more stringent than in Chile. This, he points out, is a Creole creation. A vast Spanish legislation strove to impede its growth during the Colonial period and actually succeeded in doing so. The qualification of a " unique agrarian society characterized by an extreme land monopoly and a sharply marked social stratification " is, curiously enough, more applicable to the republic than to the colony.

The abolition of the *encomiendas* that was decreed in Spain in 1720 was not made effective in Chile until 69 years after—in 1789, by Don Ambrosio O'Higgins. The *mayorazgos* (entailed estates) existed in our country until 1852, 40 years after they had been abolished in Spain and 30 years after they had been suppressed in Mexico.

"Here has existed," says Dr. McBride, "a New World country with a social organization of old Spain, a twentieth century people still preserving a feudal system." Yet, as was the case with feudalism in Europe, the Chilean social-economic formation served the purpose of cementing together the foundation upon which a real republic could be based. That republic is now in the making.

The trouble was not so much the existence of feudal land-owners who commanded and of the landless who obeyed. It was that the land system gave its " cast to the nation " and permeated the whole social structure of the country with the psychology of Master and Man. When Don Fulano became a mine operator or an industrialist, Zutano became a laborer. The same relation was transferred to the factory and the mine, but here was absent that sense of responsibility based on a personal paternal relationship that made possible an accepted dependency and a hierarchy on the great estates. The negative attitude of Master and Man, on which a feudality was originally based, was applied to the mass of the country. A negative economy, a negative education, and a negative political system were the result. The psychology of Master and Servant long survived the factors that created it.

The middle class, on which Dr. McBride bases his hopes for a reconstruction, came to life contaminated with the stigma of the *patrón* system. First it was inspired by a desire to emulate and blend with the aristocracy. It was a class in transit toward the privileged caste. Now the hardship resulting from the errors of economic policies is reducing it once again to the level of the working class. The author of this volume has seen something overlooked by the majority of foreign observers and critics, who have found the Chilean middle class confined, uprooted, a victim of doctrines and principles that it has blindly assimilated and that actually serve interests antagonistic to it.

From a purely economic point of view, it is doubtful whether a subdivision of the land would have been beneficial in the past. The author himself describes the illusory and often disturbing freedom of the class of small landowners who have emerged in the last few years. Only directive vigilance of the State can save the pathetic gains made during this period of transition.

The reader of Dr. McBride's book might well ask himself in surprise, where is that "republic" based on the equality of men? He would be even more amazed if he examined the mass of legislation formulating the principles of democratic equality for the Chilean nation. One is inclined to recall the poet who talked of the sense of frustration felt by the people in contemplating the magnitude of their rights in principle in contrast to the insignificance of their rights in fact. Zutano is the economic reality that mocks at political abstractions.

The chief accusation that could be made against the landowners and political bosses is not that they succeeded in perpetuating a system in which all the advantages were on their side, but that they made such poor use of it. With their power anything was feasible in the way of an ordained economy to give promise of wealth and welfare for the whole nation. They established an "order" but certainly not such as was deserved by the centuries of loyalty, humility, and self-denial of the Zutanos.

Dr. McBride views Chile as a curator views his museum. Each painting, each single piece of art is familiar to him. He knows how they were produced, what materials were employed, how the artist lived and worked, to what he aspired, and how the rich patrimony was built or plundered.

The fabulous wealth of Chile has been for the common people very much like those snow-capped mountains of which the author speaks. " Children," he says, " may live for years within sight of the eternal snow fields of the mountains, yet never know the sight or feel of snowflakes."

CARLOS DÁVILA

New York,
December, 1935.

PREFACE

This work is an attempt to analyze the agrarian problem in Chile. It is based on familiarity with Chilean social institutions gained during a former prolonged residence in that country and during an additional year recently spent there in gathering detailed data by interviews, visiting different kinds of rural properties, and carrying on investigations in libraries, archives, and government offices. Traveling from end to end of the republic, I was able to see the problem in its practical aspects in each of the several geographical sections. Observations carried out during these two periods of residence, separated as they were by an interval of twenty years, made it possible for me to note many changes that had taken place. Thus something of perspective, both in time and space, was secured.

Throughout the study the problem has been viewed sympathetically. It seems impossible for one to sojourn in Chile without being attracted by the natural charm of the land itself and by the people whose character is best described by their own word, *simpático*. I have felt also that I was studying the conditions in the midst of which many of my Chilean friends actually live—conditions that underlie the whole structure of their society and will, in large measure, determine the happiness and prosperity of their country. Most helpful assistance has been rendered by many Chileans, both in their official capacities and as individuals, and there has been a sustained effort to carry on the investigation in as friendly a manner as if the writer were himself a Chilean, yet with no sacrifice of frankness or loss of that perspective so difficult to obtain except as one looks on from the outside. Some years' study of similar problems in Mexico, Bolivia, and other countries of Latin America have offered a background for comparison and for an understanding of the relation between the systems of land tenure in a country and other phases of its social organization. It is hoped that this book may lead to a better understanding on the part of Americans and other foreigners of the structure of Chilean society and of the substantial transformation now taking place in Chilean life and institutions.

To the institutions that have contributed to make this research possible—the University of California, the American Geographical Society, the Social Science Research Council, the Institute of International Education, and the Carnegie Endowment for International Peace which appointed me its Visiting Professor in South America in 1929-1930—I take this opportunity of expressing my gratitude and appreciation; as also to Professor Francisco Montau of the Spanish Department in the University of California at Los Angeles for reading the manuscript and making invaluable suggestions. For the use of several photographs I am indebted to Dr. Robert S. Platt and the Pan American Union.

G. M. M.

University of California at Los Angeles.
November, 1935.

PART I

CENTRAL CHILE
THE LAND OF THE HACIENDA

CHAPTER I

MASTER AND MAN

I met them on the country road, Don Fulano and his
mozo (servant), the latter riding at a respectful distance
behind. Don Fulano was mounted on a tall, beautiful
dapple-gray mare, rather heavy for saddle purposes but
fitted for hard riding over rough roads. The mozo rode a
much smaller horse of the somewhat shaggy mountain type,
a real country nag but a good traveler withal. Both men
used Chilean saddles. Don Fulano's was made of handsome leather, and the seat was covered with the soft,
down-clad skin of a large mountain bird. His stirrups,
carved in the usual Chilean fashion out of heavy blocks
of wood, were ornamented with bands of iron and inlaid
silver. His bridle, too, with reins and headstall of neatly
braided rawhide, bore elaborate silver ornaments about
the bit and the brow band. Large-roweled spurs were worn
by both the riders. The mozo's accoutrement was simple,
a thick sheepskin covering the uncomfortable wooden
frame of his saddle, while bridle and riding whip were
made of rough-tanned leather thongs. They had been
riding for some hours when I saw them, having left
in the early morning the farm to which we were going.
Don Fulano had pushed back his flat-brimmed hat and
had thrown the blanket-like poncho, which every Chilean
horseman wears in the country, back over his shoulder
to allow his arm more freedom and to give him the benefit
of the fresh midmorning air. This revealed that he was
well clad in up-to-date riding habit with puttees and boots
carefully polished. His strong figure, sitting firmly but
gracefully on his mount and set off with the handsome
character of his trappings and his horse, made a strikingly

attractive picture of virile, prosperous, commanding manhood (Fig. 1).

The appearance of his riding companion was in sharp contrast. Not in rags by any means, but cheaply clad underneath his coarsely woven poncho, with ill-fitting trousers, the ungainly short jacket used by the men of his kind on Chilean farms, a dilapidated felt hat and well-worn shoes, the mozo could be seen at once to belong in a different class. He was well-built and muscular, though of distinctly smaller stature than Don Fulano, and his features seemed somewhat less European in cast, though both men gave evidence of a strain of Araucanian blood from some remote ancestor. The mozo waited in silence and at a little distance, allowing his horse to nibble at the bushes beside the road while Don Fulano greeted us. Then he dismounted and, hat in hand, brought over the beautifully ornamented saddlebags which he had been carrying behind his saddle, holding them up while his *patrón* stowed away the letter of introduction that we had presented. Furthermore, in the same deferential manner and with many repetitions of " Sí, sí, Señor," he corroborated his master's detailed orders for preparations to be made for our reception on the farm.

Don Fulano expressed his regrets at not being able to welcome us personally at his house, assuring us that only an unexpected matter of urgent business had called him to the city for the day. Then, with reiteration of his pleasure and that of his family at the prospect of several days' visit with an old friend of his friends, a promise to see us before night of the following day, and an evidently sincere " Hasta lueguito " (Hoping to see you very soon indeed), he touched spur to his handsome mount as we started on our way. Glancing back I saw the mozo fall into position behind his master as the two rode leisurely along between the lines of Lombardy poplars that almost met over the country road.

Fig. 1—An *hacendado* and his *mozo*. (Courtesy of the Pan American Union.)

FIG. 2

FIG. 3

FIG. 4

FIG. 2—An hacienda owner's house near Santiago.
FIG. 3—*Inquilinos'* houses near Santiago. (Courtesy of George T. Hastings.)
FIG. 4—Central Valley, near Santiago, with Andes in the background.

THE MOZO

I saw them a day later on the farm (Fig. 2). True to his word, Don Fulano had ridden back the 25 miles from town, arriving shortly after noon. He was now, in mid-afternoon, seated at a desk in his office, supervising plans for the approaching harvest. The mozo, too (whose name we now learned was Zutano), having disposed of a late *almuerzo* (eleven o'clock breakfast) and lounged about for a half hour of rest from his strenuous ride, was standing by the door, again with his hat in his hand, listening to the directions being given the foremen of the farm by the German administrator; getting his own instructions as to when the troop of half-wild horses should be brought down from the summer mountain pastures and be ready to trample out the grain on the threshing floor; occasionally also offering suggestions as to which field was ripest or how many men could be spared from among the stock hands for the harvest period (Fig. 3). He was 10 years older than his patrón, and during the latter's childhood had frequently acted in the capacity of guardian and companion of the little fellow who had now grown into proprietorship of the family estate. Zutano's father and grandfather had been born on this farm. His mother's family, too, had lived on a distant part of the same property for as many generations as they could recall. As a consequence they all felt an interest in the work to be done out of all proportion to the meager compensation they derived from it. It seemed a part of their lives and they a part of it, though, if they stopped to consider, they knew that not a foot of its land belonged to them nor were they entitled to any share of the proceeds of the place. This seemed to make little difference to them, however, for to all intents and purposes they belonged to the farm and it to them quite as fully as was the case with the patrón's own family. With a zeal bred of this long relationship and with a freedom that was surprising to the foreign visitors, yet always with a deferential manner, Zutano and many of his fellow workmen as well, took part in the direction of the *hacienda* (estate).

On this particular occasion little was required except general instructions. Don Fulano had been away from the farm most of the year, and its management had been left largely in the hands of the *administrador* and the various division foremen. When these details had been attended to the visitors were reminded that it was time for afternoon tea.

THE MASTER'S FAMILY

We followed the master of the house into the dining room, the administrator accompanying us, while the workmen answered the call of the farm bell to receive their rations of *harina tostada* (ground roasted wheat) and a biscuit of hard Chilean bread. Expecting a simple cup of tea served in the plain English fashion, we found instead a long table spread with a great variety of fruits, cakes, native cheeses, melons, and preserves, while several kinds of Chilean drinks were offered us. The Señora, Don Fulano's gracious wife, presided; and his family of eight children, ranging in age from five to twenty years, gathered quietly at their places. A French governess completed the group. Several maids assisted the Señora or looked after the smaller children. The conversation about the table was carried on in three languages, while German, too, was attempted occasionally in playful fashion by some of the family in light talk with the administrator. Refined courtesy prevailed throughout the meal, except when one or two of the younger children found it necessary to raise their voices in command when a servant demurred at complying with all their wishes.

A Tour of the Master's Estate

Meanwhile Zutano had eaten his simple food and was busy getting horses ready for the ride we had been promised over a near-by section of the farm. We found him waiting for us under the shade of a spreading horse chestnut tree in the yard, the half dozen horses tied by their bridles to rings fastened overhead to the lowest branches of the tree. Don Fulano mounted a lithe-limbed young stallion of evident Arabian extraction and led us through a labyrinth of barns, corrals, silos, and sheds, then through a young orchard of pear trees which he showed us with great pride, along a eucalyptus-lined farm road for several miles, then out through fields of alfalfa where scores of beef cattle were browsing, and at last to the brow of a hill that gave a view over many square miles of the estate. We went through many gates, at each of which Zutano came riding up from behind to open the gate and hold it until we had passed. On one occasion Don Fulano's fourteen-year-old son courteously started to perform this service but was rather sharply told to let the mozo do it. At times Don Fulano would half turn in his saddle and call back some query regarding the farm, the usual answer being " Sí, sí, Señor." On reaching the trail that led up to our point of vantage, Zutano had spurred ahead to take the lead, picking the best way, breaking off an occasional obtruding branch, or getting down to remove a fallen bush or a stone from the path. When we finally halted at a place too steep for even the sure-footed horses we rode, he dismounted, threw his bridle reins to the ground cowboy fashion, and letting his own animal stand, hurried back to hold ours while we climbed to the rock-capped top of the hill on foot. Our host had brought a rifle along, hoping to get a shot at some foxes that had been raiding the poultry yards, but unfortunately this weapon had been entrusted to the mozo to carry on the way up and two young foxes made good their escape before it could be brought up from the rear.

On the way back, as we rode along a semipublic road that crossed the farm, we passed the tenants' houses which were strung like beads on each side of the highway. At one of them Don Fulano stopped, explaining that the small son of the mozo who accompanied us had a badly broken arm which he thought might need other attention than that already given by the *curandero* (the untrained practitioner found among the tenants on most of the Chilean farms). One of our party was a physician and willingly consented to see what more might be required. Zutano at once became host. Calling to a ragged youth who chanced to be loitering in the road and telling him to hold our horses, he led the way through a gap in the briar hedge into his yard. He placed some homemade, rustic chairs for us on the clean-swept earth under a great grape arbor in front of his door, while Don Fulano, hardly waiting to be conducted by the apologetic mother, stooped somewhat and entered the dark interior of the lowly thatched hut. With a friendly greeting to the lad and a half-scolding admonition not to be such a daredevil in the future, he looked over the broken arm himself and asked the doctor to see if it was properly adjusted. Finding that the bone was skillfully set, though lacking much in the cleanliness of its bandages, he gave a few instructions to the parents, glanced about the premises as if to see that all was as it should be, and led the way to the street again.

The Mozo's Life History

Having my interest awakened in Master and Man, I gathered what data I could regarding the life history of each. Don Fulano and Zutano were both born on this farm. The latter had never lived elsewhere; in fact, had seldom been away from his home place for more than a day or two at a time. He had begun his duties as son of an *inquilino* (tenant) when about seven years old, doing such chores as a boy might about the house of the patrón. When he had reached the age of ten he was spending most of his time in care of the sheep belonging to the estate, going with them every day to the near-by foothills and spending several months each summer with other herdsmen tending the flocks that were kept during that season on the high Alpine meadows at the foot of the retreating snowline. He had thus learned to fight off the great condor when it frequently circled down out of the sky in attempts to carry off lambs or even full-grown ewes. On a few occasions he had been required to face a puma and frighten it away from the sheep corrals at night. He had learned to ride well, to know every trail through mountain and valley, to know where the best pasture could be found, to understand the secrets of the mountain weather and forecast the coming storm, to know the virtues of each plant and shrub and tree and the uses to which it could be put. This was his principal education. When he was a boy, there had been no school upon the estate and the nearest village was miles away. So he grew to manhood with no opportunity (and little need, perhaps) to learn to read and write. He was thus illiterate though far from ignorant, a man thoroughly versed in the lore of his limited habitat but knowing little beyond the bounds of the estate on which he lived. His experience in civic affairs consisted of but two incidents. Once he had been sent into town with most of the other tenants of the estate to vote on a measure that affected the property. He had for this occasion painstakingly learned to write his name and had put his signature where told on a sheet of paper. A few years later he had relearned to make his signature in order to earn a few pesos which a candidate for municipal election had offered. Such had been the life of his father, his grandfather, and of as many generations as

could be remembered. None of them had known any
other condition than that of a hereditary tenantry.

THE MASTER'S CAREER

Don Fulano began his career by learning to command.
Almost before he could walk or talk he had learned that
he could impose his will on most of the circle around him
Servants attended him from dawn until night. His parents
he learned to respect and love, and among his large family
of brothers and sisters he found that he met his peers.
Outside of this group his wish was usually law. He had no
set tasks that he must do; every labor was done for him;
he moved a small king in his small world. This was the
case whether on the farm or in the city home where the
greater part of each year was spent. The situation changed
somewhat when at an early age he was put into a private
school in the city. A servant accompanied him to the
school in the morning and was waiting for him at the end
of the day, even carrying his books the few blocks between
school and home. Inside the school, however, he found
himself in a world he could not entirely command. This
brought him some grief and several sharp clashes with
teachers (mostly priests) and fellow pupils until he gradually discovered how far his will could be imposed. Until he
was nearly twenty years of age, most of his time had been
spent in school, first under a governess in their city home,
then in the priests' school, later in the capital of his country
where also a family residence was maintained, and at last
in two years of study in France. Most of his education had
been in letters and arts. He had never studied agriculture
nor anything in the line of administration. During the
period of schooling, vacations had been spent on the farm
where, in association with his father, he had become familiar with some of the problems of its management. He
had never done any manual work. His hands had never
turned a shovelful of earth, nor had he followed a plow, nor

milked a cow, nor yoked a team of oxen. He had hardly learned to saddle and bridle his own horse without the assistance of a mozo. His training and experience had fitted him only to direct, to command. Even his ability in this was based on a meager knowledge of practical details. After his education was completed he had begun a desultory practice of law that very soon brought him into political life. Here the influence of family and friends together with the prestige of his wealth had led to rapid advance. He had occupied many official positions, most of them under the national government. He had served as prefect of his province, as deputy in Congress, and was now senator for one of the neighboring provinces in which his family was very influential. On one occasion he had been a member of an international commission appointed to settle a conflict about a boundary line. This had taken him to Europe for several years' stay while he was searching the archives there for documents bearing on the affair. His family had accompanied him, as well as a small retinue of secretaries and servants. His wife was the daughter of a distant relative. Through her he had come into possession of a second estate not many miles from his home. He tried to be at one of these estates, or both, at planting time and harvest; but even this was not always possible, and the farms were left largely in the hands of the administrators. Don Fulano was thus a city dweller rather than a country resident, a gentleman land owner rather than a farmer. This had been the character of his father before him and of each generation back nearly four hundred years to the *conquistador* from whom they proudly traced their descent and from whose grant of land from the Spanish crown their estate had been formed.

THE TWO CLASSES OF CHILEAN SOCIETY

These two characters, Don Fulano and his mozo, are composite figures to which I have given fictitious names.

The description of them is made up from actual observations of many individuals recorded during several years' residence in Chile. The form was suggested by Tolstoy's well-known little story of Russian life in former days, and the title of this chapter is borrowed from that story. These men represent the two sharply differentiated classes into which Chilean society has been divided for several centuries. Until recent years there was no other class. There was a landholding aristocracy, well educated, far-traveled, highly cultured, in full control of the national life; and, quite apart from them, a lower class, often spoken of with mixed disdain and affection as the " rotos " (ragged ones), constituting the fixed tenantry of the rural estates. This distinction, clearly an agrarian one in its origin, was carried into the social structure of the entire people. It gave its cast to the nation. There were few families in the whole country that did not find their station in life determined by this classification. Even those who had no direct relation to rural affairs were still grouped in this fashion. Whatever might be a man's occupation or wherever he might live, he belonged to one or the other of these two classes. He was either Master or Man. The laboring population was descended from and belonged to the tenant group. Those who engaged in commercial pursuits (except foreigners or persons of unusual character), those who occupied the lowest positions in public affairs, even some of those in professional ranks, also came out of and were thought of as still belonging to the lower class. The landholding gentry seldom engaged in commerce or industry. Its members did, however, control the banking systems and occupied the higher positions in some of the large-scale mining and business enterprises. From this class also were recruited most of those who entered the learned professions. The clergy, the university professors, the literary lights, the artists, the lawyers, the medical men, the politicians and statesmen were mostly drawn from this group. It was a leisure class whose members entered such careers rather as dilettantes than from the necessity of earning a livelihood.

The distinction between these two classes was not merely one of wealth. Some of the lower order, through unusual success in business, attained large fortunes. They usually found themselves still outside the ruling class. On the other hand, there were many members of the old aristocratic families whom misfortune had left in penury. They nevertheless retained their place in the upper class, often attaching themselves to the more fortunate households among their relatives or capitalizing their family connection to obtain some sinecure in public office. Rarely did they sink so low as to engage in the ordinary pursuits of the lower stratum of society.

Nor was the differentiation made wholly on the basis of race. Both classes were derived from the mixture of Spanish and Araucanian blood. Both boasted such descent. Individuals in each class showed marked similarity to one or the other race. The tenants generally were descended more directly from the Indians who had occupied the country before the Conquest, while many of the gentry gave evidence of being more nearly pure European in extraction. But all were Chileans, speaking one language and claiming no marked difference of race.

Thus there has existed in Chile a social structure built on a distinctly agrarian basis, and the nation's entire life has been molded by relation to the land. The landowner has commanded, a landless people has obeyed. A man's status has been determined by whether or not he owned an hacienda or, at least, by whether he belonged to a landholding family. Position in life, occupation, opportunity depended mainly on this. Possession of ability, attainment in education, achievement in any line, even acquisition of wealth has meant less than being born into a circle that monopolized the land resources of the nation. *El privilegio de la cuna* (the cradle, or birthright, privilege) was what counted. Here has existed a New World country with the social organization of old Spain; a twentieth-century people still preserving a feudal society; a republic based on the equality of man, yet with a blue-blood aristocracy and a servile class as distinctly separated as in any of the monarchies of the Old World. Throughout Chile's history this situation has existed. It is this social heritage that forms the background for the present-day problems of the Chilean people. To analyze this agrarian background and its influence in Chilean life is the purpose of the present study.

CHAPTER II

AGRICULTURAL CHILE

Chile is essentially an agricultural country. The world knows her best for her mineral resources, nitrate and copper in particular; but it is not in exploiting these that most of her population is employed. Relatively few of the Chilean people have ever seen those sources of national income, the *salitreras* (nitrate beds) of the northern desert and the mines hidden deep in the Andean canyons, nor have they seen the great forests that constitute the potential wealth of the south. Chile's people live on the soil. Her life is agricultural to the core. Her government has always been that of farm owners. She has never had a president, I think, who did not have a farm and spend a part of his time on it. Her Congress is made up chiefly of rich landlords. Social life is dominated by families whose proudest possession is the ancestral estate. All the élite have rural properties. The man is poor indeed who does not own at least a *chacra* (small farm). Many even of her urban dwellers—forty-six per cent of the total inhabitants—retain close relations with the farm, as owners, renters, tenants, or hired laborers. The typical Chilean of the poorer classes is a *huaso,* a country fellow accustomed to the hard life of the field. Chile's agricultural products have not figured conspicuously in her exports, but neither has she had to buy from abroad. Her farms have fed her people and made her economically independent for most of the necessities of life. The ancestors of the present Chileans had tilled the fields of Spain; coming to America they established themselves in fruitful valleys between the Andes and the sea; and during the four centuries of their life in the New World they have carried on agriculture, making that industry the basis of their entire social order.

Agricultural Areas of Chile

Yet Chile's agricultural area is decidedly limited. It lies almost wholly in the central section of the country. In 1925 her four northernmost provinces, with a total area of 266,935 square kilometers (103,064 square miles), contained only the following productive farm lands: [1]

Cropped lands	43.42 square kilometers
Artificial pasture	156.21 " "
Arboriculture	67.23 " "
Total	266.86 " "

Of this third of the republic just one-tenth of one per cent was used for agricultural purposes. The rest was desert with no water supply in sight with which to reclaim any appreciable part of it. In the three administrative divisions of the far south (Magallanes, Chiloé, and Llanquihue),[2] with a total area of 276,956 square kilometers, only the following lands were being used agriculturally:

Cropped lands	1,202 square kilometers
Artificial pasture	1,998 " "
Arboriculture	24 " "
Total	3,224 " "

Thus this second third of the national territory has so far brought into agricultural use but one per cent of its area. This will be increased; but most of the great forests that are gradually yielding to the ax and fire occupy land,

---

[1] Chile: *Sinopsis Estadística*. (Bibliographical references in the footnotes of the present work are for the most part given in abbreviated form, the titles of Chilean government publications being introduced with the word " Chile." For complete references consult the Bibliography at the end of the book.) The figures in the *Sinopsis Estadística* of course refer to the territorial divisions existing before 1928.

[2] These divisions were reorganized by a decree of 1927 as Territorio de Magallanes, Territorio de Aysén, and the Province of Chiloé (see Rudolph: New Territorial Divisions, 1929, pp. 61-77). Aysén and Magallanes were given the formal status of provinces in 1929 (Chile: División territorial de la República de Chile, 1929).

particularly south of Chiloé, that is too rough or too bleak in climate to be fit for successful farming. Two-thirds of her territory being thus of almost negligible value for agriculture, it is upon the remaining third that the country depends. This region is almost wholly agricultural.

DOMINANCE OF CENTRAL CHILE

The term Chile, unless otherwise defined, means invariably the central section of the country. The northern desert region is not Chile proper; neither is the great forested territory of the far south. Any consideration of the country, from the standpoint of its history, its human geography, or its present-day problems, takes into account primarily if not exclusively the remaining third of its territory—what is usually spoken of as central Chile. Even the casual visitor recognizes that he has not known the real Chile until he has seen the lovely rural landscapes of the Central Valley. Rich fields of alfalfa reflecting the sun in their abundant irrigation water; fat cattle wading deep in green pastures; level wheat and barley fields fringed with long rows of Lombardy poplar, weeping willow, or eucalyptus trees; and occasional glimpses of orchard and

FIG. 5—Map of Chile showing provinces. Scale, 1 : 34,000,000.

vineyard or palatial
country homes and
grounds—these, all
laid close to the
foot of the snow-
crowned Andes,
form the visitor's
picture of Chile as
she is.

The name " Chi-
le " was first ap-
plied by the Span-
iards to the Acon-
cagua Valley alone,
the last and most
important of the
transverse valleys
as one comes from
the north. The term
apparently had been
used with this limi-
tation by the Inca
invaders who had
conquered the re-
gion and had estab-
lished a loose con-
trol over it. When
the Spaniards ar-
rived they soon
came to apply the
same name, by ex-

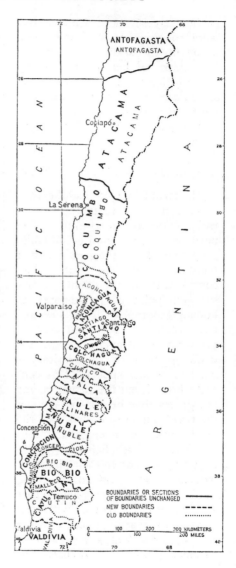

Fig. 6 (in two parts)—
Map of Chile showing the
province boundaries before
and after the decree of
Dec. 30, 1927. Scale, 1:
13,000,000.

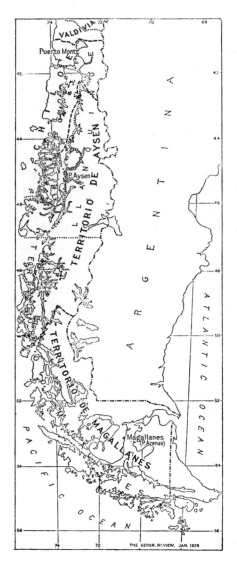

THE GEOGR. REVIEW, JAN. 1929

tension, to the country that lay immediately south, and even to include the other irrigated valley oases in the southern part of the desert of Atacama through which they had passed on their way from Peru. It is this central section of the country particularly from Coquimbo (30° S.) to Concepción (37° S.) that constitutes the real Chile. Here live more than three-fourths of the total population; here are located nineteen of the twenty-six cities of more than 10,000 people; in this region are practically all the farms of the country. Even the natural resources of the north and south are owned in central Chile; here is centered the political, social, educational, financial, and ecclesiastical control of the nation (Fig. 8). Here the laws are made and the policy of the nation determined. The rest of the country sends its tribute of taxes to central Chile and to its hub, Santiago. This region and this city in turn dominate the rest of the land. The two great universities of the nation are located in Santiago, while two others, recently founded, are in Valparaíso and in Concepción. Central Chile also contains the leading normal school, the school of mines, the school of medicine, a well equipped school of mechanic arts, and the best institutions of secondary instruction. Elsewhere there are no such institutions, and education in general is far less advanced. In matters of church, as in matters of school, central Chile dominates. The archbishop of the country has his seat in Santiago and the Papal Nuncio his official residence there. So, too, in financial affairs; the concerns, industrial and commercial, that operate in other parts of the nation, as far south as Tierra del Fuego and as far north as Arica, in most cases have their headquarters in Santiago or Valparaíso. Even the foreign firms follow the same arrangement. Furthermore, the finances of nearly all such enterprises, in so far as they are Chilean, are drawn from capitalists whose home is in central Chile. Politically the same pre-eminence is maintained. Chile is what is known in Latin America as a unitary, in contrast to a federal, republic, and authority centers in and emanates from the national capital. Governors of all the provinces are appointed by the president and are responsible to him. There are no provincial legislatures. The national Congress, meeting at Santiago, legislates for the entire nation. The country has a national police under orders from the president. So far does one section dominate the life of the nation. The seat of government could not possibly be elsewhere than in central Chile—in fact, elsewhere than in Santiago. This is the dominant district. This *is* Chile.

Northern and Southern Chile

The reasons underlying this extreme centralization in the life of the nation are mainly geographic. The northern section is not only one of the most completely desert regions of the world but is, in addition, so devoid of water that irrigation can be carried on only in a few extremely limited districts. North of Coquimbo, where the desert may be said to begin, there is no place with an annual rainfall of more than five inches (127 millimeters), while over most of the area many years go by without even a trace of rain. This aridity prevails on the slopes of the Andes as well as on the lowlands, so that there are few streams that can be used to make up for the lack of precipitation. Were it not for exceedingly rich mineral deposits the region would be almost uninhabited. In spite of the nitrate wealth of these provinces and large deposits of copper and other metals, the total population of the northernmost three provinces was, in 1930, but 353,104, an average of 1.4 persons to the square kilometer (3.6 to the square mile).[3] Moreover, a

[3] Chile: *X Censo de la Población* (1930), Vol. 1, 1931, pp. 50-51.

Fig. 7—Map of annual rainfall of Chile. Key: stipple, less than 250 mm.; horizontal ruling, 250-1000 mm.; diagonal ruling, 1000-2000 mm.; black, over 2000 mm. Scale, 1: 36,000,000. (Based on W. Knoche's map, 1: 5,000,000, *Zeitschr. Gesell. für Erdkunde zu Berlin*, 1929, No. 5-6.)

large part of these are more or less temporary dwellers
in the north, recruited for short terms of service from
the farms and towns of central Chile or from the populous
neighboring highlands of Bolivia. Such a combination of
conditions makes northern Chile a mere appendage of the
well-populated regions of the center, dependent upon these
latter in all departments of its life and activities.

Southern Chile is, in most respects, of even less significance. The islands, peninsulas, and mountain ranges
that make up the southern third of the republic are so
heavily forested, so lacking in arable land, and so inhospita-
ble climatically to a people from the mild Mediterranean
regions of Europe, that, in spite of the extensive area
in the large provinces of Magallanes, Aysén, and Chiloé,
this whole district contains a total of only 231,123 inhabitants. Southern Chile has little more weight in national
affairs than has Alaska in the United States or Baja California in Mexico.

In any consideration of important problems of the nation
these two outlying regions may be largely disregarded.
This is particularly true in reference to such matters as
agriculture and systems of land tenure. The irrigated valleys of the north have problems of their own growing out
of the peculiar conditions that exist there, scarcity of water
underlying most of their agrarian difficulties. The south,
in contrast, has too much rainfall. An excess of precipitation makes possible the extensive forests which protected
the Araucanian in his resistance to white intrusion and
impeded the cultivation of the lands from which the Indian
had been driven. Frequent summer rains made difficult the
growing of wheat and barley, without which the men of
Mediterranean descent were handicapped in their efforts
to colonize these southern lands. The south of Chile thus
remained a frontier for more than three centuries after
central Chile was occupied, with frontier conditions prevailing even in such fundamental matters as the acquisition and holding of land.

CENTRAL CHILE: TOPOGRAPHY AND AGRICULTURAL LAND

Central Chile, though important, is a small region. The serious beginning of the desert north of Coquimbo marks its bounds in that direction; the edge of the original Araucanian forest, roughly paralleling the Bío-Bío River, is its natural southern limit. This gives it a length of some eight hundred kilometers (500 miles). Its western border is, of course, the sea, while on the east the almost insurmountable wall of the Andes shuts it off from the rest of the continent. The width of this narrow strip of land is nowhere more than 240 kilometers, its average about 200. The entire area of central Chile does not exceed some 170,000 square kilometers (65,000 square miles). In size it therefore is about as large as the state of Nebraska, or a little smaller than England and Scotland.

Much of this relatively small territory is unsuited for human occupation. The broad chain of the Andes, measuring some fifty miles up its western slope, is almost entirely uninhabited, most of the area being far too rugged and high for agriculture or stock raising. The Coast Range, occupying a band parallel to the sea which maintains an average breadth of some twenty miles, offers the well-rounded contours of old mountains; but the slopes are dry except during a few months of winter, and there is little water available for irrigation. Much of this highland area also is waste land. These two mountain ranges occupy about half the long, narrow belt of central Chile. Furthermore there is no continuous coastal plain, the hills descending at most points abruptly to the shore. The only coastal lowlands occur at the mouths of rivers and at a few points where uplift has left marine terraces lying at the base of the Coast Range.

Between the two ranges of mountains there lies the long central "valley," a structural trough deeply filled with alluvial materials and offering a continuous, nearly level plain from Santiago to Puerto Montt. Within this depression lies most of the good farming land of the country. Even this area, however, is decidedly restricted. Spurs

Fig. 8—Locational map of part of central Chile. 1 : 3,000,000. This map with Fig. 5 and the maps in Chapters XI and XV indicate the locations of towns and other geographical features mentioned in the text.

from the Andes and the Coast Range protrude into it, at some points almost meeting. These intrusions of the hills from both sides have greatly reduced the agricultural land. The extent to which mountains or hilly terrain have restricted the tillable area in central Chile is indicated by figures for several of the provinces of that region. Take, for example, the well-developed Province of Santiago. Out of an area of 15,260 square kilometers (5,892 square miles) the land under cultivation in 1925 was as follows:

	Square kilometers
Cropped land	590
Artificial pasture..	502
Arboriculture	83
Total	1,175

This total is a little less than eight per cent of its surface. The Province of Colchagua

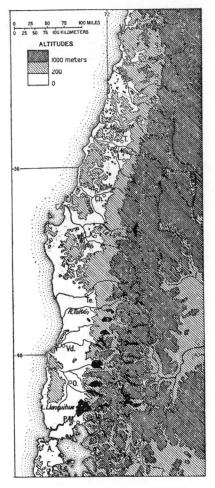

Fig. 9—Map of Chile from the Aconcagua Valley to the island of Chiloé, showing the principal relief features (Andes, Central Valley, and Coast Range) and the main rivers. Scale, 1: 9,000,000.

(Fig. 10), offering perhaps the most complete utilization of available agricultural land in the country, shows similar conditions. Of an area of 9,973 square kilometers (3,850 square miles) only the following were devoted to farming in 1925:

	Square kilometers
Cropped land	750
Artificial pasture	305
Arboriculture	55
Total	1,110

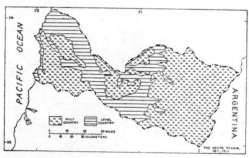

FIG. 10—Sketch map of the Province of Colchagua (before the territorial changes of 1927) showing proportion of level (ruled) and hilly country. Scale, 1:3,300,000. Only about one-ninth of its surface is under cultivation.

This is a little more than eleven per cent of its area. The Province of Talca shows eight per cent, and Aconcagua only four.[4] These examples are typical of central Chile. A few of the streams that cross this region from east to west extend the tillable area in slender lines up the old river terraces that border their mountain valleys and also offer flood plains, narrow but fertile, where they cut through the Coast Range to the sea. The valley of the Aconcagua, for example, shows a long productive strip of land a few miles wide, containing some of the finest agricultural land of the country; beyond that to the north the territory is

[4] Chile: *Sinopsis Estadística.*

so interrupted by offshoots of the Andes that it is largely a hill country, and the transverse streams contain very limited districts of alluvial deposits along their middle or lower courses.

This central district has been occupied by whites for nearly four hundred years, and it represents the most thickly populated part of the country. Some allowance must be made for the agrarian system, which has not brought all lands into the most intensive use; but there is little tillable area in the central provinces that is not included in the figures given. There are large hilly areas bearing native grass that are used for pasture; but most of such grasslands are so dry or so mountainous, or both, that there is little prospect of their ever being cultivated, and hence little reason to consider them as a part of agricultural Chile.

Central Chile: Soils and Climate

Though central Chile has a limited area of agricultural land, it has exceptionally fertile, well-mixed soil (Fig. 4). The deep deposits of silt, sand, gravel, and boulders brought by the numerous streams from the Andes into the Central Valley constitute a series of alluvial fans spread out at the western foot of the mountains. This piedmont slope contains coarse, poorly sorted material along its upper margin, but within a few miles' distance from the mountains these coarse deposits are covered with a surface layer of rich, dark soil a meter or so in thickness. Toward the center of the valley the underlying gravel is finer and is buried many feet deep under accumulated silt and humus. The deposits become of still finer texture along the western border; in fact, the material here is so small-grained as to be almost impermeable to water. In this section several extensive flats hold the surface water so completely that they become wide, shallow lakes during periods of heavy rain and dry wastes throughout the rest of the year. The central belt of deep but well-drained soil and the surface of the lower and middle piedmont fans afford the best farming land. Underneath this whole valley floor the alluvial fill is so deep as to be virtually inexhaustible in its fertility. Borings near Santiago show it to reach a depth of more than three hundred feet (*ca.* 90 meters). The angle of hillsides half buried in this deposit suggests an even greater depth. Irrigation with muddy water adds to the fertility. Though farmed for several centuries, these lands show little evidence of depletion and seldom require artificial fertilizers.

Climatically central Chile is well suited to agriculture— at least to the type of agriculture brought by the Spaniards. From the climatic point of view Chile merits better than Mexico the title " New Spain." Her position in latitude. and on the west coast has given her a well marked Mediterranean type of climate strikingly like that of Italy, Greece, Palestine, or the southern part of the Iberian Peninsula. Winter rains, a long, dry summer, and the evenly mild temperatures that characterize this region have made the Spanish people feel quite at home and have permitted the introduction of Mediterranean agriculture with little need for adaptation. Grains and fruits from old Spain have found a favorable habitat in this new land. As in Palestine and other parts of the Mediterranean region every man may sit " under his vine and under his fig tree." Wheat, barley, alfalfa, olives, grapes, figs, and citrus fruit brought from southern Europe have found conditions little different from those of their native clime, save for a somewhat greater frequency of frost, particularly near the snow-covered Andes. Snow seldom falls in the Central Valley, either about Santiago or as far south as Concepción. The higher Andes are deeply blanketed throughout the winter, and the foothills are whitened to their base after every winter rain; but only rarely does

even a light snowfall occur on the valley floor. Children
may live for years within sight of the eternal snowfields
of the mountains yet never know the sight or feel of
snowflakes. A comparison of climatic data from Gibraltar
on the coast of the Iberian Peninsula and Valparaíso on
the coast of central Chile brings out the similarity of
conditions.

CLIMATIC DATA BY SEASONS [5]

Gibraltar: lat. 36° 6' N.; elevation 15 meters.
Valparaíso: lat. 33° 11' S.; elevation 41 meters.

Average Temperatures for the Three Coolest Months
Gibraltar: (December, January, February)   Average
                                  12.6..12.2..12.8; 12.5 C.(54.5 F.)
Valparaíso: (June, July, August) 11.6..11.5..11.7; 11.6 C.(52.9 F.)

Average Temperatures for the Three Warmest Months
Gibraltar: (July, August, September)
                                  23.3..23.5..21.7; 22.8 C.(73.0 F.)
Valparaíso: (December, January, February)
                                  17.2..17.4..17.5; 17.4 C.(63.3 F.)

Average Precipitation During the Five Wettest Months
Gibraltar: (November, December, January,
                   February, March) 114..154..108..87..113 mm.
     Total winter rain, 576 mm.(22.7 in.)
Valparaíso: (May, June, July, August, September)
                                  116..162..169..99..17 mm.
     Total winter rain, 563 mm.(22.2 in.)

Average Precipitation During the Three Driest Months
Gibraltar: (June, July, August) 11..1..3 mm.
     Total summer rain, 15 mm.(0.6 in.)
Valparaíso: (December, January, February) 3..0..0 mm.
     Total summer rain, 3 mm.(0.1 in.)

Central Chile, while enjoying the advantages of a Mediterranean climate, also suffers its handicaps. During the

[5] Julius Hann: Handbuch der Klimatologie, Vol. 3, Stuttgart, 1911, pp. 107,
111, 552, 558.

long rainless summer, when vegetation becomes brown
and sere, little can be grown without an artificial supply
of water. Irrigation thus is necessary. Without it the
country could sustain but a fraction of its present population. A certain amount of wheat and barley is grown
without artificial water supply (*de rulo,* as it is called in
Chile), particularly on the slopes of the Coast Range, but
only on the southern frontier, where the cyclonic storm
régime prevails throughout the year and summer showers
are frequent, can farming be carried on without its aid.
In the rest of the country irrigation is necessary for successful agricultural development.

Central Chile: Irrigation

Fortunately, Chile is well favored for irrigation. The
deep snow beds which heavy winter precipitation leaves
on the Andes serve excellently to store the water and give
it off gradually during the warmer months. On the lower
slopes, up to about ten thousand feet (*ca.* 3,100 meters),
the snow melts rapidly with the approach of spring, but
above that height it lies in deep deposits throughout the
year. These great frozen reservoirs give a fairly constant
flow to nearly a score of small rivers that cross central
Chile to the sea (Figs. 8, 9). The most important of these
rivers are: the Aconcagua, fed by the snow fields on the
mountain of the same name; the Mapocho, which drains
the heights about Cerro del Plomo and Cerro Juncal, flows
down past the city of Santiago, and joins the Maipo; the
Maipo, receiving its supply from about the high peaks of
Tupungato and the San José and Maipo volcanoes and
crossing the Central Valley a few miles south of the capital; the Rapel, formed by the junction of the Cachapoal
and the Tinguiririca, both of which have their origin in
the series of peaks and high massifs that lie to the south
of the Volcán Maipo; the Mataquito, also formed from

two main branches, the Teno and Lontué, which unite near the city of Curicó; the Maule, drawing its water from Lake Maule and from the high volcanic slopes that surround it; the Itata, fed chiefly by the snow fields upon the volcano of Chillán; the Bío-Bío, central Chile's southernmost and largest river, which gathers its waters from a long span of snow-covered mountains between the volcanoes of Antuco and Lonquimai. No one of these streams is a large river; none is navigable except the Maule (for some ten miles from its mouth) and the Bío-Bío (which may be used by barges of three or four feet draught only). They are typical Mediterranean-climate streams, with occasional strong freshets during the winter rains or the early summer thaws of snow in the mountains. During most of the summer their supply of water is diminished, and they flow as shallow braided streams as they cross the Central Valley. The source never fails, however, and there is seldom a shortage for irrigation. In fact, so constant is the supply that, though the farmers of central Chile are often prodigal in their use of water, the channels, even in their lower sections, are never dry.

The slope of the land in most of the country is peculiarly favorable for irrigation. In the great central trough there is a general descent from two thousand feet (*ca.* 600 meters) in the north end of the valley near Santiago to sea level near Puerto Montt, eight hundred miles (*ca.* 1,200 kilometers) to the south. This general inclination, however, is of less importance than the gentle grades of the extensive alluvial fans corresponding to the numerous transverse streams. The rivers run along the crests of their fans, and water may be led north or south from these slight elevations. From east to west there is also a gradual slope, as the piedmont at the base of the Andes lies from five to six hundred feet higher than the western margin of the depression. Thus over most of the region it is possible to carry water by gravity flow to any place desired. There

is no need for the construction of expensive reservoirs, nor
for any but the simplest system of canals, nor for extensive
leveling operations. The land lies ready for the water,
and there are no serious engineering difficulties to be
overcome. In fact, so simple has been the problem of
irrigation that the government has not been called on to
undertake the task, most of the canals having been built
by single landowners or by small groups of them in
co-operation.

CENTRAL CHILE: NATIVE VEGETATION

The native vegetation of central Chile has not seriously
impeded agricultural development. The great valley, it is
true, seems to have been covered by a growth of timber
when the Spaniards arrived. Frequent mention of this
is made in the early descriptions of the region even as far
north as Santiago, but, though the district is spoken of
as being covered with a heavy *bosque* (forest), it is apparent that very little large timber was found. The need
of lumber in building operations is often referred to, and
within a few years after the founding of the city measures
were taken to preserve the timber in the vicinity.[6] It is
evident that the *bosque túpido* (thick forest) to which the
Spaniards made reference must have been merely what the
Chileans call *matorral* at the present time (Fig. 12), the
chaparral characteristic of such a climate, a type of vegetation corresponding to the *maquis* of the Mediterranean
region and still found in many unspoiled spots in the Central
Valley. It is a thick growth of small trees, strikingly like
the shrubs that cover the lower hills of southern California.
It consists of hard-leafed, brittle-stemmed trees, seldom
over ten feet (*ca.* 3 meters) high, many of them thorny
(as the *espino,* common on every hillside about Santiago)
and many of them as aromatic in their blossoms and foliage

6 Actas del Cabildo, *in* Historiadores, Vol. 1, 1861, pp. 185 and 200.

as the typical chaparral of the California slopes. After struggling through the thick growth in either of these regions, one finds one's clothing redolent of sage and other aromatic plants; while the mountain climber, descending from the clear, odorless atmosphere of the snow-field levels, discovers the lower layers of air to be loaded with the fragrance of this vegetation. Along the immediate shores of some streams and back in the numerous narrow canyons along the foot of the mountains, both the Andes and the Coast Range, a larger growth of timber is found. On the wide valley floor it is still common to see a band of willows fringing the banks of streams, while in the mountains the canyon bottoms show a stand of *peumos,* with trunks from twenty to thirty feet high and several inches or even a foot in diameter. The latter remind one of the sycamores and bay trees of the California canyons. These shady groves of peumos, frequently with limpid, cool mountain streams flowing through them, form delightful retreats from the heat of summer days in central Chile. To the farmer, with little but the soft wood of poplar and eucalyptus growing on his land, they furnish a prized store of hard timber, useful for fence posts, building material, and the making of plows, carts, and other implements. They also supply the farms and towns with charcoal, the fuel most commonly used in kitchens and in the braziers occasionally employed for warming rooms.

The mountain slopes on both sides of the great valley offer little tree growth of any kind. Above four or five thousand feet the Andes are almost completely devoid even of shrubs, and beyond some eight or nine thousand there is not even grass, one bare rocky slope rising beyond another until the fields of perpetual snow are reached. It is only in the southern section of the central Chilean Andes, from about the Maule River southward, that forests are found on either the middle or the lower slopes. The Coast Range, too, has few trees. Most of its hillsides are grass-covered from base to summit, except where, particularly on the seaward slope, the matorral finds sufficient moisture to maintain a foothold. It is common to find such growth of shrubs heavier on the shady side (in central Chile the south-facing slope) where there is less loss of moisture through evaporation. The higher summits in the Coast Range, rising to four or five thousand feet, are largely bare of vegetation or support a scant grass covering.

The natural vegetation of central Chile is thus typical of a Mediterranean climate and has offered little obstacle to agricultural development. Though in its native state it no doubt constituted a formidable obstacle to travel on horse or afoot and must have seriously embarrassed the early Spaniards in any maneuver of their cavalry, it was easily burned, was far more easily removed than a true forest, and yielded quickly to the efforts to clear the land for agriculture.

Thus it is seen that agricultural Chile is limited almost entirely to the central longitudinal trough and the Aconcagua Valley immediately to the north. This small area of Mediterranean climate and sharply restricted tillable land has constituted the basis of Chile's agricultural development—the basis, in fact, of her existence as a separate national entity. Here Chile's typical system of haciendas has grown up, placing its peculiar stamp on the agriculture and the system of land tenure of the nation. In this isolated region between the Andes and the sea Master and Man have lived together for four centuries and have built a unique agrarian society characterized by an extreme land monopoly and a sharply marked social stratification.

CHAPTER III

TYPES OF CHILEAN HACIENDAS

One of the greatest charms of central Chile lies in its beautiful farms. Every traveler who comes to know the country speaks in glowing terms of its rural landscape. Artists, national and foreign alike, find scenes in the country districts that inspire their art. The Chileans themselves are proud of their country estates, set in the attractive natural surroundings of mountains and valleys and stimulated to easy production by an ample supply of water for irrigation. The mildness of the Mediterranean climate makes possible the cultivation of varied crops, the growth of ornamental trees, native and exotic, and the production of flowers and fruits in abundance. The wealth of the landowners has enabled them to beautify their farms—in fact, one wonders whether, in the minds of most Chilean proprietors, the first thought is not for the adornment of their country estates rather than the providing of an income.

In the literature dealing with Chile there are many descriptions of the *haciendas*.[1] Some of these accounts were written years ago, when conditions were somewhat different from those at present, though rural Chile has changed but slowly through the centuries. To give a picture of them as they are now, I shall describe several haciendas typical of different sections of the country.[2]

[1] See Ruschenberger: Noticias de Chile, 1931, pp. 130-148.
[2] See also Platt: Items in the Chilean Pattern of Occupance, 1934, pp. 33-41.

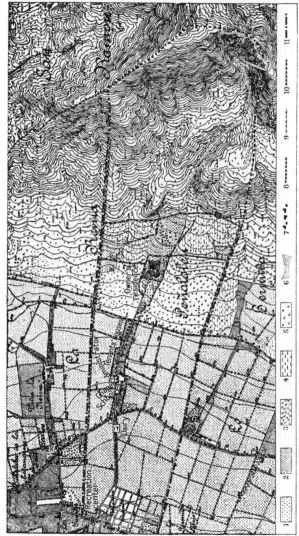

Fig. 11—Plan of a typical hacienda, Peñalolén, in the Central Valley. Scale, 1:70,893 (reduced from topographic map, 1:25,000 by the Chilean General Staff). The details of the layout of the estate, which occupies a strip of land extending from the level plain of the Central Valley (a village on the outskirts of the city of Santiago appears in the northwest corner) across the piedmont to the high foothills of the Andes, are discussed in the text.

Key to symbols: 1, cultivated land; 2, vineyards; 3, orchards; 4, meadow and pasture; 5, scrub woodland; 6, garden and other closely occupied land around houses; 7, houses; 8, trees as field borders; 9, wire fences; 10, irrigation canals and ditches; 11, property boundary.

Peñalolén: A Piedmont Estate Near Santiago

At the foot of the mountains, just east of Santiago and some ten miles (*ca.* 16 kilometers) distant from the city, is situated the well-known *fundo* [3] of Peñalolén (Fig. 11). It contains about 45,000 acres (*ca.* 18,200 hectares) and consists of three distinct divisions. A small part of it lies out on the nearly level plain of the Central Valley, about a third occupies the piedmont slope close to the Andes, and the rest extends back into the high foothills of the mountains. Its soil varies correspondingly. The lower lands have a shallow but fertile covering of loam underlain by gravel deposits of great depth; the section lying back at the foot of the mountains is too full of stones to lend itself well to cultivation; the high mountain lands are almost devoid of soil and support only a growth of chaparral and bunch grass on their lower slopes, with completely bare rock forming the highest ridges that reach to over 8,500 feet (*ca.* 2,600 meters) elevation. In this character of topography and soil Peñalolén is typical of a long series of piedmont farms that lie at the eastern margin of the Central Valley. Many of these foothill properties are among the most desirable in the country. They contain the greatest variety of lands though not the richest, they have the most independent water supply from their own springs and canyons; they offer the most sightly locations for the owners' large houses and grounds; they possess excellent drainage of water and air—hence they are among the most attractive for their healthfulness; sensitive fruits may be grown on their more nearly frostless slopes. Peñalolén combines all of these desirable features. Furthermore, its nearness to the capital makes it possible for the owner the more easily to divide his time between the city and the farm.

[3] At the present time most of the large farms of Chile are called *fundos,* only the largest usually being known as *haciendas.* However, since the latter term has come into general use in English writings about Latin America and is commonly employed in several of these countries to apply to any large farm, it will be used generally in this treatise.

THE APPROACH TO PEÑALOLÉN

There is but one entrance to the hacienda, a long road that leads up from the suburban town of Ñuñoa through double lines of tall eucalyptus trees. This is not a public highway and leads nowhere except into the farm. It is used, however, by all who come up from the city or the plain that lies about it to any part of the estate. Unpaved but usually kept in fair condition, it is traveled by the great two-wheeled oxcarts, by the lighter horse-drawn *carretas* (two-wheeled wagons) and delivery wagons, by carriages and taxis, and by limousines and autotrucks. Horsemen, too, coming from the city with immense panniers of bread, or from the fundo carrying large baskets of fruit or vegetables swung across their saddles or with great cans of milk on each side of their horses, are constantly seen along this thoroughfare. Travelers, both mounted and on foot, also move by this road from the several parts of the estate to and from the city or valley towns. It is the life artery of the farm.

In places this road is lined with high masses of blackberry bushes as well as trees, completely shutting out the view to either side. Along most of its extent, too, mud walls (in a few places, wire fence) shut it in. Running along at the foot of these high barriers on one or both sides of the road are ditches several feet deep, in which water from the upper part of the farm hurries down toward the plain. These canals serve the several purposes of irrigation and water supply for the stock in the fields as well as for domestic use by the entire population of the estate. At intervals the walls open and crude bridges of planks or logs lead across the canals to the houses of the tenants.

The first building encountered as one goes up the long slope of this piedmont road is a recreation center constructed on land (slightly over three acres, or about one and a half hectares, in extent) set aside for the purpose by the farm owner twenty years ago. As this border of the farm adjoined the then small town of Ñuñoa, this center was designed to serve both the inhabitants of the village and the farm population. A theater was built and other recreational facilities were installed. An idea of its purpose may be gained from the provision that no alcoholic beverages should be served there. It was thus intended as a place of wholesome, safe amusement for the laboring people of the neighborhood. Probably it was thought that such provision might aid in keeping order on the farm and in making the tenants more content to remain on the place.

After passing a mile or so farther along the road, one comes to the great San Carlos Canal (constructed and owned by a large group of farm owners) which for over a century has led water from the Maipo River out over the valley plain about Santiago. Just below the canal stands a dairy, with its long, low sheds and its cattle pens, where more than a hundred cows are milked daily for needs of the city dwellers below. Above the dairy the road widens out into an irregular open space around which are a number of houses. The *administrador* occupies one of these, an old rambling adobe structure which looks as if it might have been in former years the home of the farm owner. Beside it and behind stands a series of buildings and sheds, the *bodegas* of the estate, where grain and other produce of the place are stored and where the farm implements are housed. One of these buildings is used for a school maintained by the combined support of the farm and the government. Only children of the tenants attend here: there are no others living near enough. Several houses of tenants also stand about this court. From this center, rather than from the owner's house, the estate is managed.

Occupying most of the opposite side of the courtyard is a feature rather foreign to a farm but not uncommon on these Chilean estates. This is a church, the chapel of Nuestra Señora de Loreto, and an adjoining residence, the home of a small number of nuns who live here permanently and a resort for others who come out from convents in the city for rest or convalescence. This plot of ground and the buildings on it have been independent of the fundo at least since 1870, as a provision in the bill of sale of that date specified that the *capilla* (chapel) and the buildings belonging to it were excluded from the objects transferred at the time. An earlier document in the land recorder's office apparently refers to this plot as having been set aside for religious use in 1866.

A little farther along, the dwellings of the tenants begin to line both sides of the road. Here openings break the blackberry wall at distances of about a hundred yards, each giving access to a two-acre plot of ground with a small house standing close to the road. These dwellings (44 in all), housing most of the inhabitants of the farm, are mostly of adobe, some few of brick, and several with wattled walls. They are the humblest of cottages, consisting of two or three rooms at most with thatched roofs and beaten earth floors. The houses extend for a mile or so along the road, forming a long-drawn-out settlement with but a single street.

Just above this another main canal is crossed, the canal of the Perdices (partridges), which also brings water from the Maipo River to the series of piedmont fields lying too high to be reached by the San Carlos Canal. Very little land above here is cultivated, as there is no adequate supply of water for irrigation. Cattle and horses graze on this high land, though the native chaparral covers much of the area. To one side of the road the government has bought an extensive tract from the farm and has built a large military ground with barracks and officers' quarters.

THE MANOR HOUSE AND PARKS

About a mile farther up one comes to the owner's great house, the *casa de hacienda,* as the Chileans call it. The house is large but not notable either for its architecture or its construction, a spacious two-story structure of adobe and frame, with many porticos, wide hallways, a great number of rooms, and built as if wing after wing had been added as occasion required. While the house itself is not particularly attractive, the grounds that surround it are strikingly so. In fact, their beauty would make them famous anywhere except in Chile, where it is the common thing for an estate to have the owner's residence set in such surroundings. Peñalolén is a veritable park. Many a city has nothing to compare with it in size or charm. It is set high up on the piedmont slope at the very foot of the Andes, with a wide view over the entire valley of Santiago. It would be difficult to find a more picturesque location. The main part of the grounds, surrounded by a high mud wall, covers as much space as a dozen city blocks. A grove of magnificent eucalyptus trees occupies much of the area, with driveways, walks, and open gardens among them. Other trees in great variety form groves and avenues through the park, while in the outlying sections there are orchards of choice fruits. Flowers in variety and abundance are found everywhere. A canyon running for miles back into the mountains (entirely on the farm) sends its little stream out here and its waters have been led through the grounds in rills and cataracts and pools. Several small artificial lakes have been formed along its course, and their borders are studded with water lilies and other aquatic plants.

Behind this main park a second one, less ornate but more natural in its beauty, has been formed; and beyond this the canyon mouth offers trails and groves and secluded dells, and the canyon itself, with a crystalline stream of snow-fed water, leads on and up far into the bare mountain heights where small fields of snow lie even in midsummer. High in this deep ravine a group of gigantic boulders has fallen in such fashion as to afford some shelter beneath them, and a road has been constructed along the steep slopes of the valley back to this *casa de piedra,* as it is called, purely for the purpose of allowing the owner and his family to enjoy outings at this picturesque site. The natural beauties of the farm's location attract many visitors from the city, and occasional conventions and assemblies are held in the upper groves of the park; while in the seclusion of the canyon itself, a mile or so above the great house, representatives of the American school in Santiago (the Instituto Inglés) have, with the owner's consent, built a rustic stone lodge, the Eagle's Nest, where their students may taste the joys of outdoor life among idyllic surroundings.

Space is given here to a description of these recreational aspects of Peñalolén because the typical Chilean hacienda is perhaps first of all a place to enjoy life. Its economic importance is secondary, at least in many cases. It is less a place to work than a place to play. While to the tenant the farm offers all that he has, home and business alike, to the owner and his family, who spend much of their time in a city residence, the farm figures rather as a spot where delightful vacations are passed than as a place where a livelihood is wrested from the soil. The nearness of Peñalolén to the city gives it even more of this recreational character, but many farms far distant from the capital or other large centers are valued chiefly as summering places for the owners, and their families and friends.

LAND UTILIZATION ON PEÑALOLÉN

The fields of Peñalolén, however, are not unproductive. Four hundred *cuadras* (*ca.* 1,600 acres) are under irrigation and are cultivated with a fair degree of care. About one-quarter of this is planted in alfalfa, which is pastured by the several hundred head of cattle and horses on the farm or cut and baled for sale in the city. Wheat and barley constitute the next most important crops, some four hundred acres normally being devoted to these. Beans of several varieties, potatoes, corn (for household use), other vegetables, and several varieties of fruits figure among the products of the property.

Not all the land is worked for the owners. In fact, the estate is much divided in its administration. Though figuring as one property, it has virtually been partitioned among three sons and one daughter of its former owner, who died a few years ago. Of the three sons, one owns the hacienda house and the surrounding park. This section contains relatively little productive land, since most of it lies above the two canals that cross the farm and has no water for irrigating the fields except the small stream that comes down out of the canyon and carries little surface flow during the three or four months of rainless summer. Furthermore, the gravel of the piedmont is but slightly covered with soil over the greater part of this land and renders it of little use except for grazing. Indeed, even for this purpose it offers sufficient grass during the rainy winter months only.

Below the upper canal nearly all the land is under irrigation. Here good crops of alfalfa, wheat, and barley are raised. The surface is of more gentle slope; it has good alluvial soil, an abundant water supply, and excellent drainage both of water and air. This section of the estate has been divided more or less equally among the other two sons and the daughter. They, however, do not usually care for the land themselves but live in the city and rent the greater part of it, some in large blocks, some in plots of a few acres each. The small rented plots are usually devoted to the production of vegetables or corn grown for human food. There are no houses on these parcels of land nor on any other part of the farm except as described above. The renters are either some of the tenants themselves or residents of the village that lies immediately below the estate.

The total population of Peñalolén is about five hundred. This number includes the forty-four tenant families, the master, his family and servants, the administrator and his assistants, and the small group of nuns usually found in the rest home beside the chapel. A priest sometimes resides at the capilla also, and there are a few hangers-on in various capacities about the property.

The hill section of Peñalolén of course cannot be farmed. Much of it is completely waste land, the highest parts having neither trees nor grass, neither water nor soil (Fig. 13). The lower slopes, however, are brush-covered up to about 5,000 feet (ca. 1,500 meters) ; and some grass grows among the bushes, enough to afford at least scant pasturage for a few cattle. The brush itself is of some value, supplying firewood and small timbers for use about the farm. Of greater importance, still, is the protection it affords against erosion. Without this soil cover the slope would soon be deeply gullied and the land below would be covered with debris washed down from the hills. Then, too, the chaparral holds much of the rain that falls and allows it to sink into hidden springs and subterranean streams. In the bottom of the canyon, particularly in places where water flows underneath the accumulated boulders and gravel in the valley bottom, groves of trees, chiefly *peumos,* are found, while at some points quite a luxuriant growth of vegetation forms thickets that completely fill the narrow gorge down which the water runs. Two or three rude shacks have been built at the least unfavorable sites along the mountainside, little more than temporary shelters, and in each lives a tenant for at least a part of the year—a woodcutter, sheep herder, or guard to look after the little canals that bring a small amount of this clear mountain water down to the settled sections of the farm. Except for these individuals, the hills, though they constitute fully a third of the farm in area, contain no inhabitants. One may wander about over them for days and see no human being, perhaps not even a domestic animal, so worthless in general are the hill sections of such a farm as Peñalolén.

Escorial de Panquehue: A Valley Hacienda

This fine farm is located in the Aconcagua Valley, about forty miles (*ca.* 65 kilometers) north of Santiago and up the Aconcagua River some fifty miles from Valparaíso. It thus lies outside the great longitudinal valley but within the region generally considered as central Chile. It is one of a hundred or more farms that are found in the beautiful and productive valley above named and is a part of the famous great estate known as Panquehue which some years ago was divided into three sections, each of which now forms a magnificent independent property.

THE ACONCAGUA VALLEY

An old friend had invited me to accompany him to his small fruit farm in the Aconcagua Valley, and the owner of Escorial, knowing our plans, had pressed us to stop en route for a visit with him on his hacienda. We went by train from Santiago, turning at Las Vegas to follow up the Transandine line nearly to the small city of San Felipe at the junction of the Aconcagua and the Putaendo. This entire valley is one of the most important agricultural units of the country. With a floor varying from one to ten miles in width and almost level, it contains rich deposits of alluvial materials and is supplied with abundant water for irrigation by the snow-fed river itself. Furthermore, the temperatures are mild even for a Mediterranean climate, and frosts occur in the lower and middle valley so seldom as to cause little danger even to semi-tropical fruits such as lemons, oranges, figs, *chirimoyas,* and *avocados.* Farther up toward the exit of the river from the mountains the cool air sinks down from the high snow fields of Mt. Aconcagua, bringing frost temperatures not infrequently in the winter months of June and July. There deciduous fruits, peaches, plums, pears, and apples are grown. Grapes thrive throughout the valley, some of the finest vineyards of Chile being located here. Alfalfa and grains, too, are extensively produced, and vegetables of many kinds yield good returns.

As has been noted, it was this productive region, the last of the transverse valleys as one comes from the north, that first attracted Spaniards and the Inca conquerors before them and that gave the nation its present name. Irrigation, perhaps introduced by Inca civilizers a century or so before the Conquest, has been carried on here ever since. At present the Aconcagua Valley is intensively developed. It contains the towns of Los Andes, San Felipe, and Quillota and many of the best farms in the country. The greater part of the valley floor is given over to alfalfa production, though fields of wheat and barley with their rich golden hues are interspersed with the deep green of the grasslands. The main auto or wagon road and the railway, following closely along the south margin of the valley on the first slight elevation, touch and skirt the jutting spurs that descend with considerable regularity from the high bordering hills. Between each pair of promontories that protrude into the valley there sweeps back a long, curving, semicircular cove like the symmetrical scallops of a giant shell, and in each of the smoothly curving recesses piedmont slopes rise gently from the level valley floor. In these wide, sweeping re-entrants, snuggling up against the foot of the hills and protected upstream and down by the points of jutting cliffs, lie the choicest sites for fruit farms and vineyards. In such an alcove, a great natural amphitheater containing nearly a thousand acres (*ca.* 400 hectares), are situated the farm lands of the estate we were to visit, with 240 cuadras (960 acres) of fruitful irrigated ground, while back over the mountains behind this slope stretch some two million acres more of hill land also belonging to the estate.

<h3 align="center">APPROACH TO THE HACIENDA</h3>

We were met at the railway station by the owner's grown son, who was acting as administrator of the estate. In a good foreign automobile he drove us through the single street of the little town of Palomar, between rows of low adobe houses thatched with straw, then out along a country road lined with Lombardy poplars, now bright yellow in the late May days of autumn. Then, entering the farm through a gate in a high mud wall, we followed through avenues of eucalyptus, poplar, and weeping willow a couple of miles by a roundabout road to the house. Most of the land we saw was in alfalfa, with cattle and horses grazing its short-cropped growth. We passed a few fields of grain and saw well-kept vineyards rising row on row along the foot of the hills as far up the slope as canals could supply them with water. Each individual field was enclosed by rows of tall poplars, the red roots of the trees exposed along the half-filled irrigation ditches. Long lines of weeping willows, too, bordered some of the plots, and their drooping branches were neatly cropped by the cattle into an evenly barbered " bob." Mud walls some four feet ($1\frac{1}{3}$ meters) high also separated the fields, built close to the rows of trees. Each of these fields, called *potreros* and containing some twenty to twenty-five hectares (50 or 60 acres) as an average, bears its own name, we are told. One is called the Field of the Serpents, another the Field of Copper, another that of the Walnut

Trees, while several bear the names of persons, possibly former owners of the lands now incorporated into the hacienda. The naming of fields is a common practice on the larger Chilean farms.

THE OWNER, A CHILEAN OF IRISH STOCK

At the big house (*casa de hacienda*) we found the owner awaiting us. Known to the whole countryside as Don Santiago (Spanish for Saint James), he was introduced by that name. His surname was pronounced Carrayee. He professed a slight knowledge of English, but all conversation was carried on in Spanish for some time. We found, however, that he knew more English than he had at first admitted, and finally he confessed that he had been in New York, that, though his mother was a South American, his father was Irish, and that his name was mispronounced by the Chileans, being really James Carey. As his life from early childhood had been spent in South America he had come to accept the Spanish form given his name—had, in fact, made himself thoroughly South American in many ways. His wife and children knew no English, and few of his friends thought of him as a foreigner.

Such an occurrence is not unusual in Chile. A number of the leading families of the country bear English names. In a list of the most distinguished Chileans one finds such surnames as Edwards, Delano, Lyons, Wilson, Walker, Armstrong, MacKenna, MacIver, while Green and Davis, Smith and Jones, Gibson and Murphy figure in the roll of Chilean citizens. It will be recalled also that Chile's first president was Bernardo O'Higgins. While there has been no extensive immigration of English-speaking people into Chile, straggling individuals from the British Isles and Anglo-America have found their way to the country and, attracted by its natural charms and the hospitality of its people, have remained, married into Chilean families, and become thoroughly incorporated in the national group. The alliances they have formed were generally with the upper class, and, in that relatively small body, their descendants have become conspicuous out of all proportion to their actual numbers. These families have now become as thoroughly nationalized as have the second or third generation of immigrants in the United States. Many of them have as completely lost the tongue of their foreign ancestors as have their counterparts in North America. They are in every sense Chileans. Not a few of the large haciendas of the country belong to such men as our host at Escorial de Panquehue.

Mr. James Carey was as hospitable toward us as any Chilean could have been, assuring us in true Latin American fashion that his house was ours ("Aquí tiene Vd. su casa, Señor!"), and that he and his were at our service in any way in which they could be useful. His family does not live on the farm but at a city residence in the port of Valparaíso where Don Santiago conducts a large importing business. They come to the hacienda only during holidays or on other special occasions. Our host himself was up only for the week-end to see that all was running properly. The casa de hacienda is thus usually without occupants except for the eldest son, who manages the estate in the absence of his father. However, the force of domestic servants was complete, and we were at once made to feel at home. A well-served luncheon had been prepared, and we were soon seated at a typical Chilean board. The table was spread with the best products of the farm as well as with various imported delicacies. It was served by two or three maids, typical Chileans of the tenant class, trained to such tasks from early childhood—daughters, we learned, of old *inquilino* families on the farm. A Chilean hacienda seldom goes outside of its own people for such, or, as a matter of fact, for any service. Some one on the place can usually be found for whatever type of labor may be demanded. Whether blacksmith or wet nurse, seamstress or veterinary may be needed, the farm will supply it. In this, as in its material resources, it is a self-sufficient unit.

Don Santiago's house was a one-story structure of some twenty rooms. It had thick adobe walls and a tile roof, and the rooms were well floored, some with tile and some with boards. Though well kept up, the house bore marks of age. It probably had stood for a good half century or more. It stood in the midst of gardens, less spacious than those of Peñalolén but occupying several acres and filled with flowers and fruit and ornamental trees. It was built around several *patios,* or enclosed courts, as are most of the older houses in Chile, each of these open to the sky and paved with tile or cobblestones (Fig. 14). Potted plants stood about these spaces, while a small fountain and pool occupied the center of the principal court. The rooms opened on long covered porches which surrounded these patios on all four sides. Thus it was necessary, in most cases, to pass into the open air in order to go from room to room. A few of the corridors had been enclosed with glass for better protection from the cool evening air or occasional bleak weather of Chile's rainy winter. Modern conveniences, such as running water, electric lights, and a bathroom, contributed to the comfort of the house.

A RIDE OVER THE ESTATE

Soon after luncheon we were told that horses were ready to take us over the farm. Don Santiago led the way. Through a labyrinth of corrals and farm buildings, dairy barns, granaries, implement sheds, stables, sheep pens, workshops, fruit depositories, and vast wine bodegas he conducted us in a roundabout way to the public road that passes through the farm. This highway was lined much of its length by well-built mud walls, topped with tile or

FIG. 12   FIG. 13

FIG. 14

FIG. 12—*Matorral* vegetation of the central Chilean hills near Santiago at an elevation of about 4,000 feet. (Courtesy of George T. Hastings.)

FIG. 13—Upper slopes of Andean foothills in Peñalolén. (Courtesy of E. E. Wurth.)

FIG. 14—Courtyard (*patio*) of a Chilean house.

FIG. 15—Hacienda Escorial de Panquehue, looking north across the Aconcagua Valley.

hard-packed earth so high that from our saddles we could just see, as we rode along, the extensive vineyards and orchards that lay between us and the hills. On the other side of the road, reaching down to the wide gravel bed of the river, were fields of grain and rich alfalfa pastures. Some two miles from the house the road passes close to the intake of the large canal, Don Santiago's own canal, that leads his water supply from the river along the base of the hills behind his orchards. Just above this point the river bends to meet the hills, and Don Santiago's land pinches out into a narrow band. Rounding a projecting spur at this point, we turned up over some uncultivated gravelly fields and past an abandoned quarry and a small mine (still on the farm), climbed the slope by zigzag trails, and finally came out on the point of a long ridge, whence we could look over the whole valley above and below the farm.

The view was most imposing (Fig. 15). To the east, rising high into the sky, stood the Andes, their snow crowning the long stretch of massive mountain shoulders that sloped up before us from across the valley. In all that expanse of elevated and badly broken land there was nothing that suggested human occupation. It seemed a complete waste. In the valley below us, however, reaching far down toward the sea where Valparaíso stands, there lay a veritable Garden of Eden.[4] The great trough carved out for itself by the Aconcagua River is widened at this point by the entrance of a tributary stream, the Putaendo. This forms a broad, open valley where a dozen large haciendas and several towns are located, all in sight from our vantage point. The little city of San Felipe, with its narrow streets and its blocks of one-story adobe buildings lies along the curving, gravel-marked course of

[4] The name Valparaíso (Vale of Paradise) was given to the harbor situated at the mouth of this valley, partly to honor the native town (Valparaíso, Spain) of its discoverer and partly, no doubt, because of the natural beauty of the region.

the river. Beyond the town the valley of the Putaendo leads northeastward into the Andes, while to our right the deep gorge of the Aconcagua opens an avenue to the historic Uspallata Pass. At the junction of these mountain corridors the two divisions of San Martín's army had converged in their famous crossing of the Andes, and not far from here they surprised and defeated the Spanish forces at Chacabuco in the last campaign for Chilean independence.

The hacienda of Panquehue was almost at our feet, but fully three thousand feet (1,000 meters) below us. The poplar-bordered fields lay like a checkerboard on the valley floor. The highway cut the farm into two slightly unequal parts, that on the river side variegated in sharply contrasted grain and alfalfa fields, the other largely orchard and vineyard.

THE IRRIGATION SYSTEM

Down the valley we could trace the broad gravel bed of the river, a thin line of silver marking all that was left of its waters. The secret as to what had become of its full upstream supply was revealed by the canals that lay one above another like narrow parallel roads along the foot of the bordering hills on both sides of the valley. Most of the canals gave the distinct impression that they were rising rather than going downstream and recalled to mind the Chilean inquilinos' boastful saying that "the *patrón* can make water run uphill." The highest of these *acequias,* as the irrigation ditches are called in Chile, marked a neatly cleft divide between two types of growth. Above, upon the slopes of the hills could be discerned hardly a vestige of green in the prevailing brown of the chaparral. Below the canals all was the fresh green of the early spring of our middle latitudes. No effort had been made to cultivate any part not reached by these life-giving arteries. Land above was worthless—below it was the best the country affords. Water alone made the difference.

On the Panquehue side of the valley, curving in long sweeps around the upper borders of the cultivated lands, the main irrigation canal of the farm, marked by a line of tall young poplar trees, lay like a contour line upon the slope. Don Santiago's hacienda, like most Chilean estates, has an independent water supply. It has built its own aqueducts, four in number, taking the water from the Aconcagua just above the upper edge of the property and carrying it by gravity flow to all the level or gently sloping parts of the farm. These canals, each one named— El Puente (The Bridge), El Medio (The Center), Los Hornos (The Ovens), and La Rueda (The Wheel)—also provide water to run a private power plant that supplies current for the various pieces of electrical machinery about the place as well as for lighting purposes. The farm has first water rights (*primeras aguas*) from the river, and rarely if ever does the flow become so reduced as to cause a shortage. Most of the large properties in the valley and many of the smaller ones have as dependable a water supply.

ORCHARDS, VINEYARDS, AND VILLAGE

Immediately below the highest canal the hillside was planted with young deciduous fruit trees. They formed a band a few rods in width and had been set here, where the air drainage was good, to avoid danger of frosts. Don Santiago informed us that he had 28,000 peach trees and 3,000 apple trees. On the lower part of the slope vineyards began and reached completely down to the wall along the road (Fig. 16). There were 327 acres (132 hectares) in vines, and Panquehue's greatest wealth consists of the fruitage of these vineyards. Its bodegas, as the wine cellars are called, were two-story buildings, covering nearly an acre, with deep basements capable of holding 2,000,000 liters. Before we left the farm Don Santiago conducted us through these extensive cellars, indicating with pride the great casks, the provision for storing the products of his vineyards for many years, and the carefully worked out system by which the whole stock was cared for. A Belgian, expert in the production and care of wines, was employed for this task. The vintage of this farm, as that of most other Chilean vineyards, finds its market within the country. A little is exported; but the area suitable for vineyards is relatively limited, and domestic consumption is large.

Below the orchards and vineyards the hacienda house and its outbuildings could be seen almost as if from an airplane. Surrounded by gardens and groves of tall trees, the group of buildings covered enough land for a small farm. On the opposite side of the road lay the settlement of inquilinos, occupying an area about equal to the former. It contained fifty-five houses of regular tenants, while six or seven buildings occupied by the foremen or other higher employees adjoined it along the road. It thus constituted a village of some three hundred persons. The arrangement of the tenants' houses was quite different from that commonly seen. In most cases the inquilinos live in a long row of cottages stretching along the highway or the main road of the farm, as in Peñalolén. On Panquehue, however, the settlement was in the form of a square, with streets crossing at right angles, and the cottages were set close together as in a compact village. Looked at from above it appeared less satisfactory (though perhaps more economical of space) than the usual arrangement. It gave something of the character of a town to what in most cases is but a row of peasant cottages. The houses themselves were better built than is common on Chilean farms, where they are frequently miserable huts. This settlement, however, was largely bare of trees, and the dwellings lacked the homely though humble appearance given by the customary wide-spreading grapevine and great fig tree about an inquilino's house.

FIG. 16

FIG. 17

FIG. 16—Vineyards of Escorial de Panquehue. (Courtesy of Robert S. Platt.)

FIG. 17—Maipo River valley, showing terraces upon which are situated Peumo and other haciendas. (Courtesy of George T. Hastings.)

Los Peumos: An Andean Estate

This hacienda is quite different from the others described. It is one of a relatively small number of Andean valley farms. The main cordillera of the Andes is almost wholly waste land as far as either agriculture or grazing is concerned; but there are a few rivers along the bottoms of whose canyons tillable lands similar to those of the Central Valley are carried back for miles into the heart of the mountains. The Maipo is one of these rivers, the Maule is another. Both of these streams and a few others offer narrow strips of flat land along their valley floors. The V-shaped canyons in which the rivers flow apparently were lowered at some past time and have had their bottoms filled deep with coarse alluvium—soil, sand, gravel, and boulders being laid down in a more or less heterogeneous mixture (Fig. 17). Over this material a shallow covering of humus has accumulated. Later, an uplift of the whole area has set the streams busy eroding again, and they are now cutting out the deposits they themselves had built. Erosion, however, takes place principally downward, producing deep gorges and leaving the former valley floors as river terraces high above the present level of the water. On these fertile though often gravelly surfaces agriculture has been extended deep into the Andes themselves. The Maipo has such flats running back fully thirty miles from where it debouches on the Central Valley. The Maule has terraces almost as long.

Upon the strip of flat land extending back along the Maipo River is situated the cultivated section of the Peumos hacienda. The valley floor here is only about a mile wide, giving an elongated form to the properties that occupy it. Los Peumos stretches along this old river terrace immediately above and below the junction of the Colorado with the Maipo. Its cultivated fields reach from the gorge in which the river runs along one side of the valley to the foot of the hills on the other side. The farm is well supplied with water, its own canals tapping the Colorado some miles above. Minor tributaries of the Maipo also enter from the adjoining hills, bringing an additional supply from the snow fields. Wheat and barley are its customary crops, with potreros of alfalfa upon which to pasture the hacienda's numerous stock.

The owner's house is situated at the edge of the valley, on the highway that leads up to San José de Maipo and the Piuquenes Pass at the crest of the mountains. It is an old structure of a rambling character, with yard-thick adobe walls and heavy tile roof. The extensive garden that surrounds it is filled with fruit and nut trees as well as ornamental shrubs and beds of flowers. In one corner a swimming pool has been built and is filled by a canal fed from fields of melting snow not many miles away. From the same source comes the excellent supply of water for the domestic purposes of the farm's settlement. Close by the casa de hacienda stand the houses of the inquilinos, the storerooms, barns, implement sheds, and pens for cattle, horses, and sheep. The owner and his family have made no attempt to fit the place for permanent residence. It is fitted, rather, as a vacation resort. With the coming of summer and the close of schools the family (usually accompanied by several relatives and friends) moves out from the city, bringing only such effects as would be needed for a stay of two or three months. The house servants, of course, accompany them, and others are drawn from the group of tenants. Numerous horses are provided, for the favorite recreation is riding. While the master of the farm with his overseers directs the harvesting of crops, the young folks and their guests spend the days in games, picnics, excursions into the mountains, and the restful life afforded on such estates. The Andean scenery, the unbroken sunshine of a Mediterranean summer, the aromatic fragrance of the chaparral, the keen, crisp air of the mountain valleys, all make such an estate particularly attractive to the Chilean, and he prizes his farm largely for such features.

THE HILL LAND OF LOS PEUMOS

By far the greater part of this fundo, as of many others that lie near the mountains, is the hill land it contains. This extends back along the right bank of the Maipo and the Colorado and includes the extensive drainage area of several tributary streams. Up one of these, the Estero de las Monjas (a small snow-fed torrent that joins the Colorado on the upper part of the farm), a series of mountain trails leads to highland pastures some ten miles from the administrative center of the estate. Though there is little grass on the lower slopes of these mountains, good grazing is found at an elevation of about eight thousand feet (ca. 2,400 meters). At this height a common feature of the Andes in central Chile is a broad, nearly level or gently sloping platform lying halfway between the steeper sides of the river canyons and the equally steep-sloped peaks that rise out of the fields of perpetual snow. The flats apparently represent former erosion levels into whose high surfaces the streams have now, in a new cycle of erosion, incised their channels to depths of four or five thousand feet. The broad uplands of gentle contours are deeply buried in snow during more than six months of the year. In late spring or early summer the snow line retreats above them, and a thick growth of grass and flowers springs up on the frost-mellowed soil. At this time the Central Valley and its foothills, green enough during the rainy winter, are becoming dry from the long drought of the summer season. From the lowland pastures, useless now except where the land is irrigated, large herds of cattle, horses, and sheep are driven up the narrow, tortuous trails to the Alpine meadows. Here they graze in a half-wild state throughout the summer, feeding in many cases at the very foot of the retreating snow fields. The herdsmen who accompany them are compelled to live a more or less nomadic life, finding shelter where they can, or occupying such rude shacks as they may have been able to build in former seasons. All their supplies must be brought from the farm below, and only such things as can be carried on horseback are taken up. For three or four months they live here with their flocks, spending much time in the saddle, subsisting chiefly on meat and cheese and the hard bread brought up after occasional trips down to civilization. Their families are seldom taken with them, though children sometimes go to help tend the flocks of sheep. The cattle and horses require little attention. They must be kept from straying too far over the mountains, though there is little danger that they will trespass on another farm, so large are the areas included in the estate. Water is abundant in the little streams that issue from under the fields of snow or in the marshy, flower-spread plots about the springs in which other brooklets have their sources. The greatest dangers are from pumas, many of which inhabit these remote grazing lands, and from condors which nest in the almost inaccessible crags that rise out of the snow fields at altitudes above 10,000 feet (*ca.* 3,000 meters). The condors are daily seen sailing about high above the mountain tops, watching for carrion or small animals on which to prey. On one occasion while visiting these pasture lands, two of us lay motionless on the ground to see if the giant birds would be interested. One or two which we had seen circling high in the sky soon detected us and descended in wide spirals until they were so close that we could plainly see their eyes and even hear the rush of air through their powerful wings. Other condors saw them and joined in the investigation until sixteen of the birds (each measuring probably seven to nine feet from tip to tip of their wings) were circling around close above us. At a movement on our part, they swerved, rose swiftly in giant spirals, and soon were lost to sight over the distant peaks. On another occasion we saw several condors attacking a young calf. The calf sought refuge under bushes, but it took the combined efforts of a number of cows to drive the hungry birds away. These voracious creatures are a serious danger to such young animals and to goats, sheep, or pigs. In time of great hunger, the herdsmen say, they will attack even grown animals, swooping down upon them with such force as to drive or knock them over cliffs. Occasionally one hears of a man having to fight them off.

With the approach of autumn and the beginning of rains in the valleys, the herds are driven back to the lowland pastures. Care must be taken to have them out of the mountains before the first storm arrives, for on these elevated flats neither man nor beast could long survive the rigors of winter.

The seasonal migration of herds is common on most farms that lie in the mountain valleys or on the piedmont close to the foot of the Andes. The movement generally takes place within the confines of a single property. Some of the great estates recognize no eastern boundary except the Argentine frontier and make seasonal use of even small grazing lands right up to that line. Many other farms possess grazing rights in extensive mountain areas that seem to be undivided parts of former great estates now used in common by the properties into which such estates have been partitioned. On the flat lacustrine basin about Lake Maule, the main source of the Maule River, at an elevation of 10,000 feet above the sea and within the sight of the Argentine border, I found cattle that had been brought up from the Central Valley.

As may be judged from this account, Peumos is not a source of great wealth to its owner. The valley lands probably produce little more than the farm community of about a hundred souls consumes. Small quantities of grain and fruits as well as vegetables find their way to the markets of Santiago or some nearer town. But, even with irrigation, little surplus of purely agricultural products is obtained. Livestock constitutes the principal resource. The cattle, pastured on the highlands and fed during the rest of the season in alfalfa fields, yield beef and hides enough to form a small revenue. Sheep add wool and mutton beyond the needs of the farm population. Horses, goats, and swine contribute a small income. At best, however, the farm as organized with inquilino labor, a hireling administrator, and an absentee owner, can scarcely be looked upon as a paying investment. It serves to bring in a modest income and, perhaps more important still, affords a vacation resort for the family and their friends and gives to the owner the prestige of a member in the landholding class.

CHAPTER IV

THE ORIGINS OF THE CHILEAN HACIENDA

To the early Spanish settlers of America Chile was one of the least important lands discovered. It lacked the great mineral wealth that lured fortune seekers to Mexico and Peru. It contained no great native empire whose realms could be conquered for the Spanish crown, whose people could be brought to swell the population of Christendom, and whose labor could be employed in mines or fields to support the invaders. It offered nothing of fabled cities or mysterious treasures to stir the imagination of adventurers. Furthermore, it lay far off, on the most distant corner of South America, on the far shores of the great South Sea. It could be reached only by way of the dreaded passage around Cape Horn, or the still more dangerous narrow strait which Magellan discovered, or by sailing for long days against wind and current along the forbidding desert south of Peru. From Spain's other colonies it was walled off by sea and mountains and desert, all formidable barriers even today with our improved means of travel.

Conquest and Early Colonization of Chile

The first Spanish expedition into Chile, that of Almagro in 1535, left no permanent results. It confirmed Indian reports that there was such a land as Chile, but it found no dense population nor high civilization and discovered no promising sources of wealth. The new land received a bad name. " There was no man who wished to come to this land," says Pedro de Valdivia in one of his letters to the king. The reported poverty of the region and the terrible hardships encountered along the five-hundred-league march, over the cold heights of the Andes and across the waterless desert, so discouraged further exploration that five years passed before another attempt was made even to enter the country. In 1541, however, Valdivia, after a few years' experience in the conquest of what is now Bolivia and Peru, led into Chile a small army of 150 Spaniards and some three thousand Peruvian Indians, styled *yanaconas,* who had been drafted into service to accompany the expedition. They marched down from the Lake Titicaca region and by vigorous campaigning reached the spot where the city of Santiago now stands. They even penetrated the forested region of the south as far as the city that now bears their leader's name and, after defeating bands of Araucanian warriors who opposed their way, took possession of the entire territory in the name of Spain. Subsequent events, however, proved that the resistance of the Indians had been under-estimated. Their country fought for them. The deep forests that lay beyond the Bío-Bío offered a terrain that was both unfamiliar and impassable to the Spaniards. Valdivia's small force was soon ambushed among the timbered hills of the Coast Range, and few escaped from the disaster. Valdivia himself was captured and put to a cruel death. Most of the territory south of the forest's edge was recovered for the natives and, except for a few far-separated points along the coast, was held back from white occupation for three hundred years. Spanish settlement was thus limited to northern and central Chile. The towns of Santiago and Concepción, founded in 1541 and 1550, continued as the nuclei of the new colony. Little opposition was presented by the Indians about Santiago and in the desert of the north after the first fierce battles with which they met the entrance of the invaders. The natives were few in number, occupying widely separated settlements. Moreover, they were easily ousted from the areas they occupied, for most of them were not sedentary agriculturists with fixed dwellings or permanently cultivated fields. They had little hold on the

land. Nor did their territory offer the protection afforded
by the forests of their kinsmen farther south. The chapar-
ral-covered floor of the Central Valley and the grassy vales
that lay among this light timber were soon swept clear of
opposition by the mounted soldiers of the conqueror. The
colony grew slowly, however, both in numbers and importance. Its one attraction in those early days seems to
have been the opportunity for military exploits (and profit
in the form of royal favors) afforded by the long-continued
but ever unsuccessful war against the Araucanians.

Settlement of Santiago and Vicinity

The colony, well styled La Nueva Estremadura, both
because of its position at the end of the continent and because in climate it resembled the region of the same name
in Spain, early became agricultural. It took firm root in
the soil. Though producing gold in some quantity, it never
shared with Mexico and Peru their fame as mining regions.
Moreover, cut off from the other colonies, it was from the
very start forced to be self-sustaining. Its history is therefore that of an agricultural settlement. The spot selected
for the first town, Santiago, had been the site of a semi-
permanent settlement of Indians who apparently had taken
advantage of the tendency of a small river, the Mapocho,
to overflow its low banks and spread out over a broad
alluvial fan. Here, with the natural irrigation caused by
such floods aided by a simple system of canals, they were
accustomed to plant corn, beans, and other food crops.
The Spaniards took possession of their cultivated plots
and from the products, supplemented by raids on other
such Indian settlements near by, secured supplies enough
to keep them until they themselves could obtain a harvest.

At the founding of the city of Santiago on this site, a
small plot of land was allotted to each of the settlers, a
commons (*dehesa*) was set apart for the pasture of the

stock they had brought with them, and the planting of a few crops was at once begun. The Spaniards themselves and the Peruvian Indians who had survived the hardships of the campaign labored hard to render the colony self-supporting. No such efforts were necessary in Mexico and Peru where a large native population was already producing and where abundant supplies could be obtained by levying tribute on the Indian farmers. The first Chilean settlers took great pains to protect the small store of European seeds and grain which they had brought with them. No other was to be had except by a march of a thousand miles across the desert to Peru, or an almost equally difficult sea voyage up the coast. Indian corn, of course, and several other native products were put to use; but the Spaniards looked on these as fit only for their animals (and the Indians) and entirely unsuitable for a white man's food. They had brought a small amount of wheat with them; but this had been so reduced by use and by loss when the Indians had set fire to the infant city that there were but " two handfuls " (*almuerzas;* literally, breakfasts) left. This remnant and other seeds were carefully planted, and the agricultural history of the white man's Chile was begun.

The plots of ground within the town were not long sufficient for the needs of the colony. Apparently now firmly established, though in a small territory, many of the settlers were desirous of securing for themselves larger pieces of land near the town, on which they might raise more crops. Two sets of such lands were laid out, one set of lots having a frontage on the south side of the Cañada, as one of the channels of the Mapocho River (now transformed into the Alameda de las Delicias, the principal avenue of the city) was called; the other across the main channel of the Mapocho, on the north side. In both places the soil was rich though shallow, a bed of alluvium and humus underlain at a little depth by coarse gravel brought down by the stream. A reproduced plan of Santiago shows these

" *chácaras* " (i. e., *chacras*), running back from the river bank in long strips, apparently (as we may judge also from the early documents regarding them) undefined in their rearward extension.[1] It was not long before the desire for land brought about disputes over the chácaras already given. So poorly defined were the bounds of these grants that the land commissioner (*alarife*), appointed among the first acts of the Municipal Council, required assistance in deciding many of the cases and in measuring and demarcating such properties. Consequently three representatives of the municipality were given authority (1557) to settle matters and put the new properties on a more satisfactory basis.[2] These holdings sufficed for the limited food supply required at first by the few inhabitants of the little town but did not afford an adequate provision for the permanent existence of the colony. They show how promptly the Spaniards recognized the opportunity for agriculture in the mild Spain-like climate of Mediterranean Chile and how early the settlement became agricultural in character.

THE SYSTEM OF ENCOMIENDAS IN SPANISH AMERICA

Spain's colonial policy, already established in her other American possessions, provided a system devised to accomplish the threefold purpose of her expansion in America. Seeking the subjection of the conquered peoples and territories to the government of the crown, the conversion and instruction of the aborigines in the Christian faith, together with the support of the *conquistadores* themselves, she had evolved the system of *encomiendas,* or *repartimientos.* An encomienda, as the term was generally employed in the colonization of Spanish America, was a grant of Indians together with the land they inhabited, given by the king or in his name, as reward for service rendered in

[1] Thayer Ojeda (Tomás): Santiago, 1905, pp. 17ff.
[2] Actas del Cabildo, *in* Historiadores, Vol. 1, 1861, p. 571.

the conquest of the continent. As originally instituted among the islands of the West Indies, it was a mere temporary grant of the services of the Indians to provide for the sustenance of the Spaniards until they might become established in the unfamiliar conditions found in the New World. It was based on the theory that the conquered peoples of America were under an obligation to pay tribute to the king of Spain. This tribute the king farmed out to his soldiers as a recompense for the part they played in the Conquest and to enable them to live off the land they were conquering. Since the Indians could not pay in coin, the Spaniards were authorized to collect in services this contribution to the crown. At first the service was exacted wherever the Spaniards desired the Indians to work: in military campaigns, in the mines, in the fields, in the houses established by the newcomers. So heavy were the tasks imposed and so severe the conditions in which the Indians were made to labor that numerous restrictions were put upon the form in which the tribute should be rendered. Personal service was forbidden, labor in the mines was prohibited or severely regulated, and many measures were enacted to prevent the moving of the Indians from their homes and the breaking up of their families. Efforts were made to hold the encomiendas to their original character of a mere right to exact service in lieu of tribute. But the legislative authority was far away, supervision was in the hands of officials who were generally in sympathy with the colonists, and enforcement of such benevolent legislation proved impossible. As actually practiced in the New World, the encomienda came to be a form of serfdom, mild or severe according to the character of the recipient and the degree of faithfulness with which the royal decrees were carried out in a particular locality.[3]

[3] Bourne: Spain in America, 1904; Simpson: The Encomienda in New Spain, 1929; McBride: Land Systems of Mexico, 1923, Chapter 3; Douglas-Irvine: Landholding System, 1928; Keller: Agricultura chilena, 1929; González: Chilean Agriculture, 1927.

However, the Indians' service was of little value apart from the land on which they worked. Hence the colonists came to supervise their labor in the fields, and by a gradual process to look upon the fields in which their Indians labored as their own. The native people in many parts of America had little, if any, concept of individual property in land. So long as they were allowed to use it, it mattered little to them who claimed its ownership. Furthermore, the number of Indians rapidly decreased after the advent of whites, and many fields were left without their former occupants. The result was that most of the land on which the encomienda Indians lived passed into the hands of the Spaniards. Thus the system, though not originally so intended, came to represent a virtual acquisition of the land. Where the Indians were firmly settled in agricultural communities, as was the case in the highlands of Mexico to which Spanish conquest early extended, the encomiendas frankly took the form of land grants with the Indians attached, no longer being designated by the terms "Chief So-and-So with his Indians," as was customary in the West Indies, but as "such-and-such a *pueblo*" (village with its communally held area of fields and water, woods and grasslands). The encomienda thus came to give actual possession (understood to be temporary, of course) of the agricultural communities, including the Indians and the lands they occupied. This was the direction its development took not only in the Aztec Empire of central Mexico but also in the densely inhabited farming districts of the Andean tropical plateaus, whose conquest preceded that of Chile.[4]

INTRODUCTION OF ENCOMIENDA SYSTEM INTO CHILE

The conquerors of Chile had had experience in these earlier colonies, Valdivia and several of his associates

[4] McBride: *loc. cit.*

having held encomiendas in Peru. It was but natural that they should expect their services to be rewarded by similar grants of land with Indian laborers attached. Hence, within a short time after the founding of the first settlements this system was inaugurated. On January 12, 1544, only three years after Santiago had been established—as soon, in fact, as his little band of Spaniards had been able to bring the region into subjection—Valdivia began the distribution of encomiendas. Near Santiago, the only district as yet fully under the control of the Spaniards, sixty encomiendas were bestowed upon as many conquistadores, the other soldiers being assured that further grants would be made as conquest progressed southward. It was soon found that the Indian population in this part of Chile was far too small to warrant the existence of so many encomiendas, and the number was reduced to thirty-two in a re-allotment (1546).[5] Grants were given to others as the conquest advanced. Before the death of Valdivia (1553), most of the Indians in central Chile, and in the northern valley oases of Copiapó, Huasco, and Coquimbo, had been distributed among the conquerors, as had also many groups in the southern forests about Concepción, Valdivia, Imperial, Osorno, and Villarrica. Few recipients were able to take advantage of these last, inasmuch as the Indians promptly revolted and drove the Spaniards out of most

[5] A record was kept of the encomiendas granted at this time and later in the jurisdiction of Santiago. The book in which they were registered was called " El libro de repartimientos." Unfortunately it has been lost. There are, however, several lists of encomenderos compiled at different dates. One such list, given in Amunátegui Solar's " Encomiendas," Vol. 2, 1909-1910, pp. 77-85, which is based on a document in the Archivo de la Real Audiencia, Vol. 1723, enumerates the " vecinos feudatorios " (citizens holding fiefs of Indians) of Santiago, holding (in 1655) at least ten Indians each. Here are given the names, ages, dependents, etc., of all such encomenderos. The list was made in order to know from whom an army of defense might be formed against the threatened attack of the Araucanian Indians in that year. The roll contains the names of 102 men and 4 widows. Nearly all of the men are military personages, generals, captains, lieutenants, and maestres de campo. Incidentally, it reads like the roster of leading families of Chile at the present time, so largely are the terratenientes (large landholders) of today the descendants of the encomenderos.

of the southern area. A sufficient number of encomiendas survived, however, particularly from Concepción to Santiago and in the transverse valleys of the north, to establish the system as the basis of conquest and settlement in Chile.

Though introduced at the beginning of the colony, the encomienda did not play the part here that it had played in such lands as New Spain, Guatemala, and Peru. About Santiago and Concepción there was no such dense native population as on the tropical highlands. Within the jurisdiction of the first settlement it has been estimated that there were only some 70,000 Indians.[6] This probably refers to all the territory from, and including, the Aconcagua valley down to the Maule River. About Concepción the number was larger, perhaps double, within the area over which the Spaniards early established their hold. These figures, compared with corresponding data for Mexico or the Andean highlands—in each of which there were several millions of natives—reveal how much less practicable it was for the Spanish conquerors of Chile to depend for their support on Indian labor in the form of encomiendas. In fact, of such slight importance were the encomiendas of Chile as compared with other colonies that it was often said that the institution never was established there.[7] This is not strictly the case, for grants of encomiendas were made there as elsewhere, but they did not figure so conspicuously as in other lands, and, as will be brought out, they took on a quite different character.

INDIAN COMMUNITIES OF CENTRAL CHILE

The natives of central Chile, as has been noted, were not, as a rule, settled in permanent communities. From the best accounts available regarding the pre-Columbian con-

[6] Thayer Ojeda (Tomás): Ensayo crítico, Chap. 11. Thayer Ojeda (Luis): Elementos étnicos, 1919, p. 33.
[7] Torres Saldamando, in his "Apuntes históricos," 1888, p. 124, says, referring to Chile, "Allí no llegaron jamás a establecerse " (They were never established there).

dition of the aborigines of this region it is evident that most of them lived in small, scattered settlements, far less permanent in character than the towns and cities with stone or adobe structures found in the well-established centers of population in Peru and Mexico. In central Chile, the *rancherías,* as these settlements were called by the Spaniards, seem to have been mere clusters of huts, halfway between the encampments of nomads and the permanent towns of sedentary peoples. The more or less temporary character of land occupancy accounted for this lack of permanent dwellings.[8] In a few places, perhaps a score or so, between the Aconcagua and the Maule rivers, fixed agricultural villages had been established with irrigation sufficiently developed to make continuous use of the land possible. This seems to have been particularly true of the smooth valley floor of the Aconcagua River, where an abundant supply of water, gentle gradients, and extensive fertile alluvial flats offered exceptional facilities for this type of farming. Settlements of a similar character and of a nearly equal permanency may have been found along the Mapocho and a few of its small tributaries below the site of Santiago, as also in the valleys of the Cachapoal and the Tinguiririca south of the capital. On the spot where Santiago itself was founded an Indian settlement had existed, its semipermanence attested by the irrigation canals found there by the Spaniards. In many of these places Indian towns continued to exist during the colonial period, and some of them have survived to the present time, little changed except for the mingling of Spanish blood with the aboriginal Indian. These quasi-permanent towns possibly represented settlements developed under the di-

[8] Perhaps the earthquakes of the region had had something to do with the character of their dwellings, these light structures of brush, sometimes plastered over with mud, being much more suitable to such conditions than the heavy walls of adobe, brick, or stone introduced by the Europeans. In fact, Chile is now returning deliberately to this type of building as a protection against the loss of life occasioned by the seismic disturbances from which the country has suffered so severely throughout its history.

rection of the Inca Empire, a century or so before the arrival of the Spaniards, somewhat after the model of the fixed villages characteristic of that empire. They may have antedated even the penetration of Inca influence in central Chile, for in all cases they owe their permanence to a satisfactory water supply and seem to be the natural response to climatic and soil conditions found at such places.

Except for such settlements, few in number, the inhabitants of central Chile were not found so firmly fixed to the soil that the granting of encomiendas could be based on agrarian units (pueblo or community). Instead, the system turned back to its early type of grant, that of an Indian chief with his followers, and even conserved the West Indian term *cacique,* which had been used in the original encomiendas but had been little employed in the more settled areas conquered.[9] The kinship group became the common unit in the distribution of Chilean natives among the Spaniards.[10] The location of the Indians given in an encomienda was often described explicitly as being " in this valley of the Mapocho " or " in the valley of the Aconcagua," etc. Whether this was done or not, the encomiendas were always given a place character with the words " who have their seat in such-and-such a district," indicating that though most of the Indians of central Chile did not live in permanent towns they did have a certain fixity of residence within regions, usually valleys. They seem to

[9] In the south of Chile encomiendas were granted by the *levo* (clan) with its chiefs and Indians.
[10] The usual phraseology was that employed in the following grant with which Valdivia favored Juan Gómez, one of the conquistadors who had accompanied the expedition from Peru: " Encomiendo en vos el dicho Juan Gómez, en nombre de S. M., . . . el cacique llamado Millanabal e Purinabal, con todos sus indios y subjetos, . . . que tienen su asiento en la provincia de los poromaucaes " (I commit to you, the said Juan Gómez, in the name of His Majesty, . . . the chieftain called Millanabal and Purinabal, with all his Indians and subjects, who have their seat (settlement) in the province of the Poromaucaes) (Amunátegui Solar: Encomiendas, Vol. 2, Apuntaciones y Documentos, p. 62). Medina also gives the formula regularly used, in his " Documentos para la historia de Chile," Vol. 9, 1896, pp. 117, 395, 397, 410, 412, 441, etc.

have been accustomed to cultivate bits of land on the
gravelly flood plains of the streams for a few years and
then to move to some other where the soil was less depleted,
less affected by the deposits of infertile material, or better
supplied with water by the fickle braided streams. In some
cases they were said to move from one river to another as
the flow of water varied from year to year. In most if not all
settlements they must have practiced irrigation in some
form, for the seven months of the Chilean summer are
almost totally rainless, and it is impossible to grow the
main crops of maize and beans without an artificial water
supply. But in most cases the system of watering their
fields must have been of a simple, crude character, short
canals taking water from the streams and carrying it to
adjacent bits of land. Irrigation was certainly not extensively developed and had not yet greatly affected the
character of their landholding system. Of these semi-seden-
tary natives most of the Chilean encomiendas were composed. In such cases the encomiendas did not represent
land grants, and many of them continued to be merely a
right to the tribute paid by Indians or the privilege of
demanding service in lieu of such tribute. It is evident
from many references that some of the grants were purely
of this character.[11]

Early Chilean Encomiendas

In certain cases the grants of encomiendas took on something of the character seen in those of Mexico and Peru.
There were examples in central Chile of these definitely
agrarian concessions, where it is clearly stated that the
grant was a territorial one, consisting of the Indians *and
their land*. This was possible only where there were clusters
of more permanently located people, chiefly along the rivers
where irrigation had been better developed. Several of the

[11] Latcham: Organización social, 1924, p. 126; Vicuña Mackenna: Relaciones históricas, Vol. 1, 1877, p. 24.

encomiendas given out by Valdivia were of this kind. Some of them were situated near Santiago along the Maipo and the Mapocho rivers, while others were in the transverse valleys farther north where the complete dependence of the people upon irrigation made for permanent settlements.[12] While the type of encomienda that conveyed only the service of the Indians was apparently most common, this latter kind which bestowed upon the conquerors both

[12] Of this type was one of the encomiendas bestowed on Inez Suárez, the woman who accompanied Valdivia on the expedition of conquest. After assigning her certain Indians " in the province of the Poromaucaes," Valdivia adds others as follows: " y más el cacique llamado Apoquindo, con todos sus principales e indios sujetos, que tienen su asiento en este valle de Mapocho, y dáseos su tierra e indios, para que os sirvais de todos ellos " (and in addition the chief called Apoquindo, with all his sub-chiefs and Indians and subjects, who have their seat in this valley of Mapocho, and to you is given his land and Indians, that you may make use of all of them) (Amunátegui Solar: Encomiendas, Vol. 2, Apunt. y Doc., p. 8). Again, in granting an encomienda to Juan Bautista de Pastene, the Genoese sea captain who joined the small party of conquerors a few years after the founding of the colony, Valdivia, after using the customary phrase, " the chief and all his sub-chiefs and Indians and subjects," adds, " con más las tierras e asiento que tienen los dichos caciques e indios cerca del Río Maipo " (with the lands and settlement which the said caciques and Indians have near the Maipo River) (ibid., pp. 32-33). Again, an encomienda was given to Antonio Tarabajano, " con todos los indios, pueblos, tierras, términos, ríos, montes y valles " (with all the Indians, villages, lands, bounds, rivers, forests, and valleys) (Soto Rojas: Apuntes para la historia agrícola de Chile, 1915, p. 178). On another occasion, according to one of the earliest chroniclers of Chile, a certain encomienda consisted essentially of an Indian village. Valdivia was said to have given to Francisco Martínez, who had lent him twenty thousand pesos to help finance the conquest, " una encomienda de un pueblo, llamado Colina, tres leguas de la ciudad de Santiago " (an encomienda of a town called Colina, three leagues from the city of Santiago) (Mariño de Lovera: Crónica del reino de Chile, in Historiadores, Vol. 6, 1865, p. 89).

Another example of an encomienda that was clearly territorial is that of the grant to Gonzalo de los Ríos (August 1, 1549) of " la mitad de los valles de la Ligua i del Papudo, con todos sus caciques " (half of the valleys of La Ligua and Papudo, with all their caciques) (Amunátegui Solar, op cit., p. 73). This encomienda was considered as a land grant during its entire history. About 1695 this holding was consolidated into an entailed estate, and the documents recording that transaction trace the history of the holding in four stages: first, as an encomienda received by Don Gonzalo de los Ríos; second, as an estancia (ranch) held by Doña Catalina de los Ríos; third, as an estancia bought at public auction by Don Juan de Hermúa; and fourth, as an estancia y tierras bought from him by Don Juan de la Cerda and entailed in favor of his son, Don Juan de la Cerda (Amunátegui Solar: Mayorazgos, Vol. 1, 1901-1904, p. 174).

Still another example of a " territorial encomienda " is the grant by Valdivia of " half the valley of Lampa together with the Indians resident there " to Francisco Hernández Gallego (Medina: op. cit., pp. 441-442).

the Indians and their land was not unknown, though it certainly was much less common in Chile than elsewhere. The encomienda had much less of an agrarian character here than in other colonies and thus contributed in a smaller degree to the creation of large rural properties with serfs attached.

Furthermore, with the limited number of Indians available, there were not enough encomiendas to go round, even for the small group of conquistadores who accompanied Valdivia. Only those who stood highest in the favor of the leader or had the strongest claim to rewards for distinguished service could hope for such grants. The total number given in the first distribution about Santiago did not provide for more than a fourth of the original band. Even with those that were added during the subsequent conquest of the south and survived the uprisings of 1552 and the following years, there were not enough to meet the needs of the gradually increasing settlement. In 1655 it was said that there were but two hundred who held encomiendas, whereas the total number of Spaniards must have been at least double that.[13] Those who had received no Indians were known simply as *vecinos* (citizens), as distinguished from the *encomenderos,* and the two groups were rather sharply differentiated. In the Cabildo (Municipal Council) of Santiago each group had its own representative, the one being served by the *alcalde* (mayor) *de vecinos,* the other by an *alcalde de encomenderos.* The former class occupied a decidedly inferior position in the colony. They enjoyed less social distinction, had no retinue of native attendants at their command, possessed no assured means of livelihood, and as yet had been given no opportunity to establish themselves on the land except on a small scale as holders of urban lots and suburban chácaras. They scarcely figured as masters in the country they had helped to conquer.

[13] Amunátegui Solar: Encomiendas, Vol. 2, pp. 75-85.

As at first understood in the West Indies, the encomienda was a temporary concession, to be surrendered at the will of the crown. As the system became established the term of possession was defined as " *una vida* " (one life), that is to last during the life of the recipient. By 1536 the term had been extended to include *dos vidas,* that of the holder and that of his heir. It was made still more permanent in 1629 by the addition of a third life, and later, under certain conditions, a fourth and fifth life were added. The encomiendas thus came to be regarded as the actual possessions of the families which held them, being virtually hereditary.

In the early years of the colony there was much confusion in the system. Encomiendas were changed from one person to another; the governor sometimes took Indians away from one individual to bestow them upon another more deserving or closer in friendship to the donor; not infrequently encomiendas were left vacant by the death of an owner who had no heirs or by his departure from Chile; there was also some bartering of Indians in order to secure more satisfactory allotments. Evidently much disorder prevailed among the kinship groups of the natives, and it was frequently difficult for the Spaniards to ascertain to which chief a particular group belonged. Tribal lines do not seem to have been so strictly drawn as elsewhere in America; or, perhaps, the chaos brought about by the breaking up of the native social order by the Conquest was responsible for this apparent looseness of kinship ties. As a consequence, many readjustments were necessary during the first few years, and resort to litigation over Indians was common. So many disputes arose that it was found necessary to institute an orderly procedure: the plaintiff and defendant were each directed to name a representative, and the court was asked to appoint a third. This trio acted in an advisory capacity, the final decision being made by the governor himself.[14]

---

[14] Actas del Cabildo, *in* Historiadores, Vol. 1, pp. 349-351.

Additional confusion was produced by the practice of the Spaniards of moving their Indians from place to place. Such transfer was forbidden by the regulations governing encomiendas, but it continued nevertheless. The lands most sought after by the Spaniards were those capable of being irrigated, and these were the lands on which the service of the Indians was desired. But since many of the Indians had their settlements far from the lands most suitable for the European type of agriculture, the encomenderos frequently insisted on moving them from their home districts. The development of cattle raising also created such a necessity. The grasslands had been of little use to the Indians of central Chile, who had no large number of domestic animals, for the llama and the alpaca (though apparently raised in some numbers farther south) played little or no part in the central section of the country. With the introduction of cattle, sheep, and horses herdsmen were needed on the grass-covered Coast Range hills, on the high summer pastures in the Andes, and in other places where grazing could be carried on. This brought about an additional disruption of the Indian groups. Mines, too, offered occasion for the transfer of many Indians from their home regions, the breaking up of families, and the dissolution of the Indian social structure.[15]

There has been some discussion as to whether the encomiendas were really feudal in character—that is, as to whether they were given with a proviso requiring military service from the recipient. In some of the American colonies this does not seem to have been the case, in actual practice at least. Apparently a definite obligation of military service was not always assumed by the one to whom an

[15] Many instances of such transfers are found in documents dealing with this period. A case in point is that in which several Indians belonging to the encomienda of Ñingue were moved from their home district to the estancia called Maitén near Chillán, recorded in a document in the Archivo del Ministerio de lo Interior, Vol. 481, pp. 350 ff. Amunátegui Solar in his " Encomiendas " cites numerous other such instances.

encomienda was given. In Chile, however, as in some of the other colonies, the grants of Indians were plainly called *feudatorios*, and military service was demanded in return.[16] Several of the lists of encomenderos compiled in Chile were definitely for the purpose of ascertaining the military strength available through the system. An encomendero pledged himself, frequently if not always, to furnish arms, horses, and men for the service of the king, taking an oath of fealty to that obligation. Here it was not against a foreign foe in the same sense as in old Spain that the feudatorio swore to combat faithfully for his liege lord, but against the indefatigable enemy that harassed the southern frontier and from whom the Spanish armies sought in vain to wrest the land.[17]

The number of Indians comprising an encomienda varied widely. Valdivia is said to have reserved for himself some 1,500 natives at the time of the first distribution and to have presented 500 to Inez Suárez and 400 to Jerónimo de Alderete, his lieutenant.[18] Other encomiendas were much smaller, averaging perhaps some 50 to 100 each in the central part of the country. In the more populous south, as the conquest progressed there, the number of Indians included in an encomienda was usually far greater. Valdivia took some 40,000 for himself in that region and gave his brother-in-law, Diego Nieto de Gaete, more than 15,000 (at Villarrica), while at the town of Valdivia, Francisco de Villagrán received 30,000; Pedro de Villagrán, 15,000; Jerónimo de Alderete, 12,000; Pedro de Olmos de Aguilera, 8,000; Andrés Hernandes de Córdova, 6,000; and many others in proportion.[19] Unfortunately for the recipients of these prodigal favors, most of the encomiendas given in that part of the country did not materialize, as, it

[16] Solórzano Pereira: Política indiana, 1703, Book 3, Chapter 3, p. 135.
[17] An example of the oath taken by an encomendero is given in Amunátegui Solar's " Encomiendas," Vol. 1, p. 70.
[18] Barros Arana: Historia, Vol. 1, 1884, p. 282.
[19] Mariño de Lovera: Crónica, *in* Historiadores, Vol. 6, pp. 141-142.

will be remembered, the Indians soon recaptured the larger part of their territory and held it until the end of the colonial period.

Forced Labor of the Encomiendas

As originally constituted, the encomiendas were of relatively little value. Most of them lacked the element that gave value to the institution in other colonies, i. e. land. As they became more firmly established, however, and as the Spanish conquerors secured a greater and greater hold on the land itself on which Indian labor could be employed, the system provided a means whereby the newcomers might live with ease and comfort. The encomiendas containing a large number of Indians in the early days of the colony enabled their owners to work the gold deposits which the Spaniards eagerly sought in every territory they occupied. They also made possible the development of extensive stock raising on the Indians' own land, on the *estancias* of the encomenderos, or on the unclaimed public domain. Favored with this forced labor, the Spaniards were also able to bring an increasing amount of land under cultivation and to introduce such European plants as were suited to the climate of the new country. Wheat, barley, grapes, and a number of Mediterranean fruits were produced within a few years after the founding of Santiago, while maize continued to be grown by the Indians on their own account for their own food as well as to supply an increasing demand for it on the part of the Spaniards. Beans and potatoes were also cultivated by the native people.

All the necessary manual labor was performed by the Indians. The colonists loudly proclaimed that they could not possibly occupy the land and maintain themselves there except by means of the forced labor of the Indians. Chileans of the present day, though condemning the severity with which the first Chileans were treated by their conquerors, readily admit that only through some such method could settlements have been established and the country brought under exploitation. It was taken for granted, then, as it still is, that white men could never have done the work themselves, and could hardly have been expected to do so. The encomienda system provided the labor supply considered essential to the establishing of every Spanish colony.

The service rendered by the Indians of an encomienda varied with the locality in which it was situated, the character of the encomendero, and the kind of properties held by him. A detailed list of the requirements made upon Indians of a Peruvian encomienda has been preserved and shows the use made of the Indian service. This list specifies that the Indians of a certain encomienda should provide seventy-five pesos worth of gold each year, placed in the house of the encomendero; that they should make and deliver to their master a fixed amount of native cloth; that they should plant each year ten or twelve measures (*fanegas*) of maize and seven or eight of wheat, from which four hundred measures of maize and three hundred of wheat must be obtained for the master, while the Indians are entitled to any surplus produced and are obliged to make good any shortage. All that is due the encomendero is to be presented to him on demand. He himself is to attend to the threshing (with oxen or horses) on the threshing floor on his own account, but may call upon the Indians to help with the work. A small additional amount of grain is to be planted and cared for in the chacra of the Spaniard; furthermore, the Indians are to supply each month forty fowls (half of them hens) for the house of the master; forty *arrobas* of fish every year delivered to the master's house; also thirty eggs are to be brought to the master each Friday and each "fish day" and during the Lenten season, and four pounds of fresh fish on each of these days; also the Indians should supply the master each year with 250 pounds of salt (10 arrobas) and twelve sacks of charcoal; also, for the personal service about the house of the encomendero there must be maintained a force of twelve Indians, serving in relays (*mitas*), as well as a force of six Indians to tend the cattle of the encomendero in the vicinity of the city (Lima), and six more for the same purpose in the district where the encomienda was located.[20] While the details of the service demanded varied with the needs of the Spaniards in the different regions, this may be taken as typical of the requirements in most of the Spanish colonies. In Chile the personal service exacted appears to have been more extensive than in other lands, and this particular obligation survived there long after it had been abolished elsewhere.[21]

The first use made of the encomienda Indians in the early years of the Chilean colony was as laborers in the mines. Though the mineral resources here were not nearly so great as elsewhere, and though the distance from all markets for the metals made mining less remunerative than in Mexico, Colombia, or Peru, gold mining early lured some of the conquerors. Valdivia was able to secure a quantity of this metal from the mines already known to the Indians in the valley of the Margamarga, near Valparaíso; within a few years after the founding of the colony he had a force of yanaconas and encomienda Indians at work here. At several other points in northern, central, and southern Chile where gravel was washed for its gold the Indians were obliged to work back into the banks of the streams as far as their crude tools could be used. In the deep forests lying behind Osorno and Valdivia some of these ancient placer mines are now being exploited anew after the lapse of nearly four hundred years. Rough stone retaining walls show where the Indians had worked

[20] Libro Primero del Cabildo de Lima, Vol. 2, 1888, Apéndices, pp. 152-154.
[21] Amunátegui Solar: Encomiendas, Vol. 1, pp. 174-190.

in those early days. Some of the largest trees of the forest now spread their roots over the workings where swarms of Indians sat day after day with the cold water up to their knees and washed for the grains their masters prized so highly. The crude wooden picks with which they labored are still found occasionally, buried in the gravel deposits over which they toiled. Fortunately, severe restrictions were put upon labor in the mines, but not before many of the Indians had succumbed to the hardships and exposure incident to such work.

AGRICULTURAL LABOR OF THE ENCOMIENDAS

Before many years had elapsed the service rendered in the mines had become of far less importance than that in the fields. As has been stated, Chile early became pre-eminently agricultural in character. By 1630 Santiago and its environs had become " the most notable garden in the world," to use the phrase of a contemporary historian, " full of all kinds of fruits, vegetables, wheat, and barley." For some twenty leagues about the city there were " rich farms, with great harvests of grains and wine and stocked with abundance of cattle." Santiago itself was " beautifully developed with orchards, olive groves, and vineyards, the wine and the olives being better than those of Spain, while oil is produced in quantity, and dried fruits, especially figs, are yielded in large abundance." [22] The labor of field and orchard that made such development possible was carried on entirely by the Indians. There were no others to do the work. A few African slaves (so few that one seldom sees any evidence of African blood even in the common people of Chile today) and a small number of yanaconas from Peru constituted the only other labor supply. To make such production possible much pioneer-

[22] Tribaldos de Toledo: Vista jeneral, 1864, p. 8. This writer was the official Cronista de Indias, successor to Antonio de Herrera, and wrote his description between 1625 and 1634.

ing had to be done. Land had to be cleared of chaparral (*matorral,* as the Chileans call it; Fig. 12), irrigation canals had to be built or extended, the ground had to be broken (at first by hand, until oxen could be brought down from Peru and plows made), seed had to be planted and harvested, houses erected, orchards set out and cared for, fences (usually high mud walls) had to be built, and the increasing herds of cattle, horses, and sheep had to be tended. In the agricultural tasks and in the care of flocks and herds the conditions were less oppressive than in the mines. Here there was a type of labor to which the natives were somewhat more accustomed. Besides, the relationship of master to man on rural estates was usually more benevolent. Even here, however, the master was not always present. Legislation whose purpose was to protect the Indian from abuse by the Spaniards forbade the encomendero to live among his wards. His natural response was to employ an overseer. This individual was most commonly drawn from the class of *mestizos* (half-breeds) which grew up rapidly in the colony. With the mingling of the two races that took place as settlement became more general, it was not long before the owners of the encomiendas had among the Indians who belonged to them many in whose veins their own blood was diffused. They thus came to occupy the position of patriarch as well as of master and to treat their Indians with a degree of paternal regard. The longer the encomiendas continued and the more the mutual obligations of Master and Man became regulated by custom as well as by law, the greater was the tendency toward this truly patriarchal relationship. There were some notorious examples of oppression on the part of the encomendero, as in the case of the diabolically minded woman, La Quintrala, owner of a valuable encomienda in the valley of La Ligua River, whose name has become a byword and a synonym for cruelty among the Chilean people. In general, however, conditions were gradually improved, and as the colony became more completely agricultural there appeared less of such hardships as marked the first years when the Indians were employed chiefly in the mines ; but of poverty there was an abundance. The Indians belonging to an encomienda probably lived in poorer houses and were possessed of food and clothing far inferior to those enjoyed by the free Indians south of the Araucanian frontier.

As the Indian towns that existed in certain places about the Central Valley gradually disappeared, engulfed by the neighboring encomiendas or drained of their inhabitants to supply the labor required in this system of settlement, the personal and domestic service which the Indians of an encomienda were required to render to their *patrón* came to constitute a more important feature of their obligation. All the tasks of the household fell to the Indians, men and women. Each encomienda group was compelled to furnish a fixed number of servants from their company. The colony depended on these domestics for all kinds of menial labor. Repeated decrees were issued prohibiting such service, all to no avail. The colony was too far distant, the local authorities too much in sympathy with their settlers and their needs, and there was no substitute for the labor of the natives. They became, wherever the Spaniards settled, the " hewers of wood and drawers of water." No household of Spaniards was without its retinue of native servants, either living in quarters beside their master's or coming in a system of relays from their own settlements for a few days or weeks of personal service for the encomendero and his family. This domestic service (as indeed all the labor of the Indians) was sometimes sold or rented out by the owner, contrary as this was to regulations.[23] The colony members thus came to depend upon their Indians for all the manual labor to be done, in farm,

---

[23] Valdivia's widow, in her will, makes mention of a number of Indians whose service she had rented out to other Spaniards (Amunátegui Solar, Encomiendas, Vol. 2, Apunt. y Doc., p. 137).

ranch, mine, and household, and the white man came to regard such labor as entirely beneath his dignity, fit only for the subject race that had been brought into this position of servitude.

DECLINE OF THE ENCOMIENDAS

Such was the encomienda as introduced into Chile from the West Indies, Mexico, and Peru, and such was the part it played in the early days of the colony. As has been noted, however, the slightly sedentary character of the Indian population made it impossible for the system to serve the same purpose it had served among the very different conditions existing in other regions. The years immediately following the establishment of the colony made this apparent. The small number of Indians found in the central part of the country rapidly became smaller. Many of them were pulled loose from their native groups but did not become fixed on the Spaniards' holdings and thus came to constitute a floating population of little value to the new farms. Furthermore, losses in warfare were severe, and diseases introduced by the Europeans carried away whole settlements. Unaccustomed labor also decimated the ranks of the survivors. Those who could escaped into the unconquered forest country only a few score miles to the south or sought refuge in the almost inaccessible valleys of the Andes. Those who fled south frequently joined the Araucanians in the protracted warfare against the whites along the frontier. Some of these, such as the famous Lautaro and Caupolicán, taught their Indian brothers European methods of fighting and rendered still more formidable the resistance of those tribes. This encouraged still others to abandon the part of the country now settled by foreigners and to escape from the hard tasks imposed by the invaders. Thus there was a constant recruiting of the enemy's ranks from these refugees and a constant depletion of the Indian labor supply on the encomiendas. While some of the first encomiendas had contained two or three thousand Indians or even more, by 1610 there were said to be none with more than one hundred and most of them had from forty to sixty. There were at that time not over 2,899 encomienda Indians in the district of Santiago. In the whole "Kingdom of Chile" no more than 5,000 Indians were serving in the encomiendas.[24] The system gradually lost most of its value, in so far as it consisted of the mere service rendered by a group of Indians. It tended to disappear, as regards both the number of encomiendas in existence and the number of Indians serving on each.

In the meantime, the encomiendas that had survived had undergone such transformation from their original character that they little resembled the early grants or the encomiendas still existing in other Spanish American colonies In 1680 the encomiendas of Chile were described by Don Juan Henríquez, then serving as "president" of the province, as of three kinds: first, those formed of Indians belonging to a pueblo or cacique (the original type) ; second, those composed of what in Chile had come to be styled "yanaconas" (not the Peruvian Indians who had come down with the early expeditions from that country, but Indians of Chile who had been found apparently unattached to encomiendas or kinship groups and had been brought onto rural holdings, with or without official commitment) ; third, those composed of Indians who had been captured in the wars on the frontier, sold as slaves to some Spaniard, and then transformed from the status of slave to that of an encomienda Indian attached to some property.[25]

In the early decades of the colony the number of Indians available for service in central Chile had been re-

[24] Vicuña Mackenna: Historia de Santiago, Vol. 1, 1869, pp. 148-149.
[25] Amunátegui Solar: Encomiendas, Vol. 2, pp. 220-223.

plenished frequently by raids into Araucanian territory. These raids, although ostensibly for the purpose of protecting the frontier or overcoming resistance in that quarter to Spanish rule, were animated perhaps fully as much by the desire to capture Indians and sell them to meet the needs for labor among the new European settlements. This was at first frowned upon by the government but later permitted, as serving to break down Araucanian resistance and also to provide for the greater prosperity of the Spanish settlements. According to Vicuña Mackenna,[26] more than half of the Indians in encomiendas at the beginning of the seventeenth century had been obtained in this way. It was not permitted that they should be held in formal slavery, but they might be " deposited "—committed to the charge of some Spaniard who would then be entitled to settle them with other Indians on his holding. The source of supply for this third type of encomienda declined after 1650, and the practice of enslaving captured Araucanians was finally prohibited completely (1674). Besides, it was this kind of Indian who was most difficult to retain in captivity, particularly in the region of Concepción and elsewhere near the border, where escape was easy.

As for the first class, the number of Indians available from this system became increasingly smaller. The tribal and other kinship groups had been so broken up, the cacique's authority so destroyed, the established habits and customs of the natives so disturbed, and their former freedom so curtailed, that, with disease and flight further reducing their numbers, it became hardly worth the trouble and expense of having the encomiendas renewed when the term for which they had been granted expired.[27]

Furthermore, the mixing of the races brought about a steady transformation in the status of the serving class,

[26] Vicuña Mackenna: *loc. cit.*
[27] Amunátegui Solar: Encomiendas, Vol. 2, pp. 220-224.

as generation after generation made it more European. The children of Indian mothers and Spanish fathers were not held in encomiendas. Many of the descendants of the Indians originally granted in such concessions thus became exempt from such service, and many more are reported by officials to have taken advantage of this situation by asserting that they were mestizos.[28] This condition continued and grew worse with time. The report of the officials referred to shows how reduced in numbers and importance the encomiendas had become. In 1759 only four encomiendas were left in the district (*correjimiento*) of Santiago, four in that of Aconcagua, seven in Colchagua, four in Maule, and few in other sections of the country. Most of these were so small in the number of Indians that they were of little value. In several cases the report states that all the Indians were either dispersed and of no service to the owner or had secured exemption on the grounds that they were mestizos. In 1788 another report enumerated the encomiendas still existing and gave the total for the whole country as forty-nine.[29] When it is remembered that Valdivia had created thirty-two in 1546 and many more within the next few years before his death, and that, as already noted, in 1655 there had been 107 persons in the city and district of Santiago alone who had held encomiendas of ten or more Indians each, it is seen that little remained of the institution as originally constituted.

INFLUENCE OF THE ENCOMIENDAS

The influence of the encomienda in Chile, however, was not lost. Though it had proved to be of relatively little value in directly providing a labor supply, it had

---

[28] Report to the " president " of Chile, Manuel de Amat y Junient, by officials of the treasury, in 1759 (Amunátegui Solar: Encomiendas, Vol. 2, pp. 236-244).
[29] *Ibid.*, pp. 244-249.

established the type of rural holding destined to be common in that country for the next four hundred years at least. The territorial encomiendas became estates, the pride of their owners, the envy of those who had not been so fortunate as to receive them. In spite of the diminishing number of Indians included in them they became the basis for some of the most desirable of the Chilean *haciendas*. As agrarian units they were of great importance. They had brought the land itself into possession of the Spaniards, thus giving a permanence to Spanish occupation of the country. In most, if not all of them, the Spaniards had completely replaced the Indians as owners of the soil.

One way in which this transfer of ownership came about was through the intermarriage (regular and irregular) between the encomenderos and the natives. Some of the Spaniards did not disdain formal marriage with the Indians, particularly with the daughters of caciques, but far more commonly illicit unions of whites and Indians occurred. These relationships brought the Spaniards at once into the status of membership in the kinship groups with the concomitant rights to the community possessions, much as among the "civilized" Indians of the United States it was common for a white man to take an Indian woman and, by becoming a "squaw man," to acquire full citizenship rights in the tribe, with the privilege of fencing and using as much land as he might wish. The writer has seen frequent instances of this among the Choctaws and Chickasaws of the old Indian Territory. In much the same manner Spaniards seem to have established themselves in many places in Chile.

A good example of this is the case of Bartolomé Flores, the German whose real name was Blumenthal and who accompanied Valdivia on his expedition from Peru. This man received an encomienda in the angle formed by the junction of the Maipo and the Mapocho rivers, a few miles southwest of Santiago. He promptly took as his wife Elvira, the daughter of Chief Talagante, and thus established himself as a member of the group entitled to the land belonging to the tribe or clan. Elvira is spoken of as "owner of lands and valleys," with title (whether individual or collective is not certain and practically made little difference) received from the Inca Tupac Yupanqui (1453-1483) to large areas reaching from where the town of Talagante now stands to the baths of Cauquenes on the upper Cachapoal, including the districts of Aculeo and the Compañía, both now famous for their magnificent farms. These lands were said to have been crossed even in those early days by *acequias* (irrigation canals) built by the Inca.[30] It was not long before Blumenthal was in possession of some of the best lands in the region. That he obtained them through his connection with the Indians, rather than by a grant from the colonial government, seems evident both from the absence of any mention of such a grant in the procedings of the Cabildo and from the fact that many years later the best grounds on which Doña Agueda (daughter of Blumenthal and the Indian, Elvira) could lay claim to the lands was actual possession of them for "over fifty years," no mention being made of any *merced* (grant).[31] There seems little doubt that it was in this fashion that Blumenthal acquired possession of the holding that later became the basis for several of Chile's most valuable haciendas.

By such or even less regular means the land of encomienda Indians gradually passed into the possession of Spanish colonists. Writing late in the colonial period, one of the " presidents " of Chile said: " These Indians have completely lost their lands, either by having them occupied and used by the encomenderos themselves for their own profit or by abandoning them as they have been forced to

[30] Soto Rojas: Apuntes, 1915, pp. 176-179.
[31] Lillo: Mensuras de tierras, Vol. 1, 1603-1604, pp. 39-40.

move." [32] The encomienda thus, indirectly at least, became a main source of the great landed estates that have characterized the country for several centuries.

DIRECT GRANTS OF LAND

Many of the farms of Chile, however, trace their beginnings to a very different origin. They sprang from direct grants of land. Some of these grants were in connection with encomiendas, providing areas where the Indians might be worked. But many were made to individuals to whom, it seems from the records, no Indians had been given. In either case they gave rise to recognized agricultural holdings. Many of the greatest haciendas of the country were begun in this way, rather than in the form of concessions containing both the Indians and their land.

We have seen that some of the encomiendas consisted only of the service of Indians and brought no direct title to lands. The recipients of such favors were accustomed to ask and receive land grants, without which little use could be made of the service of the Indians. In such cases lands were generally given near where the Indian groups had their settlements; the natives might then remain in their accustomed *caseríos* (clusters of houses) and from there work the property of their masters. It was not uncommon, however, for the land and the Indians received by an encomendero to be widely separated, in which case the laborers were frequently transferred to the property, royal orders to the contrary notwithstanding.[33] There were many examples of this.[34] If, as not infrequently

[32] Amunátegui Solar: Encomiendas, Vol. 2, p. 252.
[33] Cédula of 1541.
[34] Francisco de Aguirre even took Indians from the region of Santiago to Serena to employ them on his holdings there (Amunátegui Solar: Encomiendas, Vol. 1, pp. 129-144; Vol. 2, Apunt. y Doc., p. 46). Numerous other instances are cited in a document in the Archivo del Ministerio de lo Interior, Vol. 481, pp. 350 ff.

happened, the Indians whose service was given in the form of an encomienda had lost any former holdings they may have had (as was the case when the town of Santiago was founded on a site occupied by a settlement of natives), their master might apply for and be given a piece of land on which his wards could live and work for their sustenance and his. Frequent instances of this are noted in the early documents.[35] Although in cases like these the encomienda often led to the formation of a rural property, the real basis of the hacienda was the direct land grant, rather than land conveyed through a concession of the service of Indians.

Furthermore, the system of encomiendas had not offered rewards to, nor provided for the sustenance of, all the conquerors. There were many not included in the limited circle of favorites who received these mercedes.[36] Such persons had to be recompensed in some other way, and other means of support had to be found for them. Of unoccupied or lightly held land there was an abundance; it had all, theoretically, passed into the status of royal patrimony, as the king of Spain considered himself legitimate successor to all former governments in the conquered continent, and all the land became, in a sense, public domain. From this source recompense was found for many of the soldiers, and with these lands provision was made for the maintenance of the mass of the people in the new province.

For some time after the founding of the colony it appears that individuals had made use of whatever land they found unoccupied in the environs of the settlement, treating it all as commons or public range. This situation could

---

[35] Actas del Cabildo, *in* Historiadores, Vol. 1, pp. 260, 262, 293.

[36] In his " Geografía y descripción universal de las Indias " López de Velasco, writing about 1571-74, says there were at Concepción 150 Spanish citizens (*vecinos*) and only 31 encomenderos; at Santiago 350 to 400 citizens and only 26 encomenderos; at Valdivia 230 citizens and but 56 encomenderos; at La Serena 80-100 citizens and only 8 encomenderos; and thus at other places.

not last long. As the colony became firmly established and more numerous, there grew a demand for larger plots of ground than the town lots and the chacras about the city, on which crops might be grown. There soon developed, too, a need for greater pastures than those provided by the common dehesa. The cattle, horses, and sheep that had been brought down the coast from the older colony of Peru or from Panama had multiplied to such an extent that extensive range lands were needed. There were frequent complaints regarding the improper use of the common pasture, and the small, unfenced plots of ground cultivated by the Indians were being invaded by the settlers' stock. As the danger of Indian attacks in the neighborhood of Santiago had become less, there was opportunity for more extended settlement.

The Spanish government was committed to a policy of establishing its colonies in an orderly fashion. No detail was too small to receive attention in a royal *cédula*. In contrast with the largely uncontrolled colonization by individual or group venture in Anglo-America, the Spanish American was an official undertaking, carried out with all the methodical procedure characteristic of government enterprise. Distance from the seat of authority made the operation of a system difficult at times; but in general the beginning of a colony, the establishment of a settlement, the founding of a city—all followed a well-regulated procedure. This was the case, too, with the setting up of an agrarian system and with distributing the land and establishing a method for acquiring and holding property.

In Chile the founding of the colony had been, as usual, an act of solemn formality. The distributing of town lots and chacras among the members of the conquering army had also been carried out in an orderly manner. As soon as the subjugation of the surrounding country had advanced sufficiently to make it possible, the formal granting of larger holdings began. By this time (1544) central

Chile, northward to the desert and southward to the edge of the forest, had been sufficiently pacified so that it was open to settlement. The area could now be occupied at greater distances from the original centers, and it was feasible for the colonists to acquire land for more extensive agricultural undertakings than had been possible at the beginning. The making of land grants now proceeded with an orderly method and with due formality.

The body upon which devolved the responsibility of providing land for the would-be settlers in the Spanish colonies varied from time to time. With the first establishment of Spain in the New World the leaders of the several expeditions, equipped with appointments from the crown as governors general, were authorized to distribute lands and Indians among their followers. However, a royal decree of 1534 had bestowed upon the new towns themselves this prerogative. In later years the procedure was modified repeatedly, but by that time most of the rural properties of central Chile had been established. In Santiago the Cabildo (Municipal Council) had been formed March 7, 1541, less than a month after the founding of the city. Valdivia, in the name of the king, had appointed eleven officials, who, with the governor himself, constituted the Council. Among the earliest acts of this new body was the assignment of city lots and the chacras, already mentioned, to the one hundred and fifty Spaniards who made up the army of conquistadores. This body undertook the distribution of land in larger blocks for agriculture. It will be remembered that the Cabildo did not distribute encomiendas. This was a prerogative of the governor acting directly in the name of the king. Thus, in theory at least, one agency distributed the land, another distributed the Indians. Only on exceptional occasions was any other procedure followed, as, for example, when the Cabildo bestowed (1554) Indians upon several persons;[37] but this

[37] Actas del Cabildo, in Historiadores, Vol. 1, pp. 417-418, 435-436.

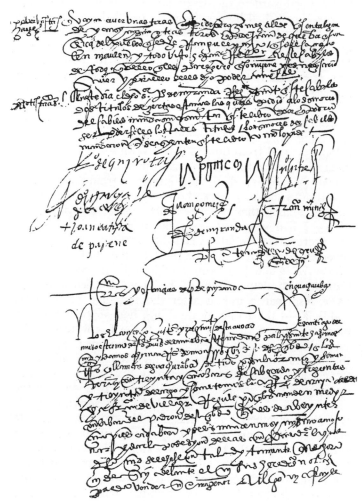

FIG. 18 (caption on opposite page).

was after the death of Valdivia, while the position of governor was still in dispute among three contestants. A record of the distributing of land by the Cabildo was carefully kept and still exists. The original record of the earliest proceedings of the Cabildo was destroyed (September, 1541) in an Indian attack upon the city when most of the houses were burned to the ground. Three years later, however, an account of these proceedings (perhaps from fragmentary data) was made into a new book of records, called the *Libro Becerro* (Calfskin Book), which is still preserved in the National Archives of Chile as one of its chief treasures. The accompanying cut, Figure 18, is a photographic copy of one of its pages.[38] In the volume

---

[38] This record has been deciphered and has been published under the title "Actas del Cabildo," as part of Volumes 1 and 17 of the series " Historiadores de Chile," to which reference has already been made.

Fig. 18—Facsimile of a page from the *Libro Becerro* (Calfskin Book), 1544, containing the early land records of Chile. The book is preserved in the National Archives in Santiago.

On the lower half of the page begins the wording of a grant of land given to Pedro de Miranda in Guachuraba near Santiago. The Spanish original and an English translation read as follows:

Tierras y estancias de P. de Miranda en Guachuraba

Nos, el consejo, justicia y rejimiento de esta ciudad de Santiago del Nuevo Estremo de estas provincias de la Nueva Estremadura por la presente hacemos merced y damos a Hernán Rodríguez de Monroy vecino de esta ciudad las tierras que llaman de Guachuraba de tierras para su labranza y sementeras y con treinta y cinco varas de cabecera y trecientas y treinta de largo y cometémoslo a Rodríguez de Araya alcalde y a Francisco de Villagra rejidor para que las manden medir con el vara del padrón de esta ciudad que es de a veinte y cinco pies cada vara y se las manden asimismo amojonar y dar la posesión de ellas conforme al derecho la cual dicha merced se le hace con tal aditamiento que ahora ni en adelante él ni sus herederos no las pueden vender ni enajenar a clérigo ni a frayle . . . .

Lands and ranches of P. de Miranda in Guachuraba

We, the council, justice and municipal board of this city of Santiago del Nuevo Estremo of these provinces of the Nueva Estremadura by these presents make a grant and give to Hernán Rodríguez de Monroy citizen of this city the lands called Guachuraba as lands for his labor and planting with a frontage of thirty-five varas and three hundred thirty in length and we commit to Rodríguez de Araya mayor and to Francisco de Villagra councilman the duty of ordering a survey with the vara certified by this city which is twenty-five feet and of ordering also that the lands be marked off and that possession be given according to law, the said grant being given with the additional proviso that neither now nor in the future neither he nor his heirs may sell or alienate them to clergy or friar . . . .

are noted many grants of land for city lots, for chacras, and for the larger properties then usually termed *estancias* (cattle ranches).

ESTANCIAS

In the creation of this third type of holding, the estancia, many Chilean haciendas had their origin. From estancias as well as from encomiendas sprang the peculiar form of property that became the basis of the country's agriculture, its most important population unit, the dominant institution in its social, economic, and political life throughout three centuries of the colonial period and a fourth century of existence as an independent republic. It is necessary, therefore, to note the character of these grants (the first purely agricultural ones made), their distribution, their size, their value as farming lands, the use to which they were put, their effect on the distribution of settlement and on the character that such settlements were to take.

The earliest grants recorded in the *Libro Becerro* were dated 1547, six years after the founding of Santiago. Earlier grants had been made, both by the Cabildo and by Valdivia. In fact, much of the land of central Chile had been disposed of in huge blocks by the Municipal Council during the absence of Valdivia on his first long march into the south (1544). Those who remained in Santiago had partitioned the whole area thereabouts among themselves. But upon Valdivia's return with reports that he had failed to conquer the Araucanian territory and thus to secure great areas with which to reward those who had accompanied him on this expedition, the distribution of land made in his absence was annulled and the process was begun anew on a more inclusive plan.[39] The first grant of land formally recorded as having been given by the Cabildo was that allotted to Ortún Jeréz (April 26, 1547) and is described as follows: "A piece

[39] Actas del Cabildo, *in* Historiadores, Vol. 1, pp. 602, 603.

of land for your stock range (estancia) and fields (*semen-teras*)." It was located not far from where Valparaíso now stands, along the Margamarga tributary of the Quil-pué Creek, and included an entire valley (*quebrada*) that comes into the Margamarga there. Its area is not specified but probably was several thousand acres. Similar grants were made the same day to three other colonists.[40] At meetings of the Cabildo during succeeding months additional grants were made to other members of the group. This process continued slowly during the next few years, resulting in the creation of some thirty estancias. To this list of formal grants recorded in the acts of the Cabildo must be added a number of confirmations given to holdings acquired already in some other fashion or not formally entered in the records. Many of these probably represent unauthorized occupation of lands, virtually " squatter " procedure. The governor himself also gave out lands, seeking confirmation of the Cabildo later.[41] He seems to have done so with such prodigality that the Council finally considered it necessary to remind him that the distribution of land was its own prerogative.[42] Judging from the frequent references to land grants for which there is no record in the Cabildo's book, it would seem that many farms must have been started in such irregular fashions.[43] With the grants being made in other sections of the country as these districts were sufficiently pacified, it seems evident that by the end of the first decade most if not all of the companions of Valdivia had been provided with rural properties. The colony thus took on from the very first the character of an agricultural and stock-raising settlement, with encomiendas and estancias, chacras and sementeras constituting the several forms of rural holdings.

[40] *Ibid.*, p. 122.
[41] *Ibid.*, p. 284.
[42] *Ibid.*, pp. 192-195.
[43] *Ibid.*, pp. 342-346.

Most of these early properties established by the Spaniards were located along the streams that descend from the Andes and the Coast Range in central Chile. The valley of the Aconcagua in its middle and lower sections, where the rich alluvial floor offered some of the best potential farm land in the country, contained a number of the grants. The valley not only contained excellent soil and a constant, abundant supply of water, draining from the great snow fields about Mt. Aconcagua, but was probably more fully developed (cleared and irrigated) at the arrival of the Spaniards than other sections of central Chile. The Inca influence seems to have been stronger there than farther south beyond the Chacabuco ridge in the Santiago district. Though the upper part of this valley, as has been noted,[44] is subject to killing frosts in winter, the lower and middle section is sufficiently exposed to marine influence to have its climate decidedly tempered. Valdivia kept a large part of this district for himself. In the region of Quillota, in the lower Aconcagua Valley, he selected the site on which he purposed to establish his hacienda and planted the two handfuls of wheat saved from the siege of Santiago.[45] The first three grants of land recorded in the Cabildo's list were all near by. Though gold mines were being worked in the valley, it appears that these grants were made entirely for agricultural and stock-raising purposes, and that climate, soil, and water supply were the factors determining the choice. The traveler in Chile today is well convinced that no better selections could have been made, since some of the most beautiful haciendas of the country are now found here. Not only do field crops characteristic of Mediterranean Chile flourish here, but the fruits also of semitropical climates thrive exceptionally well; oranges, lemons, figs, avocados, and even *chirimoyas* being found in abundance in the luxuriant orchards seen on all sides.

[44] See above, p. 46.
[45] Edwards (Agustín): Mi patria, 1928, p. 62.

As the train pulls up at the station of Quillota, one finds venders with all these fruits waiting for the eager passengers. Along the streets, as about the hacienda houses are seen palms, oleanders, magnolias, and other semitropical plants. The fields and orchards are crossed by canals carrying water from the river channels. It was this region apparently, more than the immediate district of the bay, that led the Spaniards to give the name of Valparaíso (Vale of Paradise) to the near-by port serving as its outlet. In many respects it is the choicest part of Chile. It was but natural that here should have been located the first extensive land claims of the colony.

Next in desirability appear to have been the widespread alluvial fans of the Mapocho, Maipo, Cachapoal, Tinguiririca, Mataquito, and Claro rivers, stretching from the vicinity of Santiago southward to include the present regions of Rancagua, San Fernando, Curicó, and Talca. In this wide depression between the Andes and the Coast Range, with its several transverse streams running swiftly along the crests of their alluvium-built fans, the Spaniards found excellent sites for cattle ranges and cultivated fields, though the region lacked the labor supply afforded by the denser population of the Aconcagua Valley and showed less Indian development of irrigation. There was little in the way of natural obstacles to check the advance of the Spaniards over this area or to separate the new centers founded by them. Within five years after the founding of Santiago they had, according to Valdivia's letter to the Emperor, occupied the territory for thirty leagues southward from that city.[46] Encomiendas and land grants were made in the region, and the country was quickly brought under control of the conquerors.

It is impossible now to locate with any degree of accuracy most of the individual grants made in these first

[46] Cartas de Don Pedro de Valdivia al Emperador Carlos V, *in* Historiadores, Vol. I, p. 23.

years. Many of them were designated as being in the district of such-and-such an Indian chieftain who has not given his name to a definite spot. Even in the cases in which place names were used in defining the grants, this nomenclature has long ago disappeared for most part. It would seem, however, that these lands were distributed much as were the encomiendas. Many were selected precisely because they were near the settlements of Indians that had been allotted to the men who were receiving the land. The crown steadfastly attempted to protect the Indians' land from encroachment, but the colonists just as persistently sought either the lands actually occupied by Indians or those near such native settlements. It was but natural that many of the very areas the Indians had found most suitable for their own cultivation and as locations for their settlements should be the lands most sought for by the Spaniards. This was not true of the grasslands, either the nearly treeless slopes of the Coast Range or other such districts where stock could range but where irrigation would be difficult. The Indians had had little use for such lands, and the estancias proper of the colonists represented little encroachment on the land used by the natives. But, though the Spaniards later developed far more elaborate systems of irrigation than those maintained by the Indians, the early years showed the newcomers to be governed by much the same desires as the natives in their selection of sites for cultivated fields. They were also attracted to those same sites by the supply of labor available there. Hence the early distribution of agricultural holdings closely resembled that of the more permanent Indian settlements.

SIZE OF LAND GRANTS

During the first years of the colony the grants of land alone, as distinguished from the grants of encomiendas of Indians, were generally of moderate extent. In a few instances, however, large areas were bestowed on some of the more favored of the conquerors. For example, Pedro de Miranda received a league and a half of land along the Cachapoal River (April 7, 1553).[47] If, as would appear, this was a square league and a half it would represent a territory of some 8,640 acres (*ca.* 3,480 hectares). Miranda had an encomienda (Copequén) in this neighborhood. The land is good here, with an abundant supply of water for irrigation. Such a concession, even if only a fraction of it were under irrigation, must have been of great value. A few other grants appear to have been even larger, but extensive grants seem to have been the exception. The crown had early issued specific regulations as to the size of rural grants to be made. A cédula of June 18, 1513, had fixed the standards for such grants in the newly-found territories. Men of no special rank, the *peones* (foot soldiers) and common citizens, were to be given *peonías*. This unit was probably thought of as the holdings of an individual member of an agricultural village community such as characterized Spain in common with most of the countries of southern Europe, where the farmer lived in the village and went out daily to tend his fields. Its actual extent varied according to the character of the land, as it varied also in different colonies. It was defined as made up of a building lot (*solar*) in the village, agricultural land containing 100 *fanegas de labor* for wheat and 10 fanegas for corn, 2 *huebras* [48] of land for orchard, 8 huebras for a wood lot, pasture for 10 hogs, 20 cows, 5 horses, 100 sheep, and 20 goats, making a total perhaps of something more than 100 acres (40 hectares)—much more than this where the land was poor. It would thus correspond roughly to a modest homestead allotment in the United States and was probably originally intended to be the amount a man could work without hired

---

[47] Actas del Cabildo, *in* Historiadores, Vol. 1, p. 343.
[48] As much land as a yoke of oxen could plow in a day.

help. Few of the Spaniards who took part in the conquest of America, however, were content to settle down in such humble conditions, nor did the Spanish agricultural village become common in the New World. The colonists at once assumed a superiority, quite natural on the part of a conqueror in the presence of a conquered race, and aspired to an economic position in keeping with their military status as superman. The status of a mere settler on a small farm did not attract them.

The crown had provided that those of higher rank— officers in the army or in civil affairs—and those who were rated as *caballeros* (literally, horsemen, but applied both to the cavalrymen of the army and to gentlemen in civil life) should receive a grant of land called a *caballería,* which was five times larger than the peonía, thus ranging from some 350 acres to more than 500.[49] It is doubtful if these units were strictly applied in any of the colonies of the New World. The great extent of land available for settlement in America brought into use larger units of measurement than were common in the crowded countries of the Old World. The terms peonía and caballería are seldom employed in the documents referring to land grants in Chile. In spite of the fact, too, that many of the colonists were fighting men (largely horsemen), the grants of land in the early days were not excessively large. A few examples will show the relatively small extent of those made at this time. The exact size of many of them is not given, but the following are typical.

On the fifteenth of September, 1546, two grants were made in which the dimensions are stated, the length and breadth being given in *varas* (specified to be a 25-foot,

<hr>

[49] See McBride: Land Systems of Mexico, 1923, p. 51. Gay (Historia física; Agricultura, Vol. 1, 1862, p. 77) estimates this amount to be much larger, counting the *peonía* at 341 *cuadras* (about 1,330 acres or 530 hectares). The *fanega* of land varied greatly in the different provinces of Spain and in the several colonies of America, hence the difference of opinion.

or 7.62-meter, linear measure).[50] Pedro de Miranda received a piece of land called Guachuraba near Santiago
(apparently the present-day Huechuraba) with a frontage
of 30 varas and a depth of 300, giving an area of about
52 hectares (129 acres). Adjoining this land a grant was
made on the same day to Hernán Rodríguez de Monroy,
measuring 35 varas in frontage and 330 in depth, thus
totaling a little more than 67 hectares. On June 27, 1547,
Diego Oro received a grant measuring 150 varas in frontage and 300 in depth, about 260 hectares. On September
19, 1547, the Cabildo confirmed to the heirs of Gabriel
Salazar (deceased) a grant that had been made to him at
the founding of the city, measuring 49 varas in frontage
and 300 in depth, about 85 hectares. Another grant confirmed by the Cabildo, on February 25, 1553, was one made
by Valdivia directly to his captain of marines, Juan Bautista de Pastene, seven years earlier and containing about
18 hectares. On February 12, 1557, a piece of land measuring 35 hectares was given to Antonio Miñez (Martínez).
On August 11, 1559, Padre Diego Paz received a grant
that was 90 varas wide and 350 long, about 182 hectares.[51]
Thus none of these grants of land appears to have been
excessively large, and many of them are but little beyond
the limits set for the peonía. At this stage of the settlement there was little accumulation of land in large estates,
except as the encomiendas had something of that character.

By the end of the sixteenth century, however, colonists
were finding that, in order to get service from the Indians,
larger landholdings were necessary. By this time, too,

[50] No record of these two grants appears in the regular minutes of the
Cabildo, nor is there in the *Libro Becerro* any meeting noted as having taken
place on this date. These items appear only at a later date, when the Cabildo
is requested to confirm the titles to the grants (Actas del Cabildo, *in*
Historiadores, Vol. 1, pp. 343-345).
In many of these early grants it is clearly stated that the vara was " de a
veinte y cinco pies cada vara "; thus this *vara* is quite a different measure from
the vara of today, which is 2.78 feet.
[51] All of these grants are noted in the "Actas del Cabildo" in the minutes
for the respective dates.

the Indian laborer was being reduced to a more satisfactory condition of servitude. The land grants grew in size. This is evident in a series of grants made in the Colchagua district along the Cachapoal and the Tinguiririca rivers south of Santiago. About 1600, Padre Hernández de Cáceres received a piece of land near Rancagua, containing some 1,300 *cuadras* (about 5,200 acres, or 2,110 hectares) ; at about the same time Jerónimo de Molina received 1,000 cuadras in the same region; while a year or so later 600 cuadras were given to Juan Díaz alongside the Tinguiririca River. In the following years other such grants were made, some of them reaching as much as 4,000 and 5,000 cuadras.[52]

CONTROVERSIES OVER TITLES

Among those who had received smaller grants there was a tendency to enlarge them. Owing to the small number of Indians in the region and to the light hold they had on the soil, much of the territory gave every appearance of being unused and unclaimed. Furthermore, the Spanish forces had been strong enough to break down the simple native organization of society but as yet not sufficiently numerous to effect a compact settlement of the country. Under such pioneer conditions it was but natural that recipients of land grants should attempt to extend their claims over the unused areas contiguous to their holdings. One of the early Spanish chroniclers, writing in 1646, states that " the antients who took possession of the land thought that, if they had a little footing in a valley, it was all theirs." [53] So common had this practice become

[52] Data from Santa Cruz: Los indígenas del norte de Chile, 1913, pp. 38-88, and Crónica de la provincia de Colchagua, 1927, pp. 159-178. See also Lizardo Valenzuela: El corregimiento de Colchagua, 1929, pp. 173-204.
[53] Ovalle: Histórica relación, 1649 (quotation from the English edition, 1813.) A document dated 1589 in the Archivo del Ministerio de lo Interior, Vol. 310, pp. 39-103, registers an official complaint that much land belonging to the crown was being occupied by settlers with no authorization whatever.

that much of the land claimed by the *hacendados* of Chile at the beginning of the seventeenth century could show no titles or, at the best, was held by uncertain titles and had ill-defined bounds. In fact, the situation had become general throughout the Spanish American colonies, resulting in great loss to the royal domain, a multitude of suits over property rights, and complaints on the part of the Indians who had been despoiled of their holdings. The situation finally attracted the attention of the home government. Measures were then taken to examine and revise the documents by which lands were held, to ascertain what public lands still existed, to restore improperly acquired parts of the public domain, and to establish all property on a sounder basis.

In Chile the governor general, Alonzo de Rivera, issued a decree in the name of the king (1603), appointing a special surveyor, Jinés de Lillo, to carry out this review of titles. The reason assigned for providing this survey was stated to be that the king had been informed that " by various titles and without titles much land of the Indians had been taken possession of—land that was needed for their support and for that of their cattle.[54] All such ille-

---

[54] Lillo: Mensuras de tierras (a collection of manuscript reports in the National Archives of Chile). These documents, written in quaint seventeenth century Spanish by many different scribes, each of whom had his own system of abbreviations and combinations, as well as his own style of penmanship, are all but illegible today (see Fig. 19). Several attempts have been made to decipher them and render them available to the public. Vicuña Mackenna in his " Historia de Santiago," Vol. 1, 1869, p. 151, says that in 1837 a motion had been made in the Chamber of Deputies that they should be translated by the only person in the country at that time able to read them, Don N. del Fierro. The work was not carried out, however, and Mackenna considers it fortunate that it was not; for, he says, it would have been like opening Pandora's box in the public plaza. Some have supposed that the failure to publish these manuscripts has been intentional, since they throw much light (perhaps undesired by some) on the history of rural property in Chile. Be that as it may, the task of deciphering them has now been completed, under the direction of Dr. Don Ricardo Donoso, Director of the National Archives, and the work awaits publication (1935). The set forms one of the most interesting and valuable of historical collections dealing with colonial Chile at the beginning of the seventeenth century. I am indebted to these reports (consulted in their original manuscript form) for many of my data regarding this period. It is to be hoped that their publication will not be long delayed, but it would not be surprising if influential landholders still prevent it.

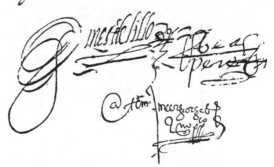

FIG. 19 (caption on opposite page).

gally-held lands, termed *demasías* (excess), were to be discovered, surveyed, and reclaimed for the crown, and returned to the Indians where it was apparent that injustice had been done. Rightful owners were to be confirmed in their possessions. During the next two years (1603 and 1604) this work was carried on by the Juez Visitador General de Tierras (as Jinés de Lillo was called), who examined into the titles presented, approved those that were in order, confirmed many that represented *de facto* hold-

FIG. 19—Facsimile of a page from the " Mensuras de tierras " of Jinés de Lillo, special examiner of land titles and surveys in Chile, 1603-1604. The Spanish text and an English translation follow:

" Medida

" Virtud del cual dicho título y merced quede su sobra incorporado el dicho Juez Visitador vista la disposición de la tierra señaló por lo que tocaba al dicho título desde el principio y cabezada que hizo la medida de la quebrada del Axí que posee Pedro de Gijón que en ella le midieron con parte del valle tres cientas cuadras y en aquella derezera está un cerrillo redondo con un árbol grande en cima de él del cual su merced señaló por tierra perteneciente al dicho título el valle arriba con todas las vertientes, enconadas y quebradas que cayen al dicho valle y hasta donde se acaba el dicho valle y enconada y desde allí vuelven estas tierras por la otra falda del costado del Pico y Pomaire hasta el mojón que está en la punta de la entrada de la quebrada que llaman del Axí con lo cual quedó enterado en este título y reservó en lo demás del dicho valle su derecho a salvo al dicho capitán Lisperger y a la dicha doña Agueda de Flores para que pidan su justicia como vieren que les conviene atento que los demás que en ellos están poblados están actualmente poseyendo y le mandó dar testimonio y lo firmó de su nombre.

JINÉS DE LILLO "

(Measurement

In virtue of which said title and grant the said Visiting Judge, having seen the disposition of the land, marked, in so far as it concerns the said title, from the beginning and head of the canyon of Axí which Pedro de Gijón possesses, which had been surveyed for him, with part of the valley three hundred cuadras, and straight in that direction there is a round hill with a large tree on top of it from which his Honor indicated as land belonging to the said title up the valley including all its slopes, inlets (?), and canyons that fall into the aforesaid valley and as far as the valley and the inlets (?) reach, and from there these lands turn along the other slope of the flank of Pico and Pomaire to the landmark at the entrance of the canyon which is called Axí with the which this survey was completed, and to the said Captain Lisperger and to the said Doña Agueda de Flores was reserved the right to seek justice regarding other rights in the valley as it might seem best to them in view of the fact that other settlers there are actually in possession, and he ordered that this should be certified and he signed with his name.

JINÉS DE LILLO).

ings for a long period even though their titles might be defective in form, and gave formal possession to the owners. He also surveyed the bounds of properties, indicating their extent and the natural features that marked their borders. These surveys were far from satisfactory compared with modern practice, as many of the bounds were left indefinite or marked by such unsuitable objects as a tree or a stump, a large stone on top of a hill, an irrigation canal, or the principal channel of a braided stream (Fig. 19). Yet they represented a decided improvement over former methods of defining properties, in which it was not uncommon to specify nothing more than the valley in which the farm was located or the Indian chief whose people had previously occupied the land. Many (probably most) of the haciendas of central Chile depend upon the surveys made at that time, as well as upon the documents issued and recorded by Jinés de Lillo. Many of them trace their beginning (in legal form at least) to these surveys.

Disputes over properties also came before Jinés de Lillo. He examined the respective claims, passed judgment on the points at issue, corrected boundaries where necessary, and gave possession to the successful litigant in the name of the king. In case of imperfect titles confirmed by him, or where some doubt existed regarding the full legality of the original acquisition of a property, he was accustomed to repeat the formal act of giving possession in the presence of witnesses. The owner would dismount from his horse and, taken by the hand, would be led over his property, where he would pull up plants, strike his knife into trees, and finally drive the officials and the witness off the place in token of his actual authority there.

The results of Jinés de Lillo's investigations showed the need for such an undertaking and revealed what had been going on since the early settlement of the colony. While the apparent intention of the government had been to form modest if not small holdings, the actual result of its efforts had been the creation of *latifundia*. Many of the relatively small grants officially made and recorded had been expanded into vast estates. The original pieces of land now represented only the nuclei about which neighboring areas had been accumulated. Yet the matter had been of such long standing that it was now difficult to correct. There is little evidence that much land was restored to the Indians or reincorporated into the royal patrimony. Perhaps there was no possibility of that. The lapse of nearly a century had probably destroyed all evidence on which the Indians could establish their claims. It had also firmly established many colonists in actual possession of crown lands. To have returned all such irregularly acquired land either to the Indians or to the crown would have wrought an injustice to the present holders. It would also have raised a storm of opposition in the province and apparently would have brought disaster to agriculture as it was being developed in the flourishing young colony. As a matter of fact, with the imperfectly defined bounds of the original grants it would probably have been impossible to determine what sections were not rightfully held. The only solution was to recognize the rights acquired by long occupation, and by the well established doctrine of prescription allow the colonists to retain the lands actually in their possession. This plan, common in the other Latin American colonies, was followed by Jinés de Lillo in Chile. The length of tenure usually recognized as giving full right to title was forty years. This was generously interpreted, since the government was as much concerned in establishing a well regulated system of land ownership and protecting the colonists in their holdings as in seeing that all illegally acquired land should be returned to its rightful owner.[55]

By these measures Jinés de Lillo settled many of the controversies between individuals as well as between in-

---

[55] Solórzano Pereira: Política indiana, Vol. 2, Book 6, Chapter 12, p. 512.

dividuals and the crown and gave to rural property a far sounder basis than it had formerly enjoyed. Furthermore, by confirming the colonists in their possession of extensive holdings he gave official recognition to the hacienda as the typical form of rural property in the country. Other confirmations of irregularly acquired holdings were made from time to time in later years, the demasías held by hacendados throughout the country gradually being incorporated into the legally constituted properties. The nuclei of original grants thus became greatly expanded. A policy of sale for a nominal price—most commonly two *reales* (some 20 cents) per cuadra [56]—also was followed during much of the colonial period. Owners of estancias were thus enabled to add land from the public domain, and others to establish new farms on the gradually advancing frontier. The large farm estates, whether based on encomienda, on land grant, on purchase from the public domain, or on " squatter " possession alone, became established as the dominant agricultural units in Chile. Almost all the best land (the easily irrigable valleys and alluvial fans) was included within the bounds of these large farms; even most of the hill and mountain country, useless for farming and of small value for grazing, was also absorbed; there was left little room for any other type of holding in the entire area occupied by whites. Chile became almost exclusively a land of great estates (established now on a legal basis) and has remained so to the present time.

Since the colony was, in early years, chiefly a stock-raising country, the rural properties were at first largely cattle ranches. There was little demand for agricultural products. The population was small; there was virtually no foreign trade. As the province developed, farming became an adjunct of stock raising, but for some two hundred years the estates being created by the colonists in Chile resembled closely the great estancias that were growing up

---

[56] The cuadra as used in Chile is 15,625 square meters or 3.85 acres.

across the Andes in the Argentine or the extensive ranchos characteristic of early-day California and Texas. Later, as we shall see, the estancias became haciendas (estates characterized by extensive farming methods), these in turn giving way to *fundos* with somewhat more intensive agriculture, and the fundos gradually yielding to the demand for smaller subdivisions, the *hijuelas,* as the need for food crops increased with the growing population.

ENTAILED ESTATES

An institution that played an important rôle in maintaining these large properties unbroken for several centuries was the system of *mayorazgos* (entailed estates). With a desire to attain high social distinction and preserve an elevated rank in society for their descendants, some of the leading families sought and obtained the entailment of their estates. The kings of Spain encouraged the transplanting of this Old World system to the New; partly for the sake of the permanence it gave society in the new oversea provinces, partly for the purpose of rewarding faithful service in civil and military activities, partly for a price. A number of mayorazgos were created among the holders of large properties in Chile, the estates being thus preserved against subdivision.[57] Although the number of these mayorazgos was not great, they represented a power and an influence far beyond their numerical strength. They not only held intact a number of great estates, but they also set a pattern that was followed by the majority of Chilean haciendas. It became the custom to hold properties unbroken from one generation to another and to pass them undivided to the eldest son. This practice greatly strengthened the system of large holdings, tending still more to concentrate land in the hands of a few. It made more per-

[57] A list of the mayorazgos and other entailed estates in Chile existing at the close of the colonial period is given in Barros Arana's " Historia," Vol. 7, 1886, pp. 364-365.

manent the properties based on grants of land to the early colonists; it still more firmly established the encomienda as a form of rural holding and effectively checked any movement toward the creation of small farms. Formal entailment of property began in Chile near the close of the seventeenth century and continued for several decades after independence had been won. It survived longer in Chile than elsewhere in the Spanish colonies or even in Spain herself. The more democratic government established in Spain in 1812 brought with it the abolition of such oligarchical institutions in that country, and echoes of this action were heard in America in the enactment of measures leading to the same end. In Mexico the mayorazgos were finally abolished in 1823. After surviving in Chile until the middle of the nineteenth century, they were finally ended by the laws of 1852 and 1857. Even then the custom of holding the large properties intact did not cease but continued to characterize Chilean agriculture for many years and to exert a powerful influence on the entire life of the nation.

Problems of Labor Supply

The ways in which labor was secured for the lands of the estancias in the early years of the colony are of interest as throwing light on the relation of the present rural worker in Chile to the property on which he lives and to the owner of the estate. The situation today is a gradual outgrowth of conditions in that formative stage. By tracing this development insight may be gained into the relationship existing between master and man at the present time.

There were several sources from which the early Spaniards obtained the laborers required to work their chacras, their haciendas, and their estancias. In the first place, they brought a few slaves and a larger number of yanaconas from Peru with them. These were not sufficient for more than the first attempts at cultivating the soil while the number of Spaniards was small. Once the number of colonists was augmented by the arrival of new settlers and of additional armed forces from Peru and Spain, additions to the labor supply were required, as it was a generally accepted principle in the Spanish American colonies that it was beneath the dignity of a European to engage in manual labor. In the presence of a subject race the conqueror must not stoop to serve. Furthermore, there was the practical reason that most of the Spaniards were engaged in the military phase of the Conquest and seldom found it safe to lay aside their arms. This was true particularly in Chile where the endless war against the Araucanians demanded an unusually large force of fighting men. Had it not been for the large number of military men and the constant call for service on the frontier, the country would have felt less need for an increased labor supply. As it was, the slaves and yanaconas were not nearly numerous enough to produce for the increasingly large number of Spaniards. The encomiendas, as has been seen, were disappointing to the colony in that the number of Indians who could be forced into service by this system was small and steadily decreasing. To augment the labor supply needed on the estancias, recourse was had to several expedients.

With the breakdown of the simple kinship organization that had marked aboriginal society before the advent of the whites, there were a number of Indians left unattached either to encomiendas or to the remaining free groups. Many encomienda Indians also took advantage of the confusion and escaped from the Spaniards to whom they had been allotted. These unattached natives were at first styled yanaconas. Their lands having been taken by the Spaniards and their dependence on tribal units made no longer possible, this floating population found lodgment on the estancias of the invaders, thereby securing homes for themselves and providing labor for the farms. Laborers of this kind had reached sufficient numbers by the early seventeenth century to warrant special legislation governing their status. According to the regulations established by the Príncipe de Esquilache, 1619, these Indian residents on the haciendas, by this time called *inquilinos* (tenants), were each to work 160 days per year for the master, receiving in return a piece of land large enough to sow one *almúd* (about half an acre) of maize, two of barley, two of wheat, a little land for vegetables (chiefly beans), and the loan of the owner's oxen and tools for working this land.[58] This became an established order in many parts of central Chile.

Another means of securing labor for the rural properties was by enslaving the Indian prisoners captured on the Araucanian frontier. This method proved to be so profitable, owing to the labor shortage in the central part of the country, that it became a regular practice to raid the Indian territory, take as many prisoners as possible, and sell them into slavery. The custom provoked much opposition on the part of the more humane among the clergy and civilians; but it continued, sometimes with and sometimes without the royal approval. It was one means of wearing down the resistance of the indomitable Araucanians. Since the colony had not developed an intensive agriculture for which actual slave labor was needed, these captives were usually settled on haciendas as laborers attached to the properties after much the same fashion as the yanaconas already referred to. Such Indians (whether yanaconas or enslaved prisoners) were not actual slaves. Neither were they free men. In fact, if not in theory, they were bound to the

---

[58] " Indigenas residentes en las Haciendas de Campo, conocidos en Chile con el nombre de inquilinos " (natives residing in the country estates, and known in Chile by the term *inquilinos*) (Gustavo Opazo: Las terratenencias del corregimiento del Maule, in *Rev. Ch. de Hist. y Geogr.*, Vol. 52, 1927, p. 100). Thus as early as 1619 the term " inquilino " had come into use. In this sense the word is peculiar to Chile.

land on which they lived, but with certain rights as well as duties. By a long process of give and take, customs became established, affected somewhat by official regulations but more by the reciprocal needs of master and man. The system became firmly rooted, and many of the farms came to depend for their operation upon this type of labor.

One other means by which labor was obtained for the haciendas was the hiring of Indians from the holders of encomiendas. In spite of royal orders strictly forbidding such a practice, the farming out of Indian labor was not uncommon. Frequent mention of it is made, particularly in the earlier stages of colonial history. An example of this is seen in the will left by Doña Marina Ortíz de Gaete, widow of Pedro de Valdivia, in which she mentions several groups of encomienda Indians rented out to others. For the services that one group of eleven of her encomienda Indians was to render during a year's time, she was to receive the sum of " one hundred pesos of good gold " and one hundred fanegas of wheat, fifty of corn, and fifty of barley, together with twenty sheep.[59]

The encomienda, as has been noted, had been looked on as a means of providing labor for the support of the conquerors. In the other Spanish colonies it had served this purpose. But in Chile, where the difference in the character of the native population had rendered it of relatively little value, the colonists, in order to assure themselves a permanent and dependable labor supply had brought about a gradual transformation in the nature of this institution. Royal decrees themselves, intended to afford protection to the Indians, had facilitated the change. A series of *ordenanzas,* issued principally between 1600 and 1635, had fixed the *tasa,* or tribute, which the Indians should be compelled to pay and the form in which payments should be made. Of money the Indians had none; there was little market for the products of their crudely cultivated fields; the only

[59] Amunátegui Solar: Encomiendas, Vol. 2, Apunt. y Doc., p. 137.

thing they could offer was labor. The result was that they were reduced to the necessity of laboring for the encomendero, practically on the latter's terms, in order to meet this theoretical tribute due the crown.[60]

On the territorial encomiendas, where a settled district had constituted the grant, the status of the Indian had been gradually changing from that of a mere ward with obligations to render certain service to his guardian, into that of a serf attached to the soil, with no liberty to engage in other pursuits than those on the owner's property, and obliged to spend his life in labor for a master, much as was the case on the encomiendas established over the sedentary peoples of Mexico and Peru. The very dependence of the Indian upon the soil in such encomiendas had resulted in virtual ownership by the Spaniard of both the Indian and his land, the two constituting inseparable elements of a single property.

In the case of encomiendas that had consisted merely of the Indians' service but had not directly conveyed land to the recipient much the same process had been going on. On land grants received from the Cabildo (or from other sources) the labor of the encomienda Indians was applied, and wherever possible these laborers were induced or compelled to live on the property. This procedure was described as "*asentar por carta*," that is receiving Indians to live upon the estate, making a permanent agreement with them before the authorities whereby a yearly wage would be paid in addition to such rights as that of using a small parcel of land for their own sustenance, the permission to build a shack on the farm, and the privilege of pasturing a few cattle on unused parts of the property. In return the Indian was obliged to do the work of the farm as it might be required. The practice of fixing Indians on the farms by such agreements became quite

[60] Barros Arana: Historia, Vol. 4, pp. 332-334. The cédulas referred to are given in Rosales' "Historia general," Vol. 3, 1878, p. 114.

common as the number of Indians who could be held for service under the original system declined.[61] The process had been going on apparently since early in the settlement of the colony. There is frequent mention among the old colonial documents of transfer of Indians from one place to another, from their native site to some other where the encomendero could make more profitable use of their labor, though all such procedure was strictly forbidden by royal decree. One of the chroniclers who went to Chile in 1628 and wrote his history in 1647 says that at that time encomenderos were accustomed to people their estancias from the encomiendas that had been given them.[62] That most of the encomiendas of central Chile had followed this development seems evident from a list given in a report dated June 3, 1788, in which twenty-two of the thirty encomiendas mentioned are stated to have been in such-and-such an hacienda.[63] A concrete example of this procedure is seen in the case of the encomienda located in the La Ligua Valley, given to Diego García de Cáceres. In 1599 an extensive grant of land adjoining the location of his Indians was made to the heirs of this encomienda, and to the estancia created there, called Pullalli, were transferred the Indians of the encomienda.[64] Such Indians became a mere attachment to the property of their masters. To comply with regulations established in favor of the aborigines a nominal wage was paid (amounting usually to about 40 *pesos* a year), and daily rations in limited amount were supplied in addition to the small piece of land allotted each family.

Accounts describing social and economic conditions in Chile about the middle and toward the end of the eighteenth

[61] Letter from Fray Diego de Humanzoro, Bishop of Santiago, dated October 5, 1666 (Amunátegui Solar: Encomiendas, Vol. 2, pp. 216-217).
[62] Santiago de Tesillo: Guerras de Chile, *in* Historiadores, Vol. 5, Part 3, 1865, p. 81.
[63] Amunátegui Solar: Encomiendas, Vol. 2, pp. 244-247.
[64] *Idem:* Mayorazgos, Vol. 1, p. 244.

century show how far this transformation of the encomienda had progressed and how little there remained of the institution as originally constituted. In 1748 Don Tomás de Azúa, Protector of the Indians in Chile, wrote as follows to the king: " The encomenderos provide the Indians with tools and the time necessary for work in their own fields; the rest of the year, with the exception of feast days, the Indians serve the said encomendero in haciendas adjoining their villages, receiving each week their daily rations of food and at the end of the year thirty-one and a half pesos for their clothing, the encomendero assuming the obligation to teach the Indians religion and to pay the tribute due for them to the crown." [65] Again, a little later, a report stated that a certain encomienda (that of Puangue) had no existence and that " each Indian constituting it was now paid six pesos a month as if he were an ordinary hired laborer." [66] A similar description of the encomiendas as they existed at the end of the century is given by Ambrosio O'Higgins, then " president " (governor general) of Chile, in a letter addressed to the king and dated April 3, 1789, in which he says: " What were called encomiendas in this region were not certain villages whose tribute the king had conceded to those citizens in return for services rendered by their ancestors but rather a number of unhappy individuals who, generally attached to the houses and establishments that form the haciendas of the encomenderos, work all year . . . . in anything that contributes toward the comfort and advantage of those whom they called their masters." [67]

ABOLITION OF THE ENCOMIENDAS

This was the condition of land and labor in Chile when the king was finally prevailed upon to abolish the entire

---

[65] *Idem:* Encomiendas, Vol. 2, p. 64.
[66] *Ibid.,* Vol. 2, Apunt. y Doc., p. 34.
[67] Amunátegui (Miguel Luis): Precursores de la independencia de Chile, Vol. 2, 1909-1910, pp. 485-491.

system of encomiendas in all the American colonies. As is well known, the government of Spain had made repeated efforts in the early history of its colonial empire in America to undo the wrongs inflicted on the Indians by the system of serfdom into which the encomiendas or repartimientos (designed for the protection of these very Indians) had brought them. The New Laws of the Indies (1542) had been drafted with the intention of completely abolishing the encomiendas. But their issuance had aroused such a storm of opposition on the part of the colonists, whose whole position as a privileged class rested on this institution, that it had been deemed unwise to attempt their enforcement. The government had been compelled to content itself with the enactment of measures to ameliorate the conditions in which the Indians served. During the succeeding two and a half centuries the privileges of the encomenderos had been repeatedly abridged, in theory at least, though many of the limitations imposed by royal decree had not seriously affected the holders of encomiendas in the distant colonies. In Chile, for example, an ordinance was enacted (1634) declaring the Indians of encomiendas completely free of obligation to render personal service and subject only to the obligation of paying a yearly tribute of ten pesos per capita—and this in the products of their own fields and flocks.[68] A contemporary historian, however, wrote that this decree, like many others, "was of little effect, for things remained in the same condition as before, as this evil had taken such deep root that no remedy can ever be found for it." [69]

A royal cédula, dated July 12, 1720, followed by another of August 31, 1721, finally decreed the abolition of all encomiendas. Even this was impossible to carry out, and fifty years more elapsed before this change in the colonial organization was put into full effect. It was Ambrosio

[68] Rosales: Historia general, Vol. 3, Book 7, Chapter 20.
[69] Santiago de Tesillo: Guerras de Chile, in Historiadores, Vol. 5, p. 81.

O'Higgins who actually brought it about in Chile. Attention has already been called to his description of the encomiendas as they existed in his time. He considered their complete abolition essential for the welfare of the province over which he presided as governor general. By an *auto* (decree) issued in Serena, February 7, 1789, and approved by the king in cédulas dated April 3 and June 10, 1791, all encomiendas existing in Chile were abolished. By this time the encomiendas had become of so little value that the measure created little opposition, and this time-honored institution ceased to exist. In its original character it had long before disappeared.

RISE OF THE HACIENDA SYSTEM

The legislation abolishing the encomiendas actually brought but slight change in conditions so far as the people of Chile were concerned. The laborers, still sometimes called Indians though most of them now had an admixture of European blood, " did not comprehend the liberty which the king had granted them and continued subject to their former masters." [70] To these laborers, attached to the estates by the several processes already described, the name of " inquilinos " (tenants) had come to be applied, generally replacing the term " *Indios.*" However, the relationship of Master and Man which had grown up during the several centuries in which the encomienda had continued to mold Chilean society was not destroyed. The encomendero disappeared but the hacendado had already taken his place. The Indio, too, had gone—fled back to the forests of his kinsmen in the south or merged by intermarriage with his conquerors. In his stead there was found to exist the inquilino, a mestizo laborer, bound by contract or custom to the soil of the great rural properties that the invading race had carved out of the lands of his Indian

[70] Amunátegui Solar: Encomiendas, Vol. 2, p. 260.

ancestors. Both master and man were now Chileans, neither Indian nor European though belonging to two sharply divided classes; one with the social, economic, and political heritage of the native, the other with that of the Spaniard. They lived together on an hacienda, a distinctly Chilean institution, under a system created by no royal decrees but evolved out of the peculiar conditions that surrounded it. The hacienda, outgrowth of both the encomienda and the land grants of the early days but neither encomienda nor land grant now, had become both a territorial and a social unit, consisting of land and the laborers attached to that land. With this dual character, it had become the dominant social institution of the country. It was the characteristic unit of population; more important by far than the few small cities that existed in Chile at that time, playing the rôle that in most other parts of the world is played by agricultural village, kinship and agrarian group, urban nucleus, or one-family farm. It served as the basic economic unit as well; about it, more than about any other form of agricultural holding, or mine, or factory, or commercial center, was organized the economic life of the people. Its separation of master and man gave cast to the entire social structure with its sharply distinguished upper and lower classes, just as the relationship that prevailed between these two individuals determined the type of governmental institutions that existed or could exist in the country, the code of laws, and the degree of participation in public affairs enjoyed by each member of the community. The Chilean hacienda had fully evolved, and about it was organized the entire life of the colony.

Independence wrought little modification in the hacienda. While it freed the colony from Spain it did not emancipate the inquilinos from their virtual serfdom, nor did it dethrone the hacendado from his position of lordship in the nation. The hacienda continued to be the characteristic form of land tenure. With the abolition of the mayorazgos in 1857 the legal obstacle to subdivision of large properties was removed, but the social motive for retaining ancestral estates unbroken was strong enough to give this legal innovation little effect, and economic reasons favoring the creation of other forms of holdings were not yet sufficient to break the customs of centuries. The growth of population brought about a gradual though slow process of subdividing large farms, but throughout the nineteenth century and well into the twentieth there was no serious break in the dominance of this historic type of rural possession. Even today, though, as will be noted later, there is now going on a somewhat accelerated process of disintegration in the large holdings, the hacienda continues to be the most characteristic feature in Chile's agricultural organization, as also in the entire social structure of the nation.

CHAPTER V

HACIENDAS TODAY

Such farms as have been described in the foregoing chapters characterize all central Chile. From Coquimbo southward to the Bío-Bío River they constitute the typical form of rural property. There are other types, small farms and collectively held properties, as will be noticed later; but the bulk of the land is in the form of *haciendas*—or *fundos,* as they have come to be called more generally in Chile—properties operated with the labor of a considerable force of dependent tenants. As one travels through this part of the country one is impressed with the large scale of the agricultural patterns: league-long rows of eucalyptus and Lombardy poplar trees stretching across the landscape; high, well-built mud walls lining the road for miles without a break; irrigation canals (*acequias*) following these walls in a single extensive system; dozens of connected fields, not large in themselves, but joined by gates showing that they all are sections of the same property; the absence of houses in most of the fields; private roads uniting the fields with an extensive central settlement perhaps several miles away; a great rambling hacienda house set in an attractive grove of giant eucalyptus trees, surrounded by beautiful Mediterranean gardens, and separated from other houses of its type by leagues of agricultural land; back of the house, covering a distance of several city blocks, granaries, storerooms, wine *bodegas,* workshops, implement sheds, dairy barns, sometimes a silo or two, stables for saddle horses and stock corrals; and not far away numerous small dwellings of laborers, strung along both sides of the main hacienda road like a village with a single street—a town of workers and their families all connected with the farm. Such is the picture one carries away of the present-day agricultural landscape (Figs. 2-4, 11).

NUMBER AND AREAS OF HACIENDAS

In 1925,[1] there were 5,396 such estates (counting only those containing more than 200 hectares or 494 acres) in the fourteen provinces from Coquimbo to Bío-Bío, inclusive. They held in the aggregate 10,377,482 hectares out of a total of 11,675,500 hectares in rural properties; that is 89 per cent of all farm land. There were 76,688 other properties, but all these combined contained only 1,298,018 hectares.

Taking the individual provinces, we note in each case this same preponderance of land in large holdings. The Province of Curicó with a total area of 788,500 hectares had 437 haciendas of 201 hectares or more, these 437 comprising 521,851 hectares out of a total in all rural properties of 622,578; that is over 83 per cent. There were 5,937 other holdings (of 200 hectares or less), but these comprised only 100,727 hectares. Aconcagua had 183 of these large estates containing in all 1,328,197 hectares, leaving but 26,451 hectares for the other 4,619 holdings; that is, three per cent of the properties contained 98 per cent of the agricultural land. In other provinces the area included in the large farms was of corresponding proportions. Statistics thus confirm what every one familiar with Chile knows, that the hacienda is by far the most important form of landholding, so completely overshadowing other forms that many persons, even among Chileans themselves, seldom have occasion to come into touch with any other types of rural properties.

[1] Chile: *Anuario Estadístico*, Vol. 7, Agricultura, 1925-1926. Data for this year are used partly because they are more complete than those for later years, partly because they are given for the provinces as they existed before the political reorganization of 1927. Most statistics issued up to the present represent that earlier organization, hence these serve better for comparison.

Statistics for 1925 showed the following grouping of these estates in the fourteen central provinces:

Haciendas with from 201 to 1,000 hectares................3,889
  "   "   " 1,001 to 5,000   " 1,132
  "   "   " more than 5,000   "   375

In each province, with one exception, the largest number of estates falls into the first category; O'Higgins, for example, showing 92 farms with from 201 to 1,000 hectares, 41 from 1,001 to 5,000, and 16 more than 5,000. A similar proportion is found in Talca, which has 325 of the first category, 89 of the second, and 13 of the third. Valparaíso alone shows the highest number in the second class. All the provinces show a smaller number in the third group than in either of the others.

In aggregate area the order of these groups is reversed, being as follows:

Area of the 3,889 farms of
    201 to 1,000 hectares....................1,785,487 hectares
Area of the 1,132 farms of
    1,001 to 5,000 hectares....................2,496,434   "
Area of the 375 farms of more than
    5,000 hectares 6,095,561   "

The first group, though more than three times as numerous as the second and more than ten times as numerous as the third, contains just a little more than one-sixth of the land held in these three classes, while the 375 large farms (constituting the third group) contain nearly 60 per cent of the total area included in all these estates. In fact, these 375 alone, constituting four and a half tenths of one per cent in number, contain more than 52 per cent of all the land held (11,675,500 hectares) in all the 82,084 rural properties of all kinds in these fourteen provinces. It is to these very extensive properties that the term " hacienda " is most commonly applied at present in Chile. Relatively few in number, they absorb enormous areas of land.

Haciendas of More Than 5,000 Hectares

Since the properties of this third group, those containing
more than 5,000 hectares (12,355 acres) each, aggregate
the largest amount of land and in general stand far above
the other groups in size, we shall consider them first.
Among the central provinces, those having the largest number of the very large estates are Coquimbo with 76, Aconcagua with 59, and Santiago with 51. The other provinces
all have less than 30, with the exception of Bío-Bío, which
has 35. In general then, as would be expected, the more
arid districts of north-central Chile have more of these
vast holdings than the districts farther south where the
rainfall is heavier. These greatest farms are not all limited
to a mere 5,000 hectares or so. Relatively few of them
rank near that figure; the average for the group of 375
is 10,921 hectares; many have double or triple that area,
and a few are far greater. It is difficult to say which is the
largest hacienda in Chile. Exact surveys of most of them
have never been made. Not even their owners know how
many square leagues of territory they hold. The following appear to rank near the top in size. The Hacienda
Río Colorado in the valley of the same name not far from
Santiago is credited with 160,000 hectares, about 618 square
miles or just about half the area of the state of Rhode
Island. The Hacienda Illapel, in the Province of Coquimbo,
Department of Illapel,[2] is estimated to contain about
150,000 hectares. The same province has also the Hacienda
La Marquesa, which covers 125,000 hectares, and the
Estancia Pajonales y Hincaguasi, which contains 120,000
hectares. In the Province of Aconcagua, Department of
Los Andes, the Hacienda El Sauce covers nearly as great
an area, as does also the Hacienda Tranquila, Department
of Petorca. Farther south, in the Province of Ñuble,

[2] Each province of Chile is divided into departments, the departments in
turn being divided into communes (*comunas*).

Department of San Carlos, the Hacienda Virhuín y Zemita
(really two in one), which reaches from the Argentine
border on the crest of the Andes to beyond the railway
that runs down the Central Valley of Chile, contains not
far from 100,000 hectares. Only a few miles from Santiago
the Hacienda Las Condes is estimated to contain almost
60,000 hectares. There are possibly other properties that
rival some of these, and there must be several score containing from 30,000 to 50,000 hectares. In Victoria Department, Province of Santiago, there are six haciendas
listed in the statistical publications with an aggregate area
of 340,209 hectares; in the Department of Illapel, Province of Coquimbo, four with an aggregate of 316,000; and
two estates in Rancagua Department, Province of O'Higgins, contain together 107,000 hectares.[3]

One must not be misled, however, by these figures. Much
of the land in most of the extremely large properties is
rough mountain terrain, totally unfit for agricultural use.
Much of it is virtually worthless for any purpose. The
largest haciendas listed lie in communes that include arid,
hilly or mountainous country, either well to the north as in
Coquimbo and Aconcagua, or, if farther south, in the
Coast Range or the Andes. In fact, large parts of such
areas are both mountainous and desert. In the case of
Peñalolén, described elsewhere, it was noted that nearly
two-thirds of its area lies back on the slopes of the Andes.
The Hacienda Río Colorado, with its 160,000 hectares,
has only 250 hectares of level irrigated land; the rest is
hills and mountains. Some of the most rugged sections of
the Andes lie within its bounds, which include enormous
areas of mountain tops and fields of perpetual snow. The
Hacienda Las Condes, neighbor to Peñalolén, furnishes
another example of this characteristic common to many of
the Chilean big farms. It lies just east of Santiago. The
main house and grounds are situated near the foot of the

[3] Data from Valenzuela O.: Álbum de informaciones agrícolas, 1925.

mountains, where the Mapocho River comes out of the Andes into the Central Valley. Out of a total extent of 58,768 hectares, by far the larger part consists of the high foothills of the Andes, and only some 500 hectares are on the Santiago plain and thus suitable for agriculture. Chacabuco is another enormous holding. Most of its 26,869 hectares lie on the rugged slopes of the Chacabuco Range, which closes the northern end of the Central Valley. These vast properties are better described by the term *estancias* (cattle ranges) formerly used in Chile when the country was chiefly a stock-raising region, and still commonly applied to the great estates of the Argentine Pampa. Much of their area, however, has no value even for grazing.

Yet there are also many large haciendas on the valley floor of the great central trough, or in the other regions of productive soil. In the Commune of Hospital, Department of Maipo, Province of O'Higgins, situated in the Central Valley some fifty miles south of Santiago, there is one estate (Aculeo) with 34,500 hectares. Graneros Commune in the Department of Rancagua in O'Higgins Province, has one holding with 15,915 hectares; the neighboring Commune of Rancagua has one with 5,400 hectares. A large part of each of these properties lies in the region of level land with, moreover, fertile soil and an abundant water supply. For example, the hacienda of Aculeo contains 3,409 hectares of level, irrigated land; another hacienda, Chada, not far away, has 2,003 hectares under irrigation, and Codao, an hacienda lying on the fertile land along the Cachapoal, has 2,750 hectares of irrigated land. A little farther south, in the Province of Colchagua, the hacienda of Almahue has 2,500 hectares under irrigation. The great double hacienda, Virhuín y Zemita, already mentioned, has nearly 12,000 hectares under irrigation. Most haciendas, even the large ones, have a smaller acreage of irrigated land than these cited, but few irrigate less than 500 or 600 hectares. Thus these great properties are seen to contain not only enormous total extent, but large blocks of excellent land as well. In fact, many of them are built around extensive tracts of the most productive soils in the country.

Many of the greatest estates average decidedly smaller than the properties just noted, ranking between these vast holdings and those (still large) that approach the minimum extent (5,000 hectares) of the third group. Widely scattered throughout the central provinces there are farms ranging from 10,000 to 20,000 hectares. So also there are numerous holdings that range from 5,000 to 10,000 hectares. These constitute more workable properties, particularly when, as in the cases just noted, their usable land is not nearly so extensive as the figures for their entire area might lead one to suppose. However, even when one takes into account only the good lands, most of these haciendas must still be classified as excessively great; since the few thousand hectares to which their size is reduced when tillable land alone is considered constitute *latifundia* from whatever angle viewed. Most of them cannot be looked upon as farms in the ordinary sense of the word, but rather as estates possessed by owners who give little thought to scientific agriculture or even to improving production under the rather antiquated methods generally employed on these great Chilean properties. They have a social and a political value to their possessors, but contribute toward the economic welfare of their owners or of the country to a degree not at all commensurate with their size. It is against these large estates, which usually produce but a fraction of what they are capable of yielding, that current opposition is being directed.

HACIENDAS OF 1,001 TO 5,000 HECTARES

The second group of large estates, that of properties of from 1,001 to 5,000 hectares, constitutes the next most important class from the standpoint of land monopoly. These 1,132 holdings, with an aggregate of 2,496,434 hectares, contain a little more than 21 per cent of the farm lands of central Chile. In the first and second groups (that is in all the properties of more than 1,000 hectares) we have far more than half of the total acreage included in 82,084 rural holdings of the central provinces. This 1.8 per cent of the farms contains more than 56 per cent of the land.

The estates of the second class are also distributed widely, though not evenly, among the provinces. According to the 1925 figures, Bío-Bío had 130, Coquimbo and Santiago 107 each, Linares 101, and Ñuble 100; while Aconcagua had 49, Concepción had but 42, and O'Higgins only 41. These farms also include within their area some hill or mountain land, though less than in the case of the largest haciendas. They are situated in the valleys of the Coast Range, along the base of the Andes, and out in the valley floor of the great central trough. Wherever located, almost all of them contain much good land. Unlike most of the excessively great estates, which are located at some distance from the centers of population, a large number of the estates of the second class are near the principal towns and cities of their respective provinces. The Commune of Santiago had one such estate, that of Valparaíso had five, that of Rancagua had four, that of San Fernando had one, that of Linares had 27, and that of Chillán had two. They are more nearly typical of present-day Chile, whereas the greatest haciendas are typical rather of the earlier pastoral stage of colonial times and the first half-century of independence.

PROPERTIES OF 201 TO 1,000 HECTARES

The first group, that of farms with from 201 to 1,000 hectares, is still more representative of the present status of landholding in central Chile. There are more of these properties than of either of the other groups just discussed—nearly three times the number of both combined —and, though they contain a far smaller aggregate of land, they probably have a larger share of the good land of the country than either of the others.

A number of the communes in the neighborhood of Valparaíso and Santiago and other towns of the Central Valley have no larger properties than those of this class, as, for example: La Calera, La Cruz, and Las Hijuelas near Valparaíso (La Calera has none larger than 200 hectares), and San Miguel and Renca near Santiago. Indeed, in the Department of Victoria situated mainly on the valley floor in the Province of Santiago there are four communes, none of which contains a farm of as many as 200 hectares. In the Province of O'Higgins, too, the Communes of Buin, Valle de Paine, Peumo, and Doñihue contain no holdings of more than 1,000 hectares. These communes all lie out in the middle of the great central trough. Farther south in the Province of Curicó two rural communes (Quinahue and Tutuquén) also contain no properties larger than those of this class. To such holdings and those somewhat smaller the term " fundo " is most commonly applied, though, as has been noted, there is no clear line of distinction between the fundo and the hacienda.

The fundo of El Salto may be taken as typical of this class of properties. Located a few miles north of Santiago on the plain that surrounds the city, it contains 600 hectares, all level land except 60 hectares on the slope of the bordering San Cristóbal Hills. The whole area, even the hillsides, is under irrigation from two ancient canals, one of which dates back to Inca times. Most of the farm is under quite intensive development, a part devoted to horticulture, a part to dairy uses, and some 20 hectares to growing strawberries. There are large fields of alfalfa, which is baled with a hydraulic press run by the farm's own waterfall.[4] The population of the fundo is some 170 souls, including the owner and his family (who actually spend most of their time in Santiago), the manager, several overseers, and the laboring population.

HACIENDAS IN INDIVIDUAL DEPARTMENTS AND COMMUNES

A more complete idea of the extent to which these properties (all those having more than 200 hectares) occupy the land in central Chile may be obtained by examining a few of the individual departments. For example, the Department of Caupolicán in the Province of Colchagua, typical of the central region of the country, contains an area of 332,300 hectares (821,113 acres).[5] Of this total, 284,503 hectares were classed as " agricultural land," [6] and of these 78,492 hectares were irrigated. This last figure represents the greater part of the good farming land, since little is expected of the soil in central Chile, however fertile, if it cannot be supplied with water during the six to nine months of rainless summer. Not even good pasture is possible during those months without irrigation. Most of the other so-called " agricultural land " is infertile, hilly terrain of little use except for winter pastures. The irrigated land consists almost entirely of the level or gently sloping alluvial deposits in the great Central Valley and along the transverse valleys tributary to the Cachapoal, which here crosses from the Andes to the Coast Range. These deposits

---

[4] Hence the name El Salto, meaning The Cataract.

[5] The Department of Caupolicán is here considered as including also the four communes formerly constituting the Department of San Vicente, which apparently for a short time were amalgamated with Caupolicán. This is the political grouping given by Benjamín Acuña A. in his " Estudio agronómico del Departamento de Caupolicán," which, with Chile: *Anuario Estadístico, loc. cit.*, is the main source of the present data. Figures for the amount of irrigated land on the fundos are taken from Riso Patrón: Diccionario, and Valenzuela O., *op. cit.*

[6] All land included in rural properties is classed in Chilean statistics as "*territorio agrícola.*" It is in this sense that the equivalent English term, " agricultural land," is here used.

are especially fertile and well supplied with water. The department ranks among the most productive in the country, and its production of wheat, barley, beans, melons, and fruits has brought fame to its farms. Its rural landscape is particularly attractive, even among the rich farming scenes of central Chile. Level, well-tilled fields with thick stands of grain, surrounded by high mud walls and everywhere bordered by rows of Lombardy poplars, eucalyptus, or weeping willows, alternate with clover and alfalfa pastures which support herds of fat, blooded dairy or beef cattle. Orchards of peach, plum, apple, orange, lemon, and olive trees with an occasional well-kept vineyard also bespeak the varied wealth of the region, one of the garden spots of central Chile.

The Department of Caupolicán is not only intensively developed but is densely populated. Within its entire area it has a population of a little more than 14 persons to the square kilometer (37 to the square mile) ; but when its irrigated area alone is taken as the basis—for outside of this irrigated area very few people live, the hills and mountains being almost uninhabited—we have a very different figure. Most of the 47,769 people live on 784.92 square kilometers, which gives an average of 60 to the square kilometer (156 to the square mile), a figure that approximates the density of population in the habitable part of the department.

In this department there are in all 4,253 farming properties. Ten of these belong to the group of largest holdings (more than 5,000 hectares), and these ten contain 176,906 hectares, equivalent to 62 per cent of the total " agricultural land "; the 28 properties in the next class (1,001 to 5,000 hectares) contain 49,073 hectares, or 17 per cent ; and the 78 properties of the first class (201 to 1,000 hectares) contain 38,579 hectares, or 13 per cent. The 116 properties of more than 200 hectares thus hold an aggregate of 264,558 hectares, or 92 per cent of the total

" agricultural land," leaving but 8 per cent, or 19,945 hectares, for the 4,137 other properties, or an average of 4.8 hectares (11.9 acres) each. The 116 large estates average 2,281 hectares, or nearly 9 square miles, each. That much of this great area is waste land is compensated for by the fact that most of the good irrigated land is also held in these large properties—a fact that is clearly evident, though unfortunately there are no official statistics to support this statement. It is notorious, however, among all those familiar with the region (as with central Chile in general) that the best lands belong to the large estates and that the small holdings consist very largely of leftovers.

It is apparent that most of the 78,492 hectares of irrigated land lie on the large properties when it is observed that, even if all the 4,137 small properties with their 19,945 hectares were under irrigation, it would still leave just about three-fourths of such land in the big estates. As a matter of fact, most of the large canals belong to individual haciendas or to irrigation associations composed mainly of large landowners, while many of the small farms get their water from less satisfactory supplies, such as small *esteros* (brooks) or springs. The great canal that taps the Cachapoal at Gultro belongs to an estate of the same name and to some of the neighboring haciendas. The fundo of Gultro has some 400 hectares under irrigation here. The canal of Requínoa, which irrigates the fundo of the same name and associated properties, is also of private ownership, as is that of Tipaume, recently constructed along the Tipaume Creek near Rengo. One of the canals (Los Boldos), built in this province to irrigate three fundos belonging to a group of brothers, is 25 kilometers long, contains two half-mile tunnels through the hills, and cost the owners a million pesos. The figures for irrigated land in some of the large properties sustain the conclusion that most of the irrigated area is on these estates. Requínoa (mentioned above) has 531 hectares under irrigation; Pichidegua has

863 hectares; Huique has 1,000 hectares; Las Esmeraldas on the Río Claro has 2,993 hectares; La Quinta, along the Chimbarongo Creek, has 1,200 hectares; while Almahue has 4,500 hectares of irrigated land.[7] Thus it is evident that these great estates occupy not only most of the land but also most of the desirable land in this department. They leave little of value outside of their bounds.

The Department of San Fernando lies just south of Caupolicán in the same province, and like Caupolicán it stretches from east to west across the Central Valley. Unlike Caupolicán, however, it reaches from the Argentine border on the crest of the Andes to the Pacific Coast. It thus represents the several types of land characteristic of central Chile. It, too, is one of the most densely populated (93,285 in 1926) and most intensively developed of the central departments. It is 6,664 square kilometers (2,573 square miles) in area, and it has 414,648 hectares of "agricultural land" and 53,812 hectares under irrigation. If we take this last figure as representing the habitable area of the department (as it does approximately) we find a population density of 173 persons to the square kilometer (448 to the square mile), a figure more nearly representing the actual situation than that based on the entire area or even on that of the "agricultural land." Taking only the rural population (1926) and the irrigated land, one finds a population of about 130 persons to the square kilometer, comparable to that of the densely inhabited rural districts of Europe and the United States. It is a fertile, well-watered country with landscapes that speak of abundant production and crops corresponding closely to those of Caupolicán.

In this productive department the land is distributed much as in Caupolicán. The 414,648 hectares of "agricultural land" are divided among 3,739 properties, which, as

[7] Mention has already been made of the nearly 12,000 hectares of irrigated land on the Virhuin y Zemita hacienda, in a similar position but farther south.

the census shows, is an average of 110 hectares each. But, dividing them into groups, we find a very different situation, for 219 holdings have 363,654 hectares, or 88 per cent of the total, while 3,520 properties have 50,994 hectares or 12 per cent. The average of the 219 is 1,660.5 hectares, over six square miles, each, while the average of the 3,520 smaller places is 14.5 hectares each, and 1,877 of them average only 1.2 hectares in extent. Two of the haciendas have 26,000 and 23,550 hectares respectively. These great properties also, as those in Caupolicán, have hundreds or thousands of hectares under irrigation, highly productive lands for hay, grain, fruits, or pasture.[8]

In the Department of Ovalle, Province of Coquimbo, the division of land is still more uneven.[9] Here there are 646,183 hectares of " agricultural land." Of this, 630,581 hectares belong to 154 properties, while the remaining 15,602 hectares are divided among 1,930 holdings: that is, 7 per cent of the owners hold 97 per cent of the land. As this is a more arid region than the Central Valley, getting usually only from 5 to 10 inches of rain a year, a large part of the great holdings is of little value, but they contain a larger proportion of the best irrigated lands, productive of excellent fruit. One fundo has 500 hectares several others 200 hectares each, and others from 100 to 150 hectares under irrigation. They control the best water supply, that of the streams fed by the Andean snow fields. One hacienda, that of Valdivia, makes exclusive use of the entire flow of a river, the Palomo, which comes down from the Andes. Many of the small properties are forced to depend on the meager and uncertain supply of water from intermittent streams having their sources in the dry hills rather than in the snow of the Andes. This is a serious matter in Ovalle, since the rainfall there is scant at best.

[8] Benjamín Acuña A. and Arturo Merino E.: Estudio agronómico del Departamento de San Fernando, 1928.
[9] Chile: Estudio agronómico del Departamento de Ovalle, 1928.

If we turn now to individual communes we find some striking facts regarding the distribution of the land. In the fertile valley of the Aconcagua, where agricultural land was selling in 1930 for 4,000 pesos ($500) a hectare and where both productiveness of the soil and the excellent water supply seem to indicate the most intensive use of the land in orchards and vegetable gardens, there were five properties in the Commune of Calle Larga with an aggregate of 35,535 hectares, while the entire commune contained only 37,664 hectares. One hacienda alone, San Vicente y Santa Rosa, contained 31,500 hectares and had 750 hectares under irrigation. In the adjacent Commune of Los Andes the total farm land (*territorio agrícola*) was 70,403 hectares; and one hacienda, El Sauce, held 70,000 of this, while 32 owners divided the small remainder among them. In the Commune of Ocoa, farther down the Aconcagua Valley, seven owners held all the 23,997 hectares. In the Commune of Margamarga, Province of Valparaíso, ten properties occupied the total 26,922 hectares; in San Francisco Commune, two owners held the whole 9,998 hectares of its extent; while in El Melón, not far away, the whole 28,260 hectares that comprised this political division belonged to one estate. This hacienda, also called El Melón, had 1,800 hectares under irrigation, kept more than 150 milch cows, pastured more than 2,000 beef cattle, some 1,200 sheep, and hundreds of horses, hogs, and goats. Many other communes showed distributions little less uneven than these. Among the fourteen provinces of central Chile there were seven communes that had no property smaller than 201 hectares; sixteen communes had not more than five properties of that small size, and one entire department, that of Valparaíso, had no holding of smaller extent than this.

FARMS OF FROM 51 TO 200 HECTARES

Analysis of data for the next lower group of farms, those from 51 to 200 hectares, reveals the fact that a great number of these rank toward the top of this bracket, have much or most of their land under irrigation, and so do not belong in the category of single-family farms but rather in the hacienda class, managed usually by an administrator and worked by *inquilino* labor. Of such dimensions and character is the fundo of El Peñón, near Malloco, west of Santiago, near the Mapocho River. It has an area of 120 hectares, all level alluvial land and all under irrigation. The work of caring for its small herd of dairy cows, its fields of barley, beans, potatoes, and corn, and its orchards of walnuts, olives, and almonds, is performed by some ten families of workmen. The owner's " big house " (*casa de hacienda*), set in its grove of shade trees and surrounded by a characteristic Chilean country garden, gives it the appearance, as it has the character and organization on a small scale, of the typical hacienda.

Other fundos too large to be worked as one-family farms are found in all the central provinces. The owner of an estate of this type is usually a man who spends little of his time on the property but follows some other career than agriculture. As does the typical Chilean hacendado, he looks upon his holding less as a piece of land on which he and his family might reside and from whose soil they might wrest a living than as an ancestral estate which has, it is true, a certain economic value but which is to be prized largely because the social stratum to which he and his family belong is composed solely of old landholding lineages. Even these relatively small holdings are miniature haciendas, and their owners belong (with rare exceptions) to the landed aristocracy.

Ownership and Names of the Haciendas

A description of the present-day hacienda system is not complete until it is noted that the number of owners is not the same as the number of properties. An individual appears, in many cases, as the proprietor of several haciendas—in not a few instances of several of the very large ones. To offset this, many large holdings belong not to an individual but to a group of several or many persons. Probably owing to the practice, strengthened if not established by the *mayorazgos,* of holding rural properties entailed, there exists the custom in Chile of holding a property together in the family as an undivided inheritance for some years, and not infrequently for a generation. This multiplies the number of actual owners, of rural properties in particular. Another practice of long standing is revealed in the clusters of separate haciendas or fundos belonging to family groups. For example, in the Commune of Chimbarongo, near San Fernando, a list of properties published in 1902 [10] showed the haciendas of Tinguiririca, Santa Isabel, La Esmeralda, another Santa Isabel, Santa Rosa, San Juan de la Sierra, San Antonio, and La Mariposa as all belonging to one family; the list of properties in the Commune of Ñuñoa (just east of Santiago) included fundos or haciendas belonging to eight members of a single family, while in near-by communes members of the same family held four other estates; another family held seven properties in the Commune of Quillota; while near Talca fifteen large properties belonged to two closely related families. Other districts reveal this same clustering of family holdings. Some of these represent the gradual acquisition of neighboring properties; many of them indi-

---

[10] Espinoza: Geografía de Chile, 1903. (References are from lists of "*fundos rústicos*" for the respective communes.) Other lists such as Valenzuela O., *op. cit.,* and the official *rol de avalúos* (tax lists) show the same grouping in most regions of central Chile.

cate the partition into *hijuelas* (small landholdings) of once great estates.

As will be observed, each of these haciendas bears a name, most commonly an Indian name derived from the place or the native people that constituted the original basis of the property, but almost as frequently the name of some saint. Indeed, the entire roster of saints seems represented. Many of these names are beautiful in sound and suggestion; as El Edén, Delicias, El Verjel (The Garden), and El Encanto (The Charm). Some are derived from natural features, such as trees, junctions of rivers, conspicuous rocks, or other landmarks. A few of them express the humor so characteristic of the lower-class Chileans and to a degree shared by the upper class. For example, one rather small property, probably the portion received through inheritance by some one glad to get even that relatively small share of the family's estate, is called " Peor es Nada " (Better than Nothing) ; another is called " El Tropezón " (The Stumbling Block, a name frequently given with greater appropriateness to saloons) ; while another is called " Kikirikí " (Cock-a-doodle-doo).

POPULATION ON THE HACIENDAS

These haciendas constitute recognized units of population, and many of their names appear on maps alongside those of cities and towns. In fact, they constitute some of the most important population units of central Chile, aside from the greater urban centers. The census for 1930,[11] counting in the rural population all those who do not live in cities or towns of 1,000 or more, divides rural dwellers into the following categories; fundos (including all agricultural properties), *aldeas* (villages), and *caseríos* (hamlets). Its detailed statistics show that the fundos account for the larger part of this rural population, though

[11] Chile: *X Censo de la Población* (1930), published 1931.

no general summary is made. There are many rural *distritos* (subdivisions of the communes for census purposes) in which there are no other inhabitants than those on the fundos; as for example, the District of María Pinto, near Melipilla, where six fundos contain the entire rural population of 1,083; or Zapata, near Curacaví, in which ten fundos also contain all the rural inhabitants; or Tunca, near Rancagua, in which eight fundos have all the 2,596 rural dwellers. There are also many districts in which aldeas or caseríos exist, yet in which the fundos account for the larger part of the population; as, for example, the District of Santa Cruz, near San Fernando, in which twelve fundos contain 2,967 persons, while the four aldeas (with 206, 316, 168, and 290 respectively) and two caseríos (with 117 and 49 respectively) account for the remaining 1,146. Only six of these twelve fundos mentioned have fewer than fifty persons apiece, while three of them had 738, 780, and 792 respectively.[12] Throughout central Chile a similar proportion exists between villages and estates, indicating that probably from sixty to seventy-five per cent of the rural population of this region (1,381,669 in 1930) lives on the large properties; that is that the haciendas in these provinces contain from 800,000 to 1,000,000 inhabitants.[13]

The Renting of Haciendas

Another characteristic development of the hacienda system of today is the practice of renting out these large holdings. This, too, marks them as being less farms than country estates whose possession the owner prizes and whose income he desires but which he has little desire himself to operate. Probably more than at any other time

[12] *Ibid.*
[13] This agrees approximately with the estimate made as to the number of inquilinos, when allowance is made for the increase in rural population from 1920 to 1930. The census of 1930 gives 1,124,306 as the fundo population for the whole country.

since the great properties of Chile were created it is now the custom thus to rent them out. With the growing attraction of city life a great number of hacienda owners have removed with their families to provincial capitals, or to Santiago, or have elected to spend a large part of their time abroad.[14] The bureaucratic government of Chile provides many positions for members of influential families and their near and distant relatives. When the family abandons country life the haciendas are either left in the hands of administrators, the more common practice until relatively recent years, or are rented. The administrator system, particularly when the owner himself is at a distance, seems never to have been very successful. In a two-class society it has been difficult to find suitable persons to act in the capacity of *patrón*. None of the lower class could command the respect necessary; few of the upper class would stoop to such employment outside of their own families. The need has been met in part by employing foreigners, sometimes highly trained ones. Throughout central Chile one finds haciendas under the direction of German, Spanish, English, Scottish, Swiss, or American managers. But this system, too, has had its drawbacks, in that the foreigners are often unfamiliar with Chilean methods of farming and are unable to handle the inquilinos and hired labor satisfactorily. These difficulties have led many hacendados to rent their estates. They have thus freed themselves of the responsibility of supervision and at the same time have acquired an assured income from the property. Where a member of the family is available it is customary to rent the property to him. This is par-

[14] Teodoro Schneider: La agricultura en Chile, 1904, p. 7. The custom of living in the cities rather than on the haciendas is shown in data supplied by Valenzuela O. in his description of rural properties. In the Commune of Teno, some two hundred kilometers south of the capital, nine of the twenty-four fundos listed gave a Santiago address as well as a local one. Even as far south as Linares, more than 400 kilometers from Santiago, the same thing is true, eight of the twenty-eight haciendas having addresses in the capital also.

ticularly true where an estate has remained undivided; one of the heirs frequently rents from the group. Otherwise, some other member of the hacienda class, or possibly some foreigner, is found as renter. An hacendado would hardly let out his property to one of the lower class, even if some unusual fortune (such as luck in a lottery or the discovery of a mine) should make it financially possible for the latter. The renter must be a real patrón in his relations to the labor of the farm.

There are no government statistics covering this phase of Chilean agriculture. By the use of unofficial data [15] an idea may be obtained of the situation. The Department of San Antonio has 27 haciendas listed, 4 of which are in the hands of renters; that of Quillota has 76 such properties, of which 22 are rented; Caupolicán (described elsewhere) has 103 haciendas, with 17 of them rented; Vichuquén has 7 of its 14 haciendas rented, while Linares shows 14 of its 49 haciendas operated by renters. These seem to be typical. From these data and from observations it would appear that some twenty-five per cent of the haciendas in the central provinces are in the hands of renters.

In many cases the renter himself does not live on the hacienda. He, too, lives in the city and entrusts the direct management of the property to an administrator; he may even sublet the farm. Quite commonly he finds some member of his own family willing to spend at least a part of his time on the hacienda and undertake the management. Foreign renters as well as Chilean follow this practice of maintaining a city residence where they may spend the greater part of their time. A number of foreign business men have taken over rural estates in order to enjoy the advantages of the hacienda system. Except that they generally give more time and attention to making their places productive economically, they follow Chilean customs.

[15] Valenzuela O.: *op. cit.*

To this tendency of the hacienda owners to leave their properties in the hands of others some students of Chilean agriculture ascribe the threatened breakdown of the historic agrarian system. Aside from the fact that neither administrator nor renter is likely to give as great care to the permanent upkeep of the estate as the owner, it is almost impossible for any one to replace the patrón in the traditional Master-and-Man relationship. With the increased movement of hacendados to the cities, the inquilinos have been left without the patriarchal authority that has largely helped to keep Chilean rural labor in its place. With the removal of this control the laboring population of the haciendas has become less stable, less submissive, more inclined to make common cause with the lower class in the cities. This is thought to account, in large part, for the strikes, revolts, and general insubordinate attitude of rural labor in recent years.

DOMINANT POSITION OF THE HACIENDA

From the foregoing descriptions of these large properties it is evident that Chilean agriculture is still based mainly upon the hacienda; that the rural population is made up chiefly of hacienda dwellers, neither small farms nor agricultural villages constituting, as in most parts of the world, the characteristic units of country life. Furthermore, it seems clear that the hacienda is the legitimate descendant of the historic *encomienda* and land-grant *estancia,* and that it is preserving the customs, methods, and social organization of former times. Its place in the nation remains the same as in the colonial period, and the relationship between patrón and inquilino is virtually unchanged. It is evident, too, that the hacienda not only occupies by far the greater part of the area in central Chile but that it concentrates in the possession of a very few families the best farming land of the country. Statistics and general observation seem to support the conclusion reached by a Chilean writer, that " In Chile there exists a greater monopolization of the agricultural land than in any other country of the world," [16] as well as the conviction that on the hacienda must be sought the forces that account for the Chile of today and the factors that determine her present-day problems.

[16] Poblete Troncoso: Problema agrícola, Vol. i, 1919, p. 31.

CHAPTER VI

LABOR ON THE HACIENDAS

With such a system of large holdings as has characterized Chile there has always been present the serious problem of obtaining sufficient labor. Whereas in Mexico, Peru, and other parts of the Spanish possessions there had existed a large Indian population which could be put to work on the properties formed by the conquerors, in Chile, as has been noted, the Indian population was small, unskilled in agriculture, and not firmly attached to the soil. A few Indian servants (*yanaconas*) brought from Peru performed the labor required at the founding of the first settlements, but there was no continuous movement of such laborers into Chile to meet the needs of the growing colony. Later, neither the *encomiendas* nor raids on Araucanian territory could supply the demand. For some reason, probably owing to climatic conditions in part and in part to the great distance between Africa and Chile, Negro slaves were never introduced in large number. Spain's contact with this region was maintained by way of the Isthmus of Panama, and the sail down the west coast of South America against the prevailing wind involved a long delay in getting to central Chile. Such a long voyage would have been fatal to slaves carried in the usual conditions. The present population of Chile shows almost no evidence of Negro admixture, and the history of labor in this region indicates that a very small number of blacks were introduced.

Origin and Development of the Rural Laboring Class

The result of this shortage of labor was that a different system grew up in Chile from that of other Spanish colonies. By the end of the colonial period, when the Chilean social structure had taken form, the farms had become dependent mainly on a type of laborer unknown elsewhere in Spanish America. The landowners had turned slaves, Araucanian captives, and encomienda Indians into *inquilinos,* tenants attached to the land by agreements, more or less unilateral, in which well established custom regulated the responsibilities of one class and the obligations of the other.

It was customary, as has been seen, for the inquilino to give about 160 days of labor a year to the *hacienda,* working all daylight hours (*de sol a sol*). For this he received either no wage at all or a merely nominal money payment; but he was given a house on the farm, constructed by the farm owner or built with his consent, and a small piece of land which the tenant might work for himself. Furthermore, the right was commonly granted the Indian to pasture on unused land of the farm any stock that he might have. The inquilino was thus not a bondsman in any legal sense; but he was not actually free, for coercion, direct or indirect, was exercised by the landowner to hold him on the estate. Besides, there was virtually no land left in central Chile on which he might gain an independent living. Once the land had been taken up by the invading race, the native had little choice but to attach himself to the haciendas on whatever terms were offered and to stay there under whatever conditions existed. Thus, out of their mutual needs—the Indian's for protection and a place to live, the Spaniard's for workmen on his stock ranch or agricultural estate—evolved this Chilean system of Master and Man. There is no evidence that it was designed by the

Spanish crown or by either party to the relationship, but it grew spontaneously out of the peculiar conditions existing in the colony.

Independence wrought little change in this situation. The distinction between Spaniard and Indian was declared abolished in 1819 and all inhabitants of the republic were proclaimed " Chileans " with equal political rights.[1] The revolution modified the form (if not the essence) of Chile's political organization but did not alter the social structure of the country. Chile freed herself from the Spanish monarchy but did not become a democracy. A landed aristocracy remained in control. The colonial relationship of inquilino to hacendado continued unchanged into the period of the republic.[2] The growth of the republic itself brought little modification of this condition. It is true, there developed a class of free agricultural laborers not attached to the estates, as were the inquilinos, but seasonally attracted to the farms from towns or cities or mining centers, as the demands at planting and harvest time became greater or as opportunities for employment in urban and mining communities decreased. The number of free laborers, however, was small and did not greatly affect the situation. The system of rural labor established in colonial times has survived to the present day, little changed by a century and a quarter of nominal democracy. The principal type of agricultural laborer is still the inquilino. The relationship is still that of master and man.

LEGAL STATUS AND PERSONAL CHARACTER OF THE INQUILINO

The inquilino in present-day Chile is neither slave nor serf, and no bondage to the land or the landowner has

---

[1] Decree of March 4, 1819.

[2] A good description of the Chilean agricultural system as it existed immediately after independence may be found in Miers' " Travels in Chile and La Plata," 1826, Chapter 21. As Galdames states in his " Estudio de la historia de Chile," 1923, p. 264, " Su régimen de trabajo y de vida no había cambiado desde los tiempos de la colonia " (The régime of work and of life had not changed since colonial times).

legal status. He is not even a peon, since the essential feature of peonage—debt bondage—is not recognized or
practiced in the republic. Legally he is free to leave a farm
at will: there is not even a written contract binding him
to remain.[3] But he is, nevertheless, in most cases quite
firmly attached to the estate on which he lives. He thinks
of himself as a part of that estate. His father was probably born on the place, and his grandfather and several
generations of ancestors spent their lives on the hacienda.
Thus, by heritage and custom he is strongly rooted to
the particular property on which he lives. Moreover, as
the system actually operates, it is difficult for him to move
to any other employment. If an inquilino decides to leave
the hacienda on which he has been employed, it is almost
impossible for him to find placement on another. An
hacendado in the same neighborhood is generally unwilling
to receive a tenant who has left an adjoining property.
Courtesy to his neighboring landowner forbids his receiving a workman who has abandoned a former *patrón*.
Even if the inquilino is able to remove into some other
province or to a great distance from his former location,
he finds that the fraternity of landowners is so strong
that it is difficult for him to obtain employment on another
estate. In city or town, with the relatively slight industrial
and commercial development, work is not abundant, and
most of the jobs open are of a kind for which he has no
training. Thus, though legally free to remove from an
hacienda, he finds himself virtually fixed on it. The turn-
over of labor on an estate is not large, and movement from
one hacienda to another is uncommon.[4]

[3] As a matter of fact, a written contract would be impossible since some
90 per cent of the inquilinos are illiterate. " Es la voluntad del patrón la
que domina sin contrapeso " (It is the will of the patrón which dominates,
with nothing to counterbalance it) (Macchiavello Varas: Política económica
nacional, Vol. 2, 1931, p. 38).

[4] This statement applies to the haciendas in the older sections of central
Chile in particular. Toward the southern frontier there is more movement
of the laboring population, as also in the immediate neighborhood of the
large cities.

The character of the Chilean laborer, whether in city or rural district, is different from that of any other Latin-American laborer. Some attribute this difference to the Araucanian blood in his veins, it being the general opinion that few of the native tribes of America equalled the Araucanians in vigor, courage, and endurance. Some think the Spaniards who settled in Chile, derived largely from northern Spain where there is admixture of Teutonic blood,[5] were a more energetic race than those who peopled other parts of Latin America. Others ascribe the peculiar vitality of the Chilean workman to the climatic conditions in which he lives. Whatever the reason lying back of it, he is noted for physical strength, endurance, bravery, loyalty, and a spirit of independence greater than commonly found among the workmen of neighboring lands. To this may be added a certain recklessness with his own life (and that of others) and a strain of cruelty, as also lack of initiative and ambition, a tendency toward drunkenness, and the difficulty with which he adapts himself to improved methods and implements. In the opinion of the average Chilean most of these better qualities, with few of the poorer ones, seem to be found in the regular inquilinos on the haciendas, while most of the undesirable characteristics and few of the good ones are common among the free laborers of the country and the common laborers of the cities. Even the outside observer is inclined to agree with this view. This may be due to the fact that the unattached laborer, in city and country is really at odds with the society in which he lives, an Ishmael with his hand against both of the recognized classes into which Chile's population is divided, an outlaw with no place in a social structure composed only of masters and men. The institutions of the country were not designed to care for such as he; he clashes with them

[5] Thayer Ojeda (Luis): Elementos étnicos, 1909. Palacios: Raza chilena, 1904.

at every turn. He is a rebel against society—such society as he knows. He probably left some hacienda for this very reason. It is hardly to be expected that he would conform to social conditions created by an hacienda régime. Rather he looks on society as his enemy and preys upon it at every opportunity. One guards against meeting him in unfrequented places by day or by night, in city or country. Only a strong police force can keep him in order; army and navy units are distributed with this in view. Let their protection be withdrawn, as occurred in Santiago in 1905, and this pariah element of the Chilean population leaps at the chance to even its score with society in looting, burning, killing, and ruthless vandalism.

In sharp contrast with this landless, professionless, patronless, lawless, unattached " *roto* " is the inquilino of the hacienda. He is respectful, loyal, faithful, diligent, honest, submissive. Sometimes quarrelsome with his equals and quick to let quarrels grow into fights, he seldom forgets himself, even when drunk, so far as to fail in deference to the upper class. He knows his place and keeps it and discharges well the obligations of that position. " There is no country in the world which has so valuable a working-class (with the possible exception of Japan and China)" wrote a foreigner after studying the country and its people. " Perhaps, economically speaking, the fact that they live and work on exceedingly low wages . . . is one of their most important characteristics." [6] This inquilino fits perfectly into the social system that has characterized Chile, both rural and urban, for several centuries—in fact, that system was built about him and his relation to the hacienda. Many of the qualities that mark him as better than his unattached brother are good merely because they fit the established régime of the country.

[6] Elliott: Chile, 1907, pp. 249-250.

Economic Status of the Inquilino

The wages received by the inquilinos at the present time are much the same as those of a century ago. The rate of pay has risen from a mere 10 *centavos* a day to something like 30 or 40 centavos, and in places at present to as much as 75 centavos. Unfortunately, depreciation of the currency and higher costs of living have greatly reduced the purchasing power of the wage. At present the centavo is worth only about one tenth of a cent in United States money. Payment is usually made by the month. The perquisites remain about as in colonial times. To each inquilino is given a *cerco,* or piece of land, usually of about two acres in extent, adjoining or surrounding his house. This he may cultivate or not, as he pleases, and may use for whatever purpose suits his needs. Generally it is devoted to truck crops: beans, onions, artichokes, red peppers, and corn (maize) raised in quantities sufficient to meet the needs of his family.[7] (In Chile corn is grown almost wholly for human food and is classed among the truck crops.) In addition it is not uncommon for an inquilino to receive a second piece of land somewhat larger in extent, but generally not over four acres, called the *chacra.* This may be utilized for crops such as grain or alfalfa. In some places it is customary for the inquilino to cultivate this second plot of ground on shares (half-and-half) with the hacendado in payment for seeds and the use of tools and oxen and as rent for the land.

The house occupied by the inquilino is not his, though he lives in it year after year, and it is not uncommon for a family to occupy the same structure for several generations, if it can be made to last so long. The inquilino's house generally consists of one or two rooms only. Most commonly it is built of canes plastered over with clay (*quincha*) or of adobe brick and is thatched with straw. It

[7] Opazo G. (Augusto): Como deben esplotar sus cercos nuestros inquilinos, 1923.

has only an earth floor and receives light through one or two doorways with possibly a small window or two. The houses are built without chimneys and with no provision for heating. There is generally a small roofed porch along one side of the house, and a brush-covered, lean-to kitchen where all the cooking is done. In almost every case there stand beside the house one or more large fig trees whose spreading branches provide outdoor shelter for the family. Just as commonly found is the grape arbor (*parrón*) usually placed behind the house and covering as much space as the dwelling itself. Every man lives under a vine and a fig tree—but not his own.

The furnishings of the house are of the simplest; a table, a few crudely made chairs, a chest of drawers, and a trunk or box for the family's clothing. An iron bedstead or two generally occupy a place in the house, though frequently during the eight or nine months of good weather they are set out under the grape arbor or under the fig tree. The table itself not infrequently stands outside. A small hand sewing-machine commonly occupies one corner of the dark room. A few pictures of saints, an image, and a candle or two complete the furnishings of the typical inquilino's home.

The cerco is generally fenced in by a tall, matted hedge of blackberry bushes. Gaps through the hedge are left open or are closed with bars set in gateposts, seldom with gates. Not far from the house is a domelike open-air mud oven used for baking coarse bread. A large black iron kettle for heating water usually stands over a few stones laid together for a fire. One or two pigs may generally be seen tied by one foot to a stake. A few hens and a number of dogs are always about an inquilino's shack. As may be surmised from this description, the premises of the inquilino have practically no provision for sanitation. The water supply for all purposes comes usually from an open irrigation ditch, common to the whole farm population and little protected from pollution. Toilets of any kind are considered unnecessary.

In addition to cash wages, the house, and the plot of land about it, the inquilino normally receives a ration of food each day he works for the farm. This is supposed to be about enough to support a man while he works. The daily allotment for each laborer n a well-managed hacienda is about as follows: one pound of *harina tostada* (wheat roasted and ground), or possibly a small loaf made from the same material or of corn meal; a pound of beans cooked with (or without) sausage; an equal amount of potato and *pantrucas* (a stew of flour and water).[8] This is served out as meals, first in the morning after a few hours' work, again at noon, and again in the evening. Most haciendas are equipped with a large bell, set high on a pole frame, which rings out the hours of beginning work, of stopping for rations, and of ending work at night. The workmen stop where they are in the fields and eat the portion of food given them, moistening the harina tostada with water from the irrigation canal. If near the big house, they pass in line before the *mayordomo's* wife (or some other member of his family), receive their rations, and sit or lie about on the ground while eating.

As an additional payment for his labors, the inquilino receives the right of *talaje,* that is the privilege of pasturing a little stock on the hacienda. Most inquilinos possess two or three horses, possibly a cow, and a few sheep. These may be allowed to graze either among the hills usually found on the large estates or even in the alfalfa pastures maintained by every farm.

Some of the less material perquisites enjoyed by the inquilino are: protection from anyone outside the farm, as indeed from any disturber of the peace belonging to the

[8] " Una galleta en la mañana, un plato de porotos a medio día, y otra galleta en la tarde " (A cracker in the morning, a plate of beans at noon, and another cracker in the afternoon) (Pinochet LeBrun: Inquilinos en la hacienda de Su Excelencia, p. 46).

farm itself; also (sometimes), medical attention and, in a limited way, security against extreme need in old age. An inquilino runs little risk of being evicted in case of disability due to illness, accident, or other cause. Arrangement can generally be made for him and his family to stay on the hacienda, some one of them working enough to keep them from serious want. Since there are generally a number of children and few, if any, of them go to school, the hacienda can secure enough service to warrant keeping them. Furthermore, the hacendado seldom fails to respond, in a measure at least, to his patriarchal responsibilities as head of a numerous community. Almost every large hacienda has its chapel where religious services are held occasionally, if not regularly, some of the cost of this being paid by the hacienda. It is becoming increasingly common to find a school maintained at the expense of the estate, or more often at government cost, for children of the inquilino families. Some slight attention may be paid to the tenants' need for recreation, though on most farms such matters are left to the tenants themselves.[9]

The obligations of the inquilino, also fixed by custom rather than by law, and based on a verbal, unwritten agreement, are much the same throughout the different parts of central Chile. Usually the tenant is obliged to supply labor for some 240 days a year. This demand may be met either by his own labor or by a substitute. Certain inquilinos are required to supply two laborers, one for the ordinary work on the farm, another, mounted on his own horse, for duties where a horseman is required. The hours of work are from sun to sun, about ten hours during the winter and more than twelve during the summer (Fig. 20). An interval of an hour at noon is commonly allowed and in

[9] The problem of the country laborer is well described in Macchiavello Varas' " Política económica nacional," Vol. 2, pp. 36ff., and in Poblete Troncoso's " Problema agrícola," Vol. 1, 1919, pp. 239ff., as also in the reports of the Primer Congreso Libre de Agricultores de la República de Chile, Santiago, 1876.

many cases a shorter recess for the simple breakfast in the field after the first two or three hours of work in the morning. The day ends at sunset, no daylight time generally being allowed for the laborers to go to and from their houses. During the planting season and the harvest extra labor may be demanded; this is commonly established by custom, the usual practice being for each inquilino to supply one or two extra hands. The women and children are frequently employed but are generally paid for their time at the rate of ten to twenty cents (U. S.) a day.

Fig. 20—*Inquilino* and *mayordomo* at work. (From an advertisement in a Chilean newspaper.)

The inquilino has no opportunity to gain further income than that supplied by the farm, as he is not allowed to utilize even his free time working on neighboring farms or at any employment outside of his own hacienda, nor is his family free to seek employment elsewhere. He may not even engage in money-making enterprises, not being permitted to buy or sell upon the farm or beyond its bounds.

As many of these haciendas are large, constituting whole countrysides, almost the only opportunity for the inquilino to spend his money is on the farm itself. Each hacienda maintains its own store; *pulpería* this is called. Here the farm population may buy cloth and clothing, food products other than those produced on their own small lands, needles and thread, soap, nails, some canned goods, and other imported objects. Tobacco and the milder alcoholic liquors are generally sold in the pulpería or in an annex to it. Since it is usually inconvenient, if not impossible, for the inquilino to leave the farm often and go to town, he spends most of his money in the hacienda store. It is a common practice for the hacendados to extend credit to their tenants or to pay them in *vales* (vouchers) which may be exchanged for goods, but only at the hacienda store. A few haciendas have made their own coins or tokens (*fichas*), which are accepted at the pulpería and sometimes even beyond the confines of the estate itself (Fig. 21). Whether the farm owner runs the store himself or lets out the privilege to some one else, the prices charged are usually exorbitant, based on monopoly of trade, and bring back to the estate a good share of the money paid in wages.

There is little opportunity for the inquilino to advance out of his present status. Wages are fixed, or nearly so. Industry or skill on the laborer's part seldom results in an increase of actual pay. The most dependable of the workmen are selected to become foremen, and these receive more in the way of perquisites but little higher cash payment. It is almost impossible on the farm for a laborer to become independent economically. Even those who rent on shares (*medieros*) have but slight opportunity to get ahead. There is virtually no chance for the laborer to acquire property and thus develop that sense of ownership considered essential as a stimulus to advancement. The rare exceptions to this possibility serve but to emphasize its nearly universal truth.[10]

[10] A description of the inquilinos' life and a severe arraignment of their treatment by the hacendados may be found in Pinochet LeBrun's " Inquilinos en la hacienda de Su Excelencia," as also in his " Oligarquía y democracia," 1917, pp. 80-87. Pinochet LeBrun, a Chilean journalist, disguised himself as a laboring man and mingled with the inquilinos on the hacienda of Camarico, near the city of Talca, belonging to the hacendado who was then president of the republic. He concludes that the rural laborer lives in worse conditions and is paid a lower wage (in purchasing power) than a century
(continued on next page)

Religious and Social Life of the Inquilino

Social life of the inquilinos is quite restricted as compared with that in town or city. Sundays are free—if labor is not urgent; otherwise harvest, or planting, or care of the stock must go on. Feast days are common and are usually celebrated on the haciendas—again subject to interruption by pressing demands of farm labor. On haciendas visited regularly or at frequent intervals by a priest the chapel (usually erected by some devout member of the owner's family) is an important center of social life, the people of the farm attending mass and loitering for visits with neighbors from distant sections of the estate. It is not customary for outsiders to attend these services, nor for the people of an hacienda to attend elsewhere. The hacendados prefer to keep their people from mixing with others. On many haciendas visits from the priest are infrequent, and the religious needs of the tenants are completely neglected by the hacendado. At best religion offers little to the rural laborer except its service at christening, at marriage, and at burial. Even these occasions often find no ecclesiastical representative present. Marriage is too frequently unsanctioned by any authority except possibly the *patrón* or his representative, with a consequent irregularity in family relations. Official statistics for 1925 show 36 per cent of the births in the whole country were illegitimate.[11] The figures for rural and urban population are not separated but probably are about equal.

The feast days are more likely to be observed than Sundays. Afternoons of free days are frequently celebrated by the men with drinking parties at some inquilino's

Continuation of footnote 10.
ago. He believes, however, that the awakening of the laboring class in Chile will soon make such conditions impossible. Scarcely less severe in their indictments of the hacendados for their disregard of the inquilino's welfare are Poblete Troncoso (El problema de la producción agrícola y la política agraria nacional, Vol. 1, 1919, Chapter 5) and Carlos Keller (El problema obrero en Chile, *La Información*, Año 14, Nov. 1929, pp. 937-942)
    [11] Chile: *Sinopsis Estadística,* 1926, p. 13.

house, at the pulpería, or at some near-by town. A common sight on such evenings is a drunken rider swaying in his saddle as his horse makes its way homeward and shouting ribald greetings to all passers-by. Their strong *chicha* (must or hard cider) is the intoxicant most generally used. Feast-day dancing on the earth floor or under the vine of an inquilino's house is usually confined to the national *cueca,* a spirited open dance of a single couple accompanied by a guitar and the clapping of hands and stimulated by frequent draughts of chicha. The *huasos* (country fellows) who are horse-minded are accustomed to celebrate any free day with races. The Chilean horses are fleet (many of them of Arabian stock), the huaso is a good rider, and the long farm avenues, lined with double rows of great poplar or eucalyptus, make excellent courses. On almost any Sunday afternoon or other holiday one may see groups of countrymen gathered for such races. It is clean sport, the chief reward being the joy and pride of winning, though the flowing bowl with which victory or defeat is celebrated indiscriminately not infrequently brings to bloody conclusions arguments over horses or horsemanship.

Another national amusement sometimes fostered by the farm, though more often seen in the rural villages, is the game of *topeo.* This is a pushing game engaged in by two or more mounted men and their well-trained horses. A long, stout log is fastened securely in a horizontal position, after the fashion of an old-time hitching rack. The horses stand side by side with shoulders pressed firmly against the smooth surface of this log. At a signal, spurred on by their riders, they throw their whole strength into an attempt to shove each other along the heavy bar. The Chilean rustic selects his mount generally for strength rather than for speed, and such horses are well suited to this strenuous sport. On every holiday one may see the topeo in full swing on hacienda or in country town. Though the game is usually engaged in with good sportsmanship,

keen rivalry between representatives of neighboring haciendas sometimes reaches the stage of serious injury to an
opponent or results in fights with whips or knives.

A few of the tasks of the farm are given a social character. The yearly rodeo on the larger haciendas, occupying
several days or possibly a week, is an occasion when the
men get entertainment out of their work. At this time the
cattle and horses are brought in from the distant pastures
and branded or marked. The task of rounding them up
and separating out any stock from neighboring farms is
made something of a gala occasion by the whole population of the place. Dancing and drinking enliven the evenings during a rodeo. Threshing time has also something of
this festive character. On many of the older haciendas
the wheat is threshed on a hard earth floor in the open.
This floor is surrounded by a fence of brush or rails, and
in the center the wheat is piled high. Half-wild mares
from the mountain pastures are brought down to the farm
and driven round and round the stack of wheat to trample
out the grain. The straw is then separated and the grain
winnowed by the simple process of tossing it into the air.
On the more modern haciendas threshing machines are
now used. However the threshing is done, the event is
one of the festive occasions of the year, a season of hard
labor but marked by co-operative effort and unwonted social
contacts.

ADMINISTRATION OF LABOR AND AUTHORITY OF THE HACENDADO

There is something of a hierarchy of labor on an
hacienda. The administration is in the hands of a body of
higher employees. Each group of laborers is in charge of
a *capatáz,* and over these there is a mayordomo. Many
haciendas, particularly the larger ones, have several mayordomos, each one in charge of some special activity of the

FIG. 21

FIG. 22

FIG. 21—Token (*ficha*) issued by the Hacienda Quivolgo.
FIG. 22—*Hacendado* and his *inquilinos*.

farm. There may be a mayordomo of the park about the "big house"; another for the orchard, another for the vineyard, another for the hill pastures, another to provide the wood supply, another in charge of irrigation, another as master of the keys (*llavero*), another to supervise the milking. One gets a vivid picture of the social organization of rural Chile on seeing these foremen and their respective squads of workmen gather on an hacienda in the early morning for instructions from the administrator or the hacendado himself and then separate to scatter over the estate from milking shed to irrigation ditch, from alfalfa *potrero* (field) to wheat field and vineyard, from Alpine pasture and mountain copse to work in the quarry, on the roads, and in the construction of houses (Fig. 22). It is interesting to note, too, that some of the mayordomos attend to their duties with little need for supervision, only occasionally coming to the big house to consult the manager. Some of them, in fact, live on distant parts of the hacienda and carry on their work almost as if they owned the place.

Until recent decades it has been customary for the hacienda to exercise a certain amount of civil jurisdiction within its bounds. Crime was formerly punished by the hacendado himself, who was looked upon, if not legally commissioned, as magistrate. Some of the farms had cells or dungeons, and some are said to have maintained stocks in which to punish their more recalcitrant inquilinos. Much of this authority has now passed out of the hands of the farm owner, but in minor matters an appeal is seldom made to public officials. Within certain bounds the hacendado's word still is law on his estate. His staff of higher employees executes his will, and against his decrees there is commonly no appeal. This power has frequently led to serious abuse. The "Quintrala," already referred to, was not the only farm owner who played the tyrant. In fact, such tyranny has reputedly been all too common. The growing organization of a national police force as well as the slowly evolving independence of the laborer have put a check to much of this unbridled power.

Hardships of the Inquilino's Life

From the foregoing description it is evident that the conditions of the inquilino's life in central Chile are very hard. The farm laborers and their families live in poverty, their economic status being far below that of the rural population in most civilized countries. They have no land of their own, little livestock, scarcely any tools, and the houses in which they live are theirs only by sufferance. Even their personal possessions are few; in matters of food and clothing they live little above the mere subsistence level. In fact, if not in theory also, they are doomed to remain in their present status as long as the hacienda continues to dominate the life of the country. It is the hopelessness of their situation, the lack of opportunity to better their condition, that impresses a foreigner most strongly.

However, the traditional relationship that exists between the inquilino and the hacendado—between master and man—somewhat ameliorates the hardships of the inquilino's condition. The landowner is not only employer, he is also patrón. The system is quite patriarchal in its actual operation. The inquilino usually feels a sense of loyalty and even of devotion to the farm owner. The latter in turn looks upon the inquilinos as his wards, almost as his children. He regards them with solicitous care. This relationship is greatly strengthened because on many a farm the inquilinos belong to families who have lived on the property for generations and because the hacienda itself has remained in the possession of a single family for centuries. In fact, some of the haciendas of Chile are said still to belong to descendants of the original grantees, and it is likely that on many properties the labor families date their relation to the farm from a period almost as remote. Furthermore, it is to the hacendado's own interest that his tenants should be happy and well provided for, according to the standards common in the country. It is recognized that no hacienda can function properly with discontented inquilinos. This relationship between the two classes on an hacienda does much to soften the asperities of the system.

FREE LABORERS

Not all of the labor in rural districts in Chile is supplied by inquilinos. There is also a class of free laborers called by several different names—*forasteros, afuerinos,* or *labriegos libres.* These workmen are not attached to the farm; they do not even live on it. They come from towns or cities and drift about the country in response to the demands of planting or harvest seasons, of periodical cleaning of the irrigation canals, and other such irregular work. They are paid by the day or by the piece (*tarea,* task), earning a wage larger than that of the inquilino, but enjoying no permanence of employment and none of the perquisites usually allowed the tenants. At the present time a free laborer may receive as much as four or five pesos a day.[12] These men are generally without their families—in fact, their family relations are most irregular. They wander from city to country, from country to the nitrate fields, as work is offered, usually with no possessions but a small bundle of clothes, and they spend most of what they earn in riotous living. The common opinion among the hacendados is that they are the most unsatisfactory class of laborers. They have the reputation of being drunken, vicious, lazy, and undependable and of

[12] Chile: *Anuario Estadístico,* Vol. 7, Agricultura, 1923-1924, pp. 123-124, lists the wages paid the *afuerinos* in different parts of the country.

provoking many difficulties in the relation between the inquilino and the farm owner. The hacendado employs as few of these wandering workmen as is possible.

NUMBER OF INQUILINOS AND FREE LABORERS

In the republic as a whole, these two types of rural laborers, the inquilinos and the afuerinos, exist in about the proportion of two to one. There is an increasing tendency of the inquilinos to break loose from the farms and move into the cities, hoping to improve their economic condition or, at least, to free themselves from what a Chilean writer calls the " heavy tutelage of the hacendado." In recent years extensive public works and the reconstruction of cities damaged by earthquakes have offered greater inducements for these laborers. When such temporary employment fails, the workmen seldom return to their status as inquilinos but swell the number of unattached afuerinos. Shortage of rural labor has reached the point where hacienda owners are considering the possibility of bringing in foreign workmen. In 1926 the suggestion was made that Italian laborers be brought over, partly to act as an educational influence among the " backward and indolent " natives and partly to supply the places of inquilinos who were deserting the farms. According to official figures published in 1929, there were 386,290 rural laborers in the country, about 130,000 being free.[18] More detailed data are not available, but the number of houses for inquilinos (73,512) is given in official publications.[14] This shows an average of three and a half inquilinos per house. Assuming that this is a fair average for each of the central provinces (as it seems to be), the approximate number of inquilinos for each province, department, and commune

---

[13] Chile: Estudio sobre el estado actual de la agricultura chilena, 1929, pp. 8-9. Pinochet LeBrun, *op. cit.*, speaks of the inquilino class as comprising a half million individuals. This rough estimate probably includes the free laborers as well.

[14] Chile: *Anuario Estadístico.* Vol. 7, Agricultura, 1923-1924.

may be estimated. Taking the Province of Colchagua as typical, we find the following relations between inquilinos, afuerinos, and total rural population. Of the 284,942 persons in the province (1920), 196,105 lived in places of less than 1,000 inhabitants and are thus classified as rural. There were 5,064 inquilinos' houses, representing therefore about 17,725 inquilino laborers. The free laborers would then be about 8,800, though the number is probably smaller in Colchagua, since it is distinctly an hacienda-dominated province. The total rural laborers would then amount to about 26,500. If we estimate each family as composed of five persons, it shows a rural labor population of 132,500, out of the total of 196,105 rural dwellers, which, judging from conditions as they appear in the province, would seem to be a reasonable approximation. Some such proportions probably exist in the other central provinces.

The number of inquilinos on individual haciendas varies not only with the size of the estate but with its character, the amount of land under irrigation, the number of cattle, and the care given the farm. A few haciendas have as many as 150 inquilino families, many have 50 to 75, while the greater part appear to have from 15 to 35. Incomplete data seem to indicate that an inquilino and his family exist for about every 15 *cuadras* (60 acres) of irrigated land on farms where there is no other kind of land. On other haciendas the number varies greatly. Contrary to what one might expect, inquilinos are found on many haciendas situated near the cities as well as on those more remote, though it has been estimated that near the larger cities from 70 to 80 per cent of the labor on farms is in movement.[15] On the more distant estates fewer day laborers are employed: the dependence is more completely upon the inquilinos.

[15] Schneider: Agricultura, 1904, p. 122.

Rise of Class Consciousness

Until recent years there has been very little class consciousness on the part of the Chilean rural laborer. He has had but slight contact with the outside world, even with the relatively small industrial class of the Chilean cities. There has never been an organization of the inquilinos. They have had no voice as a group, the relations of the laborers on a farm being restricted to those with their patrón. In recent years this situation has been changing. The industrial labor group in the cities has grown larger and, in contact with labor movements elsewhere in the world, has become more class-conscious. This was particularly true in the period of social unrest that characterized most countries after the World War. During that time foreign agitators, and native Chilean leaders as well, stirred up much discontent among the so-called " roto " class in Chile. Strikes were common in the coal mines about Concepción, in the nitrate fields of the northern desert, and in the relatively small industrial population of the cities in central Chile. For the first time in the history of the country strikes spread to the rural districts. For the first time, apparently, the inquilino realized that laborers elsewhere were not compelled to live in the conditions of poverty and servitude characteristic of Chilean country life. On a number of the haciendas, particularly near the larger cities, uprisings occurred among the tenants, accompanied by violence in several cases. In 1919 an attempt was made to organize a federation of inquilinos,[16] adherents being promised a general distribution of the land.[17] The effort did not succeed, but a dangerous situation resulted from the agitation that accompanied the strikes in city and in country. Probably more than at any other time in the

[16] On November 17, 1919, the Sociedad Nacional de Agricultura was informed that such attempts were being made in the Catemu region in the Aconcagua Valley, the intention apparently being to federate the inquilinos with an organization of miners (*El Agricultor,* May, 1920, p. 113).

[17] *El Agricultor,* May, 1921, pp. 87-91.

history of Chile the hacendados were alarmed at the prospects. Particularly they feared the very evident spread of communistic agitation. The powerful Sociedad Nacional de Agricultura, having headquarters in Santiago and composed of large landholders, discussed the critical situation at many of its gatherings, and an ill-concealed note of fear is evident in the published minutes of the meetings.[18] Many suggestions for improving the status of the country laborer were made by the hacendados themselves in a concerted effort to check the growing unrest. Better houses for the inquilinos were urged; schools for children of the country laborers were proposed in regions where even primary instruction had never been made available before; as a substitute for distinctly labor organizations many hacendados proposed the creation of *sindicatos* on individual farms. These societies were to embrace only the residents on a single estate and were to work in close harmony with the owner of the place. Recreational features such as athletics, cinematic performances, and social gatherings were suggested in the effort to keep the inquilinos contented and to prevent their incorporation into the labor unions of the cities. There was apparently no recognition, however, of any need for a basic reform in the entire agrarian system.[19]

MEASURES OF SOCIAL BETTERMENT

The whole country sensed the danger of this unrest, and social legislation became a subject widely discussed in official circles and in the press. Out of this grew a number of laws for the betterment of conditions among the

[18] *Bol. de la Soc. Nac. de Agric.*, 1919, 1920, and 1921.

[19] An editorial in *El Agricultor* (Jan., 1921) urges the hacendados to recognize the necessity of facing the situation and treating their inquilinos with " benevolencia y humanidad " in order that the traditional relation of community of interest may be preserved between the laborer and proprietor. This is the typical attitude of the Chilean hacendado. There is a similar editorial, " El bienestar en la vida rural," in *Bol. de la Soc. Nac. de Agric.*, 1928, pp. 141-144.

workers, particularly in the city. One measure provided for written contracts to take the place of the vaguely defined agreements between employer and employee; another regulated the working hours of the day; another established employment insurance. Most of these reforms were put into effect among the urban laborers but were difficult to carry out in the rural districts. The hacendados were loud in their protests that, however suitable such legislation might be for the city workers, it imposed impossible conditions on the labor of the farms. Attempts were made, however, by government officials to enforce some of these provisions among all laboring classes, and the legislation did result in decided improvement in living conditions on the hacienda.

One of the most beneficent of these measures was that relative to the housing of rural laborers. The rude thatched wattle-and-daub shacks in which many of the inquilinos have been housed, while picturesque features of rustic life photographed by Chilean and foreigner alike, are totally unfit for human habitation. They are far inferior to the houses in which many of the Aracuanian Indians live at the present time, and many of them are probably inferior to the dwellings in which the aborigines of central Chile lived in their native state. The average *rancho,* as these inquilino shacks are called, offers little protection against inclement weather. Though the Chilean climate is mild, the winter nights are frosty, and the cold rains of winter bring great discomfort and danger to health among the occupants of the poorer ranchos.

Decided improvement has been made in the last few years. Some of the haciendas now build much more substantial houses, with good adobe walls, tile or corrugated-iron roofs, and board floors. One hacendado even proclaims that in the houses constructed by him for his inquilinos each room has a window. A few houses have electric lights and running water. Sanitary conditions, too, are being improved, as are also the less material conditions of the inquilino's life. Many haciendas have done something toward providing for recreation among their tenants. It is not uncommon to find a field supplied by the farm owner for what has virtually become Chile's national game, soccer football. Some estates have organized football clubs, and their teams compete with those of other farms. A few have theaters for their people; an occasional one is found providing medical dispensaries.[20] Co-operative societies have been established by the hacendados on some farms. An example of one of the most advanced in this line is the hacienda of Calleuque along the railway from San Fernando to the coast. Upon this property, which has some 100 inquilino families, there exist a neatly built chapel, a schoolhouse to accommodate 100 pupils, a theater large enough for the whole farm population, and a *sindicato agrícola* with provisions for co-operative buying, saving, insurance, and loan funds.[21] Though these improvements have been introduced in many places, the greater part of the inquilinos still live in their miserable ranchos, with few conveniences and no comforts, little better off than were their ancestors of colonial days.[22]

It should not be supposed that the hacendados have brought about these improved conditions in their tenants' lives merely because of their fear of uprisings among the inquilinos; nor that they were prompted solely by the economic necessity of keeping the laborers contented. It is

[20] In April, 1930, the Sociedad Nacional de Agricultura organized a welfare department charged with improving hygienic and social conditions among the inquilinos (*La Nación*, April 29, 1930, p. 15).

[21] Valenzuela O.: Álbum de informaciones agrícolas, Zona Central, p. 141. A similar organization within a single hacienda is that on the Fundo de Pullalli, which was becoming in 1923 the center of social activities for all the inquilinos (*Bol. de la Soc. Nac. de Agric.*, 1923, p. 808).

[22] "El obrero agrícola aun duerme el sueño de la colonia" (The rural laborer still sleeps the sleep of colonial times) (Macchiavello Varas: *op. cit.*, Vol. 1, p. 132). The inquilinos still clamor daily for full compliance with the social legislation, for schools, and for better wages (Keller: Un país al garete, 1932, p. 123).

evident in their writings, in discussions carried on at the meetings of the Sociedad Nacional de Agricultura, and in conversations with them that they are prompted by less selfish motives as well. The hacendado does not forget that he is also a patrón; he frequently evinces genuine solicitude for the welfare of those dependent on him. However he may think of the proletariat in general, the employees on his property are his protégés—they are his own people. With many of them he played as a child (always, of course, as their superior), caroused as a young man, and worked in real community of interest through later years. Before his own generation there had existed the same relationship between his fathers and theirs. In fact, in the veins of not a few of them the blood of his own family is rumored to flow. Close association for several or many generations and a common interest in a property owned by him but cared for by them make the population of many an hacienda virtually one big family—a family composed, it is true, of master and man but nevertheless compactly knit together, the inquilino devoted to the owner, the latter in turn seriously concerned for the welfare of his people.

CHAPTER VII

INFLUENCE OF THE HACIENDA

The influence of the *hacienda* is evident in the entire life of the nation. Nearly every Chilean analyst makes mention of this fact. Foreign visitors easily note how dominant is this feature of the peculiar agrarian system. Whereas in other countries it usually requires careful analysis to detect the rôle played by any particular part of the social structure, in Chile it is patent even to the casual observer that the hacienda has strongly affected the economic, social, and political life of the people. Its influence has been far-reaching in time and space. From the earliest Spanish days through three centuries of colonial history and through a hundred years of independence its mark on the national life may be seen. Though its influence is weakening at the present time, it still has no rival. This is particularly so in central Chile, where the typical hacienda has developed more fully than in the provinces of the desert north or in the forested south. From Coquimbo southward to the Bío-Bío, both rural and urban life have been fashioned about the hacienda. The social class to which one belongs depends mainly upon one's relationship to the landholding class; economic opportunity is determined by this same relationship; one's place in the body politic, as the character of that body politic itself, is founded upon the same factor. To understand Chile one must know the hacienda—not only its prevalence as a feature of the land system, but its power in molding the history of the country, in making Chile what it has been and is today.

Influence on Economic Life

PRODUCTION FOR EXPORT AND DOMESTIC CONSUMPTION

In the economic life of the country the large farm has been the main contributor to foreign trade in agricultural products. In comparison with the Argentine, with Brazil, or with the United States, Chile has not been a great exporter of farm products. Her market for such exports has been limited largely to the other countries on the west coast of South America, mainly Peru; occasionally she has contributed to meet United States' demands, as for example during the early settlement of California before the great wheat fields of the Far West had been brought into production. There is still a small export of barley, oats, wheat, wine, beans, alfalfa, and fruit. Commodities for export come almost entirely from the hacienda; fruit, shipped from the irrigated valleys of the north and, recently, animal products from the far south are the only important exceptions. No properties in central Chile except the *fundo* and the hacienda are able to produce much in excess of their own needs.

In producing for domestic consumption the haciendas also play an important part, feeding their own population of *inquilinos,* free laborers, and administrative staff, a total of from 800,000 to 1,000,000 persons in all; contributing largely to the food supply of the city populations, which amount to somewhat more than 1,000,000 people; and sending also grains, meat, vegetables, and fruit to the mining centers of northern and central Chile, a group of perhaps some 200,000 people. In all, about half the nation's population are fed from the haciendas. The small properties mainly feed their own people and supply the needs of the smaller villages, though they contribute also, in a very limited amount, to dwellers in cities and mining centers and export a small quantity of fruit.

Livestock Production and Breeding

The haciendas raise most of the livestock of the country. From the early colonial days when European animals were introduced and multiplied in the mild climate of central Chile, the large agricultural properties have been accustomed to maintain many cattle and horses. In fact, a few of them still figure more as cattle ranches than as farms. Most of those near the mountains on both sides of the Central Valley possess great areas of mountain lands which serve for little else than pasture. Others have rights to community mountain pastures coming down from the time when some vast estate was partitioned, its highland meadows having been left for use in common. On such high summer grazing lands, on winter pastures of the lower hills which many haciendas contain, and in the irrigated alfalfa fields on large properties of the Central Valley Chile feeds the greater number of her 2,000,000 cattle and nearly half a million horses and mules. Very little stock (except sheep, and even those not in great numbers) is raised in central Chile except on the large estates.

Not only does the hacienda raise most of the livestock of the country; it has also contributed substantially to improving the breeds. The influential Sociedad Nacional de Agricultura has for years maintained an annual stock fair, with elaborate provisions for awards to owners of blooded animals. This, together with the Chilean hacendado's natural pride in fine stocks, has resulted in the introduction of many excellent brood animals from foreign lands. Not infrequently Chilean hacienda owners compete with those of the Argentine and other parts of the world at the auctions of blooded stock in Europe or the United States. Particular attention has been given to improving the type of work ox. Since the plowing on the haciendas and much of the hauling in country regions is done with oxen, development of such animals has appealed to the Chilean farm owner. Dairy cattle and saddle horses have also received attention. Though most of the stock on the haciendas is still native unimproved, recent years have seen decided advance brought about by attention to breeding. Elsewhere than on the large estates, however, little has been done.

FINANCIAL INFLUENCE

In national monetary matters the hacienda has been no less influential. Controlled by the *hacendados,* Chile generally has kept her credit sound, has insisted that the government be most scrupulous in meeting its foreign obligations, and has maintained a financial reputation higher than that of most of her neighbors. In domestic finance, however, the landholding group by dominating legislation has played very largely into its own hands. Maintaining a gold standard for foreign trade but issuing cheap paper currency for domestic use, it has received the price of its agricultural exports in gold but has met its local obligations with depreciated money. Furthermore, speculation and manipulation of the currency by the same group have caused fluctuations that have worked to the benefit of the capitalist but to the impoverishment of the common people.

In the banking system and the organization of credit institutions the hacienda also figures. Many of the banks exist largely to supply the needs of hacendados and the system of making loans is adapted to the requirements of these large owners. In fact, few rural dwellers except the hacendados make use of the banks. The credit institutions carry on a lively business in large-farm mortgages. One of the important financial institutions created by the government, the Caja Hipotecaria, was devised and established mainly for the purpose of supplying loans on haciendas. The creation of this institution was justified by the government as an aid to agriculture. Almost exclusively it is of benefit to large-scale agriculture, providing cash beyond that obtainable from the produce of the soil—cash that is often spent in maintaining expensive city residences or in travel abroad. Other institutions, such as the Banco Garantizador de Valores and the Caja de Crédito Hipotecario serve much the same purpose. Their services seldom reach beyond the hacienda or fundo class.

The systems of taxation show the influence of the same agency. Devised by hacendados, who have always constituted the majority in the Chilean Congress, the system has touched but lightly the resources of the large landowners. Until recent years land has been almost entirely free from taxation. Though Chile in the first years of independence had instituted a direct tax on land (Decree of December 9, 1817), this had not been continued, the *diezmo* of colonial days surviving until 1853. Upon the abolition of this system, a small tax (*contribución agrícola*) had been imposed, based on value of rural holdings. When Chile secured the nitrate fields of the north she found this mineral a prolific source of revenue, and the landowning legislators gladly allowed it to provide the greater part of the national income. An income tax, too, which in Chile would fall almost exclusively upon the large landowners, has been avoided until recently. In fact, on one occasion the aristocratic Senate, rather than approve an income tax proposed by the administration, refused to vote the annual budget and deliberately forced the nation to the brink of bankruptcy if not revolution. With its influence in government circles, the hacendado group has laid the burden of providing government expenses almost wholly upon other shoulders than its own, mainly upon the foreign exporter of minerals and the native consumer of imported goods. In 1923, for example, out of a total revenue of 857,710,239 pesos [1] the export duties on nitrate brought 227,439,246,

---

[1] A peso in 1926 was worth approximately 12 cents (United States currency).

import duties brought 184,071,795, and taxes on tobacco and alcoholic beverages amounted to 25,748,838—these three items totaling 437,259,879; while all real estate brought the government but 15,561,803 pesos.[2] According to the law of 1916 the maximum tax the national government was authorized to lay on real estate amounted to two per mil. With the decrease in the revenue derived from nitrate, new land taxes have been levied but only over the strenuous opposition of the landholding class. The law of 1925, which greatly increased taxes upon real estate, exacting 9 per mil of the declared income from rural properties, was the subject of constant complaint from the hacendado group.[3] Deriving the lion's share of benefits from government, the hacienda has exerted its influence on every occasion to evade paying the bill, and during most of the history of the country has escaped almost entirely from the burden of taxation.

LAND UTILIZATION AND AGRICULTURAL METHODS

A further economic effect of the hacienda has been its influence against the most efficient use of the land. With large holdings, it has been both unnecessary (from the viewpoint of the owner) as well as impossible to keep all the productive land under cultivation. No figures are available to show how much of the good land of the country is actually being used effectively, but in traveling through central Chile one is impressed with the large number of fields given over to grazing or to the production of hay or left unused as compared with the number under intensive cultivation. To the visitor looking down from the neighboring hills upon haciendas about Santiago it appears that about one field in ten is being utilized for cereal production, the others lying fallow or devoted to

---

[2] Chile: *Sinopsis Estadística, 1923.*
[3] *Bol. de la Soc. Nac. de Agric.,* 1925, p. 91.

hay, or grazed by small herds of cattle or horses—this, even though the soil on these farms is the most fertile in the country and an abundant supply of water is available for irrigation. It also appears, as one would expect, that the smaller the farm, the larger the percentage of land under cultivation. Moreover, the visitor to Chile, after seeing her modern cities and their up-to-date living conditions, her well-organized mining enterprises, her transportation system with its good steamship lines, its electrified railways, and its aviation service, is astounded to see on many of her great rural estates agricultural methods that remind him of ancient Egypt, Greece, or Palestine. On haciendas that measure many square miles in extent, that contain large tracts of the most fertile land on the continent, that belong to men who count their wealth in millions of pesos, one can daily see wheat being cut with the sickle and the sheaves, bound by hand with ties of wheat stalks, carried in the arms of laborers (men and women), and set in shocks as on poverty-ridden farms in other lands. From the car window on any railway in central Chile may be seen the ox-drawn plow, an old-fashioned homemade implement, followed by a barefooted " clodhopper " who prods his beasts along with a goad and guides them with the Spanish equivalent of " gee " and " haw." While much of the threshing is now done by machinery, it was not adopted by the great estates of central Chile till long after it was commonly used in southern Chile and other progressive lands. Even today the ancient method of trampling out the grain with oxen or droves of mares on an old-fashioned threshing floor is still employed on many of these haciendas. Until the last twenty-five years this was the most common method.

Though improvements, such as threshing machines, silos, sanitary arrangements for dairy cows, and up-to-date stables for blooded horses have been introduced on some estates, the average hacendado would be convulsed with laughter at the thought of putting a *huaso* (country fellow) on a riding plow or setting an inquilino to run a tractor. In many lines these large estates are operated now almost as they were in colonial times. The hacienda must be held responsible for much of this inefficient use of the land [4] and backwardness in agricultural methods. So serious is the failure to utilize the soil resources efficiently that Chile, though essentially an agricultural country, yearly imports large quantities of agricultural products. In 1925, for example, 5,500,000 pesos worth of animals and animal products and 29,103,672 pesos worth of cereals, forage, fruits, etc., were imported. Though these figures are counterbalanced by Chile's exportation of other farm products, they show a lack of productivity on the part of her farms, a lack that, coupled with a not very efficient distribution of products, has resulted in high costs of many food materials. With the land available, Chile should be able independently of agricultural importations to provide abundantly for a decidedly larger population.

PROMOTION OF IRRIGATION

One important economic contribution made by the hacienda is the construction of irrigation canals. Until recent years the government had taken little part in the extension of irrigation. If canals were to be constructed, they must be built by the individual hacienda or by groups of large properties in co-operation. Thus one may look upon the irrigated land of central Chile as a direct and most valuable contribution made by these large holdings. There were in the fourteen central provinces (1925) 1,059,098 hectares

[4] " Present conditions of land tenure and methods of cultivation prevent agricultural commodities from figuring prominently in the export trade " (Jones: Commerce of South America, 1928, p. 170). " El latifundismo se ha convertido en el peor enemigo del progreso " (The latifundian system has become the worst enemy of progress) (Keller: Un país al garete, 1932, p. 123). Pinochet LeBrun in his " Oligarquía y democracia," 1917, pp. 89-93, also ascribes the backwardness of Chilean agriculture to the system of landholding.

(2,617,031 acres) of irrigated land. By far the greater part of this lies in the row of provinces from Santiago to Ñuble, that is, in the northern part of the Central Valley. Santiago, Colchagua, Ñuble, and Linares rank above the other provinces. Within these provinces the departments and communes with the greatest extension of irrigation are in the nearly level land on the wide alluvial fans that form most of the valley floor in the great central trough. This is the region where many of the largest and oldest haciendas are located and where the greater part of the land is occupied by large properties. These great estates have had resources of labor and capital sufficient to enable them either singly or in co-operation to construct the canals that have made this extension of irrigation possible. The San Carlos Canal, which irrigates a large part of the agricultural district in the vicinity of Santiago with water from the Maipo River, was constructed in this fashion. It was begun in colonial times on a small scale by hacienda owners. When the need appeared for extension, the government attempted to enlarge the canal sufficiently to irrigate a large area about the city. It found the cost beyond its resources, sold shares (*regadores*) in the water of the canal to properties that might profit from its use, and finally turned over the entire undertaking to a group of landowners (1827). The canal, along whose course the sediment-laden waters of the Maipo have flowed without interruption for a hundred years and which now holds rights to one half the total flow of the river, has been kept up and is still owned and operated by a private association of hacendados. This group—at present with many small holders and even owners of city lots added to its number, as properties in the suburban districts holding water rights from the canal have been subdivided—maintains headquarters in its own building in the city of Santiago, as has been noted. Here an administrative staff is engaged in maintaining and operating this great canal and a series of others that also bring water to the Santiago plain.[5] Irrigation in the fertile Aconcagua Valley is organized in like manner,[6] while southward from Santiago there exist a number of canals constructed and maintained by similar irrigation associations or by individual haciendas. To the hacienda then, irrigation in central Chile owes almost all its present development.

Influence on Social Life

In any consideration of the social influence of the hacienda one must note that this form of landed property constitutes the most common social unit of the country. Chile is not a land of large cities: Santiago and Valparaíso are the only ones. Neither does the country population live verly largely in towns, agricultural villages, or single family farms. The population of the rural districts centers chiefly around the settlements of inquilinos on the large estates. Such settlements constitute the principal units of social organization. As we have noted in the description of some individual estates, the life of most country residents contains little beyond what the hacienda offers. Labor, love, recreation, and the religious life of the inquilinos, all are circumscribed largely by the bounds of their individual haciendas. It is not surprising that the social influence of the hacienda has been strong in Chilean life.

MAINTENANCE OF FAMILY UNITY

One of the marked social effects of the hacienda is its influence in holding the family together. Few countries of the world today show family ties so little broken as in Chile. This is true both among the landowners and among the laboring class. The hacienda has been looked on as

[5] Sociedad del Canal de Maipo: Antecedentes y documentos, 1902.
[6] Claro Solar: Río Aconcagua, 1917.

a family estate coming down from generations past to be kept in the family possession if possible and to provide a home, or at least an income and the prestige of land-ownership, for all members of the family group. While most of the hacienda owners and their families live during most of the year in the cities, they regard the great house on the estate as their home and return there on special occasions, particularly during the summer season when the climate of central Chile becomes too warm for comfort in the cities. On such occasions family groups, near relatives and far, are accustomed to gather on these paternal estates and renew and strengthen the kinship ties. As the family has grown, it has been customary to divide the large estates into what the Chileans have come to call *hijuelas*—that is the possessions of *hijos* (sons)—or to acquire adjoining properties where possible and thus expand the group of related holdings while keeping it together.

Not only among the landowning group, however, has the hacienda tended to keep the family united; its influence in this direction is perhaps even more marked among the inquilinos. As has been noted, these laborers move very little from one property to another. Many of them spend their entire lives on a single estate, and it is almost equally common to find families on an hacienda that have lived there for a number of generations. Some of the young men and young women drift into the cities, the mining centers, or the nitrate fields of the north, in response to the call of greater freedom and better wages; but the number of these is not great, and they come back frequently to the estate where their families belong. It is true also that the class of free laborers already noted has been recruited in part from individuals or families who have become discontented on an hacienda or have been expelled for insubordination. In general, however, the tendency has been for the farm laborer to stay on an estate, for the family to remain together. Thus, both among the upper class and the lower, the hacienda has been a strong force for maintaining the family unit.

STABILITY OF SOCIAL STRUCTURE

The influence of the hacienda has counted for stability in the social structure of Chile. One of the greatest differences between the history of Chile and that of many other Latin-American countries is that the former has been marked by very few revolutionary disturbances. Social and political disorder has been rare in this country. The hacienda group has so fully dominated the life of the nation that it has been able to maintain a stability of society rare in Latin-America. This has favored economic progress and has set Chile apart as one of the most advanced countries in the New World. The Chileans themselves have taken great pride in this stability of their institutions, and foreigners too have loudly acclaimed it. This may be partly due to the character of the people themselves, who are frequently spoken of as " the English of South America," or " the Yankees of South America." Those who analyze the history of the country, however, are agreed that most of the stability of the social structure in Chile with the consequent progress along material lines is traceable to the firm control maintained by the upper class, the landholding gentry. In spite of the benevolent patronal system, which has led the typical hacienda owner to regard with solicitous care his inquilino population, the common people have recognized that there was an iron hand beneath the velvet. If occasionally some of the more obstreperous spirits forgot this fact, or concluded to disregard it, they have been reminded quickly and effectively that the government and governing class were committed to the task of maintaining the inviolability of property and preventing any movements that might disturb the social order.

STRATIFICATION OF SOCIETY

Probably the most striking effect of the hacienda on the social organization of Chile has been the part it has played in the stratification of society. Reference has already been made to this separation of the classes. It is a conspicuous feature of Chilean society. To one visiting the country for the first time, particularly if coming from the Anglo-Saxon countries, it is the thing that most distinguishes Chilean life. Nowhere among the other countries of Latin America does one find its parallel. Monopolization of the land has been the main factor in producing this marked cleavage in the social structure. Moreover, the hacienda system has tended to maintain the separation of the classes. It has kept the lower class down and has made it servile at the same time that it has fostered aristocratic tendencies among the landholding group. Almost as sharply separated as our own southern plantation owner from his negro tenant are these two social groups in Chilean society. The hopelessness of rising out of his " roto " status is also comparable to the condition of the negro in the South. Limited opportunity in the way of advancement into better economic conditions, or of better education, or of improved social conditions has consistently tended to depress the lower class. On the other hand, wealth, opportunity for travel, unlimited educational advantages, and increased luxury of living have tended to raise the standards of life among the landowners. There has been nothing to bridge this gap between the two social groups, nothing to bring them together. In so far as a middle class has existed at all, it has existed only in the cities. In rural life it must be master or man. There has been no alternative. The hacienda has divided the Chilean people and perpetuated the division.[7]

[7] See Pinochet LeBrun: *op. cit.*, pp. 109-130; Edwards (Alberto): Fronda aristocrática, 1928; and also MacKay: That Other America, 1935, pp. 62-65. For a discussion of the social evolution of the Chilean people and the influence of their system of land tenure, see Amunátegui Solar: Historia social, 1932, and Vicuña Subercaseaux: Socialismo revolucionario, 1908.

The hacienda system has contributed largely to making manual labor in Chile dishonorable, as has its counterpart in other countries of Latin America. The upper-class Chilean does not lack energy: he is virile, active, full of life, enterprising, as compared with the corresponding class in most of the neighboring countries. Yet too often he is given to idleness, to dissipating his vitality in useless amusement rather than employing it in labor. When urgent demands are put upon him, he is found to be not lacking in either energy or ability. Yet he has been so accustomed to have all work done for him by the lower class that he now disdains to exert himself except, perhaps, in administrative undertakings, professional pursuits, or politics. With the common tasks about the farm and the city residence taken care of by the laboring people, the men and women of the upper class are accustomed to an excess of leisure that is too commonly frittered away in frivolous social engagements or in dissipation. The system of landholding must be charged with encouraging, if not actually causing, this situation.

EDUCATION, ALCOHOLISM, RECREATION

Upon educational matters, too, Chile's agrarian régime has left its mark. The system is top-heavy. Until relatively recent years schools have existed mainly for the upper class. In fact, in rural districts few of the lower stratum of society today have opportunity for even elementary education. The higher phases of learning have been well provided for in Chile's educational system. Her National University, founded in colonial days, has produced distinguished scholars. Schools of mining, of medicine, of theology, and of law have existed for many years, are well-equipped, well-manned, and have provided the professions with many learned men. The National Library is one of the best on the continent. The National Archives are rich in treasures, excellently organized, and well administered. For the higher class there has been abundant opportunity for education. The hacendado class has provided the best for itself. Seldom, however, has similar attention been given to educating the common people. Attempts have been made by the more enlightened leaders from the time of independence to the present to provide the lower class with educational facilities. O'Higgins, dreaming of making Chile a real democracy, fostered common schools in the first years of the republic. Others have followed him in devotion to the ideal of an enlightened common people. Any advance in this direction, however, seems to have been made in spite of the hacienda and the hacienda's influence, rather than because of them. A great part of the Chilean population has remained illiterate until the present time. Money that might have been spent for education of the common people has been devoted to improving the appearance of cities, the building of government palaces, and the employment of a large body of bureaucrats. Particularly is the lack of elementary schools felt in the country districts where the hacendados, if they had so wished, might have completely abolished illiteracy. Whether it has been the deliberate aim of the hacienda owners to keep their tenants ignorant, or whether they have simply neglected such things, the result has been the same. Though separate statistics in regard to the rural population are lacking, it is commonly asserted that from 75 to 90 per cent of the inquilino class still does not know how to read or write.

Recent years have produced some improvement in this situation. Either because the hacendados have been driven to provide better living conditions, including education for their laboring class, or because they have become inspired with more real interest in the welfare of their people, elementary schools are being established on a number of the large properties. One wonders what the effect of any general extension of education among the inquilinos would be. Perhaps the hacendados are right in feeling that an enlightened laboring class could not be held on the haciendas with their present organization. One is inclined to think that the success of the hacienda system depends on an uneducated lower class and that this lies back of the prevalent illiteracy in rural districts.

Legislation looking to the improvement of social conditions both in city and country has been long delayed by the hacienda-controlled state. The regulation of hours, of wages, and of conditions of labor, the employment of women and children, the protection of family life from the corrupting influence of intemperance have lagged far behind other countries no more progressive nor prosperous than Chile. As has been noted, the conditions under which the inquilinos labor are the conditions inherited from early colonial days. They have been improved hardly at all. It would seem that the hacienda system is mainly responsible for this situation. In particular, alcoholism has remained uncurbed, apparently owing to the influence of the great vineyardists. In recent years many attempts to regulate the sale of alcoholic beverages have met stubborn resistance on the part of the winegrowers and the wholesale beverage dealers. The great deposits of alcoholic liquors both in city and in country are mainly in the hands of the vineyard owners, who are inclined to put economic gain ahead of the social welfare of the people. Efforts made by some of the Chilean leaders to check the growing degradation of the masses by alcoholism have been largely thwarted by those who have funds invested in vineyards and wine bodegas.

In the matter of recreation, also, the insignificance of the advance that has been made among the farming population seems to be due to the agrarian system and its accompanying limitations. While in the cities athletics have come to take a prominent part in the life of the youths—football, tennis, track, basketball, and other such games introduced from abroad—little of this has penetrated rural life. The cinema too, has come to the common people in the cities, but only in rare cases is it seen on the farms. In almost every feature of social welfare the hacienda has been slow to move, if it has not actually impeded improvement. The hacendado-inquilino system has concerned itself little with social welfare.

Influence on Political Life

The encomienda was devised in Spain's New-World colonies as an instrument of conquest. The Spanish invaders took over the land and its people, brought them under political control, and maintained themselves by means of the resources of the land and the labor of the people. As a method of bringing the newly acquired territories into subjection to the Spanish crown, the *encomienda* and the land grants accompanying it were eminently successful. In Chile, as in the other colonies, within a few years after the first invasion the land was fully subjected to Spanish authority. A beginning was made also in the introduction of Christianity among the natives and in the inculcation of European culture. As time advanced, the same system of large landholdings in the hands of the Spaniards or of Creoles held the country firmly attached to the Spanish crown. In Chile, as elsewhere, the encomienda and the hacienda were powerful means in the hands of the conquering race to bind the new country to the old.

The War of Independence Not a Revolution

When agitation for independence began in the American colonies of Spain, many of the landholders of Chile, both Spanish-born and Creole, remained loyal to the crown. Their interests were in large part identical with the interests of Spain itself. They had inherited Spanish cul-

ture and had introduced Spanish social institutions into
the colony. Many of them were loyal monarchists. They
had little sympathy for democratic tendencies. Probably
more than in any other Latin-American colony this sentiment of loyalty was manifest among the Chilean hacendados.[8] When Chile finally revolted from Spain it was
not in response to the very wide democratic agitation that
was moving many of the other colonies and still less, perhaps, to a desire to follow the footsteps of the English
colonies in North America in establishing democracy or
to emulate the French republicans. Chile broke away
from Spain but not from Spanish institutions. She sought
independence but not revolution. Throughout most of the
years of struggle for political freedom there was little
evidence of an attempt to extend that freedom to the
masses. The success of Chile's War for Independence
consequently brought a transfer of authority but not a
political reformation. It did not produce a social upheaval
in any sense. The War for Independence was in no way
a revolution.[9] There was less social disturbance in Chile
than in any other Latin American country. The system
on which Chile had been organized was continued and
gave little opportunity for social transformation.

The leaders in the revolt were almost without exception
hacendados. The campaigns were fought by them and by
inquilinos under their command—the latter fighting either
for Spain or against her, according to the wish and the
order of the patrón. Furthermore, in Chile less than in
most other Latin-American countries the War of Independence was not a long-drawn-out struggle which shook
society to its foundations. It consisted mainly of a few

[8] Some hacendados opposed the movement for independence, and their
properties were seized (Amunátegui Solar: Mayorazgos, Vol. I, 1901-1904,
pp. xvi-xviii).

[9] " El movimiento popular de 1810 no tuvo la más leve apariencia de una
asonada " (The popular movement of 1810 did not resemble a revolution in
the least) (Salas: Memoria sobre el servicio personal de los indíjenas y su
abolición, p. 16).

campaigns, a few sharp battles, now in favor of the patriots, now against them; but it gave little opportunity
for turmoil or for the rise of leaders among the common
people. There were few *caudillos* (military chieftains)
brought to the fore. The hacendados kept firm control of
the country while the conflict was going on. The laboring
classes, usually called " Indians " up to that time, did render enough service to the patriots to win a new designation
in common with their masters, that of " Chileans," and
actual slavery (which had never existed to a great extent
in Chile) was declared abolished. This was about as far
as the social changes went. To be sure, democratic ter-
minology was adopted and some democratic forms of government; but in most cases these were, as one of the recent Chilean writers graphically says, " palabras, simples
palabras " (words, only words).[10]

In the social structure of the Chilean people there was
no preparation for a real democracy. The encomienda
and the hacienda had built up an aristocracy which, once
the government of Spain was overthrown, stepped into
the place vacated by representatives of the crown and set
up a new government in harmony with the existing social
order. The common people took virtually no part. They
continued as they had been during the colonial days.[11]
As it was the hacendado group that had revolted, it was
they who now took over the reigns of government. The
new political organization was therefore a government
of the hacendados, by the hacendados, for the hacendados.[12]

[10] Cabero: Chile, 1926, p. 194. Galdames, in his " Estudio," 1923, p. 217,
says that the revolution had engendered almost unconsciously ideas of liberty
and equality but " en nada afectó a las instituciones en que se fundaban la
propiedad, la familia, el trabajo, la religión, el derecho " (in no way affected
the institutions on which property, the family, labor, religion, and the law
were founded).

[11] " As for the inquilinos in the country, their conditions of labor and
of life had not changed since the times of the colony " (Galdames: *op cit.*,
p. 264).

[12] Espejo, in his " Nobiliario de la antigua capitanía jeneral de Chile," 1917,
depicts the social heritage of the Chilean people.

Bernardo O'Higgins and Liberal Reforms

It is true that a few of the early leaders in Chile looked upon the War for Independence as an opportunity for social reform. Most conspicuous among these was Bernardo O'Higgins. This young military leader, to whom more than to anyone else had been due the success of Chilean armed efforts, was the son of Ambrosio O'Higgins, viceroy of Peru. It will be remembered that it was this royal official who finally brought about the abolition of the encomiendas. The son no doubt sought to carry still farther this type of reform in behalf of the common people of Chile. Moreover, Bernardo O'Higgins had traveled somewhat widely in Europe and had been educated in England. He must have observed society of a more democratic character than that of Old Spain or of the Spanish colony in which he had been born. He had also abundant opportunity to see the results of the French Revolution. Furthermore, in the years he spent in England he had become acquainted with both Miranda and Bolívar, as well as others of that group from Latin America, ardent apostles not only of political revolution but of at least limited social reform. Even at this time (while the young Bernardo's father was still viceroy of Peru) these young patriots were plotting revolt in Spain's American colonies. O'Higgins shared their ideas and evidently came to understand that their plans involved substantial social changes as well as political independence. He even belonged, with them, to that mysterious but influential society, the Logia de Lautaro, named for the noted Araucanian leader who had fought against Valdivia. In fact, he probably had much to do with the christening of the lodge, since the name adopted could have come from no one better than the Chilean youth who was born in the very district where Lautaro had operated and had met his tragic end. Hence, it was but natural that O'Higgins should have been inclined to go farther than the Chilean hacendados with whom he had struggled to win independence for the country. Though owner himself of a large estate in south-central Chile, and belonging in a measure to the hacendado class, the varied experience of this man, whom all Chileans delight to honor, gave him a somewhat different point of view from that of his associates. He seemed to comprehend better than others of his day that a political democracy could not be built upon the social foundation inherited from colonial times.

It was with this background that O'Higgins came to the headship of political affairs in Chile. Once victorious over monarchical Spain and established as Director Supremo in the new government, he set himself to the task of fitting Chile for a real democracy. Several measures introduced during his administration seem to show that he considered basic reforms in the social structure essential to the formation of a democratic government. He decreed the abolition of the *mayorazgos,* those entailed estates that had given such a strong aristocratic caste to Chilean colonial society. He forbade the use of titles of nobility and coats of arms, styling the latter " meaningless hieroglyphics and intolerable in a republic." He initiated a movement for popular education, opening public schools and encouraging the creation of schools on the Lancaster plan then being introduced by a group of Englishmen into South America. He ordered monasteries and convents to maintain private schools for the education of the common people. He re-opened the Instituto Nacional of secondary education at Santiago, and founded a Liceo for the northern provinces in La Serena. He established the national theater and reorganized the national library in Santiago. He also inaugurated many measures looking to the betterment of living conditions among all classes, improving sanitation in the cities, paving streets, converting the Alameda from a public dump into a wide thoroughfare, extending the lighting system of the municipalities, creating a general cemetery as opposed to those controlled by the Church, and curbing practices of the clergy which he regarded as inimicable to public welfare.

Two definitely agrarian measures were initiated, which revealed a possible conviction that the land monopoly characteristic of colonial Chile did not afford a satisfactory basis for the building of a true democracy and looked to the creation of small farms to offset if not to replace the influence of the hacienda. One of these measures was local and on a small scale. The other, if carried out, would have been of far-reaching effect.

To the south of Santiago there existed a dry, gravelly plain called the Llanos del Maipo. This belonged to the San Juan de Dios Hospital, but as it was of little or no value to this institution, O'Higgins ordered its sale at popular auction in parcels of 25 *cuadras* (about 100 acres). The buyers were to get water from the newly opened San Carlos Canal which, largely through O'Higgins' efforts, was now ready to convey water from the Maipo River to irrigate the region. Each buyer was to obligate himself to fence his lot and build a house on it within a year; also, never to entail the land nor allow it to pass by any means into possession of *manos muertas* (mortmain). Space was left for the founding of a small agricultural town (which came to be called San Bernardo in honor of its originator), and small sections were designated as *propios* (municipal lands) for the support of the town administration. This effort of O'Higgins to establish near Santiago a colony of small proprietors had unsatisfactory results. Few of the common people could pay for the land and water, even though the land was sold at first for as little as eight pesos (about $2.50) a cuadra on an easy payment plan. None of the upper class apparently cared to obtain these small plots of land and work them for themselves. Some foreigners later did secure holdings, but little if anything remains today of this early venture toward democracy. There are few such small properties in the vicinity of San Bernardo at present. Apparently most, if not all, of the original lots have been incorporated into the adjoining fundos or haciendas. The land is excellent, enriched for a century with the silt brought down from the Maipo River, and well supplied with water for irrigation by the system of canals that take off from the main channel or from the San Carlos Canal. It would seem to be an excellent region for the development of small holdings, but whatever properties of this kind were created have apparently been unable to compete with the neighboring haciendas in a society made to order for the latter.[13]

The other plan contemplated the creation of *colonias agrícolas* in other parts of the country, apparently somewhat on the plan recently being tried out. These colonies were proposed by a visitor to Chile, a Dutch traveler named Peter Schmidtmeyer, and probably would have resulted in the early creation of a large body of small farmers, particularly in the still undeveloped regions of the country. Unfortunately, the project was not carried out.[14] One can only conjecture why, but there seems little doubt that the same interests that determined the course of events in other matters prevented the execution of this plan. It was not at all in line with the type of organization that characterized Chile in colonial times, nor with the ideas of the *terratenientes* for the new republic.

Probably for the same reasons Chile did not reward the soldiers of her patriot armies with grants of land from the public domain, as did many other American nations. True, she had no such frontier as that of the United States or the Argentine. In every direction there were natural obstacles that tended to block expansion of settlement. Only to the south was there land that could have been utilized, but there the forests and the Araucanians

[13] Barros Arana: Historia, Vol. 13, 1894, p. 585.
[14] *Ibid.,* pp. 590-591.

stood in the way. Any other lands for soldiers would have had to come from the vast areas to which the haciendas laid claim. The owners of those haciendas were directing the government.

Moreover, in Chile's armies there had been few of the kind of soldiers that would have fitted into such a scheme of freeholds. Most of her patriots were either master or servant. The entire training of the inquilinos unfitted them for the independent life of frontier farms. They were as ill-prepared to take advantage of such opportunities as were the slaves in the United States at the time of Emancipation. Then, too, they were needed on the haciendas. To put them on lands of their own would have been to deplete the supply of labor on which the already-established agricultural properties had long depended. In fact, to any one familiar with the social structure of Chile the whole idea is incongruous. Here again the stamp of the hacienda is clearly seen on Chilean life.

The efforts of O'Higgins to make Chile more democratic met with little success. His decree abolishing the mayorazgos was not even promulgated. Several of the individuals who had enjoyed possession of these great entailed estates had co-operated with the Chilean patriots in the War for Independence, or had swung over to the winning cause after the defeat of the Spanish forces. They exerted great influence among the Chilean leaders, naturally opposed any disentailing of their estates, and succeeded in thwarting all the efforts of the Director Supremo in the direction of breaking up these great possessions. The small holdings created were soon swallowed up by the adjoining large properties, and few features of his attempted reforms persisted.[15]

[15] This characterization of Bernardo O'Higgins is different from that often given him. His association with San Martín has made it appear that he, too, favored a monarchy for the new nation. The arbitrary methods he employed in getting the new government established gave some grounds for the suspicion that he harbored monarchical ambitions. These things, it seems to me, have obscured the truly democratic character of many of his pro-
(continued on next page)

ADMINISTRATIONS OF FREIRE AND PINTO

O'Higgins' advocacy of these and other such reform measures caused his downfall. The hacendado interests leagued with the clergy took alarm at the liberal tendencies manifested by the Director and set to work to undermine his prestige. Students of Chilean history are generally agreed that the abdication of O'Higgins was brought about by the landed aristocracy.[16] The agitation that led to his resignation was engineered by this group. The *cabildo abierto*, which demanded his abdication, was dominated by "prominent citizens of Santiago and vicinity." Anyone familiar with Chilean society appreciates that this is equivalent to saying, "by leading hacendados." A Commission of Ten was named by Mariano Egaña to act as spokesmen for the concourse assembled in the cabildo. Such names as Errázuriz, Infante, de la Cerda, and Mendiburu, all of them familiar in the ranks of the Chilean aristocracy, figured in this Commission. The junta that received O'Higgins' resignation and took over the reigns of government was composed of representatives of the same class. A commission, appointed to decide the form of government which was to be substituted for O'Higgins' rule, was composed of Don Juan Egaña, Don Bernardo Vera, and Don Joaquín Campino, all "leading citizens." [17]

Continuation of footnote 15.
posals. Ernesto de la Cruz, in his annotations to the letters of O'Higgins, says: " O'Higgins' ideal for the system of government which should be adopted in Chile was always the same: the republican " (Cruz: Epistolario, 1916-1920, pp. 152-153).

[16] " La caída de don Bernardo O'Higgins se debió esclusivamente a las clases altas de nuestra sociedad " (The fall of Don Bernardo O'Higgins was due exclusively to the upper classes of our society) (Amunátegui Solar: Mayorazgos, 1901-1904, Vol. 1, p. xix). " La fronda aristocrática no tardó en derribarlo " (The members of the aristocracy did not take long to overthrow him) (Alberto Edwards: Fronda aristocrática, 1928, p. 33). " La aristocracia pelucona que derribara a O'Higgins " (the bigwig aristocracy which overthrew O'Higgins ") (*ibid.*, p. 48).

[17] Barros Arana: *op. cit.*, pp. 817-834. The conservatives had already given secret instructions to a Chilean delegate in Europe to seek a monarch from among the royal families of the Old World. See Cruz: Epistolario, pp. 144-149.

The leaders in this movement were obliged to accept Freire, the military *caudillo* from the south, as head of the government being organized. He did not represent their views and was an outsider to this clique of influential landholders; but he was the only leader in sight who could be counted on to maintain order in the emergency. Freire's government attempted to continue the social reforms of O'Higgins. From the standpoint of the agrarian program the most important measure adopted during his administration was the decree issued in 1823 signed by Freire and Egaña, providing for the distribution in small holdings of all public lands. A survey was to be made in all the provinces, lands properly belonging to Indians were to be assigned to them, and the remaining public domain was to be disposed of on convenient terms in small parcels to persons who would occupy and develop them.[18] Though this measure was nominally approved by Egaña, it is likely that he had no heart in what was contemplated and that he blocked its execution, as he is said to have blocked many another move toward social democracy during his period of influence. In only one province was the measure carried out—in the island of Chiloé. The results seen there at the present time, a century after the legislation, lead one to suppose that if this measure had been carried out in the other provinces Chile would early have created a large body of small farmers. The blocks of land given out in Chiloé were occupied by individual holders and have contributed to the creation of a real agrarian democracy in that island.

Among the measures taken by Freire's government that were contrary to the usual proceedings of the conservative aristocracy and their allies, the clerical group, was the confiscation of properties held by the regular clergy. The legislation by which this was achieved ostensibly was intended to free the clergy from the burden of attending

---

[18] Donoso and Velasco: Propiedad Austral, 1928, pp. 249-275.

to their landed estates; but without doubt it was inspired by the same desire to get property out of the hands of the church that had, a half century before, prompted the confiscation of all Jesuit holdings by the Spanish government.

Under Freire and Pinto, his successor, " a distinguished member of the liberal group which aspired to transform the country into a democratic republic," [19] much power was taken from the aristocratic class centering largely about the capital and was vested in the local governments of provinces and municipalities. All such reforms, however, were swept away within a few years by the restoration of the landed aristocracy to power.

CONSERVATIVE REACTION AND THE CONSTITUTION OF 1833

During those first years, even after the abdication of O'Higgins, Chile bade fair to become a democracy in fact as well as in name. The constitutions of 1826 and 1828— the latter drawn up in large part by a famous liberal leader, José Joaquín Mora—were decidedly democratic in their governmental provisions. Furthermore, in elections the voting was heavily in favor of the liberal element. But the conservatives were not to be balked by any such situation. When they lost the election of 1829 they organized an uprising, defeated the liberals at the battle of Lircay, and seized the reins of government. Undoing the work of O'Higgins and Freire, they restored the mayorazgos as an established feature of the social organization of the country. Led by the owners of these great holdings and others of similar interests, the aristocracy set to work to organize the nation after their own ideas. Diego Portales rose to leadership of this group. " The colonial aristocracy . . . . needed some one to dominate the evil and disturbing passions and found this person in Portales." [20] Under his guid-

[19] Galdames: Estudio, 1923, p. 246.
[20] Ibid., p. 255.

ance the Constitution of 1833 was now adopted. This
was dictated largely by Mariano Egaña, spokesman for
many years for the landed gentry, and his hand and that of
Portales are clearly seen in its provisions.[21] It served as an
effective instrument for an oligarchical control of government. An American diplomat has characterized this document as " the most aristocratic and centralized of American
constitutions. . . . . Political power originated in the oligarchy." Though theoretically vested with great authority,
" the executive was in practice dependent upon the oligarchy
as represented in congress." [22] The Constitution began
by limiting the franchise to holders of property or those
with a substantial income. It also eliminated from suffrage
those who could not read and write, at that time about
ninety per cent of the population, and gave little opportunity
for improving this situation. It virtually abolished all local
government, creating a strongly centralized system with
a large measure of control in the capital, the president
naming the governors (*intendentes*) of provinces, they
in turn the officials of the departments, subdelegations,
and districts. Santiago became the hub; all authority radi-
ated from there. So strong was the conservative control
established by this Constitution that the landed aristocracy
completely dominated government and country. For more
than a decade their power was virtually unchallenged. In
fact, though slightly altered from time to time, the Constitution of 1833 has given permanent cast to the nation,
surviving until 1925 with no important modifications.
The period of its creation and early operation is known
in Chilean history as the period of the " República
Autocrática." [23]

[21] The Constitution of 1833 was signed by four mayorazgos and one " título
de Castilla " (Amunátegui Solar: Mayorazgos, Vol. i, p. xx).
[22] Dawson: South American Republics, 1904, pp. 196-197.
[23] Evans, in his " Chile and Its Relations with the United States," 1927,
gives a sketch of Chilean political history and the part played by the
landholding class. A description of the Constitution of 1833 and its part
in Chilean history is contained in papers published in *Rev. Chilena de*
(continued on next page)

There were, however, attempts to loosen the strangle hold of the landed gentry upon the country. In 1836 Freire himself attempted to regain power but failed and was banished. In following years repeated efforts were made to wrest control from this strongly entrenched group of families. The most important leaders in these attempts were José Victorino Lastarria, Francisco Bilbao with his " Sociedad de la Igualdad," Eusebio Lillo, editor of the periodical *El Amigo del Pueblo,* and José María de la Cruz, opposition candidate (1851) to Manuel Montt, leader of the conservatives. These leaders of the opposition demanded electoral reform, more especially a wider extension of the suffrage, and persisted in a determined protest against the extremely unequal distribution of property and the oligarchical system of government maintained by the ruling caste. Political opposition grew into armed revolt on several occasions (particularly between 1850 and 1859), and a number of severe battles were fought; but in each case the entrenched, well-organized conservatives, representing the " established institutions, property, and social order," won the day and retained control of the nation.[24]

Second Administration of Montt, 1856-1861

Liberal ideas, however, were growing and were gaining recognition. During the second presidential term of Manuel Montt (1856-1861), substantial modifications were forced upon the reactionary group. Montt was strongly absolutist in his ideas of government. " He was the great apostle of government of the masses by the classes." [25] With his

Continuation of footnote 23.
Hist. y Geogr., Vol. 74, 1933, pp. 231-416, namely Gana: La Constitución de 1833 (pp. 231-345); Guerra: Origen y caída de la Constitución de 1933 (pp. 346-364); Galdames: Los dos primeros años de la Constitución de 1833 (pp. 365-409); and Roldán: El centralismo en la Constitución de 1833 (p. 410-416).
[24] Pérez Rosales: Recuerdos del pasado, 1882, pp. 244-249. This author, writing only a few years after these events, gives a good account of the social unrest. See also Barros Arana, *op cit.,* for further light on these attempted reforms.
[25] Hervey: Dark Days in Chile, 1891-1892, p. 305.

minister, Antonio Varas, he wielded a rigorous control over the country, putting down opposition with severity and in general supporting the cause of the aristocracy. Montt's administration enacted several legislative measures that favored the landholding gentry. Chile's great national credit institution, the Caja de Crédito Hipotecario, was created at this time, facilitating loans on farm mortgages. This, of course, was of little benefit to any except the hacendados. The old colonial tax, the diezmo, was abolished, and a light tax on agricultural production took its place. The former had become quite a burden to large landowners. In most respects, during the Montt-Varas government the oligarchy remained at the controls. However, with something of the patriotism, broad vision, and spirit of compromise that has characterized many Chilean leaders of all parties, Montt proposed or accepted some important modifications of the established system. He had already turned some of the hacendados against him by pushing the construction of railroads from Santiago toward Valparaíso and toward the south. Both in the Chamber of Deputies and in the Senate these progressive measures had aroused opposition from large landholders who disliked to see these iron roads cutting their great estates into sections.[26]

Supported by moderate liberals and moderate conservatives in a combination which they styled Partido Nacional, the president carried out some substantial reforms.[27] He abolished, this time finally, the mayorazgos and thus broke down the system of entailed estates which had occupied the very peak of the aristocratic social structure and had constituted the core of resistance to every effort at a wider distribution of privilege. Montt's administration also did away with the *alcabala,* a heavy tax hitherto imposed upon all

[26] Galdames: *op. cit.,* p. 307.
[27] Galdames' " Decenio de Montt," 1904, contains many details regarding political developments during Montt's administration.

transfers of landed properties and intended to keep inherited estates intact. New legislation exempted from this
tax all transactions leading to a real division of holdings.
Of almost equal importance, in laying the foundation for a
modification of the agrarian system of the country and in
weakening the landed aristocracy's monopoly of government control, was the beginning of active colonization on
the southern frontier. During Montt's administration the
age-long resistance of the Araucanians was partially broken
down, and much of their land was made available for settlement. The president and his minister fostered the immigration of German colonists as well as the settlement
of Chilean citizens on these Indian lands. The many small
independent farms thus created formed the first important
body of such holdings in central or southern Chile.

The Period of the " República Liberal," 1861-1891

After Montt there followed a series of " Liberal " party
presidents, Pérez, Errázuriz, Pinto, and Santa María; but,
while their administrations nominally espoused the cause
of liberal government, they did not make substantial con-
tributions toward more democratic institutions. Chilean
writers class these administrations as progressive and style
the period that of the " República Liberal." As compared
with its predecessors it merits such classification. But the
conservative Constitution of 1833 was still in force, virtually all leaders were still drawn from the hacendado
class, and a small group of aristocratic families continued
to dominate in the affairs of state. To the outside observer
this period seems only a little less conservative than the
former one: the hacienda is still in undisputed control;
the liberalism of the leaders has not gone deep enough to
effect any basic social reform.

One reform was brought about in the period of the
" República Liberal " which, though signifying little at the

time, was to bear important fruit in the years to come. This was the legislation whereby the right to vote was extended to all male Chileans of twenty-five years or over who could read and write, regardless of income or of the possession of property. This is spoken of by a Chilean writer as "the first step from an oligarchy to a polygarchy."[28] Public education had gradually advanced, and though a large proportion of the common people, particularly among the inquilinos of the country, were still illiterate, this measure prepared the way for a larger participation of the common people in their government.

These reforms were not sufficient to satisfy some members of the liberal element. Educated abroad, or having had experience abroad during periods of exile from their own land, a number of young aristocrats were able to look on their native society with clearer perspective than others. Constituting only a small group and powerless except as prophets of reform, such leaders as Manuel Antonio Matta, Pedro León Gallo, Benjamín Vicuña Mackenna, and Miguel Luís Amunátegui kept up an agitation for more democratic government. Vicuña Mackenna, in particular, seeing his country "governed patriarchally, as if it were a great hacienda," wrote and spoke and worked to establish more liberal principles.[29] Much of this discontent emanated from the arid provinces of the north, where the landed aristocracy had never been able to establish its system or to impose its will so fully as in the central region. In spite of the strong-arm methods employed to silence this opposition, it succeeded in gaining a recognition for some of its principles and a slight relaxation of the former autocratic rule. Furthermore, with the spirit of tolerance and the practical common sense characteristic of many leaders of the upper-class Chileans, the dominant group itself introduced more liberal features into their govern-

[28] Cabero: Chile, 1926, p. 252.
[29] See Donoso: Vicuña Mackenna, 1925.

ment. There was always, it is true, an obstinate inner circle, jealous of their *privilegios de la cuna* (privileges of the well-born), which opposed every measure tending toward a lessening of their grip on affairs of state. Side by side with such ultraconservatives always stood the hierarchy of the Church. Clerical bodies were themselves great landowners. Some of the richest of Chilean haciendas belonged to these organizations, and the Church held mortgages on many other great properties. These two groups constituted the most solidly united single interest in the country. Against their opposition progress was most difficult. The reformers, furthermore, like the earlier " liberals " already noted, were most of them hacendados or of the hacendado class, and their aims were rather for reducing the dominance of the small ultra-conservative group in political matters than for bringing about any drastic social change. The common people themselves took little or no part in the agitation for reform, though a dawn of class consciousness is seen at this time in a few poorly organized strikes (1870).[30] The middle class was so small and so inert that it exerted little influence. One Chilean student styles this period that of the " Liberal Oligarchy." [31] Oligarchy it still was.

BEGINNINGS OF A MIDDLE CLASS

In the meantime, the structure of Chilean society was gradually changing. During the larger part of the nineteenth century there had existed almost no elements in the population outside of the landed proprietors and the laboring class. The only group that could oppose the hacendados was the politically and socially voiceless " roto " masses. Little by little, however, new elements were appearing. A middle class was gradually being evolved. Popular edu-

[30] Galdames: Estudio, p. 364.
[31] Cabero: *op. cit.*, p. 193.

cation was lifting a few of the lower ranks out of their depressed condition. Trade was creating a larger body who belonged neither to the terratenientes nor to their servant class. Mining and industry, too, were forming a nucleus of citizens who were somewhat independent of the hacienda. A few foreigners were finding their way into the country; and these, too, constituted an element apart from the historic two-class society that had characterized Chile. The new farms of the south were adding their quota of individuals who were neither master nor man. True, many of the miners and business men who made quick fortunes invested in haciendas and joined, in community of economic interests at least, the upper ruling class. Many of the foreigners intermarried with the cultured hacendado families and made common cause with them. Enough recruits, however, were added to the small nucleus of a middle class to yield by the end of the century a body of citizens, inert and unorganized, it is true, but of some weight in economic and social matters.

Balmaceda and the Civil War of 1891

The first occasion on which the common people of Chile, even in a measure, found a voice and gave political expression to their aspirations, was in the election of Balmaceda to the presidency (1886). Balmaceda was a Liberal, and the Liberals had not ceased to combat reactionary features of the old aristocratic régime. Yet Balmaceda himself was a rich hacendado, and the bitter party struggles that marked his administration were mainly differences between men of the same social class who held opposing views regarding certain practices of their aristocratic government. Looked at from the outside and at this distance in years, the civil war that wrecked Balmaceda's administration appears to have been largely a dispute as to whether the president or Congress better represented the landed

gentry and could be more safely entrusted with the interests
of that ruling caste. To the foreign student of Chilean
history that civil conflict seems to have been mainly a
struggle between one group of hacendados and another.
True, there was an element of liberalism (or, at least, of
anticlericalism) in Balmaceda's program, and in general
the liberal forces sided with his cause. Even in the armed
contest there was a division on the basis of liberal and conservative; since the army, recruited from all classes, stood
with the president, while the navy, composed largely of
officers and men picked from the aristocratic families, represented the more conservative element. Yet, even so, the
conflict did not cease to be mainly a clash between rival
factions of the upper class who differed as to how the
oligarchy, of which they both formed a part, should be
organized. There was no great social reform involved.
Neither Congress nor the president really spoke for the
lower class. Both represented the landed aristocracy.

The outcome of the civil war was like that of every preceding armed conflict in Chilean history, a victory for the
more conservative faction. Balmaceda fell. Though he
had been elected by a large majority, the will of the more
conservative minority prevailed by intrigue, by propaganda,
and by force of arms. The cause of Chilean liberalism
appeared to have fallen with him. Yet in that spirit of
conciliation that has characterized Chilean politics, by which
rival factions of the governing class have repeatedly patched
up their slight differences in order to retain control of the
nation within their own ranks, some of Balmaceda's reforms were retained by the victorious conservative element.
In fact, the following administrations are generally classed
as " Liberal " by Chilean writers. They were liberal hacendado governments, as some of the preceding ones had been
conservative hacendado governments. By repeated alliances, coalitions, and combinations the landed gentry maintained its position at the controls—liberals, radicals, and

conservatives alternating in command, but forming a solid
front whenever their cherished social institutions were
threatened.

As for the interest the common people had taken in the
civil war, aside from obeying orders of both sides in the
military engagements, their action in the days immediately
following the final battle spoke in unmistakable terms. Between the fall of the government and the setting up of a
new régime, mobs of " rotos " overran and sacked both Valparaíso and Santiago, smashing windows, looting stores,
warehouses, and wineshops, scattering the furnishings of
Chile's finest residences through the streets of the capital,
and spreading a reign of terror throughout other cities
of the central region. The war had not been their war.
This was the way they would speak when their turn
should come—in an outburst of destruction possible only
under a system of government that develops in its common
people no sense of proprietorship in the government itself
and no civic responsibility. The upper class, however, soon
regained command. Citizens armed themselves and banded
together with a civil guard, which put down disorders in
the cities with little compassion for rioters and held control
until the triumphant forces of the revolution could arrive
and re-establish authority. In this outburst, it should be
noted, the inquilinos of the rural districts took little or no
part. With the attitude that has always characterized the
feudal laborers of the country, they remained loyal or at
least submissive to their masters.

Under the new parliamentary system of government
that was set up after the revolution the president's pre-
rogatives were strictly limited and the power of the hacienda class was strongly reasserted, now through Congress, particularly the Senate. While the congress in a
republic theoretically represents the people even more directly than does the president, in Chile both president and
congress have always represented almost exclusively the

upper class alone. The common people have had little to choose between the two. The defeat of Balmaceda probably set back for some years the cause of liberal government, yet it is doubtful if success by his party would have brought Chile much nearer to true democracy. In neither case would the hacienda have been removed as controlling factor in the political organization of the nation. There was a feeling, however, in the middle class and even in the small class-conscious part of the lower social stratum that Balmaceda had been the champion of the masses, and this feeling has done much to make him a national hero among them. They look upon his tragic death by his own hand (1891) as the sacrifice of a martyr in the cause of popular rights. Though the reforms he introduced were mainly anticlerical (civil marriage, civil registration of births, lay cemeteries, etc.) rather than directly *pro-populo,* his tradition has strengthened the gradually developing class consciousness among the workers and has stimulated them to seek some voice in determining the conditions under which they must live.

RESURGENCE OF HACENDADO CONTROL, 1891-1920

It was not, however, until after the World War that the hacendado class received any direct challenge to its authority. During the intervening thirty years the common people had little part in the government. The oligarchy held things strongly in its own hands. It was sometimes said that there were two Chiles: the larger unit, comprising the nation as a whole, and little Chile, consisting of a small group of influential families centered in Santiago and its vicinity; in fact, so strong was the dominance of this small aristocratic clique that it was not infrequently said that four city blocks in Santiago controlled the nation. The dominant landholding group directed affairs of state with little regard for any but their own class. Social legislation lagged. The national currency was manipulated to make greater fortunes for those who had fortunes with which to speculate. The poverty of the poorer classes was accentuated by the circulation of cheap paper money and by an attendant rise in prices. The vast income from the nitrate fields of the north provided during much of the period more than half the government revenue and made possible extravagant public expenditures which redounded chiefly to the benefit of those influential in government circles and members of their families, who found lucrative employment in public sinecures. Furthermore, this same great income from exports made it unnecessary for the government to secure revenue by taxing property or levying duties on incomes. As a matter of fact, taxes were actually reduced in various ways. The tax levied on the renting of real estate was eliminated; the *estanco de tabacos,* an institution for farming out the revenues from tobacco importation and sales, was abolished; and a variety of taxes that had been enjoyed by the national government were turned over to municipalities. All of these measures lightened the burden mainly of the well-to-do property owners.[32] It was a period of great prosperity for the upper class, but the common people had little share in this bonanza. The " rotos " of the city *conventillos* (tenement houses) and the inquilinos in their humble ranchos upon the haciendas, continued to live much as they had since Conquest days.[33]

Several developments, however, were leading toward a new situation in Chilean national affairs. A greater degree of local government had followed from the legislation reorganizing the municipalities in 1891. By these measures the country was divided into *comunas,* each of which was made largely self-governing. As these comunas even directed the elections for provincial and national offi-

[32] Macchiavello Varas: Política económica, Vol. I, 1931, pp. 146-147.
[33] " The lower class did not participate, except in the smallest degree, in the progress of the republic " (Galdames: *op. cit.,* p. 320).

cials, they thus gave the people of the towns and villages a nominal power in national affairs greater than they had ever enjoyed in Chile before. The overshadowing social and economic influence of the ruling caste, however, and the inexperience of the common people in public affairs made the municipalities slow to take full advantage of this opportunity. Extension of popular education also fitted an increasing number of the people to exercise their privileges as citizens. Industrial development, though still not great, was adding to its quota of semi-independent workers, while from the south the second generation of Chilean and foreign colonists was now taking its place in the national life. Out of this body of German, English, French, Italian, and Chilean citizenry had emerged a number of able leaders unfettered by the ancient handicap that had held down the common people of central Chile. The combination of these factors had now produced a middle class of appreciable numbers and had awakened much of the city population of the " roto " element. Though the inquilino continued in his age-old apathy regarding political matters, the mass of the country's population, for the first time, was finding political expression.

Rise of New Liberal and Radical Elements

These new elements in Chilean society were gradually bringing about a realignment in the political parties. The " Liberal " party which had existed from the days of O'Higgins had had as its main purpose opposition to the ultramontane program of the conservative group. However, while committed to a cause and on occasion ready to suffer for the cause, it had been for the most part but mildly liberal. At times it had embraced actually radical elements, but more frequently it had been willing to unite with the more open-minded conservatives and in a few instances had allied itself with the most reactionary of this latter body. While holding different views on certain political questions, the two parties had been brothers-in-land in so far as any radical modification of the agrarian oligarchy was concerned. The new elements in the Liberal party were less tolerant. Many of the individuals composing this group had no economic or social affiliations with the aristocracy. The industrial laborers of the city, the nitrate workers of the north, the small trade class of the growing towns owed no allegiance to the hacienda. Whatever loyalty to a patrón or dependence upon one their ancestors may have acknowledged had long ago disappeared. The new citizenry from the south, while mainly agricultural in interest, had no love for the great absentee landlords of central Chile with whom they had to compete on unequal terms. As for the descendants of foreigners in the group (not numerous but influential), they had a political heritage quite different from that of colonial Chile. All of these factions had become increasingly restive under the rule of the land barons. A measure of sectionalism also entered into this situation, for neither the dwellers in the towns, mines, nitrate fields, and irrigated valleys of the north nor the residents of Concepción and its sister provinces of the south have ever been too well pleased with the dominance of the central region; they have repeatedly befriended, if not actively seconded, subversive movements. They have even, on a few occasions, started revolts of their own against the hegemony of Santiago and its satellite provinces.

Most of these elements among the opposition would be classed as moderate conservatives in other parts of the world. They were made up either of small property owners or of men with investments in business that made them averse to any serious social disorder. Neither the doctrinaire liberals nor the middle class recruits to their standard favored violent measures. In contrast to these moderate liberals were their new associates from the laboring class. These were legitimate descendants of the landless inquilino and the homeless " roto." Their group was made up largely of those who still had neither homes nor land, neither investments in trade nor a stake in industry; with nothing to lose by political or social upheaval and with at least a chance of bettering their present low economic status; with no great love for life and still less fear of death; with memories of occasional riots in which they had managed to salvage some prizes from the looting or satisfy their lust for wine and rapine with no law to exact a penalty; with, moreover, vague but persistent rumors of what their kind were doing in Russia and other dimly envisioned lands—these were radicals. Reds, communists, syndicalists, anarchists, nihilists, no one of these terms expresses too strongly the political tendencies of the typical Chilean " roto " when released from the restraint of an imposed authority, nor the utter destructiveness to be expected from the mass of this population. They have never been schooled in citizenship nor have they learned even the rudiments of civil responsibility. The only government they have known was that of the patrón, imposed from above—mild and benevolent, to be sure, so long as they were completely submissive, but merciless if they undertook to assert even a measure of independence, either individually or *en masse*. No better school for radicals could be found than the Chile of the hacienda régime. The radical in politics is as much a product of the social organization in Chile and of the agrarian system which underlies it as is the aristocrat. He is just what might be expected from the training he has received. When emancipated economically from the hacienda, he joined neither of the historic parties (Liberal and Conservative) but swung far to the left and embraced the most radical doctrines. It was this element of the population that added its new-found strength to that of the liberals and the doctrinaire radicals and made a formidable party of opposition.

Up to 1920 the laboring man in rural districts had taken virtually no part in the increasing protests of the working class. He had left such matters to his fellow "roto" of the cities, mines, and nitrate fields. The inquilino's world had been limited by the bounds of his patrón's hacienda. If he voted at all, it was merely to carry out instructions of his patrón or possibly to make a little money by the sale of his vote in a close election.[34] But, with the growing unrest in the proletariat the world over, some echoes of social disquiet reached even the isolated groups on the large estates. Insubordination among the inquilinos was reported from several districts. Joint protests against conditions of labor and of living were presented to some of the hacendados. Strikes were declared on several haciendas, a thing unheard of in Chile from the time of the Conquest. The minutes of the Sociedad Nacional de Agricultura make frequent mention of these disquieting occurrences. The inquilinos, totally unorganized and effectively cut off from the activities of labor groups elsewhere, had no direct political power, but their murmurings had decided influence, alarming the conservative aristocracy and heartening the more radical groups in national politics.

DEMOCRATIC UPHEAVAL OF 1920

In the 1920 presidential campaign the several varieties of liberals and radicals had united into what was known as the Liberal Alliance, while the different branches of the conservative group had formed the National Union.

---

[34] " I have seen the inquilinos and laborers on certain great haciendas rounded up and taken in groups under guard to exercise their right of citizenship. . . . I know concrete cases in which it was stipulated in the lease for a rented property that the owner reserves to himself the right to dispose of the 300 or 400 votes of inquilinos on the hacienda " (Poblete Troncoso: Problema agrícola, Vol. 1, 1919, p. 244). Alessandri, in a communication to the Sociedad Nacional de Agricultura in 1921, said, " I want also that, once for all, an end shall be put to the common practice of the patróns of putting pressure upon their inquilinos and workmen to make them vote for specified candidates " (El Agricultor, May, 1921, p. 90).

When the election returns were counted, it was found that the Liberal party had gained such strength that for the first time in Chilean history a candidate with a truly radical program of social reform was evenly matched with a conservative. Arturo Alessandri, son of an Italian immigrant and senator for the far northern desert province of Tarapacá, where the hacienda has had relatively little influence, was the candidate of the Liberal Alliance, while Luis Barros Borgoño, scion of an old patrician family of Santiago and a leading hacendado, was candidate of the conservative National Union party. The vote was so close that it was impossible to tell which had won. The issue was decided by a specially constituted Tribunal de Honor and the Liberal candidate was declared to have won by a single electoral vote.

Alessandri's program as enunciated in his first message to Congress, on June 1, 1920, included such radical proposals as decentralization of national and provincial authority, a greater degree of local self-government, abolition of parliamentary government as it had existed since Balmaceda's defeat, separation of church and state, a stabilized money system, employment insurance, an income tax or higher land taxes to balance the budget, government control of banks and insurance companies, election of the president by direct popular vote, improved legal status for women, better living conditions for the laboring class, and wider extension of popular education. Such a program naturally filled the old landed class with alarm. If carried out, it would greatly weaken their hold on government, perhaps permanently so. Further cause for concern was the fact that the lower house of Congress also had passed into the control of the Liberal Alliance. Traditionally both houses have been composed very largely of hacendados most of whom could be counted on to support conservative plans.[35]

[35] " It is commonly said that 70% of the Congress is made up of hacendados " (Circular de la Unión Agraria, No. 1920, *El Agricultor*, Nov., 1920, p. 235).

The liberals had never before enjoyed such power. The conservatives had never before faced such a serious threat to their century-long dominance.

The Senate, however, still remained conservative. Composed as formerly of the more aristocratic representatives of the upper class, it continued to function as the organ of that element. It refused to confirm Alessandri's cabinet appointments, a number of which went to leaders of the radical group. It stubbornly opposed the creation of an income tax (December, 1923), even refusing to approve the budget for the coming year with that measure incorporated. The reactionary senators came to terms only after the garrison of Santiago, left unpaid because of the obstructionist policy in the Senate, had evacuated the city, leaving it threatened with an outbreak of the proletariat, and an income tax was approved for the first time in the history of Chile. Friction between the executive and the Senate continued now over the matter of an increased land tax, until finally Alessandri was forced to withdraw from the presidency. His resignation was not accepted, but he was given a leave of absence and decided to retire from the country. It looked like the traditional victory of the conservative group, and recalled the observation made regarding Chilean politics by a foreign diplomat: " The instances in which a president has tried to rule in defiance of the wishes of the aristocracy have been rare, and never successful." [36]

CONSTITUTION OF 1925

However, a group of the younger liberal military leaders, led by Carlos Ibáñez, in order to save the results of the peaceful revolution which had brought Alessandri into the presidency, forced the resignation of the conservative governing junta and recalled Alessandri from Europe.[37]

[36] Dawson: South American Republics, p. 197.

[37] There seems to have existed at this time a self-constituted and well-knit " Commission of Lieutenants " which had undertaken the task of ridding

(continued on next page)

In despair of achieving successful democracy under the Constitution of 1833, the historic bulwark of oligarchical rule, these leaders had a new Constitution drawn up. Submitted for popular approval, this was adopted (August 30, 1925) in spite of determined opposition from the conservatives.

This new Constitution, whatever direction Chilean government may take in the future, must rank as the most important document appearing in the country's history for a full century. It marks the end of an old régime and the beginning of a new one. Chile can never go back, it seems safe to assert, to the old patriarchal system in which a small group of powerful landholders ruled the whole country " as though it were but a great hacienda." The common people of the land have tasted of freedom and will not be denied. A middle class, too, unknown in the old days and quite outside of the hacienda system, now asserts its determination to have a voice in the affairs of their state.[38] Whatever setbacks may come, the new fundamental law of 1925 has put its seal of greater democracy upon the country.

The new Constitution abolished the old parliamentary system of complete congressional control which had grown out of the law of 1833. It made the president virtually independent of Congress, authorizing him even to adopt the national budget over the head of an obstructionist legislature. It created provincial assemblies with right to override the veto of the president-appointed prefect. It empowered the government to secure a " convenient di-

Continuation of footnote 37.
Chile of oligarchical control as also of preventing a violent social upheaval. Its activities still are quite completely veiled in secrecy, but to the energy and patriotism of its members are generally ascribed the repeated *golpes de estado* (*coups d'état*) which thwarted every attempt of the conservatives to regain their power and also held in check the extreme subversive elements.

[38] In 1919 there was founded a Federación de la Clase Media, which proposed to group the middle class into " a powerful nucleus to work for popular welfare, independently of the aristocratic class " (Figueroa: Diccionario histórico, 1925-1931; reference under " José A. Arias Pérez ").

vision of property " (El estado propenderá a la conveniente división de la propiedad), though maintaining the inviolability of property subject to the rules and limitations required for the maintenance and progress of the social order. Suffrage was conceded to all male citizens over twenty-one years of age who could read and write. Church and state were completely separated. The president, the Senate, and the Chamber of Deputies were to be elected by direct vote of the people.[39] These liberal measures were fortified by a provision whereby the president might appeal to the people in a general plebiscite in case Congress should attempt to force an amendment to the Constitution. By these provisions it would seem that the people of Chile have secured a guarantee against any possible return to an oligarchy.

FIGUEROA LARRAÍN, IBÁÑEZ, AND THE REVOLUTION OF 1925-1927

Upon the adoption of the new Constitution, Alessandri resigned—after appointing Luis Barros Borgoño (his defeated opponent in the election of 1921) to succeed him until a new president could be chosen. In a typical Chilean political compromise all parties except the so-called " Radicals " now agreed upon Emiliano Figueroa Larraín, a moderate conservative, as coalition candidate. He was elected (October, 1925) ; but the real radical element, composed largely of laboring men, protested in a two-days' general strike which brought all business to a standstill and caused the government to respond by declaring a fifteen-days' state of siege in the whole country. When the general Congressional elections took place in November (1925) the progressive elements matched their strength in numbers against the influence of the conservatives and

---

[39] Chile: Proyectos de reforma de la constitución política de la República de Chile, 1925.

secured virtual control of both houses of Congress. Figueroa Larraín, typical representative of the hacendado group and of the old system of government, though apparently well-intentioned and desirous of harmony, attempted to rule by the now discarded " parliamentary " method of political intrigue and combinations. Under his leadership the government was fast moving back into the hands of the conservative elements. Ibáñez, now the strongest leader of the group that had determined to have done with both conservative and radical extremes, forced the resignation of the president, called for a new popular election, and himself was chosen (May 22, 1927) by 220,000 votes out of a total of 230,000. While this election was dominated by Ibáñez and his associates, it probably represented quite fairly the preponderance of sentiment in favor of the middle-of-the-road liberals.

Throughout this three-year period of revolution and counter-revolution, there had been no blood shed in government circles. Radical laborers in the north had been shot down on one occasion—no one seems to know how many of them—but the changes of government had been brought about by political strategy (and threatened coercion). After one such *coup,* a foreign lady, a resident of Santiago, asserted she did not know a revolution had occurred until reports of it were seen in her home papers a month later. Yet this revolution swept away the power of the oligarchical group that had dominated Chile for a hundred years and put the government into the hands of the people. It made Chile politically what it had already in large measure become economically and socially, a democracy. It reflected the profound changes that had taken place in Chilean society since the Constitution of 1833 was adopted. It revealed what even many Chileans, particularly the aristocracy, had not realized: that the nation was no longer the Chile of colonial times, but a twentieth-century people, resolved to abandon the old-fashioned chariot of former days and move forward in a twentieth-century model.[40] There were thoughtful hacendados who had not been blind to these changing conditions. An editorial in the organ of the Sociedad Nacional de Agricultura in 1921 states that members of the Society (almost all of them hacendados) must recognize that such developments as are taking place among the working people are inevitable, that they form a current which cannot be opposed. Hacendados must face the new problems with a united front, but with "benevolence and humanity." "It is necessary to foresee and provide for the exigencies which are certain to come."[41] At the same time it was evident that the upper class as a whole had no intention of yielding without a struggle to the demands for a more even distribution of either wealth or opportunity, nor of surrendering its "privilegios de la cuna," the dominance which it looked upon as its birthright.

DICTATORSHIP AND REFORMS OF IBÁÑEZ

For several years after Ibáñez came into the presidency he governed the country as virtual dictator. He put down all subversive movements with severity, cracking down hard on extremists among both the old conservatives and the radicals. Many were exiled, more were arrested, every one was under strict surveillance. His government, however, did not limit itself to mere repression. With that repression went an attempt to cure the ills of which the social unrest was but a symptom. Social legislation more advanced than in any other American republic was enacted. Much of the program outlined by Alessandri upon his ac-

---

[40] A summary of political events in this period may be found in Haring's "Chilean Politics, 1920-1928," 1931. For a history of political development in Chile, see Alberto Edwards: Los partidos políticos chilenos, 1903; and for constitutional history, see Galdames: Historia de Chile, La evolución constitucional, 1810-1925, 1925; see also Cox: Chile, 1935.

[41] El Agricultor, January, 1921, pp. 1-2. See also Aguirre Cerda: Problema agrario, 1929, pp. 241ff.

cession to the presidency was put into operation. Education was made compulsory from seven to fifteen years of age, and child labor was much restricted. The laboring class, for the first time in the history of Chile, was invited to take its part in the government of the republic, and the organization of a labor party with strong constituent syndicates was fostered.

" But the most sweeping and comprehensive reform movement undertaken by the new administration was that intended to make a literate nation of Chile's almost four million inhabitants. Large numbers of teachers were sent to the United States and other countries to study and bring back new educational ideas, and teacher-training schools were reorganized. In 1928 nearly one hundred million pesos was assigned to the support of primary education, which represented the largest effort ever made by the Chilean government in this regard." [42] Contracts were let for the construction of some six hundred school buildings, most of them rural schoolhouses, in an attempt to wipe out Chile's high illiteracy (25 per cent in 1930). Coupled with this went a comprehensive program, the first ever deliberately undertaken, intended to abolish the underlying evils of Chile's historic agrarian system.

The main features of this really heroic agrarian program were these: colonization of the remaining public lands; extension of irrigation; provision of rural credits, particularly to small proprietors; development of agricultural co-operatives; clearing of titles to property in the already settled sections of southern Chile, coupled with the abolition of still-existing Indian communities there; subdivision of large rural properties in the central part of the country and founding of agricultural colonies on their lands. As might be expected, such measures alarmed many of the hacendado class. Some of them, however, realizing that a change was inevitable, preferred to have it come about

[42] Williams: The People and Politics of Latin America, 1930, p. 616.

under the direction of a strong and moderate government rather than in a violent upheaval which seemed certain if the more radical elements should obtain the upper hand.

Ibáñez called to the government few of the elder statesmen of the aristocracy, making up his Cabinet and filling important positions chiefly with men from Chile's newly formed middle class. Some of these, engineers rather than lawyers, had occupied subaltern administrative positions in government. Many of them were the public servants who had been doing the actual work of the government continuously through the kaleidoscopic changes of ministries and presidents. A number of them represented the smaller propertied class, owners of *funditos* (small fundos) or *chacras,* related to the hacendado class but gradually grown away from it. Others came from the second or third generation of foreign families that had settled in Chile during the nineteenth century. Ibáñez himself, though owner of an hacienda in Linares, represented the less aristocratic element of the landholding group and, moreover, had broadened his point of view and cleared his perspective by service abroad.

Surprise is often expressed that Chile's democratic movement should be led by military men and that the army should be the agency for effecting a social revolution against an oligarchy. The fact that, for the last ten years, the army has been leading the movement in Chile, has led people to consider it a veiled reactionary development and to speak of it as an anti-bolshevist movement.[43] It is true that Ibáñez did issue a declaration in which he expressed determination to put down "communism and anarchy," which at that particular time were a real menace to the country. But that was only one of the dangers that threatened the nation—the most alarming at that particular moment. The other danger against which

[43] Collings: Chile's New Anti-Bolshevist Government, *Current History,* Vol. 26, 1927, pp. 108-109.

his program and that of his associates was directed for a decade of revolution was the land oligarchy whose power over the country he considered must be broken. That the army should have undertaken such a campaign is not strange to those familiar with Chilean history or with the constitution of the army itself. It will be remembered that in Balmaceda's struggle for liberalism the army had supported him, while the navy sided with the reactionaries. This alignment is typical. The Naval Academy receives its students largely from the upper class. The navy recruits its officers largely from the same group. A naval career has always appealed to the Chilean aristocracy. It is only natural, therefore, that in a politico-social conflict the navy should side with the conservatives. It has never failed to do so. On the other hand, service in the army holds less distinction. The Military Academy has never enjoyed the prestige of the naval school. Many of the officers are drawn from the middle class or the lower ranks of the landholders; many also come from either north or south where social cleavage is not so marked. Hence the army has always been far more inclined to favor the liberal cause. As an American student of contemporary history states, " The revolution was really a popular revolution, although its instrument was the army." [44] In Chile in 1930 I frequently heard the government of Ibáñez spoken of as " our socialist state."

ECONOMIC AND SOCIAL CONDITIONS UNDER IBÁÑEZ

In 1929, after two years of Ibáñez rule, economic and general social conditions in Chile seemed better than they had ever been before. The strong force of carbineers not only prevented political disturbances; it maintained order throughout the country. Travel was safer than at any time probably since independence; life and property were

[44] Haring: *op. cit.*, p. 26.

better protected, both in city and rural districts, than ever before. Moreover, there were almost no unemployed and few idlers in town or country. General prosperity and an extensive program of public works gave labor to all and made for good wages. Furthermore, the social legislation that had been enacted in Alessandri's administration and under Ibáñez was bringing benefits to the common people. The writer spent nearly a year in Chile at this time, returning after an absence of twenty years. The progress made during that period reminded one of the changes that surprised Rip Van Winkle after his long sleep. Santiago and Valparaíso had become modern cities: their quaint provincialism was gone; reinforced concrete buildings, six and eight stories high, were replacing the old one- and two-story adobe or brick structures; streets were well paved and shops were modern and attractive. What was more striking still was the improvement in general welfare of the common people. The old " roto " class, as it had existed at the beginning of the century, had almost disappeared. The common people were no longer in rags; they were as well clad as common people elsewhere; few conventillos existed in Santiago or Valparaíso; hundreds of small houses had taken their place. Public utilities no longer served the wealthy alone. Autobusses were crowded with laboring men and small-salaried employees. Theaters, formerly attended only by the well-to-do, were now filled (the cinemas, of course) with the working class. The thousands that attended football games (soccer) were obviously from the same walks of life, but were well dressed and mingled indiscriminately with those of the middle and upper classes. In the spring festival truckloads of young people from all social strata drove about the city throwing confetti and dancing in the plazas and parks. In the promenade about the Plaza de Armas (main square of the city), once the rendezvous only of the élite, all classes shared. There was little evidence of the barefoot " roto " who used to slink about the shadows of the streets surrounding the plaza, afraid to set foot on that sacred precinct reserved at such times for the families of the patróns. On frequent occasions there were mass meetings of laborers and their societies in public halls, while in two or three large residences which had come into possession of the government *casas del pueblo* (houses of the people) had been established, with assembly halls, reading rooms, physical education apparatus, sewing rooms equipped with scores of machines free to any poor woman who had none of her own, and gardens for social recreation. One such house (on Augustine Street) was the former residence of a distinguished capitalist, hacendado, publisher, and diplomat. The situation reminded one of the new use being made of famous buildings in Russia; yet in Chile this was being done by a military dictator.

The Economic Depression and the Fall of Ibáñez

When the world economic crash came it found Chile deep in debt, with heavy loans contracted for public works with which to prolong the prosperity that had already begun to fade. Ibáñez' socialist-republican military dictatorship was caught in the maelstrom of world finances and went down. The landed aristocracy was the only group in the country not gravely affected by the general economic situation. With their self-sustaining haciendas they were largely proof against depressions. When the government of Ibáñez was forced to resort to heavier taxation, reduced government personnel, and drastic cuts in salaries in order to meet the crisis, the landed aristocracy took advantage of his weakened prestige and struck swiftly and hard.

It seems that they had already been boring from within for some time. When Ibáñez first came into control, they either opposed him openly or withdrew from their usual active participation in government affairs. In 1930 there was hardly one of this old guard who occupied an official position except in Congress. Even there their number was greatly reduced, and they perfunctorily passed the measures sent down from the president's offices in the Moneda (Capitol). In the Cabinet were men drawn largely from the middle class that is making its influence felt along many lines. Not one of them belonged to the old aristocratic families of central Chile: most of them were, originally at least, from the provinces of the north or the south; several represented the new foreign settlers. With such associates, the president had been able to proceed with confidence in his programs of reforms. But Ibáñez had already begun to slip. In 1927 he had married into one of the most distinguished of the hacendado families. This had brought him into a very different position in his relations with that group of intermarried lineages. It was noticed that some of the hacendado class now began to co-operate, in a measure at least, with the dictator's government.[45] Perhaps a laudable desire to win the assistance of all classes in the economic crisis prompted Ibáñez to entrust official positions to opponents; perhaps, in the financial troubles that confronted the country, he was forced to appeal to those who controlled a large measure of the nation's wealth. Whatever the reason, when the crisis came, it found a number of old families already in positions of confidence with the president. Upon the resignation (July 9, 1931) of the Cabinet, which had worked loyally with Ibáñez for several years, a typical representative of the aristocracy, nominally liberal but closely associated with the conservatives, was invited to head the new government. When he declined, another of similar position was offered the place and accepted. This man had been, under the old régime, director of the state railway system and was possessor of fundos in the Aconcagua Valley and south of Santiago. He called to the Cabinet a

[45] Haring: *op. cit.*

very different group from that already noted as associated with the president a year before. Such names as now began to appear at the foot of the government documents were well known among the landed gentry, and most of them equally well known among the strongly conservative elements or the liberals who worked hand-in-glove with the former. The premier at once restored the freedom of the press, which Ibáñez had kept muzzled for several years, and secured a proclamation of amnesty to political exiles. He also pressed down still harder on the burden of economic retrenchment. Though the country in general bore its hardships stoically, the Cabinet again resigned and again a member of the hacienda class was asked to form a new one. This lasted a single day, just long enough still further to embarrass the president. At last, but too late, Ibáñez turned back to one of his old lieutenants. But his prestige had been too greatly undermined. A university students' strike resulted in two students being killed. The bar association, the medical organization, engineers, teachers, and clerks now turned against him. Powerless to apply force to such opposition, Ibáñez made a final appeal to a group of " leading citizens " to help him save the nation from anarchy. They refused to lend their support. There was nothing now that the president could do but turn over the government to those who had wrecked his organization. The president of the Senate, distinguished representative of the landed aristocracy, took over the reigns of government and named as Acting President another hacendado, Juan Esteban Montero Rodríguez, who had served as Minister of the Interior under Ibáñez for a short time. Congress declared the presidency vacant, a new election was called for, and Montero was elected (October 4, 1931) by a combination of conservatives and " radicals " who united as they had done on many an occasion before to save the social order of which both groups formed a part.[46] Montero's only strong opponent was Alessandri, who ran as Socialist candidate and polled 100,000 votes against the 180,000 cast for Montero. There were two communist candidates, who between them, received 3,785 votes.

IS THE HACENDADO STILL IN THE SADDLE?

Montero's administration lasted just six months. Elected for the regular six-year period, he attempted to govern as a moderate conservative. His cabinet was made up of conservatives, " liberals," and " radicals " but tended more and more to run true to form as a government of the classes. It seemed again that the old group was back in the saddle. The program of colonization undertaken by Ibáñez was abandoned. The attempt to put southern frontier titles in order was discontinued: no more *colonias agrícolas* were organized; the hopes for an expanded public education faded. The president announced that Chile would redeem her credit abroad by renewing payments on her debts. He declared at first for the gold standard but finally decided to let the peso shift for itself, as had been customary in the old days of the " one big hacienda." This last measure sent the price of commodities skyrocketing and brought the poor into serious plight, though it enabled debtors to evade heavy obligations. A run on the Bank of Chile was brought about by a Congressional discussion over the gold standard. The situation so alarmed the country that a new *coup* took place, " Montero's constitutional government . . . . has been forcibly ejected, and the long reign of the aristocratic oligarchy has been superseded by the Socialist Republic of Chile," wrote the British Commercial Secretary at Santiago.[47] Montero was

[46] Keller: Un país al garete, 1932, pp. 17-18.
[47] Quoted by G. B. Roorbach in his " How the Chemical Revolution Changes Foreign Trade," 1934, p. 78.

succeeded by Carlos Dávila, a trusted associate of Ibáñez, for years editor of the progressive daily paper, *La Nación,* and later Chilean ambassador at Washington. Dávila frankly advocated a more radical policy than that of Ibáñez. He proposed a state socialism but insisted that property rights would be respected and a private economic system would be permitted to operate side by side with the projected " collective economy." To provide for the unemployed he planned to open public lands to settlement. Unfortunately, however, he found that there were no longer public lands of any importance, as all such were covered by claims of inidviduals. As the country had no funds available with which to buy land, the project was abandoned.[48] When he tried to secure funds for government expenses by increasing the taxation of the landholders, the one group in Chile that owns anything of importance to be taxed, " he was immediately overthrown," says a keen Chilean student, " for having dared to touch the interests of our oligarchy which considered such interests the most sacred rights that exist." [49] A fusion cabinet was formed (October 4, 1932) and a new election called for. Here again the people won the day. Alessandri, running as a moderate socialist, received more votes (183,-744) than all the other four candidates (Conservative, National Socialist, Agrarian, and Communist) combined (152,422). Many conservatives supported him as the safest of the liberals, some one of whom was certain to win. In such an emergency party lines mean little in Chile. When the historic social order is in danger it is not difficult for the several groups to unite. " There are no political party principles in my country," Don Carlos Dávila, able journalist, ex-ambassador, and short-time president, assured me. "All parties are under the domination of our old conservative element."

[48] Interview with Don Carlos Dávila in Los Angeles, Cal., 1934.
[49] Keller: *op. cit.,* pp. 110-111.

THE SOCIEDAD NACIONAL DE AGRICULTURA

One thing that makes the Chilean people's struggle for control of their government seem still doubtful of success is the strongly organized agency through which the hacendado class has exerted its influence. While Church and press and social system have all been used to support the established feudalistic order, the agency that has probably been most effective in maintaining the conservative cause has been the Sociedad Nacional de Agricultura (National Agricultural Society). This organization formed in 1838 by a group of influential landholders has, since that time, taken part in most of the agricultural development of the country. Like other agricultural societies, it has fostered improvement of farming conditions and has encouraged the application of scientific methods to agriculture. It has maintained an experiment station, a biological institute, and model farms. It has conducted stock fairs. It has aided the farmer (in Chile the only farmer worthy of consideration has been the hacendado) in securing good seed and in disposing of his surplus crops in foreign markets. More important, however, than these activities has been its influence in a political way. From its well-housed headquarters in the capital this society has watched over the interests of the hacienda owners and the class to which they belong. If a tax was being considered by Congress an influential spokesman of the hacienda was at hand. If a railway was being planned or the opening of a port contemplated, the bearing of such a prospect on agriculture was laid before the government. If social laws were being enacted the Society guarded the interests of its members. It not infrequently initiated measures looking toward more favorable legislation (or interpretation of the law) in behalf of agriculture.

Since, as has been noted, the governing group and the hacendado class have been practically identical in Chile, it has frequently happened that leaders in the government were also prominent in activities of the Society. On occasion (as in 1925) the Minister of Agriculture has been also the president of the Society. Members of its council have also occupied other positions in the Cabinet. In fact, the list of the Society's officers reads not unlike a roster of influential political leaders. Its headquarters are located within those few dominating blocks in Santiago that constitute the so-called Little Chile. From these headquarters it has sought to weld the hacendado class of the whole country into a compact body and throw the full weight of that body into any political struggle that might affect the interests of landholders. Looking over the published record of its activities, one finds much of its attention given to political affairs. In recent years this has been most marked. In 1921 it brought its influence to bear to prevent the attempted organization of rural laborers, particularly their affiliation with city workmen's groups. A communication was sent to President Alessandri warning him of the dangers involved in such unionization of the rural laborers.[50] In 1924, a summary of recent activities of the Society in behalf of its constituents included a successful campaign against the construction of a railway that would have facilitated the importation of Argentine foodstuffs into the northern desert regions, an equally successful endeavor to retain the duty on cattle being brought over the Andes from the Argentine, opposition to a proposed tax on agricultural implements, and the thwarting of a radical movement among the laborers of the country.[51] On the eve of the Constituent Assembly of 1925 the Society circularized its members, urging that every effort be made to send a large and powerful representation of agriculturists to that Assembly.[52] Again in the congressional elections late in

[50] *El Agricultor,* May, 1921, pp. 87-91.
[51] *Bol. de la Soc. Nac. de Agric.,* 1924, pp. 756-761.
[52] *Ibid.,* 1925, pp. 303-305.

the same year the Society was active in seeing that those friendly to its interests were seated.[53] In a session of the Society on December 28, 1925, the president (who was at the same time Minister of Agriculture) assured his fellow members that he hoped to be able to secure a modification of the social laws recently enacted, in so far as they applied to rural laborers.[54] He seems to have been successful in this attempt; at least, the Society's influence has helped to prevent the application of these laws to inquilinos,[55] and the hacienda laborers have profited far less than their industrially employed fellows. The Society's report for the year 1933 admits that it has opposed the application of the nation's advanced labor laws to rural employees and has sought to bind all landholders (*agricultores*) of the country together to guide the *política agraria* of the nation.[56]

In view of these political activities of the Sociedad Nacional de Agricultura, some of them directly in opposition to the government's program of social betterment, it seems strange that the Society should enjoy a subsidy from the national treasury. Yet such is the case. In 1925 an appropriation of 50,000 pesos was granted for its use. A smaller subsidy was enjoyed by the two affiliated agricultural societies, that of the north at Copiapó and that of the south at Osorno.[57] Such grants are, of course, in recognition of other valuable services rendered the country, but the political influence exerted is by no means the least important of the societies' functions. The century-old National Society in Santiago, in particular, has been one of the principal agencies by which the hacendado class has maintained its hold on the nation and prevented a solution of the land problem.[58]

[53] *Ibid.*, p. 826.
[54] *Ibid.*, 1926, pp. 312-315.
[55] *El Mercurio*, June 14, 1933, p. 11.
[56] *Ibid.*, January 4, 1934, p. 3.
[57] *Bol. de los Servicios Agríc.*, 1925, p. 226; 1926, p. 823.
[58] A brief history of the Sociedad Nacional de Agricultura and its achievements may be found in Schneider: La agricultura en Chile, 1904, pp. 165-203.

Alessandri's Second Administration

On December 24, 1932, Alessandri took office. He selected his cabinet to represent the several strong parties of the country and appealed to all factions to unite in a truly national administration under the Constitution of 1925. Up to the present (1935) he has succeeded fairly well in holding the various factions together. Attempts have been made, both by the extreme radicals and the extreme conservatives, to embarrass his government, but he enjoys great popular favor and has survived. His success is due in large part no doubt to the support received from the conservatives in the interest of their own institutions. With such an alliance he has not been able to go far toward social reform. Yet in the present government the hacienda has had to give up its former absolute control of the country. Politically, Chile has ceased to be the oligarchy of the past. It is doubtful whether this change can be made permanent, with the hacienda still in existence and without a reduction in the social and economic power of the landed class.[59]

[59] Thomson in his " Chile's Struggle for National Recovery," 1934, tells the story of the last few years in Chilean political and economic history.

...

CHAPTER VIII

THE SMALL FARMER: A THIRD ESTATE

In this land of Master and Man I recently met an individual who was neither *hacendado* nor *mozo*. He was
dressed in most respects like an *inquilino,* but he talked of
" my land " as does the patrón. He was on his way to the
country and was riding second class on the local train. In
the course of our conversation he explained that he had
gone into town to see about marketing a crop of peaches
and pears that his *chacra* near Melipilla had produced. It
developed that the chacra contained two *cuadras* (about
8 acres) all irrigated from a canal, a few shares of which
had come with his land. The plot was fully cultivated,
about half in vegetables and half in fruit. He lived on the
place, in a three-room house built by himself. His wife
and family of seven children helped him with his chacra.
Only occasionally did he need hired assistance; in fact, he
himself worked out at times, as did the oldest son, a robust
fellow of eighteen years. All of the children could read
and write, and even the parents could make out the occasional newspaper that fell into their hands, though with
great difficulty. I shall give this man no name—shall hardly
dare to call him a Chilean, though he is Chilean to the core
and though his class have been full fledged citizens for a
hundred years. His like is well known in the north and the
south, but in the land of Don Fulano and his mozo one
must search to find him. Yet he represents a class—a class
that is small in central Chile and so obscure that it is
seldom recognized even by those familiar with Chilean
life. It is a class, however, that has grown in importance
in the last twenty years.

It is commonly said that there is no middle class in Chile; that between the aristocrat and the " *roto* " there is no third estate. This has been the historic condition and, in a broad sense, is still the case, particularly in central Chile. However, there is, even in that section, a body of citizens ranking somewhere between the upper and lower strata of society, an element in the population composed of small independent farmers.

Little has been written about this element. In most accounts of the country, whether by foreigner or Chilean, no mention is made of any other form of rural possession than the *hacienda,* or of any other rural proprietor than the hacendado. Chilean writers on agricultural subjects or related themes frequently discuss the advantages of small holdings and the need for them in their country but, beyond citing a few statistics, they give little evidence that properties of this kind already exist.[1] As a matter of fact, the *pequeña propiedad* is not at all a conspicuous feature of Chile's land system. Only when a search is made will it be found—so completely does the hacienda overshadow all else. Furthermore, most of the small holdings lie off the beaten trails, in out-of-the-way corners of the Coast Range or deep in the narrow defiles of the Andes. A few groups of such properties are located in districts through which railways have been built, and a small number of them lie near the large towns of the Central Valley. But it is only when one examines them closely that most of these holdings can be distinguished from the tiny " possessions " of the inquilinos. In size and possibilities many of them are not very different from the latter, and their owners live on a plane little above the servile labor of the haciendas. They occupy but an inconspicuous place in the life of Chile. They

[1] Keller: Eterna crisis, 1931, pp. 279-282; *idem:* Un país al garete, 1932, pp. 122-127; Poblete Troncoso: Problema agrícola, 1919, Chapters 3 and 4; Macchiavello Varas: Política económica nacional, Vol. 1, 1931, pp. 349-360.

produce little beyond their own needs and generally market this little near at home. Their owners are not persons of influence in affairs either national or local.

NUMBER OF SMALL HOLDINGS

No very complete data exist regarding these small properties. In official reports they are either neglected entirely or are confused with the large *fundos* on the one hand or, on the other, with the small rural settlements whose inhabitants are engaged in business, industry, or mining. Yet an analysis of agricultural and population statistics reveals their presence and throws some light on their distribution and character.

It seems well to define what is meant by the term " small property." In a land where holdings run into thousands of hectares and are most conveniently measured by the square mile or the square league, the term may be misunderstood. As distinguished from the hacienda with inquilino labor, it refers to the properties sometimes described in Chile by the term *propiedad familiar* (a one-family property).[2] Such a classification is necessarily elastic as regards the actual acreage included. A single family (with occasional hired labor, of course) can normally operate not more than 50 hectares of irrigated, nor more than some 200 hectares of unirrigated, land, the extent naturally depending somewhat on the use to which the land is put. Since, as already noted, most of the properties in the central provinces ranging from 51 to 200 hectares are wholly or in large part irrigated, owned by city dwellers, operated by an administrator, and worked by inquilino labor, they are not thought of as small farms in the above sense. Actually some of the properties measuring from 21 to 50 hectares are also oper-

[2] This definition is in accord with Keller: La eterna crisis chilena, 1931, p. 281.

ated in the same way [3]; but since the great majority of them are worked by the owners themselves, it seems proper to include the group with the small holdings. This leaves the following three groups, as given in the Chilean statistical reports for the fourteen central provinces:

SMALL HOLDINGS IN CENTRAL CHILE (1925-1926) *

PROVINCE	LESS THAN 5 HA.	5 TO 20 HA.	21 TO 50 HA.	TOTAL LESS THAN 51 HA.
Coquimbo........	4,871	544	113	5,528
Aconcagua........	3,895	447	167	4,509
Valparaíso........	1,517	410	176	2,103
Santiago..........	1,746	422	227	2,395
O'Higgins........	2,450	283	90	2,823
Colchagua........	5,439	1,396	492	7,327
Curicó...........	3,389	1,301	695	5,385
Talca............	2,349	1,159	564	4,072
Maule...........	3,765	3,444	1,569	8,778
Linares..........	2,715	1,789	745	5,249
Ñuble...........	4,061	3,166	1,331	8,558
Concepción.......	3,410	2,888	1,114	7,412
Arauco..........	293	517	684	1,494
Bío-Bío..........	1,405	1,802	921	4,128
Total.........	41,305	19,568	8,888	69,761

* *Anuario Estadístico de la República de Chile*, 1925-1926, Vol. 7, Agricultura, pp. 4-13.

As may be seen from this table, the number of small properties is much greater than the number of large ones (the haciendas) already considered. For example, Coquimbo has 5,528 properties of less than 51 hectares as compared with 341 of more than 200 hectares; Santiago has 2,395 small ones as compared with 403 large ones; Maule has 8,778 small ones to 506 large ones. Some such proportion exists in the other provinces. These statistics

[3] Advertisements carried in a recent issue of a Santiago daily paper offered fundos and chacras for sale; one of 40 hectares, one of 50, and one of 125, each of them containing inquilinos, the second said to have " numerosas posesiones de inquilinos," and the third to have eight such tenants.

are often quoted to indicate the extent to which the land is already subdivided in Chile. They show nearly thirteen times as many small holdings as large ones.

SIZE AND DISTRIBUTION OF SMALL HOLDINGS

A different story is told, however, when the area of land included in small properties is compared with that in large ones. It has been seen that the 5,396 haciendas (those containing over 200 hectares) hold 89 per cent of all farm land in the central provinces. The 69,761 small holdings now under consideration aggregate only 558,333 hectares (less than five per cent of the total area in rural properties) and average just eight hectares each. Furthermore, 41,305 of these holdings, constituting 60 per cent of the entire number, consist of farms measuring less than five hectares and, aggregating only 61,786 hectares, actually average less than a hectare and a half each. From such diminutive properties the large number of small proprietors and their families, amounting to a total of 350,000 or 400,000 persons, are attempting to eke an existence. Only those in the upper half of the group can obtain anything more than a bare subsistence. For most of them the standard of living must remain low with little opportunity for cultural or educational advantages and with little opportunity to improve their economic condition, at least in so far as they depend on their farms.

Further light is thrown upon the existence of the small farm by statistics in the 1930 census.[4] Here the population is classified according to the type of unit to which individuals belong, showing the number on each fundo and for each city, town (*pueblo*), village (*aldea*), and hamlet (*caserío*). It is explained that the aldeas and the caseríos generally consist of "groups of small agricultural holdings" and that the term "fundo" is employed for all single

[4] Chile: *Resultados del X Censo de la Población* (1930), published 1931, Vol. 1, pp. 10 and 118.

agricultural properties. In addition, the number of dwellings (*viviendas*) in each unit is given and the number of persons (male and female separately). Several place units in the District [5] of Pocochay in the Commune of Quillota, Department of Quillota, Province of Aconcagua, may be cited as examples of small rural properties. In addition to a pueblo, several aldeas and caseríos, and thirteen fundos with occupants varying in number from 24 to 192, there are two properties (also called fundos in accord with the census practice) consisting of one dwelling each, the first (Santa Teresa) with five persons, and the second (Victoria) with ten. In the District of Santa Cruz, in the commune and department of the same name and the Province of Colchagua, in addition to many fundos proper, one of which has 55 houses and 435 inhabitants, there are three " fundos " with but a single dwelling each, housing ten, nine, and nine people respectively. In many of these single-dwelling fundos the number of occupants is smaller, ranging generally from four to eight. They are true one-family properties.

Analysis of statistical data for central Chile shows that these small farming plots with a single house are found in all the central provinces. The 1930 census [6] gives the following numbers for the respective political units:

Coquimbo	233
Aconcagua	60
Santiago	67
Colchagua	81
Talca	178
Maule	1,356
Ñuble	726
Concepción	832
Bío-Bío	1,540
Total	5,073

[5] A district is a subdivision of a commune.

[6] The territorial re-organization of 1927 incorporated in others the provinces of Valparaíso, O'Higgins, Curicó, Linares, and Arauco. The nine in the table contain the same territory as the fourteen used in other lists.

Single-Family Holdings in North-Central Chile

As will be observed, the vicinity of the capital has relatively few such holdings, while both to the north and the south the number increases. Somewhat the same distribution was apparent in the figures indicating all small-size properties. Both sets of data point to Santiago and its neighboring provinces as the stronghold of the hacienda, in which the large holdings have absorbed the greater part of the usable land, leaving little for anything else. The Province of Santiago, with its 15,260 square kilometers of area and a population of 967,603, shows only 67 one-house fundos and only 2,395 properties of one-family size. Aconcagua and Colchagua are not much better in this respect. To the south of Talca the small properties increase rapidly. Here neither *encomienda* nor extensive land grant played such an important part in the creation of the farms. The Maule River for many years marked the beginning of the Araucanian frontier or, at best, a danger zone in approach to that frontier. Here settlements took on somewhat more the character of pioneer communities with more small holdings and fewer great estates of the aristocracy. Side by side with the hacienda, in many of these districts, particularly at a distance from the larger centers, small farms exist, inconspicuous still in the shadow of their great neighbors and largely under the domination (economic and political) of these estates but leaving the field less completely to the hacienda than in the vicinity of Santiago. Northward in Coquimbo and beyond, the increasing aridity confines agriculture sharply to the narrow irrigable valleys, and farming becomes far more intensive. There is less space for the development of any kind of agricultural estates, but the small holdings, though not so numerous as in south-central Chile, are more numerous than in the provinces about the capital.

Within most sections of the north-central provinces the one-family fundos are found in the more remote regions, most commonly where small valleys penetrate the Coast Range or far back in the deep recesses of the Andes. For example, the Commune of Vichuquén, lying among the hills near the coast, had 43 such farms, while the Commune of Talca had but six, and the Commune of Curicó (also in the Province of Talca) had but seven. In the Province of Colchagua the Commune of Rancagua, about the city of the same name, had two; and that of Santa Cruz, in the hills between the Central Valley and the coast, had ten. Far back among the foothills of the Andean Cordillera also such tiny holdings are found, though control of water supply and high summer pastures have led the haciendas to include much of this mountain area.

While most of these one-house fundos are located in out-of-the-way districts and on poor soil, there are a few, where land is good and water sufficient, in thickly populated parts of the country. One of the best examples of this is in the Aconcagua Valley, near the small city of Los Andes (12,352 population) (Fig. 24). Here in a region where the level floor of the middle Aconcagua Valley offers deep, fertile alluvial soil, where the canals enjoy the right of "first waters" from the river, and where climatic conditions are well suited to truck crops and deciduous fruit, the land is much subdivided. In the Commune of Calle Larga there were (in 1925) 709 properties of less than five hectares; in that of Rinconada de Silva, 461; in Curimón, 410; while in the neighboring Commune of Santa María (Department of San Felipe) there were 570, and in Las Juntas near by there were 492. Farther down the same valley in the vicinity of Limache there were two communes with 592 and 380 properties of less than five hectares. These properties are very small, the 1,606 in the Department of Los Andes averaging only about half a hectare and the 1,260 in San Felipe about a hectare each.

They are intensively cultivated. They market their produce locally, seldom taking it even to Santiago, some forty miles away over a fairly good auto road leading over the Chacabuco ridge, or to Valparaíso some sixty miles down the valley. This is probably the most productive and prosperous group of small holdings in Chile. But for their extremely small size they should make valuable properties capable of supporting a thriving community. As it is, few of the owners get more than a most modest living from their land.

SINGLE-FAMILY HOLDINGS IN SOUTH-CENTRAL CHILE

In the south-central provinces the one-house farms are so much more numerous than in the region about the capital, as are also small properties of all kinds, that one might think they are the characteristic type of holding until the area they include is compared with that of the haciendas (Fig. 23). Such a comparison shows that, though the land of these southern provinces is decidedly more subdivided than that of the north-central region, the small holdings are far from dominating the landscape. Although in Linares (1925 data) there were ten times as many properties of less than 51 hectares (5,249) as of more than 200 hectares (515), yet the group of small ones held only 6 per cent of the land while the large ones held 85 per cent. In Bío-Bío, though the ratio in numbers was not far from the same (4,128 to 579), the small ones held only 4 per cent of the land while the large ones held 88 per cent. Where the small holdings lie in the developed parts of the country, they are little more than fragments wedged in the interstices among the large ones. Only far from the beaten trails are they notably more conspicuous than in the central region. The relatively large number of one-house farms, however, does represent a difference between the small holdings of this region and many of those near Santiago.

Those of the south are more characteristically homesteads, those of the center are more generally agricultural plots cultivated by individuals living in village or town rather than on the plots themselves. The former more nearly provide an entire living for the owner and his family; many of the latter are too small for this. Comparison of numbers and areas of the group of smallest properties makes this apparent. In the Province of Aconcagua the 3,895 holdings of less than five hectares aggregate only

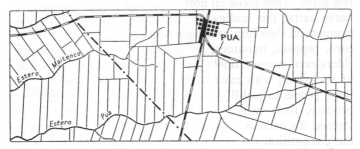

FIG. 23—Much-subdivided land in south-central Chile. Based on Carta General de Colonización, 1917. The land is not irrigated, depending on the 40 to 60 inches of rain, most but not all of which falls in winter. Wheat is the main crop. The majority of the lots are 20, 40, or 60 hectares in area. There has been a steady process of combining several (in some cases many) of these *hijuelas* into one farm. (Reproduced from *Geographical Review*, Vol. 20, 1930, p. 582.)

3,715 hectares, showing them to average less than a hectare each. In the Province of Valparaíso they average barely over three-fourths of a hectare.

SUBSISTENCE FARMING ON SMALL HOLDINGS

Only where these tiny holdings contain excellent soil and a satisfactory water supply is it possible for them to support a family, and even then they provide little more than mere subsistence. Many of the owners make intensive use of their small plots, growing vegetables or fruit (Figs. 25 and 26). The middle and lower Aconcagua Valley has many little chacras or *huertas* (orchards) devoted to tropical or deciduous fruits. Figs, grapes (generally for the table rather than for wine), peaches, pears, avocados (in Chile called *paltas*), *chirimoyas,* and strawberries are produced and sold, usually in the neighboring towns. Every such town has its municipal market into which produce is brought from the surrounding farms both large and small. Any early morning at these markets one may see the owners of the small rural properties bringing in the yield of their few acres. They come on horseback or in two-wheeled, one-horse carts, the bodies of these carts or the cow-skin panniers on their horses loaded with onions, carrots, ears of corn, peppers, tomatoes, potatoes, or fruit. Some of the riders even carry crudely constructed chicken crates made of sticks tied with rawhide thongs. It is not unusual for these people to peddle from door to door the things they produce, their musical cries echoing along the narrow streets. To make it possible for the small producer to meet the competition of the hacendados on more equal terms, recent administrations that have been freer from hacienda dominance have encouraged the organization of agricultural co-operatives. No great success has as yet been attained, but in a few districts the small holders are beginning to respond.

At best it is usually necessary to supplement the produce of their little plots with earnings from some other employment. One man I met, owner of a few hectares of beautifully productive land, was driving a truck to add to his income; another was teaching school; another was engaged in marketing fruit from the orchards of his neighbors; several others were renting additional land in order to raise enough to maintain their families even in very modest conditions.

FIG. 24

FIG. 25

FIG. 24—*Fundito* (small farm) in the Aconcagua Valley. The owner (in the background) is teaching school until he can support his family by working the farm.

FIG. 25—An intensively cultivated small farm (*fundito*). The man on the right is the owner.

PLEASURE GARDENS

Some of the one-house possessions which appear near cities are not true agricultural properties but pleasure gardens (chacras or *quintas*) belonging to city dwellers. The upper-class Chilean is fond of occasional visits to the country and takes great satisfaction in being a proprietor, even if the land he owns is scarcely larger than a city lot. It places him where he belongs by family, among the *terratenientes*. Many of these suburban quintas are delightful spots, their owners lavishing care and money to make the rich soil, abundant water supply, and favorable climate produce to their utmost. However, the city-owned holding generally has at least two dwellings, one for the patrón and a separate one for the tenant.

The general aspect of the quinta is also quite different from the single-family farm. The owner's house is large and substantially built; the plantings are primarily of an ornamental rather than an economic character. Moreover, there is usually an air of age and permanence that the true small farm of central Chile does not have. Large trees, old grape arbors, well-established gardens, and substantial surrounding walls mark these properties in contrast with the small agricultural plot which, because of its relative newness, the limited resources of its owner, or the insecurity of possession, is characterized by few large trees (except perhaps a fig tree or two), by small, flimsily constructed dwellings with no air of permanence, by makeshift fences— by every evidence of recent creation or temporary existence. Few of these small farms have the appearance of the old peasant cottages of Europe, the modest homesteads of New England, or the time-marked possessions of Indians in the highlands of Bolivia, Peru, Ecuador, Guatemala and Mexico. Only in the upper Elqui Valley, on the very northern edge of central Chile, does one find an atmosphere of age and permanency.

Village Settlements of the Andes and Coast Range

From a comparison of the two lists already given it is evident that most of the small holdings are not accounted for by the relatively limited number of one-house farms. There are 69,761 small properties (less than 51 hectares) and only 4,865 single-house places. As has been observed, some small holdings are operated on the inquilino system and so do not belong in the classification here considered. The number of these is probably not great. The rest are houseless holdings, tiny plots of ground held and cultivated by those who live in near-by settlements. Most of the settlements are small clusters of dwellings, the aldeas and the caseríos already defined.[7] Such little groups of houses are widely distributed in out-of-the-way sections of central Chile. Some are found far up the deep canyons that penetrate the Andes, where the valleys narrow so much that the feeble owners of the tiny plots have escaped the encroachment of the haciendas. In isolated recesses along the upper valley of the Maule and its tributaries, where few outsiders penetrate, I found such settlements while making a horseback trip across the Andes via the Melado River and Lake Maule. The upper reaches of the Maipo hold a few settlements of similar character, as do the Cachapoal, the Aconcagua, and the Elqui. The owners of these diminutive farming plots live in the crudest conditions, suggestive of mountain whites in isolated valleys of the southern Appalachians. Their lands are either poor, stony deposits left beside a mountain stream or else more fertile spots at the foot of the great talus slopes that clothe the base of the Andean cliffs. The climate is severe; snow blankets their settlements occasionally during storms in the mountains, and cold, drizzling rain falls for days at a time when clouds gather over the Andes during the winter months. Even in summer, though the days are sunny, the

---

[7] See above, p. 236.

air is chill in the shade, and cold air from the near-by snow fields moves down the valleys at night, sometimes with almost hurricane force, and whistles through every crevice in the poorly constructed houses. Meager crops of potatoes, beans, hardy wheat, and a stunted variety of corn, small flocks of sheep and goats, and a few scrawny specimens of poultry provide these families with scant sustenance but give them little to exchange for what they cannot produce. The children grow up in ignorance, as their parents have done, for there are no schools within miles of these isolated settlements.

The intricate network of valleys that characterize the old worn-down hills of the Coast Range offer more numerous sites for little hamlets. In every province the communes that reach back over the rounded slopes contain many aldeas or caseríos. The railway from Santiago to Valparaíso passes within sight of some settlements of this kind, as does also the auto road between the two cities. Almost any second-class road or trail that penetrates this range leads through some such group of cottages. Sometimes there is an appearance of simple comfort in the settlements; more often the houses are mere shacks, the land poor, the crops stunted, the flocks of sheep and goats half-starved, and the people poorly clad and dejected looking. In general these small holdings, whether single or in clusters, are but the leftovers after the haciendas have selected their fill of the better lands.

Village Settlements of the Central Valley

In rather striking contrast with these caseríos are the established towns (largely of the aldea class) found on the floor of the Central Valley and in other regions of denser population and better agricultural conditions. Some of these lie near the principal cities of central Chile. These, too, are agricultural centers. Both the caseríos and the aldeas perhaps quite closely resemble in general character the settlements maintained by the aborigines before the arrival of the Spaniards. The more substantial of the aldeas in particular can be traced definitely to Indian villages existing in colonial times, either created by Spain in its efforts to subject and civilize the natives or possibly antedating the Conquest itself. Among such are a number of settlements known late in the colonial period as *asientos de indios* (settlements of Indians) and still sometimes so styled.[8] Such are the little towns of Pomaire, Talagante, Llopeu, Conchalí, Chalinga, San Isidro, Valle Hermoso, and many others, particularly along the banks of rivers and creeks from Coquimbo southward to the Mataquito. Some of these have lost almost all their early character as agricultural groups, some still retain much of it. Pomaire, for example, with about 700 inhabitants, consists of small tilled lots lining the two streets of the settlement, much like the one-acre farm subdivisions of southern California. Talagante, though now classed as a pueblo with over 2,000 inhabitants, conserved its character as an Indian agricultural town until well along in the nineteenth century and was described in some detail by an English traveler of the early part of that century.[9] The actual holdings of some of these towns are known to date to 1604 when Jinés de Lillo surveyed lands for them, assigning to each Indian man four cuadras (about 16 acres), to each widow two, and to each *cacique* eight.[10] The viceroy, Ambrosio O'Higgins, when he abolished the encomiendas that remained to his time, settled still other small groups of Indians, bestowing upon them parcels of land.[11] It was the fate of not a few of these Indian towns to be absorbed into adjoining haciendas, as was the case with Pelvín el

[8] See Asta-Buruaga: Diccionario geográfico, 1876; and Riso Patrón: Diccionario jeográfico, 1924, under the names of the towns mentioned.
[9] Graham: Journal, 1824.
[10] Amunátegui Solar: Mayorazgos, Vol. 3, p. 321.
[11] Galdames: Estudio, 1923, p. 108.

Nuevo (later called Chiñihue), whose 373 cuadras of land were sold by the colonial governor of Chile (1787) to the owner of a neighboring fundo.[12] Among those that have survived, these plots constitute the basis of their present independent holdings. After the formation of the republic their little " possessions," as they call them, were confirmed (June 10, 1823) to the settlers by Freire, successor to Bernardo O'Higgins, in continuing the democratic policies of Chile's first president.[13]

In the valleys of the Cachapoal and the Tinguiririca, some 75 miles south from Santiago, there are a number of such towns and villages, mainly Indian in origin and still showing some marked Indian characteristics. These include Roma, Aguas Buenas, Malloa, Pichidegua, Lihueimo, Placilla, Nancagua, and many others, and are surrounded by smaller agricultural settlements, half village and half rural. These caseríos occupy a region of fertile soil, though generally crowded off the larger tracts of good land by haciendas; they irrigate their lands from canals constructed and maintained by co-operative effort, but are limited as to their water supply, being located chiefly along the small uncertain tributaries of the main rivers. Their diminutive fields are spread up the slopes of hills as far as soil and water are available and are intensively cultivated with truck crops and fruit, this being one of the regions where frosts are light enough to make citrus fruits possible. Products of their fields are marketed locally or in such towns as San Fernando, Rengo, and Rancagua; and one may see scores of these small farmers crowding the boxlike third-class cars of the railways, each one with his big basket of fruit, vegetables, chickens, or eggs. An index to the small size of these properties is seen in the fact that they often are measured, not by cuadras or by hectares, as are the haciendas, but by square meters. In the Commune of

---

[12] Amunátegui Solar: *op. cit.,* Vol. 3, pp. 296-297 and 321.
[13] Macchiavello Varas: *op. cit.,* p. 95.

Malloa the group of smallest properties (those of less than five hectares), numbering 708, covers an area of only 498 hectares. In the vicinity of Machalí, back in the hills from Rancagua, I learned of two rural properties measuring 676 and 1,357 square meters respectively. In such districts there are thousands of families who are dependent for their living mainly on the produce from such holdings. Necessarily they live little above the inquilinos. Within a few miles are the great haciendas of Los Perales with 40,000 hectares, 1,000 of which are under irrigation, and boasting an *inquilinaje* of 476 people; El Manzanar, with 25,000 cuadras, 300 of which are under irrigation, and with 153 inquilinos; and many other estates which count their irrigated lands by the hundreds of hectares or cuadras.[14] One needs only to analyze official statistics to see that the mere number of small properties does not indicate the degree to which the land is subdivided.

COMMUNITY HOLDINGS

Classified according to the legal titles to their lands, the agricultural clusters are of two kinds. Some consist of groups of individual properties in which each person is actual owner of a plot of ground. Throughout most of central Chile this is the form of possession. Other villages are collective in ownership, resembling somewhat the pueblos and *rancherías* of Mexico, or the agrarian communities of the central Andean plateaus in the republics farther north.[15] About the organization and operation of this latter kind little is known even in Chile. No one has yet made an intensive study of them. Until recent years they had not even been taxed. I was told repeatedly by

[14] Valenzuela O.: Álbum de informaciones agrícolas. The statistics are from the census of 1930 and from Chile: *Anuario Estadístico*, Vol. 7, Agricultura, 1925-1926.

[15] Described in McBride's " Land Systems of Mexico," 1923, and "Agrarian Indian Communities of Highland Bolivia," 1921.

well-informed agents of the government that there were no such collective holdings in the central part of the country. It was known that in the Araucanian territory there were many undivided *reducciones* held collectively by kinship groups and that in the far north where Inca influence had reached far down the western slopes of the Andes vestiges of the *ayllus* still remained; but that any such communally held possessions existed in central Chile was unknown, even to most of Chilean officialdom. However, following a suggestion made some years ago by a friend who had traveled into some out-of-the-way corners of the central provinces in connection with religious activity, I continued the investigation and finally found a tax-department officer who assured me that there were a number of such collective properties still existent. So long as government revenue was derived principally from nitrate exportation there was little occasion for officials to come into contact with the communities in remote recesses of the hills or to inquire into their system of ownership. But when the nation was forced to extend its taxation to replace the diminishing income from nitrates an effort was made to list all properties and to exact the corresponding tribute. This revealed the fact that in a number of isolated communities there was no individual who could be taxed as the owner of the land. This was collectively held, being subdivided, either permanently or temporarily, only for use. Title, in so far as title existed at all, was in the community. A study of tax lists and detailed maps has shown the existence of many of these collective holdings, known among the inhabitants themselves and now styled officially as " *comunidades.*"

One of the largest and most important of these, the community of Caleu,[16] is located in the Province and Department of Santiago, in the Commune of Tiltil, constituting an

[16] This is also spelled " Caleo " and in the census of 1930 is misspelled " Calén."

entire district of itself. The district contains no fundos or haciendas of any kind, and no cities or towns, but consists of 12 caseríos with a total of 769 persons. According to the census of 1930, the largest hamlet has 44 houses with 196 inhabitants, another has 33 houses with 164 persons, and a third has 23 houses and 121 persons. None of the others has more than 20 houses nor more than 100 inhabitants: two of them have but two houses each, with nine and sixteen persons, respectively. From what my informants told me, it is likely that the population is decidedly larger than the figures given in the census, probably being not far from 2,000. While the region is not rugged, it consists of a labyrinth of little valleys, and there are probably a number of hamlets or individual houses that escaped enumeration. Within this community there are two main divisions, little valleys separated from each other by a ridge of hills, and to most of the inhabitants the surrounding hills are the borders of the universe. In fact, they even speak of going to " the other world " when they pass from one valley to the other.

It is said that the Comunidad de Caleu was established about a century ago by a man named Astorga and that most of the inhabitants of the district are his descendants. By far the larger part bear his name, the rest being mainly members of closely related lineages, with a few recent additions from the outside. Most land titles in this community, as in others, rest in a single name, though some individuals have separate deeds to their own parcels. Except for these, a leading member of the family group holds deed to all the property and acts as agent for all.[17] He pays taxes to the government, which lists the property as

[17] I was told that in the National Library there exists a document, many years old, giving data regarding the origin of the Caleu Community, but I was unable to find it; also that there was a description of the community in a recent (1928 or 1929) " Memoria del Consejo de Defensa Fiscal," but this, too, I did not discover. My best information was derived from Señor Gualterio Looser, of the Museo Nacional in the Quinta Normal in Santiago, and from an associate of his, Señor Machado.

a single individual unit, and in turn he collects from the rest their individual shares. Members seem to occupy their agricultural plots permanently, but all use the hillside grasslands in common: water rights probably go with the individual parcels of land; wood, stone, and other resources of the hills belong to all.

On their tiny agricultural plots the citizens of this community raise wheat and barley, potatoes and beans, as well as peaches, grapes, and figs. They depend mainly on the rains of winter to water their fields, but they use some small springs for a little irrigation. There is little land in the bottom of the valleys, most of the fields being on the hillsides. Once the winter rains have ceased, these slopes become dry and brown for six or eight months. If winter rain is scarce (as happened disastrously in 1924-1925) the crops suffer severely. The hills and valleys occupied by the community are better adapted to grazing than to agriculture, and the settlers depend to a great degree on stock raising. They have a few cattle, quite large flocks of sheep and goats, and a number of donkeys which are used for transporting within the colony and for shipping any surplus to Santiago or Valparaíso. They produce mainly for their own sustenance and in favorable seasons suffer no serious want. They are not accustomed, as are the holders of small properties in most other parts of the country, to supplement their meager agricultural income by working out. In fact, they are said scarcely to know the use of wages. Within their own community they aid each other gratuitously and in many of their tasks they work in common. It is said that the builders of a road near their little towns sought to recruit laborers from the community. No wages would tempt them. "We have food and clothing and shelter," they said. "Why should we want your money? If you really need help, we shall be glad to assist you; but not for pay." It was the opinion of my informants that these community dwellers were much better off than inquilinos. "They are proprietors of their own lands," I was reminded, and that in itself was apparently sufficient to lift them above the inquilino class. It mattered little that their holdings were mere pocket-handkerchief farms, many of them less than a hectare in size; every plot was dignified with a name, like the great haciendas on the plains below, and the holders of these parcels, though possessing only a title in common, were real *propietarios*. As the name of the principal caserío (Capilla) suggests, there is a church in the community, as there is in most of the agricultural clusters; but the religious influence does not seem very impressive in Caleu, as only one among scores of holdings bears the name of a saint. A school is maintained also; and a post office, located in one of the main units, serves the neighboring hamlets as well. These, too, are common features of such settlements. Apparently there is no formal organization of the group, some one of the older members acting for all by common consent. The complete government of the district seems to lie with the people themselves—with their simple family organization, neither national nor provincial authority intervening, it would seem, except in the matter of collecting taxes and, presumably, in case of serious disorder. It is thus a simple kind of kinship unit, perhaps only in process of taking final form.

Another community that may formerly have rivaled Caleu in importance is that at Tiltil. It occupies a dry little valley, with gently sloping, round-topped hills on every side. The construction of the railway from Santiago to Valparaíso through this region destroyed its isolation and has brought disaster to it. The lands, though poor, became of some value, and neighboring haciendas have been squeezing the community between smaller and smaller limits. Once occupying most of the valley, it has now been reduced to seven families with only a few hectares of land left, except for the poor grasslands still supporting a few flocks

FIG. 26

FIG. 27

FIG. 26—Owner of a *fundito* and his home. This man owns and lives on the small farm pictured in Fig. 24. He has the appearance and bearing of a *propietario.*

FIG. 27—Remnants of the Community of Tiltil; but one house remains on this collective holding, haciendas having encroached upon it from every side.

FIG. 28—The German colony at Peñaflor, as the colonists found it on their arrival.

of sheep and goats. This community, too, retains its simple collective organization, one member representing the group in the payment of taxes and any other matters of common interest (Fig. 27).

Other communities are found in the rough hill country of the Chacabuco Range that closes the Central Valley in the north; in the lower La Ligua Valley, and in the narrow upper Aconcagua Valley along the trans-Andean railway and road. Farther north in the valleys of the Choapa and the Limarí numerous caseríos exist, some of which hold undivided properties in common.

There are no definite data indicating the proportion between individually and collectively owned small properties. It seems probable that the former greatly outnumber the latter. Not only the single-dwelling " fundos " but many of the properties constituting aldeas and caseríos are possessions of individuals. Apparently few properties other than those in out-of-the-way districts are held in undivided ownership. Even the towns of distinctly Indian origin seem now to have lost that character, though they were originally held communally by kinship groups as are today the Araucanian lands farther south.

A Chilean Middle Class

In rural central Chile the holders of these several kinds of small properties are all that exists of a middle class. They constitute the nearest approach to that

> ". . . . bold peasantry, its country's pride,
> Which, once destroyed, can never be supplied."

These seventy thousand owners of holdings averaging less than eight hectares, three-fifths of whom own an average of less than a hectare and a half, are the only representatives in central Chile of the class that in many other countries constitutes the bulwark of democratic institutions, standing between the dominance of a social or economic aristocracy and the mass of the proletariat. It is evident that, while their holdings greatly outnumber the large properties, they occupy but a tiny fraction of the land. The latter fact, rather than the former, is a fair index of the part that these landowners have played in the life of the nation. The vast majority of their properties are so small, and, in general, their resources of soil, water, and location with respect to markets have been so inferior to those of the hacienda, that they have remained almost hopelessly poor. In a society fashioned only for an upper and lower class, they have been forced to share the life of the lower class. Though they have been largely free from the servile status of the inquilino, they have enjoyed few of the advantages of the patron. Though owners of property, they have shared few of the benefits of proprietorship. Education has been beyond the reach of their own resources, and the state has not provided it for them except in limited measure. The door of economic opportunity has been closed against them. Thus handicapped, members of this relatively numerous class of free Chilean citizens have not been able to rise above their present status. I think no man or woman of note has risen from the ranks of the small farmer in central Chile. There has been no Chilean Abraham Lincoln, no Benito Juárez. They have contributed little if anything to the nation. Even in local affairs they have had little more influence than the inquilinos—perhaps not so much, since the hacendado has been interested to a degree in the welfare of his tenants, and some progress has been made because of that interest. The small farmers have contributed, no doubt, in man power both to the army and the navy. They have supplied some of the free laborers. They have fed some of the dwellers in town and city and mining camp. But, if they should all disappear overnight and their lands fall back to disuse, the country would not greatly feel their loss. In political lines they have been no stronger. The government of landowners has always had to think, in a measure at least, of the inquilino class and has never felt it safe to forget completely the " roto " element of the cities. There is little evidence, however, that it has ever given a thought to the several hundred thousand owners of small properties in the country—nor have those small proprietors ever raised their voice in united protest. The peasant proprietor of central Chile has been, up to the present, little above the inquilino. With democracy apparently dawning, the votes of common people will count for more, and perhaps the small proprietor's day is at hand. A third estate is slowly coming into existence.

CHAPTER IX

SUBDIVIDING THE HACIENDA

If Chile is to increase the number of her one-family farms, the great *haciendas* must be divided. There is no other source of land. As has been observed, Dávila's plan to settle the unemployed on public domain failed because there was almost no public domain. The lands on the Araucanian frontier have virtually all passed into private ownership except the small amount reserved in *reducciones* for the Indians themselves. The land farther south, the uncertain amount that still remains in possession of the state, is mainly unsuited for agriculture because of its mountainous relief, its heavy forests, and its excessive rainfall. On the other hand, desert conditions, with extremely limited water supply, make the north equally impossible for colonization on any scale sufficient to relieve the situation in central Chile.

Chileans of all classes recognize the need of providing land for the common people. Most of them realize that there is no land available outside of the haciendas. They see, too, that the great estates are not making the best use of the land they hold. The country is lagging in agricultural development, mainly because of the latifundian system. While the Argentine farms are producing extensively for export and enriching the republic, those of Chile are yielding little more than they did a generation ago. In fact, in some respects they are falling behind. Argentine population, too, is growing rapidly; Chile's remains almost stationary. No great tide of immigration has set Chileward; there is no land to induce it, not even enough for the proper support of her own people. The haciendas have monopolized it. If production is to be augmented, if the population is to increase, if immigrants are to be attracted, if the common people are to have land and be given a chance to develop into real citizens instead of remaining the submen, as Pinochet LeBrun calls the *inquilinos,* the haciendas must be partitioned. This is the opinion frequently expressed by Chilean writers, both theorists and practical men of affairs. A review of some of these opinions will reveal how general is this conviction.

Some Chilean Views on the Subdivision of Haciendas

Ambrosio O'Higgins, governor general of Chile in the last years of the colonial period and later viceroy of Peru, called attention to the evils of such large holdings and urged their division.[1] Manuel Salas also favored the reduction of the haciendas of his day. Darwin ascribed the extreme poverty of the rural Chilean workmen to the " feudal-like system on which the land is tilled." [2] Claudio Gay, author of the two-volume work on Chilean agriculture, part of his monumental " Historia física y política de Chile," as far back as 1862 wrote of the need of small properties and the ill effects of the large.[3] In 1875 a General Congress of Agriculturists, organized and directed by the influential Sociedad Nacional de Agricultura, which is composed of leading *hacendados,* went on record as opposed to the heavy tax (*alcabala*) on partitions of property, which made it advantageous to preserve estates intact rather than divide them among heirs ; and, regarding the division of rural holdings, expressed itself (somewhat vaguely, it is true) as follows: " The Society has great interest in seeing property distributed in such fashion that its possession and enjoyment shall be in the hands of

[1] Gay: Historia física; Agricultura, Vol. 1, 1862, pp. 86-87.
[2] Darwin: Voyage of the Beagle, 1909, p. 284.
[3] Gay: *op. cit.*

individuals who . . . . are capable of raising production
to the greatest degree possible." [4] In 1920 and 1921 there
was much discussion concerning the more general distribution of land, some of the workmen's organizations going
as far as to demand a wholesale forcible division. This
greatly alarmed the members of the Sociedad Nacional de
Agricultura; but many of the leaders of the nation recognized that there was some ground, at least, for the popular
dissatisfaction with the system. This was expressed in
1923 by a writer in one of the agricultural journals: " How
few [of the rural properties] there are that produce an
income equivalent to a third or a fourth of what they
should!" "The great extensions of uncultivated or
poorly cultivated lands are the worst obstacle to agricultural progress"; the " economical and rational division of
agricultural property " is much to be desired.[5] This same
sentiment found echo in the Constitutional Assembly in
1925, in which it was stated that " it is indispensable that
subdivision of property be undertaken at once." [6] In considering this position on the part of the government, the
writer of an editorial in the publication of the Sociedad
Nacional de Agricultura readily admitted that " rural
property is on too large a scale to be conveniently cultivated. . . . . Only ten per cent of those who work in
agriculture are owners of the soil; the great majority is
composed of renters, inquilinos, peons, and vagabonds who
cannot have immediate interest in improving property that
does not belong to them. . . . . In the subdivision of rural
property is involved a problem, both economic and social,
and of the highest interest." [7] The new constitution (of
1925), as has been noted, clearly states that the matter of
" equitable division of property " and, in particular, provision for *propiedad familiar* (family homestead) are

[4] Congreso Libre de Agricultores . . . en 1875, p. 156.
[5] *Agronomía*, 1923, pp. 123-124.
[6] *Bol. de la Soc. Nac. de Agric.*, 1925, p. 472.
[7] *Ibid.*, Vol. 45, 1915, p. 649.

proper concerns of the nation. From the north and the south, too, voices were raised advocating " the diminishing of the size of the *latifundios* " [8] and approving government efforts in this direction as " a strongly-felt necessity for the real development of agriculture in this country "; while an editorial in the periodical *Agronomía,* of Santiago, hailed the new law of colonization on hacienda lands as " one of the greatest events in the history of agricultural organization in our country." [9] A few years later, one of Chile's leading agricultural engineers, in discussing the " human factor in agriculture," said: " How much better it would be if, instead of these enormous *fundos* which we have in our country, we had only small holdings such as those in Belgium or Holland, where the human factor is the most important consideration," since the owners of these large haciendas are " entirely unfitted for expert agriculture." [10] In November 1928 another agricultural engineer wrote that the creation of small properties represented " one of the most longed-for democratic aspirations. . . The subdivision of property on the ground of public utility " is " clearly provided for in our constitution." [11] From the University of Chile have come similar opinions. The distinguished professor of political economy of that university writes in his two-volume study of the problems of Chile: " The problem of the division of agricultural property is of transcendental importance " and proceeds to show many ways in which the small holding has advantages over the large one, and by what means Chile may achieve a more equal distribution of agricultural lands. He maintains that in the solution of both of Chile's two great problems, those of greater economic production

---

[8] Cabero: Chile y los chilenos (a series of addresses given under the auspices of the Extensión Cultural de Antofagasta), 1926, p. 324; *Bol. Soc. Agric. del Norte,* January, 1929, p. 10; *El Agricultor Chileno,* March, 1927, p. 1.

[9] *Agronomía,* February, 1929, p. 344.

[10] Julio Chacón del Campo in *Revista Agronómica,* July, 1927, pp. 18-22.

[11] *El Agricultor Chileno,* November, 1928, pp. 1-2.

and of greater social equality, the first step to take is " division of the agricultural property." [12] Also, in a study already referred to, prepared as part of the series of a Seminar of Economic Sciences at the University of Chile, another author states the theme of his work as follows: " A greater subdivision of agricultural property will intensify production, increase the population and the national welfare, and will realize a democratic ideal in the distribution of wealth." [18] Carlos Keller, of German descent but Chilean by birth and training, one of the leading statisticians and a clear-sighted analyst of his country's problems, devotes much of two recent volumes to a discussion of the evils inherent in the hacienda system and frankly advocates the subdivision of the large holding. " Its days are numbered," he says. " The Chilean landholders are face to face with the alternative of giving up a part of their lands voluntarily and without compensation or losing them entirely." [14]

Still more notable is the proposal of subdividing the haciendas advanced by a senator, scion of an old aristocratic family that has held its great estates for several centuries. He introduced into Congress (1922) a bill authorizing the purchase or expropriation of lands to be divided into small parcels and sold on easy terms to constitute one-family farms, and took advantage of an enforced absence from his country to write one of the most widely-read of the books on the subject.[15]

Of still greater import is the declaration made by former President Ibáñez in his message to Congress on May 21, 1930,[16] and repeated in even stronger terms by President Alessandri four years later to the day,[17] that the govern-

[12] Macchiavello Varas: Política económica nacional, 1931, Vol. 1, p. 349; Vol. 2, p. 62.
[13] Poblete Troncoso: Problema agrícola, 1919, citation given on title page.
[14] Keller: Eterna crisis, 1931; *idem:* Un país al garete, 1932 (citations from the latter, p. 124).
[15] Aguirre Cerda: El problema agrario, 1929, pp. 245-249.
[16] *La Nación*, May 22, 1930, pp. 17-19.
[17] *Ibid.*, May 22, 1934, pp. 13-28; reference on p. 24.

ment was definitely committed to the undertaking of subdividing excessively large holdings. Referring to the subdivision of property and the creation of the propiedad familiar, the Minister of Labor in 1933 spoke of this as one of the principal aims of the Constitution of 1925 and said (rather too inclusively) that it is "an ideal of all political parties that the head of every Chilean family should be owner of a piece of the soil of his native land." [18] Many other citations might be given, showing that the subdivision of the large landholdings is widely considered an essential measure for correcting the evils of Chile's present social organization. In Congress, on the streets, in clubs, the matter is being discussed; periodicals, newspapers, and books make frequent reference to it; liberal elements urge its necessity, the conservatives fear its inevitability.[19]

As has been seen in the opinions quoted, such a conclusion is not entirely new. For a full century and more, liberal-minded critics of the existing social order have advocated this remedy. In fact, mild measures have been adopted by the government at different times to correct the evil inherent in monopolization of the nation's land. The abolition of the *mayorazgos* was brought about to do away with extreme entailment of agricultural holdings; the abolition of the alcabala, also, was intended to facilitate the division of estates; taxes on land (in so far as they have been imposed) had the same purpose in part. The colonization of the frontier by the granting of lands in relatively small parcels, begun as far back as the middle of the nineteenth century, established a form of property that was a departure from and has always been antagonistic to the great hacienda.

[18] The Demócrata Convencionalista party in its convention held in Temuco, in November, 1934, voted to favor "the expropriation of the land in behalf of the laborers, the extension of the system of colonization to the Magellan region, the protection by the government of the squatters on fiscal lands," and even "the expropriation of all church holdings" to further the distribution of the land (*La Tribuna del Sur*, Nov. 24, 1934, p. 4).

[19] *La Nación*, May 25, 1933, p. 1.

EXAMPLES OF SUBDIVISIONS OF LARGE HOLDINGS

Under the pressure of such measures there has been going on for many years a gradual reduction in size of the large holdings and a distribution of their lands among a larger number of individuals. The history of many haciendas reveals this process. They have been partitioned into *hijuelas* and some of these in turn have been divided again and again, in spite of the tendency engendered by the entailing of estates in colonial times and during the early years of independence and in spite of the family pride which leads to maintaining a property intact. A few examples of such breaking up of large holdings will serve to illustrate this process (see also Figure 29).

The Hacienda La Compañía in the Department of Rancagua, one of the most famous of the Chilean estates, is said to have contained, at a time when it formed one of the many great holdings in the hands of the Jesuits, not less than 80,000 hectares, extending from the Argentine border on the crest of the Andes to the middle of the Central Valley, and to have included nearly 9,000 *cuadras* of level irrigated land. After the confiscation of all Jesuit properties (1767), this was sold at auction (October 24, 1771), its sale arousing great interest among all the hacendados. In 1874, when its entail terminated, it was divided among eleven heirs and apparently has been much subdivided since that time. Another great estate which formerly belonged to the Jesuits, the hacienda of Longaví, of almost equal extent, has been divided into eight hijuelas, each of them forming a large fundo. Six of these contain respectively 4,800, 7,800, 5,300, 2,476, 2,200, and 4,800 cuadras, about half of each being under irrigation. The Hacienda Carén in the Department of Melipilla has been dismembered to form the following: Lo Salinas, Queserías, Pincha, Alhué, Peral, and Culiprán, all large properties; one of them contains 1,400 hectares (mostly without irrigation, it is true)

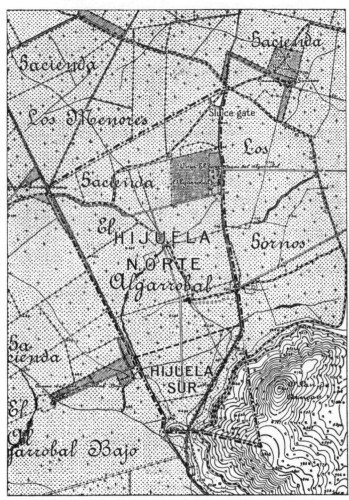

Fig. 29—Plan of the *fundo* El Algarrobal, divided into two *hijuelas*. 1:54,500. (Reduced from topographic map, 1:25,000, by the Chilean General Staff; property lines from plan supplied through courtesy of the Caja de Credito Hipotecario). See Figure 11, p. 36, for key to symbols, except dash line, which represents boundary between the two hijuelas.

FIG. 30—Advertisement of subdivision and sale of an hacienda in *hijuelas*.

and one has 1,600 cuadras under irrigation. Few of the great haciendas of former days have not been subject to such partitioning among heirs or have escaped subdivision for purposes of sale. The process is still going on, in fact much more rapidly in recent years. The groups of fundos belonging to members of a single family, already referred to, are in part the result of this movement. It is becoming rather common also to divide large properties and sell them in many small parcels of 5, 10, 15, 20, and 30 hectares (Fig. 30). Some of these are offered on easy terms of payment, much as urban subdivisions are in California. The fundo of Santa Fé, just outside the city of Curicó, was recently advertised for sale in this fashion, as was also La Florida near Santiago, Quilpué in the Department of San Felipe, and a number of other large properties (Fig. 31).

In 1930 I saw advertisements in the press and on great bill-boards announcing that one of the famous old haciendas not far from the

División de Fundo

en Curicó

FUNDO SANTA FE

A tres cuadras de la Estación de Curicó

A dos y media cuadras de la Feria y siete de la Plaza de Armas; tierras de primera calidad y con abundancia de agua.

Se dividirá en lotes de 5, 10, 15, 20 y 30 hectáreas.

PRECIO: $ 3,500 hectárea

CONDICIONES DE PAGO: 20 por ciento al contado

y el resto a 30 años plazo.

DIRIGIRSE:

OFICINA AGRARIA

MORANDE 440, tercer piso, oficinas 48 y 49. TELEFONO 80174

y para visitar el fundo, a Curicó, Fundo Santa Fe, señor Juan Antonio Fuenzalida.

Fig. 31—Advertisement of a voluntary division of an hacienda, the Fundo de Santa Fé.

capital was being subdivided and sold in small hijuelas. A real estate concern which I visited had four large fundos listed for sale in this manner. Dealers in rural properties, hitherto confined almost exclusively to large transactions (only large properties being offered and only the rich buying), were now finding a ready sale for small plots. Renters were seeking lands of their own; *medieros* (rural laborers who had been cultivating on shares) also were buying the small plots offered, while numbers of professional people, government employees, and the more prosperous of the artisan class were eager to buy a small fundo or chacra to augment their income and provide them a place for retirement. Many of these persons had never been financially able, so long as large properties only were being offered for sale, to satisfy the craving for proprietorship that seems to characterize every Chilean. The prestige of the hacendado has given a charm to the word "proprietor."

An old friend took me to visit his recently acquired *fundito* in the beautifully fertile and attractive upper Aconcagua Valley, near the town of Los Andes. This man was a teacher in the capital but, having had experience in the management of an hacienda, longed to obtain a small farm of his own on which he could live with his wife and four children. The plot was a four-cuadra section of a larger property that was being subdivided. Water rights from a community canal came with the land. The new owner had inclosed the place with an imported woven-wire fence, was planting it with deciduous fruit trees, and was planning to build on it a modern cottage, with conveniences unheard-of even on most Chilean haciendas. He expected, as soon as the fruit trees were bearing, to give up his teaching position and live on his little farm. In the meantime, a caretaker lived in the tiny house already on the plot and tended the plantings. In the Rinconada Commune, in which this property was located, there were people occupying one-house funditos and *caserios* holding an aggregate of 1,649 hectares.[20] A few of these holders were city dwellers who left their properties in the hands of employees, came only occasionally to visit them, and apparently had no intention of ever living there permanently. Most of them, however, were genuine small farmers, living on their holdings, some with an *inquilino* family or two, some with hired day laborers from the neighborhood, some doing most or all of the work themselves. The little farms were intensively cultivated, with no land lying idle. Most of them were devoted to fruit growing, a few had dairies, some produced vegetables. In education, culture, and standards of living, the owners were decidedly below the average of such farmers in most parts of the United States, as well as below the hacendados and typical city dwellers in Chile; but they were above the typical inquilino of the haciendas and vastly better off than the " *roto* " of the Chilean city slums. Some of them would rank, in general intelligence and agricultural skill, with representative farmers in any part of the world.

RECENT LAND-REFORM MOVEMENTS

The growth of small holdings has been generally at the expense of the hacienda. Since most of the land in central Chile had long been incorporated in large estates, it is mainly by the disintegration of these that smaller properties could be formed. Thus the number of little farms represents a slow but gradual subdividing of the haciendas slightly facilitated by the legislative measures noted. No serious land reform, however, has been attempted until recent years. The power of the landholders has been too great to make such reforms possible. It was only after the popular revolt which first brought Alessandri into the

[20] The figures for area and number of holdings are taken from Chile: *Anuario Estadístico*, Vol. 7, Agricultura, 1925, and the population statistics from the 1930 census. In this commune there were also 27 properties of more than 200 hectares, aggregating 43,265 hectares.

presidency (1920) that the influence of the landholding aristocracy was sufficiently weakened to permit the passing of legislation definitely looking toward the breaking up of the large estates. The first important step taken in this direction was the principle embodied in the Constitution of 1925, that a proper distribution of the land resources of the nation was a legitimate concern of government. This principle has been given substantial expression in terms of the agrarian program undertaken by the liberal administrations following the 1924 revolution. The main features of this program are colonization of the remaining public lands by small farmers, extension of irrigation to provide lands for additional holdings of reduced size, provision of rural credits as an aid to small proprietors, development of agricultural co-operatives, clearing of titles to properties in the already-settled sections of southern Chile coupled with the substitution of individual holdings for the still-existing Indian communities there, and, most important of all so far as central Chile is concerned, the acquisition of haciendas by purchase or expropriation in the central section of the country for the purpose of dividing them into parcels for agricultural colonies. All of these measures were directed against the hacienda system, and the last one was intended to accomplish the dismemberment of these great estates in the region where they had long been the prevalent form of holding.

IRRIGATION, RURAL CREDITS, AND CO-OPERATIVES

In the carrying out of the program of irrigation development between 1924 and 1927 more than sixteen per cent was added to the irrigated area of the country. Projected works should bring under cultivation within the next few years some 200,000 additional hectares. These new lands lie both in the northern desert section and in the central region where intensive farming is impossible without irrigation. Homesteads for some 12,000 families will be provided and will thus afford a small outlet for the increasing population and materially enlarge the food production of the country. More important still, they will bring to most of these families the first opportunity they have ever had to enjoy economic and social independence. The nation will profit by having so many more independent citizens. Indirectly at least, such holdings will contribute to reduce the dominance of the hacienda in the national life.

The securing of rural credits is both fostering the creation of small properties in all parts of the country and is making for more successful operation of the small farms already in existence. In particular, it makes it possible for the small proprietor to weather a series of bad years, such as occasionally come to central Chile with her scant and variable rainfall. Heretofore such seasons have been tragic for the small farmers, especially for those in the valleys and on the slopes of the Coast Range where irrigation either is not practiced, or is dependent upon rain-fed brooks and springs. In the excessively dry year of 1924-1925 hundreds of such farmers without means of securing credit became bankrupt, while the hacendados with their greater resources, easier command of credit, and water supply drawn mainly from the rivers that have their sources in the fields of perpetual snow on the High Andes, were able to withstand the drought. The few agricultural co-operatives already formed, though not yet widely effective, are giving the small proprietor the advantages of large-scale expert marketing, thus enabling him to compete with the hacendado.

DIRECT SUBDIVISION OF LARGE HOLDINGS

The problem of direct subdivision of large agricultural holdings in the central part of the country is the most delicate but the most important phase of the government's agrarian program. Under the terms of the law promulgated December 10, 1928, a Caja de Colonización Agrícola (Bureau of Agricultural Colonization) was created and provided with an appropriation of 100,000,000 pesos to be used in the founding of agricultural settlements mainly in the central part of the country. Land for these colonies was to be acquired by purchase if possible; but, failing that, the president of the republic was empowered (with proper limitations) to expropriate the necessary areas on the grounds of public utility. Lands were to be acquired in this latter fashion only within fifteen kilometers of railways, stations, and ports or within five kilometers of principal roads, navigable rivers, and lakes. Furthermore, all properties north of the Bío-Bío River of not more than 300 hectares and all south of that river of not more than 500 hectares, and properties already intensively cultivated anywhere in the country, were to be exempt from such expropriation. The lands set aside for colonization were to be divided into parcels not to exceed twenty hectares each and sold on easy terms to either foreigners or Chileans. No colonist might acquire more than one parcel unless he had three or more children, in which case he might secure another parcel for each three children. The plots were not to be subdivided either by inheritance or sale. The colonies were to be developed under the control of the Caja, the government retaining the right to enforce certain restrictions as to the qualifications of the new buyer and also regarding the use to which the property was to be put. The purpose was to conserve the character of the colonies as distinctly small-scale agricultural units (*propiedad familiar*), devoted to the production of crops most needed by the population of neighboring centers.[21]

This legislation was further strengthened by the second Alessandri administration, once it became firmly established. New measures were enacted in 1933, providing

[21] Chile: Ley No. 4,496 y su Reglamento, 1929.

for the creation of other *colonias agrícolas* and the further colonization of far southern lands. Alessandri's message to Congress, May 21, 1931, led the government organ next day to say: " It is seen that the *parcelación de las tierras* has begun " and a few days later to head its leading editorial: " Alessandri will impose the subdivision of the land." [22] His message a year later emphasized the same intention and advocated further legislation to bring about what he termed one of his principal ambitions, that of the solution of the land problem by creation of a large number of small farms.[23]

The expropriation feature of this legislation was bitterly opposed by the hacendados, who considered it a violation of vested rights and thought they saw in it a threat to the whole established social order.[24] Probably this, more than anything else, led to the movement that brought about the overthrow of the Ibáñez government. The president had never made use of the authority given him by this measure to condemn property for the purpose of colonization. There were many fundos on the market, and the government secured the needed land by direct purchase. Its practice was to solicit offers of properties or buy those already put up for sale. However, the authority was there to take by expropriation if necessary. This was alarming to those whose properties might stand in the way of carrying out the agrarian plan. Furthermore, the entire program of land reform threatened the social, economic, and political dominance of the hacienda. Its primary purpose was the democratization of the country. Only those of the aristocracy who could see the need for this and were willing to put the nation's need above their own, or those who saw the trend as inevitable and chose this rather than to face the danger of more radical demands, were willing to acquiesce in this program.

[22] *La Nación*, May 22, 1933, p. 5; May 29, p. 3.
[23] *Ibid.*, May 22, 1934, pp. 24-25.
[24] *Bol. de la Soc. Nac. de Agric.*, August, 1928, p. 547.

Work of the Caja de Colonización

The first colony under the Caja de Colonización was formed with forty-three German families selected by the Chilean consul in Hamburg, with the hope that they would thrive as their compatriots in southern Chile had done. A fundo, Santa Adela, some 15 kilometers southwest of Santiago on the level floor of the Central Valley, containing 344 hectares (*ca.* 850 acres) of fertile, irrigated land suitable for the raising of wheat, barley, maize, potatoes and other truck crops, as well as alfalfa, fruits, and nuts, was purchased in open market for this purpose. The land was divided into small plots, mostly of ten hectares each, and these were sold to the immigrants on a partial-payment plan, the purchaser to receive his deed when payments were completed. A comfortable house was built on each parcel by the government; and roads, fences, canals, electric lighting system, and water supply were provided (Fig. 28). It will seem strange that the government, with the avowed purpose of providing land for its landless laborers, should bring in foreigners who would actually compete with the native population. The intention was to create—with these intelligent, thrifty Germans—a model after which the small farms provided for Chileans might be patterned. The presence of these German farmers in central Chile introduced an element quite strange for that part of the country. It was interesting to see the reaction of Chilean visitors to the colony. The newcomers could not be treated as inquilinos nor as other members of the lower class, usually associated with such tiny holdings; yet neither could they be looked upon as hacendados, though they were educated, and, some of them, possessed of gentle manners. Their houses, too, were like neither the *ranchos* of the inquilinos nor the *casa de hacienda* of the patrón. Small, but neat and clean, with imported furniture and sanitary fixtures, with books, periodicals, music, and objects of art, there was nothing in rural central Chile with which to compare them. Those familiar with southern Chile and its many modest homesteads of Chilean and foreign farmers, or with life in northern Europe or the United States, found this middle-class colony easy to understand; but to others it was a revelation.

Several other such properties have been acquired, amounting (up to May, 1934) to more than 160,000 hectares, and twenty-four colonies accommodating 8,000 persons, mostly Chileans, have been established on them.[25] The law gives the Caja authority to obtain land in the same way to accommodate any group of not less than ten experienced agriculturists who might wish to establish small farms to be cultivated by themselves and their families. The Caja ascertains their needs, their experience as practical farmers, their health and physical fitness for agricultural work, and their ability to meet the easy terms of payment required for the acquisition of *parcelas* (small farming plots). Each applicant must show that he has no criminal record, and an effort is made to see that each head of a family who applies is legally married.

Several of the great properties acquired for colonization have been set aside for experiment in collective farming under state management. These places serve principally as training grounds for individuals who have received plots in the colonias agrícolas but who need further instruction in agriculture, particularly in modern methods. As soon as they acquire the necessary training, they are transferred to other lands, which are to be their own. There has been no attempt to socialize agriculture to the extent of abolishing the system of individual holdings.

In all these colonies the individual allotments are small, varying from 10 to 40 hectares (*ca.* 25 to 100 acres) of irrigated land and not exceeding 500 hectares where irriga-

[25] President Alessandri's message to Congress, May 21, 1934 (*La Nación*, May 22, 1934, pp. 13-28; reference on pp. 24-25).

tion is not employed. The number of applicants is much larger than was anticipated, the demand coming from the same groups that are seeking the plots offered by dealers. Up to the present, few inquilinos have obtained land in these colonies, in spite of the fact that they daily plead for

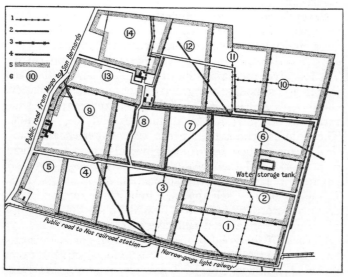

Fig. 32—Plan showing the subdivision of the Hacienda San Juan de Nos by the Caja de Colonización Agrícola into smaller parcels for settlers. Scale, 1 : 24,600. The new parcels follow rather closely the old field divisions of the *hacienda.* Key to symbols: 1-3, existing wire fences, namely 1 on old field borders, 2 on new parcel boundaries, 3 newly erected; 4, irrigation ditches; 5, parcel boundaries; 6, parcel numbers.

parcels of the subdivided properties, gathering in groups in many parts of the country to urge their claims for lands of their own.[26] This class in particular most needs land, and they, too, with their practical knowledge of farming could make best use of the land. Most of them, however, lack the funds with which to acquire parcels even on the

[26] Keller: Eterna crisis, 1931, p. 271; *idem:* Un país al garete, 1932, pp. 123-125.

easy terms available. Some other provisions will have to be made before many of them can take advantage of the opportunity offered.

Rise of Small Farms

Disturbed political and economic conditions within the past few years have slowed up the program of creating colonias agrícolas, and many difficulties have been encountered in the selection of colonists and the organization of communities; but a beginning has been made toward both the introduction of small farms into the very home of the hacienda and the breaking up of the haciendas themselves.[27]

Thus it would seem that the end of the excessively large property has arrived or at least that, even if some of these great estates continue to exist, beside them will be created a multitude of small farms which will carry on a great part of the agriculture of the country. This will undoubtedly end the extreme dominance of the haciendas in Chilean affairs. Independent small farmers, it would seem, will never allow the conditions in which they live to be determined by a small number of great hacendados. There is being developed a true middle class in the rural districts, a middle class that will make common cause with the small farmers of the south and the few of similar class among the more intelligent in the northern valleys; that will, moreover, greatly strengthen the corresponding group in cities. In many things this middle class has community of interest with the laboring class. Together, by influence and by electoral strength, they should be able to give Chile a degree of democracy never yet experienced there. As has been pointed out, this element is already making itself felt in many ways. Unless a strongly reactionary element obtains control of the government it would seem likely that this

[27] The *South Pacific Mail,* English language weekly paper published in Valparaiso, in its issue of August 15, 1935, stated that up to July 1st 625,000 acres (ca. 253,000 hectares) had been given over to small holders.

agrarian reform movement will give rise to a gradual growth of democratic institutions. This should be of great advantage to the entire country, except the relatively few of the old aristocracy who refuse to fall into line.

The program, however, has only begun. Not more than a few thousand small holdings at most have been created. To carry out the program a full half-million should be formed. Many of these will be carved out of haciendas voluntarily divided by their owners. That process has been accelerated by the menace of possible expropriation. The Church has foreseen the danger of losing its large holdings and is said to have disposed of most of its haciendas. Private dealers in lands have reacted to the stimulated demand for small holdings, and among real estate advertisements one now frequently encounters offerings of parcelas. These are from one hectare up, with improvements already installed (fences, irrigation canals, drinking water, and electric lights) and thus closely duplicate the small farms of the colonias agrícolas. To anyone familiar with the real-estate transactions common in former days when fundos and haciendas were the only rural properties offered, this appears as a distinctly new departure. Should the conservatives get back into the saddle and halt the process of land reform or attempt to undo what has been done in that direction, violent revolution, such as devastated Mexico for a decade, would seem inevitable. The warning of one of Chile's own writers may well be repeated here, since, as seen from the outside also, the situation seems to warrant such forecast.

Insisting that the common people of Chile in their aspiration to become proprietors of land are but trying to recover what was wrongfully taken from them in the colonial period; that this injustice should have been rectified at once with the founding of the republic; that only the availability of new lands on the frontier postponed until the present a reckoning in this matter; that the solution cannot be put off longer; and asserting that the problem cannot be solved by the slow and costly process of buying back the land and distributing it, he reaches this solemn conclusion: " I am not in favor of confiscation of property, I am not in favor of violent measures; but I have observed that history is inexorable in its progress and knows no mercy. The Chilean landholders face the alternative of turning over voluntarily and without compensation a part of their lands or of losing those lands completely. . . . . The days of the latifundia are numbered." [28]

[28] Keller: Un país al garete, 1932, pp. 124-125.

PART II

SOUTHERN CHILE
A FRONTIER REGION

CHAPTER X

CHILE'S FOREST LANDS

To the visitor from north middle latitudes southern Chile (from about the Bío-Bío southward) is the most attractive part of the country. To the typical Chilean it is a forbidding land. The Anglo-Saxon finds the region suggestive of northern Europe or Oregon, Washington, and Vancouver Island. Forty degrees south latitude has much in common with forty degrees north. Green grass and trees, refreshing rains—yes, and dreary, soaking rains—make him think of home. Central Chile sets the Californian's heartbeats faster for its eucalyptus trees and the incense of their burning leaves, its citrus groves, its figs and olives and grapes, its long, sunshiny summer with brown, aromatic vegetation. This Spain-like central region the man of Spanish descent has understood and occupied; the south to him is a foreign land. Relatively few Chileans even visit it, although foreigners acclaim the forests, lakes, and volcanoes as unsurpassed upon the globe.

As one travels southward from the region of Santiago the landscape gradually changes. The level floor of the Central Valley continues; the great snow-topped wall of the Andes shuts in one side while the Coast Range still follows on the other; one's view is still limited to the narrow central trough. But though these topographic features remain the same, the scenery slowly takes on a different aspect. The familiar trees of central Chile—eucalyptus, Lombardy poplar, and weeping willow—grow fewer, while native Chilean species take their places. Wheat fields continue, but green irrigated alfalfa fields are no longer seen; pastures of native grass dotted with wild flowers like the prairies of Kansas replace them. Clumps of forest begin to appear, while in an occasional field are seen the gaunt, stark trunks of deadened giants or the charred stumps of their companions that have yielded to the axe (Fig. 33).

The high mud walls that surround the fields of the north are gone; in their stead about the farms run wire fences, and these too give place, as one goes farther south, to board or rail or even logs and stumps. Here and there may be seen a stockade of short stout logs set upright in the ground. The railway-station yards are surrounded by fences made of heavy timbers. The northbound freight trains draw flatcars loaded with lumber. The houses, too, change character. Frame structures with shingled roofs replace the characteristic adobe walls and tile roofs of Mediterranean Chile. The homes no longer hide their intimate life behind high walls of mud; light wooden fences of boards or palings are all that shut them off from the curious gaze of the outside world. They draw a thin veil of shrubs and flowers about their nakedness or attempt to conceal themselves in little groves of trees. More significant still from the social viewpoint, the houses have changed in size. A *casa de hacienda* is seldom seen; nor do miserable ranchos of *inquilinos* line the roadside. The medium-sized rural dwellings and their wide distribution over the countryside give the social landscape a different aspect from that of the hacienda-land farther north. This is clearly a country of smaller holdings, of more equal distribution of the land. In a region whose basic wealth is the soil this means less inequality of economic status among the inhabitants. Social and political conditions must follow the lead of this land distribution, and the traveler realizes that he has left the home of the Chilean aristocracy and has moved into provinces marked by far more democratic ways. Natural conditions have placed their distinctive stamp on the life of this southern region, setting it apart from the typical Chile we have seen farther north.

Fig. 33

Fig. 34

FIG. 33—Recently cleared lands in southern Chile, with stumps and girdled trunks not yet removed.

FIG. 34—Farms of south-central Chile. The Malleco Valley, on the border of the formerly forested region.

Land, labor, society, government have a character all their own; and, in consequence, the problems that confront southern Chile are also unique.

In value of its resources the south is probably not a whit inferior to the nitrate regions of the north. Its importance should be more lasting by far. Constituting Chile's one source of forest products, it is now annually yielding over 1,500,000 cubic meters of lumber, whose exploitation represents a capital investment of more than 90,000,000 *pesos*. Its wheat crop amounts to some 10,000,000 bushels, about a third of the total production of the country. It also produces annually (exclusive of the Magallanes region) about 100,000 head of stock,[1] while in the territory about the Strait of Magellan there exist several million head of sheep, yielding an important export of wool and meat. Much of the nation's future prosperity is bound up with progress in this new Chile of the south. The utilization of natural resources here, particularly the land resources, will greatly affect the country as a whole.

There are four distinct phases of the land problem in southern Chile. First and most important today is the question of land titles in the region generally called the *Frontera,* or district beyond the line of old forts that for several centuries guarded the white man's Chile from Araucanian raids. As we have seen, the Bío-Bío River is generally recognized as the northern boundary of this frontier region, but a truer border is the beginning of the heavily forested lands which in turn represent climatic conditions differing from those of central Chile (Fig. 7). This actual border of the Frontera has shifted southward from time to time as both forest and aboriginal forest dweller have been pushed back by white aggression. The Frontera now includes most of the old provinces of Malleco, Cautín, Valdivia, and Llanquihue, the territory

---

[1] Chile: *Anuario Estadístico,* Vol. 7, Agricultura, 1923-1924; Roberto Opazo G.: Desarrollo de territorios al sur del río Bío-Bío, 1920.

of the valiant Araucanians, only recently opened up for settlement. The whole question of titles here is generally referred to as that of the *Propiedad Austral,* to a discussion of which the next chapter will be devoted.

In the same territory is found the second phase of the problem of the south, that of lands still held collectively by the Indians, which will be discussed in Chapter XII.

The third and fourth phases of the problem present themselves southward from the mainland in the island of Chiloé and in the provinces of Aysén and Magallanes. Cut off from the rest of the country, Chiloé has developed difficulties of its own and does not share those of the neighboring region. A heavy forest blankets the surface and has made agricultural progress all but impossible (Chapter XIII).

Beyond Chiloé stretches the long coastal belt now formed into the two provinces of Aysén and Magallanes. Here the main question is that of colonization. Much of the land has not passed definitely into private ownership and is awaiting settlement. Distance, climate, relief, and forest offer difficulties that have hitherto prevented occupation. Before the expanding population of central Chile, however, this region may yet yield a limited area of land for settlement (Chapter XIV).

CHAPTER XI

PROPIEDAD AUSTRAL

Next to the matter of subdividing the haciendas, the feature of Chile's agrarian problem that is of greatest present concern is that of the *Propiedad Austral*. The question of land titles here is acute. While the rural properties of central Chile have long been firmly established and many of them are based on documents that date far back into colonial history, the entire south is disturbed by insecurity of tenures. This situation is profoundly affecting the prosperity of the region, is responsible for a multitude of litigations, occasions violent disputes between rival claimants, and recently resulted in an armed uprising of farmers (June and July, 1934).

The foreign press reported these disturbances as radical revolts against the government. They were really armed protests of farmers who saw the farms and homes established by them on this frontier menaced by what they considered fraudulent claims. The problem was made difficult of solution by a tangle of successive legislative measures enacted in far-away Santiago without much knowledge of the local situation. In 1929 the government had confirmed title to an enormous extent of land, amounting to more than 175,000 hectares (*ca.* 432,000 acres) in the remote upper valley of the Bío-Bío and claimed by a single Chilean hacendado. Much of the area is virtually worthless mountain country, but it contains also a strip of tillable bottom land. The concession was desired obviously for speculation, and there was serious doubt as to the grounds upon which the confirmation had been based. This decree was later suspended at the solicitation of many small holders, who asserted that they were the real occupants of parts of the land, that they had developed there fields and

FIG. 35—Locational map of Chile between the Mataquito River and the island of Chiloé. 1 : 7,800,000.

homes as *bona fide* colonists,[1] and had even received their parcels of land directly from the government. In the political confusion of the last few years the affair apparently had been forgotten. Recently, however, at the behest of the rival claimant, an order for the eviction of these settlers was issued. This brought on the conflict. The group of colonists had in the meantime, perhaps under the leadership of radical agitators, organized into a "syndicate" of several hundred members, had armed themselves, and were ready to defend their holdings. A clash with government police resulted. Other colonists joined the revolt, and there was real fear lest the movement should become general. Several battles were

[1] *La Nación*, March 27 and April 5, 1930; *El Mercurio*, July 3, 1934, p. 3; July 4, p. 19; July 5, p. 19. See also *Bol. del Ministerio de la Propiedad Austral*, Año 1, 1930, No. 2, pp. 42-46.

fought before the uprising was put down. Such armed movements are but outbursts of an unrest that is wide-spread in all the provinces of the Frontera, owing to the same cause: conflicting claims of actual occupants with those who claim legal title.

Early Settlements in Southern Chile

The history of settlement here is very different from that of central Chile. In the latter region the Indians yielded quickly to Spanish conquest, and white occupation was accomplished within a few years. South of the Bío-Bío, owing in part to the prowess of the Araucanians and in part to the existence of extensive forest protection for their defensive warfare, white settlement was suddenly halted. The first few years saw this region penetrated by armed Spanish forces and the land and Indians distributed among the favorites of Valdivia and the crown. The towns of Valdivia, Imperial, Villarica, Angol, and Arauco were founded before the death of Valdivia himself (1553), and within a few years more Osorno, Cañete, Castro (on the island of Chiloé), and a number of forts and smaller settlements.[2] This occupation, however, did not last. Almost the whole of the Araucanian territory was regained by the Indians in repeated attacks and in a general up-rising that took place in the years 1600 to 1602. The inhabitants of all the region south of the Bío-Bío, except Valdivia and Arauco on the mainland and Castro on Chiloé, abandoned their towns and farms and took refuge in central Chile beyond the reach of Araucanian raids. Not for nearly two hundred years were any of these cities reoc-cupied, while some were not restored for another century. Valdivia remained in Spanish hands, its retention made possible by easy access up the river from the coast. Pro-tected by heavy stone fortresses and towers that still stand,

[2] These cities were commonly referred to as the "upper cities" (las ciudades de arriba), i. e., upward in the higher latitudes of the southern hemisphere.

the town and a small surrounding district resisted all Indian attacks, though for several centuries it was necessary to maintain a sea line of supplies (the *real situado*) from the north. A few tiny settlements were made by refugees along the southern coast of the mainland. The rest of the Araucanian territory was definitely surrendered by the whites. Not until after the middle of the eighteenth century was even a line of communication by land established across this Indian territory. The ruins of Osorno and Villarica (the former not more than sixty miles from Valdivia) were overgrown by thick forests and not rediscovered for fully two centuries.

During these two hundred years, though almost constant warfare was kept up between whites and Indians, there was a slow but gradual creep of white population into the fringe of the Indian territory that little by little forced the border southward beyond the line of forts fixed by the Treaty of 1641 along the Bío-Bío. Not, however, until toward the close of the colonial period was any substantial advance made into the Araucanian lands. The latter part of the eighteenth century saw the following towns established south of the Bío-Bío: Los Ánjeles (1742), Nacimiento (1749), Antuco (1756), Santa Bárbara (1758) ; while on the southern margin of the Araucanian territory, Osorno, Río Bueno, and San Pablo were founded, representing white occupation of some of the choicest open grasslands (*llanos*) in the southern forests. Sufficient advance was made in this region by the time of independence to make possible the creation of the two provinces of Chiloé and Valdivia (1826), though the occupied area of each included but a fraction of its present territory.

Advance of Settlement in the Nineteenth Century

Little formal advance was made on either frontier of Araucanía until the middle of the nineteenth century.

White squatters, nevertheless, had been filtering into the Indian territory, settling among the Indians and inter-marrying with them, while Chilean outlaws found the region a haven of safety from prosecution. Little by little the more venturesome of the Araucanians also became accustomed to visit the adjacent white settlements. Thus gradually was weakened the resistance between the two races.

Under the energetic administration of President Manuel Montt the gains made along the two frontiers (north and south of the Araucanian territory) were further advanced and consolidated. A few Germans and other north Euro-peans had found their way into this southern region and had been attracted by the beautiful forest country, its open glades, its fertile soil, its abundant streams, and its mid-latitude climate, where the Chileans had been repelled by these natural conditions. They had secured lands from the Indians or from the government and had induced some of their compatriots to join them. Political conditions in Germany led many of the liberals of that country to seek a home elsewhere, and southern Chile offered them an asylum, as did southern Brazil and the United States. Chilean immigration agents took advantage of the op-portunity to secure some of these intelligent, hard-working, thrifty people to colonize a region which their own citizens had been slow in occupying.[3] At the same time, native colonists were also encouraged to settle in this frontier region. The two national groups entered Araucanía by different avenues. The Germans, coming by ship, landed mainly at Valdivia and the newly created Puerto Montt on the recently explored Gulf of Reloncaví. The Chileans pushed forward by land, advancing southward, step by step, along the plain of the Central Valley. The Germans

[3] To Vicente Pérez Rosales goes much of the credit for the colonization of southern Chile as planned and initiated during the administration of Presi-dent Montt. See his works on the subject: Ensayo sobre Chile, 1859; and Recuerdos del pasado, 1814-1860, published 1910.

were plunged at once into some of the deepest forests;
but they found openings of grassland, as well, that were
more easily farmed, and discovered particularly attractive
sites for their settlements along the shores of Lake Llanquihue. In a climate

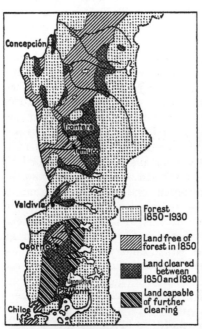

in which roads are dif-
ficult to build, equally
hard to maintain, and
almost impossible to
use during all but a
few months of the
year, travel and trans-
portation could be car-
ried on with little in-
terruption on the lake.
Timber for boat-build-
ing, for houses and
barns, for fences, for
fuel, was abundant.
The soil, though rain-
soaked much of the
year, is fertile and
on the better-drained
slopes well adapted to
cultivation. While the
climate is excessively
rainy, particularly in
winter, it is not greatly
unlike that of the mild-
er parts of northwest-
ern Europe, except
that the winter season

Fig. 36—Map showing the progressive
clearing of the forest in southern Chile.
1: 7,800,000. (Reproduced with permission
of the publishers, from map by Dr. A.
Matthei accompanying *Die Ernährung der
Pflanze*, Vol. 31, No. 18, Sept. 1935).

is less severe. People with the forest economy characteristic
of northern Europe found little difficulty in adjusting themselves to natural conditions in southern Chile. Furthermore
they gloried in the abundance of virgin land, virtually free,

and in the relative independence they found on this distant
frontier. Favored officially on every occasion over the more
or less irregular colonization of native Chileans, they made
this southern land their own. While they gave no place
names to the region and quickly forsook political allegiance
to their homeland, the culture they introduced was distinctly
Teutonic, from the German schools, Lutheran churches,
and *Turnvereine* to dwellings of north-European architec-

Fig. 37—Farm in Cayutué in the lake region of southern Chile. Notice the
high wooden trough that carries water to the wheel of the sawmill to the
right. The river seen is Cayutué which connects Lake Todos los Santos with
Lake Cayutué. (Courtesy of Mr. E. E. Würth, Santiago, Chile.)

ture, immaculately kept homes, long, four-wheeled *Acker-
wagen* along the road, and geese waddling about the
farmyard.

The foreign and Chilean immigration into the extreme
south of the Central Valley, formally begun in 1850, resulted in the founding of many towns during the first few
years (Baja Imperial on the Pacific coast north of Valdivia, 1852; Puerto Montt, 1853; Puerto Varas on Lake
Llanquihue, 1854; Carelmapu on the southern coast facing
the island of Chiloé, 1855; Cancura in the interior south-

ward from Osorno, 1857; and Toltén at the mouth of the Toltén River, 1867). It resulted also in the addition of two new political units to the Chilean republic, the provinces of Arauco (1852) and Llanquihue (1861).

Penetration from the north, mostly Chilean, came more slowly. In fact, it was not until after the Nitrate War (1879-1883) that the movement southward along the Central Valley became of great importance. The armies that returned from Peru were thrown into the conflict on the Frontera, finally breaking the line that the Araucanians had held for centuries. Moreover, the war tore many of the lower-class Chileans loose from their hereditary moorings on haciendas and in the towns of the central provinces and started them on independent careers that carried them to the frontier. Had Chile taken advantage of the situation, she might have settled thousands of these ex-soldiers on lands of their own in the south; but an hacienda-controlled government was more interested in keeping laborers on the estates than attracting them to new regions. As it was, some six thousand colonists (Chilean and foreign) were located on land by government agencies. The clandestine infiltration of Chilean squatters continued, probably bringing many more settlers than those officially established.

HIJUELAS AND LARGE ESTATES

The government attempted to protect the Indians against unfair encroachment of the whites and at the same time to open their unused areas to certain kinds of white settlement. Efforts were made also to prevent unauthorized occupation of lands that were being added to the public domain. The law of 1868 had provided for the establishment of Indians on reservations (*reducciones,* they were called). The rest of the land was to be opened for settlement, the government adding still other areas by purchase from the Indians. To provide against any possible raids by disaffected Araucanians, a line of forts was constructed along the Malleco River, which now became the frontier border. Some of the lands thus secured were divided into *hijuelas,* of twenty hectares (*ca.* 50 acres) in good agricultural zones and forty hectares elsewhere, and sold on easy terms to individuals who would occupy them. Implements, stock, and even supplies for the first year or so were provided in the same manner. This type of holding became the common one, particularly in the Province of Malleco and parts of Cautín. However, as there was no restriction against selling these plots once they were paid for, many of them were promptly disposed of to those who sought to build up haciendas. Throughout this district one finds occasional large farms composed of a number of hijuelas. One southern property with which I became acquainted is typical of such. Its area of 1,546 hectares is made up of three *fundos* combined. One of the three, containing 376 hectares, consists of seventeen hijuelas brought together by purchase, most of them having been incorporated into the present property within ten years of the time they were obtained from the government. A number of them had already changed hands several times before being acquired for this farm. In the Commune of Lonquimai in the upper Bío-Bío Valley—where the recent agrarian uprising, already adverted to, took place—something of this kind was going on. In the District of Rahue of the above commune there were in 1930 25 one-house fundos, four with only two houses, and only one property that could classify as an hacienda. It had 21 houses and 176 persons. As offering a possible explanation of the discontent in the region, it may be noted that in the adjoining District of Lolco, in which the disturbance really had its origin, there are four fundos with 13, 49, 47, and 50 houses respectively. When one remembers that only a few years ago the region was divided into small parcels for settlement by individuals who were willing to face the difficulties of establishing homesteads in this remote valley far back in the Andes, and when one sees that some of these small farms have already been combined into large estates, the cause of dissatisfaction does not seem obscure. Many other districts in the old Araucanian territory present similar situations, but the southern landscape is still characterized by a prevalence of small farms with little of the social organization that marks an hacienda region.

After the period in which there was active colonization on the hijuela basis, legislation was enacted whereby land that had not yet been taken up (and some already occupied by squatters) was offered for sale at auction, generally in blocks of several hundred hectares. This resulted in the accumulation of decidedly larger holdings as well as in active buying for speculation. Still later, large "concessions" were made to individuals who contracted to settle colonists on the land they received but did not always fulfil the terms of the contracts. Some of the concessions still exist, virtually without inhabitants. Their main effect has been to prevent settlement. Some of these holdings appear on the present-day maps as great islands of almost uninhabited lands.

Even if the large holdings are developed, there is no such fixed population as that characterizing the agricultural regions of the center. There are few inquilinos proper in the south. Much of the labor is secured only as needed, particularly at the wheat harvest. It is supplied largely by migrant harvest hands who come in from the provinces of Ñuble and Bío-Bío farther north and from Chiloé in the south. Some landholders attempt to assure a permanent labor supply by inducing workmen to settle on the farms, and advertisements for inquilinos occasionally appear in the southern papers. Where laborers live on the large farms they bear little of the traditional relation to the patrón that exists in central Chile. On the fundo of El Vergel near Angol, now owned and operated by American missionaries, forty per cent of the labor was permanent, but none was definitely contracted. The laborers were paid a cash daily wage varying from a 2.50 summer rate to a 1.50 winter rate (in pesos of about 12 cents each) plus certain perquisites, such as a house, *chacra* (some of them), ration of beans, toasted wheat and bread, and the privilege of pasturing a few head of stock on the farm. This fundo maintained two schools, open without cost to the children of the workmen. It is more customary in the south for the laborers to rent land on shares from the hacienda, and on El Vergel about half the workmen were *medieros* (share renters, croppers) as well. This population (renter and resident laborer) in part takes the place of the inquilinos farther north but is not so permanent. Hence the large holding rather hinders than helps settlement.

Settlement After the Nitrate War (1879-1883)

The advance into northern Araucanía during and after the Nitrate War is represented by the founding of the following towns: Victoria, Temuco, Lautaro, Cholchol, and Carahue (1881); Nueva Imperial, Freire, Pitrufquén, and Maullín (1882); while in 1883 the old site of Villarica was reached, and a new town of the same name established. Reference to Figure 35 shows that the whites had now penetrated into every section of the old Frontera. The Araucanian lands had at last yielded to Chilean occupation. Lines of communication in the form of roads or trails crossed and recrossed this long-defiant region. Small blocks of territory, chiefly in the foothills of the Andes and in the deeper forests, still harbored clusters of Indian families who clung to their native speech, apparel, and customs. But from the centers of Chilean or foreign occupation and along the trails that pierced the forests white settlement was gradually spreading. This influx of popu-

lation led to the organization of three new Chilean provinces in this period, each one representing a southward
march of the frontier. Bío-Bío was created in 1875, thus
adding most of the drainage area of the Bío-Bío River as
far as its southern tributary, the Renaico. By 1887 the
resistance of the Araucanians had finally ceased and settlement had penetrated their territory sufficiently to warrant
the formation of the remaining area into the two provinces
of Malleco and Cautín, the latter extending southward
to meet the territory of Valdivia. Thus the whole of the
Frontera was incorporated in the organized national
domain.

The relative ease with which much of the northernmost
region (particularly in Malleco) could be mapped—since
some of it contained extensive grasslands, although other
districts were forested—made possible here more careful
surveys and more accurate determination of property
bounds than farther south. Wherever this was possible,
it has greatly simplified the matter of land titles. A Chilean
statesman writes: " The law of property is almost perfect
in Malleco." [4] Had colonization in the region farther south
been handled as effectively, there would not now exist
the difficult problem of the Propiedad Austral.

Settlers have continued to move slowly but steadily into
this southern region. The 1930 census gave the following
figures for the population of the political units carved out
of former Araucanian territory:

Province of Bío-Bío	180,688
Province of Cautín	383,791
Province of Valdivia	236,115
Province of Llanquihue [5]	92,528
Total	893,122

[4] Edwards (Agustín): My Native Land, 1928, p. 188.
[5] Before 1927 the Province of Llanquihue, now a department of the Province
of Chiloé.

A large part of this population represents actual migration from the north-central provinces. The movement of the Chilean people southward has been slow and largely unauthorized, hence it has not attracted much attention; but it has been substantial. In fact, it represents a migration not unlike in proportions that which carried the inhabitants of the Atlantic seaboard in the United States across the Appalachians into the Mississippi basin. In Chile the movement involved not far from a fifth of the entire population. During some years it brought about an actual decline in the population of several of the older provinces.

Foreign Colonization of the Frontera

The colonization of the Frontera, as has been seen, has not been by Chileans alone. Foreigners of several nationalities joined in the movement. German, Swiss, English, French, and Spanish colonists penetrated the Araucanian country and established farms. Some of the new arrivals were officially located by the government; others, from families already settled in the ports, cities, and mines farther north, secured lands on an equal footing with their Chilean neighbors. Traveling through the old Araucanian territory, one not infrequently comes upon farms whose owners bear such names as Turner, Shaw, Smith, Williams, MacDonald, Bunster, Depallens, Dumay, Ravet, Keller, Rossellot, etc. Some of these families have become quite Chilean, some keep in contact with others of their nationality and retain much of their European heritage. Present statistics (1930) show only 9,808 foreigners in this region, but a count including descendants of recent immigrants would probably raise the figure to 30,000 or 35,000. The largest foreign national group at present is the German with 3,000; the Spanish follow with 1,819; the French show 819; the Italians 596; the Swiss 593. There are also several hundred from Palestine and Syria, nearly as many British, with Austrians, Dutch, Czechslovaks, Yugoslavs, and others in smaller number.

Though in recent years, as Mark Jefferson [6] has pointed out, greatly outnumbered by Chileans who have followed them into this region, the Germans continue as a dominating influence, particularly about Valdivia and Lake Llanquihue. It is a curious sight on this lake to see the small freight boats that ply its waters, each commanded by a German captain, filled with German passengers picked up as the vessel stops at wharves built out from German farms, while the crew that loads and unloads the heavy cargo and carries the luggage of the passengers is composed entirely of Chileans. On one trip across the lake a lone Chilean traveler from the northern provinces was the only non-German person (except myself) other than the crew. Among the passengers, he was the foreigner. To him it seemed strange that here in this part of his native land foreigners were the commanding and his fellow countrymen the serving class. It is this situation that has made the foreign element seem so conspicuous in the southern provinces, out of all proportion to its numbers. Whether in the cities or on the farms, foreigners are in command. The Chileans are mainly laborers, retail merchants, small proprietors, or government employees more or less temporarily located there. While the native Chilean element is steadily growing stronger, the situation remains much as it was in 1903, when all but two of the 34 fundos in the Commune of Valdivia valued at over 40,000 pesos belonged to men with foreign (chiefly German) names, such names as Roepk, Schuler, Anwandter, Hoffman, and Kuntsmann predominating.[7] As late as 1925 only five of the 36 important fundos in that commune were not owned by men with German names.[8] Much the same situation prevails

[6] Jefferson: Recent Colonization in Chile, 1921, pp. 8-12.
[7] Espinoza: Diccionario geográfico, 1903.
[8] Valenzuela O.: Álbum de informaciones agrícolas, 1925.

at Puerto Montt and Puerto Varas. Other communes of the south are not so thoroughly dominated by foreign elements, but relatively few of the larger rural properties or of the important business concerns in southern Chile belong to men of Chilean extraction.

SQUATTER COLONIZATION OF THE FRONTERA

The country into which the movement of settlers, foreign and Chilean, took place, was largely an uncharted wilderness. Part of it had never been explored. The 100,000 Araucanians who lived in little clusters of thatched houses widely separated in the forest, though no longer actively resistant, were still resentful of the intrusion of the whites. Scattered throughout the region, also, were whites who had forced their way into the Indian territory and had settled there in violation of treaty and law. Some of these, refugees from justice or from social ostracism in the provinces farther north, true frontier desperados with reputations that reached as far as Santiago, lived by plundering the Indians or the white settlements nearest the Araucanian border. They constituted one of the dangers against which travelers were warned as late as the beginning of the twentieth century. Others were merely adventurers, seeking a liberty unknown in the established society of central Chile or an opportunity for acquiring land by the simple process of occupying it. Some, mere " rotos " in their early days, had grown rich in lands and cattle. There must have been several thousand such intruders before the first formal settlement took place, for the earliest colonists found them at many points. By the time the last provinces of southern Chile were created, there were probably many thousand more. Though their presence was unrecognized by government, and though their holdings had no legal status, these settlers were real pioneers. They had blazed the trails through the deep forests, building crude bridges across the streams and laying plank roads in the boggy woods; they had learned the secret of clearing the damp timber by fire and girdling the trees too big to burn; they had made friends with the fierce Araucanians or fought them off, not infrequently intermarrying with the Indian families and raising families of half-breed children; they had overcome some of the Indian's opposition to the whites or worn down that opposition by persistently refusing to be driven out. They had learned to substitute lumber for adobe as building material for house and fence (Fig. 38), and had discovered what crops could best be grown in the cloudy weather and soggy soil found in most of the region; they had learned how to survive the dangers, real and imagined, of a vast forest and the rigors of an excessively rainy climate feared by all their ancestors.

GOVERNMENTAL LAND POLICIES

When the government undertook the formal colonization of this region there were several methods by which land might be obtained. It might be received directly from the government, usually by outright gift conditional upon effective " proving up," but in later years more commonly by purchase at public auction; it might be obtained from the Indians, generally by purchase approved by a government official; it might be bought from the white settlers already there, some of whom laid claim to extensive holdings; or, finally, it might be secured in the same way by which most of these earliest pioneers had secured it, by merely occupying what no one else was using or had laid claim to. Though the government recognized only the first two methods, it proved impossible to prevent land from falling into private hands in irregular ways. Large extensions of land were bought from the Indians without the formality of government approval. In such transactions the Indians frequently suffered fraud or not uncommonly sold lands not belonging to them. Speculation was the motive for some of this irregular acquisition, but many of the lands obtained were actually settled by the new owners. All of these provinces show a decided growth in population during these years, Valdivia, for example, rising from 8,860 in 1835 to 53,090 in 1875, and 133,443 in 1907. Most of this increase was due to migration from the provinces farther north, a large part of it wholly spontaneous ; and much of the new population settled on what the government considered public domain without troubling to secure deeds from government officials.

By 1851 the colonization agent who was seeking lands for German immigrants reported that " the State, which with just title should be considered owner of the larger part of the lands in Chiloé and Valdivia, has today no more than exceedingly small areas in both of these provinces." [9] Similar observations were made regarding lands in the Province of Llanquihue. Even those that were left were of uncertain size and bounds. In the Province of Arauco the government (1853) retained only 13,654 *cuadras* [10] (*ca.* 54,616 acres, the area of a fairly large fundo). In the other southern provinces the public domain disappeared in much the same fashion. While this has seriously embarrassed the government in its plans for systematic colonization, it must be recognized that it represents, in most parts of the Frontera, a spontaneous movement of Chilean people in search of better living conditions than those found in the older sections of the country. Unfortunately it left the settlers with no formal recognition on the part of authority and with no regular titles for their holdings.

Since most of this frontier region was not surveyed or mapped, demarcation of individual properties was necessarily imperfect. The *intendente* of the Province of

[9] Donoso and Velasco: Propiedad Austral, 1928, p. 107.
[10] *Ibid.*, p. 39.

Valdivia reported in 1857 that the boundaries consist of "imaginary lines which traverse dense woods where the foot of man was never set." [11] Others were completely unmarked, not even the approximate extent being known. The properties of the white settlers were little better defined than those of the Indians. To add to the confusion of titles, some of the Indians who held land collectively [12] had pretended to sell their parcels. This was quite contrary to the Indian concept of property rights, and they not only could not give proper deeds to the lands they sold but in many cases could not even give possession.

The government has generally taken a generous attitude regarding irregularly constituted properties. There has been for the most part no disposition to dispossess *bona fide* settlers. On the contrary, there has been a desire to rectify conditions and not to disturb those who have enjoyed possession for "a long time," have held properties for three generations or as a result of three transfers of ownership, or have made improvements sufficient to evince an intention to occupy the lands as permanent homesteads.[13] In some cases, however, in order to obtain suitable land for its formal colonies, the government has evicted numbers of squatters, even ousting Chileans from holdings they had improved to make place for foreign colonists.[14] So long as there was an abundance of land in proportion to the population, and so long as transfers were not extensively made, this indefiniteness of boundaries and titles had little serious effect; but with the continued immigration into the southern provinces and with repeated transfers of properties the situation has become greatly aggravated.

[11] *Ibid.*, p. 19.

[12] See the discussion of Indian holdings in Chapter XII, below.

[13] Instructions given to the government agent who was seeking fiscal lands on which to locate the German colonists (Donoso and Velasco: *op. cit.*, p. 98).

[14] Jefferson: *op. cit.*, pp. 37-39 and 46-49; Palacios: Raza chilena, 1904, pp. 613ff.

Fig. 38

Fig. 39

Fig. 38—Settler's house in southern Chile, near Temuco, showing development of a forest economy. Note use of wood for house and fence.

Fig. 39—Indian houses and lands near Temuco. Originally little of the
Araucanian land was fenced, but the introduction of stock has made it necessary to protect the fields.

FIG. 40—The edge of the forest in southern Chile, near Valdivia, in 1903. Much of this land has now been cleared and settled.

Since 1900 the southward movement of native Chilean settlement has been going on with increasing momentum. In 1903, when the railway was built through this territory from north to south, the writer traveled on the first through train and found the country, except for a few localities such as Temuco, Valdivia, Osorno, and Puerto Montt, an almost uninterrupted forest in which few inhabitants other than Indians were seen (Fig. 40). Recent tours made through the same country have shown large parts of it cleared, fenced, and cultivated; and in one railway journey through the whole of the old Araucanian territory not a single Indian, at least in native costume, was seen. One is reminded of the rapid transformation of eastern Oklahoma that followed the opening of that district to white settlement.

THE MINISTRY OF THE PROPIEDAD AUSTRAL

In the problems presented to the government, however, this southward movement more resembles the expansion of the American colonies into the trans-Allegheny territory; for settlement here, as was the case there, has far outrun government provision for it. From the irregularities resulting from this spontaneous and largely undirected movement of the Chilean population into their southland has grown the now vexing problem of the Propiedad Austral. In 1929 there were estimated to be some 47,000 properties in the southern provinces, involving about 20,-000,000 hectares (*ca.* 77,200 square miles), whose titles were in doubt.[15] In addition to the inconvenience of uncertain titles and indefinite bounds, the situation gave occasion for many abuses. It seemed that no property was safe. False claims were rife and could not be successfully contested. Even the laborers, both Indians and whites,

[15] Preamble to Decreto número 4,770 creating the Ministerio de la Propiedad Austral, October 31, 1929 (Chile: *Diario Oficial de la República de Chile*, Año 52, Núm. 15,513, November 4, 1929, p. 6143).

took advantage of the helpless condition of landowners. It became a common practice for a workman to get himself established as renter, hired laborer, or inquilino on a farm, and then assert a claim to the land he occupied, knowing that the proprietor could establish no conclusive evidence of ownership. The confusion regarding titles resulted in frequent violence, sometimes on a large scale. So profoundly was this affecting the prosperity of the region that after eight different laws had failed to solve the difficulty and the problem seemed too extensive for ordinary court procedure, the unusual measure was adopted of creating a special cabinet department to deal with the situation. This Ministry, entitled that of the Propiedad Austral,[16] was to attempt to bring order out of existing chaos in the matter of land titles and bounds. Organized with a surveying division and a department of justice, the newly created Ministry at once set about its task, not in the capital as is frequently customary, but on the field, through eight officers in as many southern cities. The aim was primarily to put property titles there on a sound basis rather than, as had been the case in other such attempts, to recover for the government lands irregularly obtained. The several laws and decrees dealing with this matter provided that all land titles in the southern provinces were to be filed (many of them never had been); owners of land who lacked documents but who could prove their legal rights were to be accorded deeds; and squatters' claims to the lands they occupied were to be recognized by acceptance of actual occupation for a period of ten years and due improvement of the property in lieu of formal deeds.[17]

[16] Decreto Núm. 4,770 (Chile: *op. cit.*, pp. 6143-6144).
[17] Decreto Núm. 171, Jan. 8, 1929, and Ley No. 4,660, Sept. 25, 1929 (Chile: *Diario Oficial*, Año 52, Núm. 15,483, Sept. 27, 1929, pp. 5307-5308).

The Establishment of Titles

The Ministry of Propiedad Austral, after lasting for less than a year, ceased to exist when the Ibáñez government was overthrown, but in that time it made a substantial contribution in the establishment of hundreds of titles, covering many thousands of hectares. It granted " definite titles " to some whose documents were faulty, recognized the validity of the holdings of others, and sold to others at low cost the land they had been occupying irregularly. Most of the properties to which titles were given in any one of the three ways were less than 100 hectares (247 acres) in extent, and the greater part were lands occupied by Chileans. In the published lists there were, however, many German names, while a few English, Italians, and other foreigners were also included.[18] With the restoration of liberal government under Alessandri the work has been continued under the Ministry of Lands and Colonization. During 1933 " definite titles " to their lands were granted to 3,019 families, covering 58,000 hectares, the validity of 498 titles to 261,204 hectares was recognized, and 8,863 hectares were sold to colonists. Provisional titles were extended to 131 families.[19]

These properties are being surveyed and mapped as their titles are being awarded. The Inspección General de Colonización e Inmigración has charge of this and has done some excellent work.[20] The process, though slow, should in a few years more remove most of the complicated problems of the old Frontera region. An orderly system such as this, adopted when settlement began in the south and carried on as new lands were opened up, would have

[18] Partial lists as published in *La Nación*, April 27, and May 9; *Bol. del Ministerio de la Propiedad Austral*, Año 1, 1930, Nos. 1-5; particularly Año 1, No. 5, p. 30.

[19] President Alessandri's message to Congress, May 21, 1934 (*La Nación*, May 22, 1934, p. 25).

[20] Carta general de colonización de la Provincia de Cautín, scale 1: 100,000, Santiago, 1916; Carta catastral de la Provincia de Malleco (same scale), Santiago, 1917; and others.

avoided most of the uncertainty now involving property claims. But the opposition of the Indians to the presence of all whites in their territory made this difficult if not impossible, while forests and rainy weather added further obstacles. Furthermore, the influential hacendados of central Chile, who controlled the government, were not greatly interested in efficient colonization that would win their laborers away from them. Out of these causes arose the muddle of land titles that has so perplexed the south.

NEED FOR SECURITY OF TITLES

It is important to Chile that the problem of the Propiedad Austral be solved as rapidly as possible. The area must be freed from the incubus of uncertain titles, or its development cannot proceed as it should. This can be accomplished, it would seem, only by carrying on the policy of recognizing effective and *bona fide* occupation as equivalent to a title, an orderly recording of deeds as issued, and a careful mapping of the whole territory and in particular of the lands to which deeds are given. This last is, perhaps, the most important. Since there are so many small properties, the number of boundaries is greatly multiplied, with a consequent increase of causes for disputes. There would seem to be no way of fixing these numerous property lines except by a careful and accurate mapping of the region. The pioneering citizens of the south, who have reclaimed a wilderness and are making it into one of the most attractive regions of the country, deserve the guarantee of secure land titles from their government.

Furthermore, to an outsider regarding Chile's slow but steady advance toward democracy during a century of independence, it would seem indispensable that the policy of forming small properties be continued in the little government land still left and that these properties be protected. The transformation of central Chile and its haciendas into anything like a fully democratic society will probably be a long and difficult task. The south suffers no such handicap. Its preservation as a land of small holdings will give to the nation a guarantee of a large body of independent middle-class citizens. The south should be the bulwark of Chile's democratic institutions. Without a secure title, however, the land of the small proprietor is in danger of being lost and of being incorporated into large haciendas. Without such small holdings democratic society can hardly survive. The most vital phase of the land problem in southern Chile is the menace to her agrarian basis for democracy.

CHAPTER XII

SUBDIVISION OF INDIAN COMMUNITY LANDS

Closely coupled with the problem of the *Propiedad Austral* is that of land still belonging to the Indians in the provinces of the old *Frontera*. The amount is not large now, but the time is thought to have come when it must be put on the same basis as other lands in the republic. The Indian, as a separate racial group, has almost disappeared: he is fast becoming amalgamated with the rest of the Chilean people. He is no longer to be treated as a minor, nor are his lands to be regarded as different from those of others. The hundred thousand Araucanians are to be incorporated as rapidly as possible into Chilean national life. To this end their lands are being individualized, any residue to be disposed of as public domain.

THE ARAUCANIAN SYSTEM OF LAND TENURE

The Araucanian system of land tenure was originally much like that of natives in other parts of the country. It was a typical American Indian system, in general character resembling that of the Aztecs, Mayas, and Quechuas, but more closely paralleling that of the Iroquois or Choctaws, who lived in a somewhat similar natural environment. The Araucanians were an agricultural people; tilling the soil was their chief means of making a living. They also raised stock but never developed pastoral economy. They raised (and still raise) corn, potatoes, and other crops for their own use and, since coming into contact with Europeans, have taken to producing wheat for sale. Small kinship groups claimed exclusive right to the areas occupied by them for pastoral or agricultural purposes.

Such rights existed, however, only so long as the land was in use. In case the site was abandoned, another group might occupy it. Within the group domain each family might use for agriculture whatever it needed that was not utilized by another. The rest of the land was public range and used by all in common. There does not seem to have existed any system of periodical redistribution of agricultural plots, as had become the custom in Mexico and Peru. It is even doubtful if any fixed practice of inheriting individual holdings had become established, though probably a family remained in possession as long as it desired. There was an abundance of land; new fields could be made whenever necessary; fences, if built at all, were simple and easily made; there was no need for irrigation; apparently natural glades were used rather than artificial clearings; hence the little investment of labor and the few improvements made gave little warrant for permanent rights to a particular piece of land. After the Conquest, and possibly also before it, the chiefs (*caciques*) held the lands of their respective family groups, but these were thought of as collective holdings, neither the chiefs nor any one else having the right to alienate them.[1]

RESERVATION OF INDIAN LANDS

The government of Chile has respected this native concept of property, as have other nations including the United States. When systematic colonization of the Araucanian

[1] Some have thought that the Indians of Chile before the Conquest held, bought, and rented land virtually as allodial. The evidence of this does not seem conclusive to most of those who are familiar with the American Indian's concept of property. For a discussion of this question as it applies to Chile see R. E. Latcham: Organización social, 1924, pp. 245-868; the same: La existencia de la propiedad, 1923; R. A. Latcham (hijo): La propiedad entre los indios del valle central de Chile, 1922, pp. 17-20; Guevara: Historia de la civilización de la Araucanía, 1898-1912; the same: Las últimas familias i costumbres araucanas, 1913. A critical discussion of aboriginal Mexican land systems is found in Bandelier's " On the Distribution and Tenure of Lands, and the Customs with Respect to Inheritance Among the Ancient Mexicans," 1878, pp. 385-448.

territory was undertaken, the land actually occupied by the various Indian kinship groups was set aside by special grant (*título de merced*) as reservations (*reducciones*) for their exclusive use. To each chief was assigned the land upon which he and his people lived, with as much more as was considered necessary. This he was to hold according to Araucanian custom in his own name but for the use of his entire family group. These groups were usually not large, ranging normally from five to ten families. The members lived in little clusters of houses, too small and too widely spaced to constitute villages. The Araucanians have never formed compact settlements. Each family group lived apart from the rest, commonly at a distance of a mile or more from others, apparently preferring to be out of sight of other groups. The population of Araucanía was thus widely disseminated over a large extent of land.

The area of the reducciones varied greatly, depending mainly on the number of families to be provided for. When they were first established, there was no scarcity of land for individuals or groups, but as the whites continued to move into the Indian territory some of the reserves were encroached upon until there were left but a few hectares of pasture and tillable land to each family. The Indians frequently complained that they lacked enough room for their cattle and their fields, one old chief saying that his people were all pressed together (*apretados*) like the grains on an ear of corn. On the other hand, they did not produce on a large scale, and on many of the reducciones there was land that was not in use. With each advance of white colonists the government has sought more land for settlement and in particular any parts of the Indian reservations that were not being used. To this end legislation has been enacted at various times (notably in 1866, 1874, 1927, 1928, 1929, and 1930) seeking to divide the collective holdings of the Araucanians, to assign adequate lands in severalty to each individual of the kinship group, and to dispose of any remainder for white colonization.[2] The Araucanians, though at first strongly opposed to the breaking up of their communal holdings, have at last recognized for the most part that there is no other way to prevent the complete loss of their lands. They realize that they must stand on an equal footing with other citizens of the republic.

In a general congress of Araucanians, which I attended in 1930 on the historic battleground of Boroa not far from the center of the old Araucanía, the problem of protecting their lands was one of the matters most eagerly discussed. Some six thousand of these distinguished Indian caciques and their followers came long distances to attend these gatherings. Most of them arrived on horseback (Fig. 42), many with splendid mounts. Some came in ox-drawn two-wheeled carts (Fig. 43). They built arbors for their families and a great central one for the meetings. Dressed in the typical fast-disappearing Araucanian costumes, men, women, and children spent four days in the encampment, daily discussing in long-drawn-out but thoughtful addresses the problems which their race was confronting in its new rôle as a body of Chilean citizens. The meetings were preceded by a martial parade of thousands of mounted men who, first at a walk and then at a gallop of thundering hoofs, reminded themselves and the few white spectators that the Araucanians of the old days still lived. A quiet respectful Indian religious ceremonial then followed, after which the assembly settled down to a consideration of their serious problems. The discussions were conducted with dignity and decorum and gave one the impression that the republic was receiving a most valuable contingent of new citizens, not only for their well-known valor in warfare but also for the sobriety and intelligence

[2] Chile: Ley número 4,169 y reglamento sobre división de comunidades y radicación de indígenas, 1928; and Ley número 4,802, in *Bol. del Ministerio de la Propiedad Austral*, Año 1, 1930, No. 2, pp. 8-16.

with which they considered their new duties and responsibilities. In resolutions adopted by them and sent to the president and the Minister of the Propiedad Austral, they respectfully urged that their race should be given the full protection of the law, particularly against illegal encroachment on their lands, and that the partitioning of the reducciones should be carried on with no further relaxing of protective measures.

Subdivision of Indian Lands

The process of subdividing the community lands and assigning them in severalty has advanced rapidly in recent years. Government offices (*Juzgados de Indios*) have been established in five of the southern cities (Victoria, Temuco, Nueva Imperial, Pitrufquén, and Valdivia), each authorized to carry out this individualization of Indian land. Early legislation (1866) had provided that a reducción should be subdivided individually at the request of one-eighth of its members. Many Indians had asked that this subdivision be carried out and had received their lands in severalty; but in 1928 there were 3,278 of these collective holdings still in existence, affecting 80,661 persons and consisting of 503,343 hectares (1,243,760 acres) valued at 150,000,000 pesos.[3] The new laws and new conditions in the south have accelerated the process. By 1930, according to the census, 1,768 more had been subdivided, leaving but 1,510 still to be partitioned. Those still in existence were distributed among the southern provinces as follows:[4]

Cautín	1,308
Valdivia	105
Bío-Bío	82
Concepción	10
Chiloé (all on the mainland)	5
	1,510

[3] Chile: *Memoria del Ministerio de Fomento,* 1928, p. 196.
[4] *X Censo de la Población* (1930), published 1931, Vol. 1, pp. 297-298.

FIG. 41

FIG. 42

FIG. 43

FIG. 41—Indian wheat fields near Temuco.

FIGS. 42 and 43—Araucanians gathered at Boroa to discuss the loss of their lands and other problems brought about by the opening up of their territory to white settlement.

The departments showing the largest number of these collective holdings were those of Temuco (with 400), Nueva Imperial (with 351), and Valdivia (with 303), all of them districts of the more dense Indian population and more complete conservation of aboriginal civilization. Each year brings further reductions of such holdings. In 1933 there were 38 of them, containing 14,716 hectares divided into 830 family hijuelas; and 170 others covering 45,341 hectares were surveyed preparatory to a subdivision to be carried out in 1934. That this is not purely an attempt to take more lands away from the Araucanians is evidenced by the fact that in one year (1928) over a million hectares of land illegally occupied by whites were restored to aboriginal holdings.[5] Some Indians also are given holdings from the public domain. In 1933, 45 received such lands, amounting to 3,146 hectares in all. It is an effort to put all property upon an individual basis by doing away with collective holdings, and thus to make possible a tax income for the government and municipalities estimated at about 1,000,000 pesos a year.[6] The Indians will suffer exploitation under such a modification of their traditional system of land tenure in spite of the provision that they may not dispose of their holdings for ten years. The change, however, seems inevitable, and, since many of the Araucanians are becoming educated, have adopted European ways, and are already carrying on successful farming, they may fare no worse than under the former protected arrangement. They still hold some of the best land on the Frontera, and many of them should be able to compete with the whites on equal terms (Figs. 39 and 41). The abolition of their agrarian communities is, however, an important event in the history of Chile, representing the virtual extinction of the long-maintained Araucanian independence as well as the disappearance of the last remnant of lands available for settlement north of the archipelago and the Province of Magallanes.

[5] Chile: *Memoria del Ministerio de Fomento,* 1928, p. 196.
[6] *Ibid.,* p. 197.

CHAPTER XIII

CHILOÉ'S STRUGGLE WITH THE FOREST

To one who has not visited the island of Chiloé it seems strange that the nation should still be talking of its colonization. For four centuries there has been no human resistance to such settlement. The native people of the island were weak in numbers and in spirit. They offered no such opposition as did the Araucanians on the adjoining mainland. True, their island position isolated them, but it also exposed them to easy attack on the part of the invading Spaniards. Furthermore, it separated them from the Araucanians and prevented their making common cause with those stout defenders of their native territory. In fact, the people of Chiloé yielded to the very first assault on the part of the Spaniards and became at once a subject people, their lands open to whatever use the invaders might care to make of them.

Retarded Colonization of Chiloé

Yet in four hundred years the white man has hardly got a foothold on this island. Only about one-tenth of its area has been occupied. Chiloé figures among the least inhabited sections of the country, its density of population being a little more than six to the square mile. There are but two towns of more than 2,000 persons each, less than a score of villages whose inhabitants number 500, and the rural population is exceedingly sparse. In 1930 the total population for the main island and the neighboring islands to the east and south was but 90,971. The occupied land on the main island is limited almost entirely to a fringe along one coast, and the greater part of the island remains today as little developed and as little occupied by man as in the days before the discovery of America.

The reason that colonization in Chiloé has been almost at a standstill for four centuries seems to be found in nature rather than in man. It is the forest that has resisted. The history of settlement here has been chiefly that of a struggle with the forest. One has but to see the island to appreciate this fact. The forest is Chiloé's greatest problem. It affects the life of her people, the development of her resources, the part she plays (or does not play) in national affairs, more vitally, it seems to me, than anything else. For centuries this has been the problem that nature has presented to man in his attempt to gain a foothold on this island. Until this problem is solved (if indeed it can be solved) Chiloé can hope to be little more than she is at present—an outlying province of slight significance in the number of its inhabitants or in its importance to the nation.

Topography, Climate and Vegetation

The island of Chiloé, Chile's principal insular possession, is about 90 miles long by 35 miles wide (*ca.* 145 by 56 kilometers). Its position, stretching from latitude 41° 50′ S. to 43° 20′ S., corresponds to the coast of northern California and southern Oregon. The backbone of the island, the western part, consists of a southward extension of Chile's Coast Range, much broken by transverse valleys and nowhere more than 1,000 meters (3,281 ft.) in elevation. The eastern two-thirds of the island is mainly a gently rolling plain, apparently (with the numerous islets that lie east of Chiloé) a continuation of the great Central Valley of Chile, which here has become broken into many segments by the invasion of waves and currents through such gaps as the Chacao Channel, north of Chiloé. The Isla Mayor (as the Chileans often call the island of Chiloé to distinguish it from other smaller neighbors) contains the larger part of this residual Central Valley floor, but the islands in the gulfs of Reloncaví and of Ancud are also remnants of the same feature and show on their surfaces much the same contours as are seen in the Central Valley. The cliffed shores of these islands seem to give evidence also in their structure and material that the islands are but the residual blocks left by progressive action of currents and waves. Most of the Chiloé section of this plain is between 100 and 200 meters in elevation. The island thus presents no very formidable topographic barriers and would seem to lend itself as well to agricultural development as the central plain farther north.

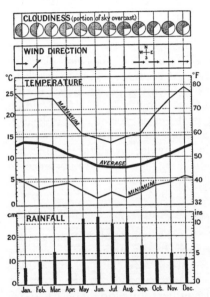

FIG. 44—Climatic graph for Ancud. Based on W. W. Reed: Climatological Data for Southern South America, *Monthly Weather Review*, Supplement No. 32, 1929.

The climate, as would be expected in such a location, is mild throughout the year and excessively rainy. The summers are cool, while the winters seldom show freezing temperatures; a winter mean of about 7° C. (45° F.) being typical and a summer mean of 15° C. (59° F.). Exposed throughout the year to the full force of rain-bearing winds, from the west and northwest in particular, the island gets a rainfall amounting to more than

80 inches (2,032 mm.). This is not concentrated in any one season, as is the case in central Chile with its Mediterranean climate, but falls during the whole year in rather even distribution (Fig. 44). In fact not only every season but every month in Chiloé is rainy. Precipitation is heavier in winter months; June, July, and August often showing as many as fifteen rainy days each and not infrequently even more. The summer months have almost as many. One year is on record in which three months showed respectively 24, 25, and 26 rainy days.[1]

Under such climatic conditions one is not surprised to find a rank growth of vegetation. Chiloé is almost completely forest covered. While some of the small islands that lie to the leeward show much land that is now clear of timber and perhaps has always been so, there is little of the main island that does not have a heavy forest. The west coast and the mountains are blanketed with an almost impenetrable growth. Even the sections that lie behind the wind shield of the Coast Range are also heavily timbered.

The trees of which this forest consists are predominantly broad-leaved evergreens. In this land of little seasonal rhythm the vegetation takes on something of a tropical character in that, though not coniferous, its trees retain their foliage throughout the year. Many of these belong to families which in middle latitudes are known as deciduous, but here they have developed a character in harmony with the climate and stay green at all seasons. Among the most common trees are the *alerce* (*Fitzroya patagonica*), the *ulmo* which the Chilotes call the *muermo* (*Eucryphia cordifolia*), the *ciprés* (*Libocedrus chilensis;* Chilean arborvitæ) and the *roble* (*Nothofagus obliqua;*

[1] The stormy character of the weather may be appreciated from the following data given as typical: number of days in a year marked by *tempestad* (tempest), 17; *temporal* (storm), 25; *chubasco* (squall), 93; *lluvia* (rain), 108; *nublados* (cloudy weather), 20; *variables* (variable weather), 93; *sol* (sun), 51 (Weber: Chiloé, 1903, p. 17).

Antarctic oak). There are also many *avellanos,* or filberts (*Guevina avellana*), *canelos,* or cinnamon trees, and *tepus* (*Tepualia stipularis*). Most of these are broad-leaved but evergreen. They all grow to large size. The alerce in particular is an imposing tree. It has been known to reach a height of 150 feet (46 meters) and a diameter of from 10 to 15 feet. Others are not far inferior in size. Along the coast the best of these great trees have now been cut, but many large ones are still to be found in the interior. Even near the coast the forest contains some magnificent specimens.

In spaces among the large trunks of the varieties mentioned there grows a mass of small trees, vines, and shrubs. The most common plant here is the *quila,* a Chilean bamboo, which grows to heights of 15 to 20 feet and forms almost impenetrable masses of intertwined growth. These and other small fast-growing plants contribute greatly to making the forest difficult to clear and in rendering it an obstacle to all penetrations from the coast.

INDIAN SETTLEMENTS

Man lived in Chiloé long before the advent of the white race. There is some evidence that a colony of Peruvian Indians, perhaps a *mitimaya,*[2] was established there, and some have supposed that Chiloé's chief crop, the potato, was introduced into the island at this time. The district was too far away, however, and too isolated by the sea and by the forests on the adjoining land for extensive modification to be made either by an increased number of inhabitants or by the introduction of many cultural features from Inca Land. Even earlier than this the island had supported an aboriginal population sufficient at least to attract the attention of these conquerors. The Indians

[2] A group of subjects transplanted into a newly conquered region to prevent uprisings and also to diffuse their culture.

of Chiloé in those remote times were able to make little headway into the interior. Without iron they found it difficult to clear the ground, nor could they burn the wet forest to make land available. They held but a slight hold on the land and had developed only a simple form of communal tenure. They lived close to the sea, produced meager crops of maize, potatoes, and quinoa, supplementing these food articles with fish and shell-fish found along the shore. As would be expected under such conditions, they were expert seamen, making boats (*bongos*) of hollowed trunks or from the large boards split from alerce logs. They were accustomed to travel from their island home to adjoining islands of the archipelago, as also to the mainland.

THE SPANISH RÉGIME

The Spaniards approached the settlement of Chiloé handicapped by a heritage of life in a nearly treeless land. They were unfamiliar with forests, unattracted by forest conditions, indeed fearful of and unprepared to cope with the difficulties a forested land presented, nor did they feel need for the timber resources that a forest land affords. Coming from a Mediterranean climate and a country largely devoid of timber, they found central Chile with its similar climatic conditions and even the small irrigable valleys of the northern desert more to their liking than the heavily wooded lands that occupy the southern part of the country. These colonizers from old Spain thus generally shunned such areas as Chiloé, leaving them to the same fate as the other forested lands of the south.

Some effort, it is true, was made to conquer this outlying island and to establish settlements on it. Moving southward by sea or following along the coast on land, the Spaniards crossed the narrow Chacao Channel, utilizing the native boats for the soldiers and forcing the horses to swim the distance of more than a mile to the island. Outposts were established at several points along the shores of Chiloé, settlements that survive to the present day, though they have grown very slowly. The Spaniards even went so far as to partition the lands of the island among those who took part in the conquest. They gave little heed to the aboriginal claims to certain fields the Indians had cleared and kept clear from the rank growth of timber that covered the rest of the land; but they divided the greater part of the island into large sections and distributed these, with their inhabitants, as *encomiendas*. By this system the native population was brought into subjection to the conquerors and the Spanish crown. However, the system did not accomplish much toward the actual settlement of the island. The native inhabitants were overcome, it is true, and the island was definitely incorporated into the colonial system of Spain; but the recipients of the encomiendas gave little attention to occupying their concessions and settlement of the island was but slightly affected.

In addition to these great concessions, grants of land alone were given later (chiefly in the period 1670-1696), the size of these *mercedes,* as they were usually called, being from 50 to 80 *cuadras* (*ca.* 200 to 320 acres). In a few cases grants of 300, 400, or even 1,000 cuadras were made.[3] Some few Spanish colonists were brought into the island by such measures, but those who actually occupied their lands did little more than settle down to a life similar to that of the aborigines. Contact between island and mainland remained slight; no roads were cut through the forests to connect the scattered settlements, communication still being limited to a coastwise navigation or to travel along the natural highway of the beach. In fact, so difficult was the task of beating one's way through the forest that when at last an Indian did succeed in cutting a fifty-mile trail across one corner of the island with axe and

---

[3] Donoso and Velasco: Propiedad Austral, 1928, pp. 234ff.

machete to connect the two main settlements, Castro and Ancud, the government rewarded him well by grants of land and gave his name, Caicumeo, to the road, a name which it bears to the present time.

Little land was cleared for agricultural use. A Spanish chronicler asserts that even as late as 1789 less than a score of settlers could be found living more than half a league from the shore. In fact, so bitter was the struggle with the forest that, if we may credit the enumerations made, the population actually decreased after Spanish occupation. It has been estimated that the aborigines numbered, at the time of the Conquest, some 70,000. A census taken in 1713, after 150 years of Spanish domination, showed a total of only 59,000 inhabitants; one in 1772 gave a total of 32,000; and in 1789 a count showed but 26,689, only 5,000 of these being of European descent. At this last date there were but three towns on the island—Castro, San Carlos (Ancud), and Chacao—the second of these having been founded only some twenty years before.[4] Such was the result of two centuries of Spanish attempt to settle Chiloé. The forest gave promise of choking out the human intruder.

LAND POLICY AND SETTLEMENT UNDER THE REPUBLIC

The first years of independence brought little improvement in the situation. No new colonization was undertaken in Chiloé. In fact, Chile deliberately faced northward to the desert, turning her back upon this forest region in the south. As the years passed, it is true, she extended her political claim to the south and established her hold as

---

[4] Moraleda y Montero: Memorias. There seems to be no vestige of an Indian system of landholding in Chiloé, unless the numerous small holdings represent such a survival. This is strange in view of the slight Spanish influence; yet neither has the aboriginal language survived. Other cultural vestiges are marked.

far as the Strait of Magellan region and Cape Horn; but little attempt was made to colonize either Chiloé or the rest of the country south of the Bío-Bío.

There was one general measure enacted by the republic that set a peculiar stamp upon the settlement of Chiloé. This was the decree issued in 1823 ordaining that, after lands occupied by Indians had been ascertained and secured for them, all public domain of the country be sold in parcels of from one to ten cuadras. As has been seen, this measure was not carried out in the other provinces, but in Chiloé it was put into execution and resulted in the creation of many small holdings. In the district (*partido*) of Castro more than seven hundred and in Chonchi nearly a thousand cuadras were thus allotted, most of the land in both districts being sold in the small lots mentioned. By 1837, as many as 2,249 cuadras had been laid off and most of it disposed of in the form of small farms. This, with the somewhat similar method employed in the early colonial régime, has left a permanent mark in Chiloé upon rural property and upon settlement itself. There are few extensive holdings, most of the farms containing from four to ten cuadras. In 1854 it was stated by a public official that on Chiloé " There is not a single hacendado; all are properties of four or more cuadras." Another writer, in 1859, notes this wide distribution of holdings and remarks: " Todo Chilote es propietario " (Every Chilote is a land owner).[5] He gives the number of rural proprietors as 4,263 and the total population as 39,866 or one owner of rural property for every nine persons, a far higher proportion than in any other part of the country. Present figures indicate this same marked subdivision of the land. According to official statistics for 1925, there were the following rural holdings: [6]

    [5] Pérez Rosales: Ensayo, 1859, p. 277.
    [6] Chile: *Anuario Estadístico*, Vol. 7, Agricultura, 1925-1926, p. 13. These data include the several small islands lying close to the east coast of Isla Mayor.

Less than 5 hectares (12.35 acres)................ 2,158 properties
From 5 to 20 hectares......................... 4,148   "
From 21 to 50 hectares......................... 371   "
From 51 to 200 hectares........................ 208   "
From 201 to 1,000 hectares.................... 31   "
From 1,001 to 5,000 hectares.................. 21   "
More than 5,000 hectares...................... 11   "

    Total 6,948   "

Throughout most of the nineteenth century progress in colonization in Chiloé continued to be extremely slow. The colonization of the southern mainland by Germans and other foreigners and the opening up of the Araucanian territory to Chilean settlement had little effect on the island. Toward the end of the century, however, after the foreign colonies established on the adjoining continent had proved their success, attempts were made to bring settlers from Europe to Chiloé. In accordance with the plan adopted in the colonization of the mainland forested regions, people were sought in the countries of northern Europe more or less accustomed to such climatic conditions as are found in Chiloé, and, incidentally, descendants of forest dwellers.

THE FOREIGN COLONY AT HUILLINCO

In 1895, 320 families were brought in by the Chilean government and located on lands set aside for the purpose. Among them were English, Dutch, Germans, Belgians, and some Austrians. In an effort to prevent the formation of solid national blocs, different nationalities were mixed in the colony. In spite of this policy, one group composed chiefly of families from the British Isles (85 in all) became known as the Scottish colony, because of the larger number of Scots composing it. It was located not far from the city of Ancud, in the northern end of the island and bore the name of Huillinco. Many of those brought out for this venture did not stay—in fact, many remained only long enough to see the lands which the government had set apart for them. Some returned to Europe, some settled in other parts of Chile. Only those stayed on, I was told, who had no means of getting away, some dozen families in all.

The government in its desire to push settlement into the interior had chosen for this colony a location back from the coast a few miles, in the heart of the dense forest. Each head of a family had been promised a free grant of seventy hectares (173 acres) of land for himself and thirty additional for each son over twelve years of age; each family was to receive a yoke of oxen, a cow, 150 boards with which to build a house, and some of the essential implements such as an axe, a plow, etc. When the colonists arrived they found the land, to be sure, but found it covered with a heavy forest, with only a trail cut through to give access to the several farms. So compact was the growth of timber and quila that cattle and even men got lost in it, and stories are still told of members of the colony who wandered for days almost within hearing of the settlement but unable to find their way out of the woods. It is said that one youth, going into the edge of the clearing in search of stock, lost his bearings and, unable to find his way out, died of exposure and starvation within a few miles of his home. The danger of their children being lost in the forest was a constant source of worry among the families.

It was October when the colonists arrived—mid-spring and high time to put in crops; but there was a delay of six or seven weeks in getting the land distributed. No land was cleared and there were no houses in which to live, no roads built, no supplies nearer than Ancud, 22 kilometers away. The government, however, in addition to paying the passage out from Europe, provided free maintenance for one year, this debt to be paid back during a five-year period. Even with these facilities it is not surprising that only the most hardy or those with no other possibility before them remained to go on with the attempt at building homesteads in the wilderness. The first few years were times of great hardships. The work of clearing the forest was most difficult and proceeded at an exceedingly slow pace (Fig. 45). Even after a whole year of hard labor they had been able to clear only small areas for the planting of potatoes, wheat, and corn. Many of the colonists were not experienced farmers. They came from the cities or towns of the British Isles. To them it appeared an almost impossible task to create farms in this wilderness. In addition they must build their houses, fence their lands, and care for the stock they had brought with them. All of this had to be done with the poorest of equipment and when needed supplies were difficult to obtain. There was no road to Ancud or to the coast, only a narrow trail cut through the forest. Frequent heavy rains rendered this trail impassable for any kind of wheeled vehicle and almost impassable for horses or men. As a consequence of the rains, the ground is always soft, and during the winter months of June, July, and August, when it often rains for days at a time, every road becomes a quagmire. The description of the Chiloé roads written by Darwin in 1835 was still true of them in 1895 and is true of most of them today. " Even where paths exist they are scarcely passable from the soft and swampy state of the soil." " The road itself is a curious affair," Darwin wrote of the old Caicumeo road from Castro to Ancud. " It consists in its whole length, with the exception of a very few parts, of great logs of wood, which are either broad and laid longitudinally, or narrow and placed transversely. In summer the road is not very bad, but in winter, when the wood is rendered slippery from rain, travelling is exceedingly difficult. At that time of the year the ground on each side becomes a morass, and is often overflowed; hence it is necessary that the longitudinal logs should be fastened down by transverse poles which are pegged on each side into the earth. These pegs render a fall from a horse dangerous, as the chance of alighting on one of them is not small. It is remarkable, however, how active custom has made the Chilotan horses. In crossing bad parts, where the logs had been displaced, they skipped from one to the other, almost with the quickness and certainty of a dog. On both hands the road is bordered by the lofty forest-trees, with their bases matted together by canes. When occasionally a long reach of this avenue could be beheld, it presented a curious scene of uniformity: the white line of logs, narrowing in perspective, became hidden by the gloomy forest, or terminated in a zigzag which ascended some steep hill." [7]

During the summer it was possible for the colonists at Huillinco to bring provisions on horseback from the city. But in the constantly rainy weather of winter they were almost cut off from communication with other places. In order to get supplies from town they resorted to the contrivance which the native Chilotes had long used, a short, broad, hollowed-out log canoe with a knoblike projection left at one end to which a pair or two of oxen were hitched to drag the boat through the mud. I saw some of these still in use in 1930 (Fig. 46). It was as difficult to get produce out to a market as it was to bring supplies into the colony. As a result, the group was forced into typical pioneer conditions and became self-sustaining to a large degree. Though this must have severely taxed the ingenuity of colonists unaccustomed as most of them were to frontier life, they persisted and gradually improved their condition. Within a few years enough land had been cleared and put into crops to support the group—meagerly it is true. Several of them had acquired small herds of cattle. Their houses were built, some of the land fenced, a church and a schoolhouse had been erected. A little social

7 Darwin: Voyage of the Beagle, 1909, pp. 310-311.

FIG. 45

FIG. 46

FIG. 45—Colonist's house and farm in the Huillinco Scottish settlement.
FIG. 46—Mud sled used by the people of Chiloé and adopted by Scottish colonists for transporting goods to and from Ancud.

FIG. 47

FIG. 48

FIG. 47—Chilean settlement on the coast of one of the inner islands east of Chiloé proper (the island of Huar).

FIG. 48—Recently married couple's new home being built in the colony of Huillinco.

life was maintained by parties organized from house to house or in the two public buildings now available. Some of the places, surrounded by fences of boards or palings, took on the appearance of real homesteads, with fruit trees, shade trees, lawns, vegetable and flower gardens, out-houses. The houses were built to resemble the cottages with which the settlers were familiar at home. A few of the families moved into town, and some have prospered there; but most of them stuck to the land. The children brought out from the British Isles have now grown up and married, usually within the colony, though not always within their own national group.

A Scottish Family at Huillinco

A Scottish family, with whom I became acquainted in Ancud and by whom I was entertained there, was typical of the best of the colonists. The head of the house, who had borne the brunt of the struggle in settling the land, was now more than eighty years of age. In the old country he had been administrator of a Scottish estate, and so was better prepared than some of the others for the problems encountered. With his wife he had attempted to carve out a future for his six children from the thick Chiloé forests. One of his sons had left the island and ultimately had found his way into the British Navy. The others had stayed on the 200 hectares (494 acres) of land they had received, had succeeded in clearing 100 hectares, and had put about 50 of these under cultivation; the rest was left as pasture. They had several hundred head of cattle on the place when I visited it. One of the sons had married a daughter of another Scottish family and, after more than twenty years on the farm, had moved into town and gone into the meat business. In this he had prospered. With their family of seven children, he and his wife lived in a modest but attractive English cottage in

Ancud. It was an interesting sight to see this fair-haired, blue-eyed family group settled in that far-away corner of the world, not as most of the English-speaking people of such countries who merely sojourn in foreign lands for a few years for business or professional reasons, but regarding Chiloé as their home and with no thought of returning to the land of their fathers. The children were Chileans by virtue of their birth there; they thought of themselves as such. They used the language of Chile, as most of them had not even learned English. In many ways the process of Chileanization was far advanced. Yet though these children did not understand a question put to them in their parents' tongue or at best only imperfectly, the parents still spoke with a strong Scottish burr. In other ways, too, the family remained Scottish, keeping their connection with the struggling little congregation of Protestants in Ancud and clinging to the custom of Presbyterian ancestors in having grace at the table before each meal. The children have been well educated in the local schools, and their manners were as refined as one would find in such homes anywhere. None, however, have been out of Chiloé and even the parents have never traveled farther than Santiago.

The youngest brother in the original family stayed on the farm until a few years ago. He had married a Norwegian girl who had come out to visit some of the colonists. He had been but three years old when he had left Scotland and now spoke Spanish more easily than English, though he used both languages well. The process of Chileanization is well illustrated in his case: his associates found his given name, Malcolm, too hard to pronounce, and he is now known everywhere as " Marco " and even signs that name in place of the one with which he had been christened. In recent years this man, too, has grown weary of the unending struggle with the forest and has crossed the Andes into the Argentine, where he has been employed as administrator on one of the great sheep *estancias* there. In that region, where scores of other Scots are engaged in raising sheep, he spends part of each year, returning to his family and his farm seasonally, and keeping supervision of the land on which his father's family had settled.

OTHER SETTLERS AT HUILLINCO

Some of the settlers in the colony of Huillinco had not done so well as these brothers. Several of them had been unable, because of illness or lack of equipment or ignorance of how to deal with the forest, to clear more than a small part of the land they had received. They had barely contrived to grub a living from the soil that lay among the stumps and fallen logs and were living when I saw them in little better conditions than when they started, thirty-five years before (Fig. 48). A few of them had been so hard pressed that appeals had been made to their fellow countrymen in Santiago and Valparaíso for food and clothing. About the properties of such individuals the forest wall was relentlessly crowding; and the ground, even where cleared, was springing up again with a new growth of bamboos and sturdy young trees. In some cases this was taking place before the logs of the former occupants had been disposed of.

The colony in 1930, thirty-five years old, consisted of about two dozen families, mostly Scottish, but with a few English, Germans, Austrians, and French, and one or two Chileans who had come in later. Such names as Brown, Gilchrist, Leyton, Rutherford, Lindsay, Turner, and Dobson figured in the original list, and families with these names still are found in the colony. The lands occupied consist of a strip twelve kilometers long from west to east and four wide. About half of this has been cleared. The farms front on the trail leading through the length of the grant and now, for the first time, being made into a road that can be followed by wheeled vehicles. About half of the cleared land is under cultivation and the rest is used for pasture. The forest primeval makes an unbroken wall on all sides of the clearings.

THE STRUGGLE WITH THE FOREST

Chiloé's eternal problem, that of getting rid of the timber, is by far the greatest one faced by these settlers. The forest is seldom dry enough to burn even after the underbrush has been cut and left to die. When the dead small growth can be burned it still leaves the trunks of the larger trees standing. By hard labor these can be felled, but it is difficult to dispose of them except by letting them rot slowly as they lie encumbering the ground. Even then the stumps remain. It has taxed the patience and ingenuity of the settlers to eradicate them. The problem is common to all and has brought about one of the few measures of co-operation in the colony. The men have frequently banded together in stump-pulling bees, combining their efforts and those of their oxen. The roots are cut and grubbed out as completely as possible, and the stumps then extracted by trained teams of oxen. Accustomed to being yoked by the horns, the oxen lower their heads while their horns are bound securely to the base of the stumps. By united lifting and pulling the stumps are raised out of the ground. All this process of clearing takes several years, and by this time the second growth, particularly of quila, has again covered the ground. I was assured that it costs from 600 to 900 pesos to clear a hectare of ground, and when ready for cultivation it would bring little more than the cost of clearing.

There has been little market for the lumber yielded by this clearing process, and, furthermore, without roads or rivers or snow it has been practically impossible to get the timber even the few miles to the coast. Hence the only use to which the lumber can be put is to meet the needs of the local community. Here wood is used in multiple ways: in the building of houses, barns, and out-houses, in the making of fences, in the paving of roads (corduroy fashion), in the making of tools and implements of all sorts. The dwellings are of frame or log, the roofs of clapboards or shingles made by hand; the fences are constructed of split pickets or rails or, as is frequently the case, of short sections of logs set in the ground like heavy, low stockades. All of these uses combined dispose of but a small part of the timber cut from the clearings—the rest must be burned or allowed to rot on the ground. As a consequence, in every field stand the stark, ghost-like forms of girdled trees, while blackened stumps stud the more thoroughly cleared areas, and the ground is littered with charred, decaying logs, or cluttered with great trunks of fallen trees lying in tumbled confusion like giant jackstraws. Behind all this rises the almost impenetrable wall of the living forest, as if but waiting until man's energy shall be exhausted in the futile struggle before it makes a new advance to reclaim the land.

It is true that one of the things for which Chiloé has been noted is the lumber it has supplied. From very early colonial times, even from before the Conquest, the Chilotes have been famous for the splendid planks or boards of alerce and the boats they built from this timber, as well as for the wood they supplied other parts of southern Chile for boatbuilding. Many of the barges still used along the coast of central Chile were built in Chiloé from native lumber.[8] But these uses have not created much demand for the timber yielded in the clearing of the interior forests.

[8] At San Carlos, now Ancud, there was built in 1771 a small frigate, the *Favorita,* which was sent north for use along the Peruvian coast and from there found its way northward to " Nueva California " in one of the exploratory expeditions along that coast (González de Agüeros: Descripción . . . de Chiloé, 1791, pp. 80 ff.)

Other Colonies in Chiloé

Conditions in this colony are typical of those found in all the newer settlements of the island, the chief difference being that few other settlers have ventured to undertake the clearing of the forest on so large a scale or the establishment of homes so far inland. A small German colony was begun at this same time on the north coast at Chacao, and there is also a nucleus of German settlers at Mechaico, inland a short distance from Ancud. A small group of Belgians established themselves at Quetalmahue near the coast a few miles west of Ancud, and enough of them have remained to give the name " Belgian " to a tiny settlement there. These lands, too, are but partially cleared of the dense timber and are still littered for the most part with stumps and decaying logs.

Chilean settlement has been very slow to enter Chiloé.[9] Where it has come it has mixed with that of the old-time Chilotes and has followed much the same lines. Along the eastern coast a string of diminutive villages reaches from Chacao Channel nearly to the southern end of the island. They vary in size from a few families to 600 persons, and there is only one larger place, Castro with 2,700 inhabitants. All of them are directly on the shore. They are agricultural villages, with fishing a supplementary occupation. Most of Chiloé's population lives in *aldeas, caseríos,* or single-family *fundos*. As seen from our steamer each settlement consisted of a church, a schoolhouse, and a half dozen dwellings. Every house faces the water, for in Chiloé travel is mainly either by foot or by horse along the beach or more commonly by boat along the shore. " The Chilote farmer has no wagon," a friend assured me, " he does all his hauling on land by mud canoe, while to go to market he has the sea." At any such settlement one sees a number of

---

[9] One setback it received was the ousting of squatters from lands the government had selected for foreign colonists (Weber: Chiloé, pp. 153-194). See also Jefferson: Recent Colonization in Chile, 1921, pp. 31ff.

canoes drawn up on the beach or else men or women rowing
out to meet the passing coastwise steamer or collecting boat-
loads of seaweed (*lamilla*) for fertilizer. All the houses are
of frame, usually shingled, roof and sides, with home-split
"shakes." They bear much more resemblance to English or
Norwegian cottages than to the houses one sees in central
Chile. Fences of split palings or of upright stakes surround
the houses, shutting out pigs, cattle, and horses which
enjoy free range. In front of each village, on the beach,
a low circular fence runs out into the water, and in this
enclosure fish are trapped at low tide. Clams, too, are
taken in quantity from the shallow water along the shore.
Behind the houses a few patches of potatoes or larger fields
of grain occupy the cleared land, and beyond that, in an
irregular arc, the thick woods shut out the little settlement
from landward connections with the world. Up and down
the coast for several miles the timber is unbroken and the
forest comes down to high-water line. Then, farther along
the shore another clearing may be seen and a small farm
lying close beside the sea, with its modest shingled cottage
surrounded by a simple garden and little fenced fields. Except for such interruptions the forest descends compactly
to the water's edge. The agricultural land tributary to
these houses in no place reaches back more than five or
six miles from the sea, except along the old Caicumeo
road and the railway which follows approximately the
same route between Castro and Ancud. Here a thin and
frequently interrupted line of farms and tiny settlements
is strung between the two towns.

At the narrowest part of the island, where a trail has
been forced through the forest past lakes Cucao and
Huillinco [10] to the Pacific, there is one small settlement
on the banks of the latter lake. Along the whole west
coast there are but three small hamlets and a few tiny

[10] Note that this lake lies at some distance from the settlement of the same
name referred to on pages 327-330 above.

farms, but no other population. This coast, in contrast with the eastern shore, is rugged, in most parts rising abruptly from the sea and offering little level land on which settlements could be located. Almost no effort has been made to colonize this side of the island. Exposed to the full effect of the stormy westerly winds and favored with not a single satisfactory harbor, the area is forbidding. Heavy timber covers the slopes down to the water's edge. It is not surprising that neither native Chilotes nor imported colonists have been able to settle along this coast.

The older settlements in Chiloé have, of course, grown out of the raw stage of recently won land, but they also still give evidence of close dependence upon the forests. In sharp contrast with the type of dwelling seen in central and northern Chile, where adobe brick is the usual building material and tile or thatch the characteristic roofing, the houses in the towns, such as Castro and Ancud, are of frame construction with shingle roofs. The sidewalks are of wood with heavy planks for curbing, whereas in other Chilean towns they are of cobblestone, brick or flagstone. Houses must be heated in winter, generally with open fires, and the use of wood in construction has exposed the settlements to the danger of fire common to such regions. Serious conflagrations have occurred at different times. One of the important events in the history of Castro was its destruction by fire in 1643 when, as capital of the island province, it was captured by the Dutch invaders under Brouwer. It also suffered severely from the same cause in 1857 and again in 1895. Ancud, too, has been partially destroyed by fire on several occasions, once in 1844, again in 1859, once more in 1871, and finally in 1879. Since this last date additional precautions and better fire-fighting equipment have checked such serious disasters. The smaller places also have frequently suffered from the ravages of fire.

The small area of land which the Chilote has been able to wrest from the forest, the unfavorable climatic conditions for agriculture, and the limited grasslands available have forced the people of this island to seek some way of augmenting their income. In response to this need the Chilotes wander far from home during the summer. Bands of them cross the Chacao Channel to the mainland and journey northward by rail into the harvest fields of south-central Chile. Every summer one may see small groups of these short, swarthy men, with bundles of clothes under their arms or swung over their backs, moving from station to station in the wheat region as their services are required. They seldom get farther north than the Bío-Bío or the Maule but contribute an important element to the labor of the southern provinces. They are excellent woodsmen also and find employment in the logging camps and the lumber yards of the old Araucanian districts. Skilled boatmen as well, they follow their own barges up the coast and may be found in small numbers as far north as Talcahuano or even Valparaíso and Peruvian ports, though they seldom seem to compete with the aggressive longshoremen in the ports of central Chile. Many Chilotes also go south to work at the newer settlements of Aysén and Magallanes. They may be seen as far from home as the Strait of Magellan. This exodus from the island, beginning in September or October each year, involves thousands. They nearly all return to their little island homes and fields of potatoes in February or March and spend the rest of the year seeking a living from their native habitat of narrow coastal strip and shore-line fishponds or in dangerous voyages across the stormy waters of their channels with boards of alerce, sides of bacon, home-made woolen blankets, or sacks of seed potatoes to market on the mainland.[11]

[11] Cavada: Chiloé, 1914, p. 15. See also Schwarzenberg and Mutizábal: Monografía geográfica . . . de Chiloé, 1926, pp. 259-261.

COLONIZATION OF NEIGHBORING ISLANDS

Most of this description refers only to the Isla Grande, the island of Chiloé. On the adjoining islands conditions are quite different. Some of those that lie farther south have topography and vegetation much like those on the main island, but little effort has been made by civilized man to get a foothold on them. They are still occupied by a small number of aborigines who live in close contact with the shore, securing their living more from the sea resources than from the land. In years to come, when the frontier of the mainland becomes inhabited, these islands may offer some room for expansion and will probably go through much the same process that is taking place on Chiloé. In the meantime they play little part in the life of the Chilean people.

Eastward from Chiloé and extending northward toward Puerto Montt lie a number of small islands of quite a different type. They correspond topographically to the plains country of the great longitudinal valley of central and southern Chile and, vegetationally, to the *llanos* or meadow lands of the Araucanian territory and the Osorno region. On most of them there now exists no timber, and apparently they never had anything like the growth of forest that characterizes the main island, or, if so covered, they were more easily cleared because of their smaller size. At any rate they are now quite fully occupied by farms that reach back from the shore. Few towns or even villages have grown up on the islands; in some of them, it is said, there is no store or other place of business and all marketing is done by boat trips to the mainland or to Chiloé. A characteristic sight along the shores is a group of buildings consisting of a church, schoolhouse, and residence or two (of priest or teacher), each surrounded by its fence of palings or boards (Fig. 47). Along the trails that lead off by the beach or into the interior lines of school children may be seen going homeward after lessons, or, on Sunday, groups of the faithful strolling to or from mass. The whole picture is as unlike central Chile as if in another part of the world. The green landscape, the rolling lands covered with small farms, the frame buildings, the wood fences, the simple, but cozy, shingled farm houses scattered over the countryside suggest northern Europe or the United States. But the population is almost wholly Chilean. The region's likeness to these other lands merely results from the development of similar ways of living in environments of strikingly similar character.

SMALL AREA COLONIZED

Under the presidency of Ibáñez, in 1929, a new attempt was made to colonize Chiloé. The plan was to expropriate 500,000 hectares (1,235,500 acres) of the undeveloped parts of the main island, divide 200,000 hectares of this into parcels of 200 hectares each, and offer these parcels free to any suitable Chilean or foreigner who would settle there. To discourage speculation these grants of land were to be inalienable for a period of time. The rest of the land expropriated was to be held by the government for five years and then sold in blocks of the same size as the colonists' holdings, and the resulting funds were to be used for redeeming bonds issued to finance the enterprise. The government undertook to construct roads through the forest, to clear a part of the land, and to build small frame houses in advance of bringing the colonists to the island. Disturbed political conditions in Chile and the general economic situation have made it impossible to carry out the project.

Except for the few invasions of the interior already noted, settlement of Chiloé is still limited to the narrow fringe that skirts the east coast. The rest of the island is devoid of towns or farms or even roads. Few trails penetrate the forest depths, and the only occupants are scattered bands of cattle, half wild and seldom rounded up, that wander through the dense timber, subsisting upon the tender leaves of the quila and the grass found here and there in open spaces among the trees. Occupation of the land by man is little farther advanced than before the advent of the whites or before the conquest by the Incas. The forest is holding its own against the human invaders. Neither Indian nor Spaniard nor Chilote nor Chilean nor even the descendants of hardy forest peoples from northern Europe have as yet succeeded in wresting the land from the forest's tenacious grasp.

CHAPTER XIV

THE FAR SOUTH

The Strait of Magellan is a long way from central Chile. Aysén is not quite so far, but it is equally difficult to reach. These two territories constitute the new *Frontera*. The old frontier is no longer a haven for those in quest of free land and pioneer conditions. It is virtually all taken up. Here and there are small areas which the government asserts are still fiscal lands, but most of them are already occupied by squatters. The *reducciones* of the Araucanians are yielding additional bits for settlement. But frontier opportunities have all but disappeared before wheat fields, wire fences, roads, railways, towns, and cities. To the Chilean who seeks an escape from crowded civilization, the far south (and the forbidding parts of Chiloé) are all that remain. What do these new territories contain and what do they offer toward a solution of Chile's problem of land for her people?

Population and Natural Resources

Magallanes and Aysén provinces occupy nearly one-third of the entire area of the nation, 235,188 out of the 741,767 square kilometers (90,810 out of 286,405 square miles). It has been noted that they have a little more than one per cent of the population, or 47,624 out of the 4,287,445 inhabitants. This would seem to indicate plenty of room for expansion. A region with but two-tenths of a person to the square kilometer would appear to offer abundant opportunity for colonization. Yet, so far, the Chileans have not gone there in large numbers. This territory has belonged to Chile since 1843. For nearly three centuries before that time it had nominally formed part of the Spanish colony. However, its first city was founded less than a hundred years ago and has now but 24,000 inhabitants. Outside of that city (Punta Arenas; Sandy Point to foreign navigators) there are fewer people than within it in all the expanse from Cape Horn to Chiloé. The raw frontier that the region has been for four centuries it would appear still to be.

Natural conditions in the far south have held back its settlement. It lies in the opposite direction from that in which Chileans normally travel. Punta Arenas is more than two thousand kilometers (1,200 miles) from central Chile, as far as Sitka, Alaska, is from San Francisco; there will probably be no land route connecting them for many years because the intervening land is virtually impassable. The coast of the Chonos Archipelago is rugged, fog-wrapped and storm-swept during much of the year, and almost uninhabited. Aysén, while only a few hundred miles beyond Puerto Montt, presents a bold, heavily forested, rain-drenched, and stormy coast. The Andes throw barrier after barrier across the route thither and allow no coastal plain by which travel might follow southward.

The lands of these southern provinces are largely mountainous; the Coast Range is continued southward in the archipelago and the Andes on the mainland. The floor of the longitudinal trough between these ranges has disappeared under the sea or has been removed by glaciers, tidal currents, and wave action, leaving as remnants only occasional level-topped islets like those east of Chiloé. No one of the three longitudinal divisions of which Chile consists offers in this southland substantial foothold for settlement. Added to this there is a steadily increasing rainfall as one proceeds southward, with dense forests like those against which Chileans have struggled so hopelessly in Llanquihue and Chiloé. It is no doubt possible for Chileans to survive in such a habitat, but to live there they must leave behind them much of their Mediterranean culture. They must become " gringo " in their ways of living. The vine and the fig tree must be abandoned ; beans, wheat, alfalfa, maize, melons, citrus, and tropical fruits are no longer possible. They must take to the unaccustomed use of the axe, to artificial heating of their houses, to sou'westers and rainproof footwear, to being drenched with rain in spite of every precaution. Against these odds, repugnant to people from the sunny lands of a Mediterranean climate, the Chileans have been loath to struggle.

Yet there is now in the settled part of Chile much talk about Aysén and Magallanes. Visiting officials from those outlying districts find the people of Santiago eager to hear about the climate, soil, and opportunities there. The press frequently mentions the problems of colonization and administration in those far-away regions. Books calling attention to this part of the Chilean territory have been published and widely read.[1] When I was in Chile a few years ago, the American Ambassador thought it worth his while to visit this southern land that he might better understand Chile's problem there. The government has considered it advisable to reorganize the whole vast area, at first by creating the new Territory of Aysén and fixing new bounds to that of Magallanes (1927) and then by giving them both the status of formal provinces (1929).[2] Steamer service is being improved and extended to points never before reached. Roads and bridges are being constructed, and exports from the far south are arriving at ports in the central part of the country. The nation, not many years ago, was ready to go to war to protect its claims to what was then often called the Chilean Patagonia, or Patagonia Occidental.

[1] Guerra: Soberanía chilena, 1917; *idem.*, Geografía de la Tierra del Fuego, 1922; Steffen: Westpatagonien, 1919; Fuentes Rabe: Tierra del Fuego, 1922; Edwards (Alberto): Territorio de Aysén, 1928, pp. 39-43.
[2] Chile: División territorial de la República de Chile, 1929.

For several centuries the far south was a virtually un-known coast past which European pirates and privateers fought their way against the elements, suddenly to appear before the Spanish ports and cities of central Chile and Peru. Explorers such as Magellan, Drake, Sarmiento de Gamboa, FitzRoy, King, and Charles Darwin told of its imposing scenery and its intricate waterways but gave little except adverse opinion regarding its possibilities as a place to live in. Later, twenty years after Chile had become an independent republic, it offered the site for a penal colony (at Punta Arenas, 1851). When steam navigation made the Strait safer for shipping, it became a transit region with a coaling station and a base of supplies for vessels passing from ocean to ocean. For-eign adventurers discovered gold and grass and began extensive exploitation of the region, with enormous " con-cessions " of pasture lands and millions of head of sheep.[3] It is now becoming, in sharp contrast with all the former phases of its existence, a place for settlements of Chilean citizens. The conspicuous present development is almost wholly foreign, but the bulk of the laboring population and much of the small business is Chilean, and the concerns, large and small, are organized as Chilean corporations. A part of the capital invested in these concerns also is Chilean, though the management of large-scale business is chiefly in the hands of foreigners, English, Yugoslavs, Germans, and Spaniards predominating. Here, as in the Llanquihue region, the Chilean is like an alien in his own country and complains that men from abroad are extracting the wealth of the land.

Chilean statesmen, however, are thinking of it as a field for colonization from the central provinces, and the common Chilean people are talking of the opportunities to secure free land in this remote section. The Minister

[3] A description of one of these concessions may be found in Pomar: La concesión del Aisén, *Rev. Ch. de Hist, y Geogr.*, Vol. 45, 1923, pp. 329-368, Vol. 46, 1923, pp. 432-478, and Vol. 48, 1923, pp. 160-200.

of Fomento writes of the "necessity of fixing definite norms for the renting, alienation, and colonization of the Magellan lands," [4] the president proposes a law to govern that colonization, and the national Congress is sufficiently

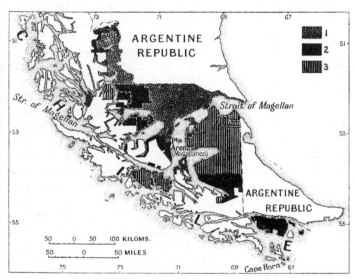

Fig. 49—Map showing the status of land tenure in the Magellan region of southern Chile. Scale, 1: 9,400,000. Key to symbols: 1, lands definitely alienated and now in private ownership; 2, lands given in "concessions" by the government; 3, lands leased by the government. Within 2 and 3 the areas surrounded by a broken line represent lands which will revert to the respective types of tenure indicated after certain contracts and leases now in force shall have lapsed.

(Based on the Plano de parte del Territorio de Magallanes con la subdivisión de las tierras, 1: 500,000, prepared by the Departamento de Tierras, y Colonización, Ministerio de Fomento, Santiago, 1928.)

impressed with the necessity to enact the proposal into law.[5] A map is issued showing the lands definitely alienated, those given in "concessions," and those rented (Fig. 49).

[4] Chile: *Memoria del Ministerio de Fomento*, 1928, p. 198.
[5] Chile: Ley No. 4,547 sobre arrendamiento de terrenos magallánicos, 1929.

GRASSLANDS EAST OF THE ANDES

While large parts of the region are still marked " *ines-plorado* " on the best maps, Chileans have discovered that there exist in the far south districts quite unlike the rest of the region. Behind the rugged wall of the Andes, at the eastern base of the mountains and in the rain shadow of those ranges—where the winds and storms of the Pacific coast, if they reach it at all, arrive with much diminished effect—there are lands that are nearly level, that have no forests and are not drenched with rain. Both in the Aysén region and in Tierra del Fuego they are found, and these lands are Chilean. Though east of the Andes, they were awarded to Chile in the arbitral decision of King Edward in 1902. That award was, however, but a recognition of a geographical fact. The great wall of the Andes has gates—gaps that make it easier to reach these eastern foothill plains from the west coast than from the far distant shore of the Atlantic beyond the wide pampas. Fed by the heavy rains of the west coast, numerous rivers emptying into the Pacific have eaten their way headward into and then through the mountains and now spread their upper tributaries about the eastern foothill region. The valleys through which these rivers flow have been fiorded by ice and partly submerged, so that arms of the ocean enter far into or even pass through the Andes. In many places where such fiords and inlets do not reach, the valleys still afford fairly level passageways, narrow and interrupted at intervals, but passable. With its barriers thus pierced, the Andes range has offered less of an obstacle to penetrating these piedmont districts than has the broad expanse of the Patagonian plateau. In recognition of this fact and because the Chileans had moved into this region in greater numbers than the Argentinos, the award drew the boundary line beyond (eastward of) the headwaters of most of these rivers.[6] As a consequence,

[6] Holdich: The Countries of the King's Award, 1904.

Chileans have found, within their own national domain, dry but fertile grasslands in this southern section. About the upper tributaries of the Palena, the Cisnes, and the Aysén rivers, and about the eastern reaches of the Valdés Canal and the Strait of Magellan, lie these level to rolling grasslands, green enough for grazing all the year round and generally free from destructive storms (see Fig. 5).

Here Chilean population has been gathering in very recent years in sufficient numbers to present problems of administration and land titles. The most important center is Punta Arenas (the city and surrounding commune) near which more than half the population of the entire far south (Aysén and Magallanes) is located. There are plains and rolling country here, with no real mountains and no forests about the city. Grass and shrubs cover the ground, since the rainfall is not heavier than that of central Kansas. Far north is the second most important of the small southern settlements, in the narrow glaciated valley floor and along the upper reaches of the Aysén River. The Commune of Aysén, including the capital of the province of the same name, in 1930 contained 6,835 inhabitants. Here, too, little of the torrential rain of the west coast penetrates. It is a grassland, and in many ways not unlike the Central Valley of Chile or the Meseta of Spain. A recent traveler describes it as " a level pampa . . . . well grassed, undulated ground." . . . . " We passed a flock of ten thousand sheep . . . . but they raised a terrible cloud of dust. . . . . As for ' guanacos ' and ostriches the place was alive with them." And then, on turning westward toward the Andes, "As we were again in well-watered country, we could dispense with the water tin." Like Magallanes, it is quite different from the west coast which Chileans have considered so forbidding. Next in order comes the cluster of settlements about the port of Natales, chief center of the region now known as Última Esperanza but long figuring on the maps with the name Last Hope. The commune of this name has 4,987 inhabitants, and the immediately adjoining commune (Cerro Castillo) raises the figure for this district to 5,639. Here too is a rolling, grassy plain. A small section of territory just across the Strait from the city of Punta Arenas, centering about the port of Porvenir, also contains a nucleus of population amounting to a little more than 2,000. There are several other settlements of secondary importance, some of them about sawmills on the west coast but more of them along the eastern base of the mountains. It will be seen that, while the population of the far south is widely scattered, at several points colonists have gathered in sufficient numbers to make an orderly system of land tenure imperative. This is the more urgent because the region is being occupied by squatters at many points.

As would be expected, these settlements in far southern Chile are established in areas relatively easy of access. Travel and transportation in the whole region is mainly by water, the labryinth of channels largely taking the place of roads. All of the above-named centers are either on the coast or within easy reach from it. A port, however small, is an essential feature here. Yet much of the population is disseminated over the interior. In the Province of Aysén eight-tenths of the inhabitants are rural; in Magallanes, two-thirds of the population outside of the capital are rural. Probably nowhere else in the republic is the rural population so widely distributed.

SIZE AND CHARACTER OF LAND HOLDINGS

The majority is engaged in the one typical occupation, that of herding sheep, and some 2,000,000 head of sheep are pastured on the grasslands of the two provinces. From the port of Punta Arenas as base, *estancias* (ranches) averaging some ten thousand hectares (24,710 acres) in area stretch back into the interior. From Natales other such sheep farms spread out. But these are relatively small holdings in this land of wide spaces. In 1925 there were 73 properties which averaged 73,015 hectares each, while one company, the Sociedad Esplotadora de Tierra del Fuego, operated 1,895,770 hectares, owning outright 945,-770 (181,655 across the border in the Argentine) and renting 950,000 from the government. Another company, the Sociedad Industrial y Ganadera de Magallanes, had a lease of more than 500,000 hectares, and another a similar lease of about 700,000 hectares. The people employed on such holdings are mostly men and live in barrack-like structures very different from the usual type of single-family house found on the haciendas of central Chile. One estancia had thirteen *viviendas* (dwellings) which housed 123 persons, only eleven of whom were women. Another had twenty-nine houses to 223 persons. In each case the figures probably represent a few family residences and great " quarters " where the employees, mostly transients and many of them foreigners, were lodged.

In contrast, there are also in both Aysén and Magallanes many one-family *hijuelas,* represented in the statistics by a single house and a few occupants. In the District of Mañihuales, for example, not far from the port of Aysén, there were 23 *fundos* listed in the census of 1930, and all but two of these were one-vivienda farms. Much the same was true of several other districts in each of the two southernmost provinces. This is the type of holding that the present government of Chile is trying to develop in this frontier region. Its recent legislative measures, particularly the law of the *Propiedad Austral* and laws governing the land in the far south, point in this direction. Since this is a grazing country, the individual holdings are far larger than in the center of the country. Many of those sold at auction to actual settlers measure from 5,000 to 10,000 hectares, but a smaller holding of 500 hectares, called the *hijuela ganadera* and intended for stock raising, is being tried out in some places. The policy of making the extensive leases just referred to is being abandoned in an effort to get the land into the hands of small proprietors. For the same purpose, an attempt is being made to ascertain the extent and character of still-existing fiscal lands, as well as to explore unknown sections, particularly in the Province of Aysén.[7]

THE FUTURE OF THE FAR SOUTH

Much of the far south can never be occupied to any great extent. It will remain, like the Andes and the Coast Range farther north, of little importance for settlement. But the better areas, such as northern Tierra del Fuego and the lands at the eastern base of the Andes, should be capable of still greater development. They are already producing extensively, and Chile now exports notable quantities of wool, mutton, and other sheep products. If the government carries out its avowed policy of recovering the public domain (at least those parts that are not supporting a *bona fide* settlement) and disposing of it in relatively small parcels, these areas will probably attract many thousands of the more venturesome in the central Chilean provinces who seek an independence greater than can be found in an hacienda-fashioned society. It would seem important for Chile to foster this settlement, if for no other reason than for the protection of its sovereignty there. Foreign domination is likely to increase unless the region is well filled with permanent Chilean citizens. Transient labor will not hold it; neither will temporary residents engaged in trade or government affairs; no more will the holders of great concessions who reside in distant cities. History shows that eventually land passes to those who actually settle it. The British yeomen were stronger in the long run than the Norman conquerors. The meek inherit the earth. Genuine settlers in Chile's far south will provide her surest guarantee of permanent sovereignty.

[7] Chile: *Memoria del Ministerio de Fomento*, 1927, pp. 128-130; 1928, pp. 197-199. Chile: Ley No. 4,547 sobre arrendamiento de terrenos magallánicos, 1929. Barclay: The Land of Magellan, 1926. Sociedad Esplotadora de Tierra del Fuego, 1928 and 1929.

PART III

NORTHERN CHILE

AN ARID REGION WITH SCATTERED SETTLEMENTS

CHAPTER XV

DESERT FARMS

Toward a solution of Chile's agrarian problem northern Chile has little to offer directly. North from Coquimbo stretches one of the most unredeemable deserts on the face of the earth. For years at a time no rain falls. When it does occur, it usually comes in fierce downpours that send torrents of water coursing madly down the dry canyons and out over the alluvial fans, too often sweeping away whatever crops may have found footing in small, moist flats along the stream beds. The only dependable supply of water is the meager runoff from the light snows and rain that fall on the Andes. Precipitation is so slight at this latitude, even on the high Cordillera, that only small streams are formed and there is not even a ground-water supply of any great importance, so far, at least, as has been discovered. Under such conditions, permanent occupation of the land has been severely restricted to the very limited areas which can be irrigated from the few small streams of fairly steady flow. Elsewhere all population is unstable.

Temporary and Permanent Population

Northern Chile has two distinct kinds of inhabitants: one transient, the other permanent. The transient is composed of workers in the nitrate *oficinas* (establishments) and in the mines, together with many others dependent on these extractive industries. About half the population of the north normally belong to this class. Their stay depends mainly upon the degree of activity in these industries. Exhaustion of minerals or a shutting down of production due to market conditions sends many of them out of the region. Even temporary suspension of activity starts some on a return to the populous centers of middle Chile, to adjacent districts of Peru and Bolivia, or, in the case of many of the higher employees, to Europe and the United States. Residence in the desert of northern Chile is considered temporary even by many whose connection with mining or nitrate exploitation is quite indirect, since most of the general business of the region is contingent upon prosperity in these special lines. The population of such cities as Iquique and Antofagasta is far from stable; that of the actual mining centers still more shifting. As many as 100,000 people moved out of the northern region when the depression of 1930 closed down many of the nitrate oficinas.

This temporary population has little direct relation to agricultural land. It is mainly urban, residing in the ports and mining establishments, which are located without regard to agriculturally productive areas. About many of the cities and towns not a farm or a garden can be seen. Food is brought largely from outside: most of the meat driven on hoof over the Andes from the Argentine or brought by ship (but still on hoof) from central Chile; most of the flour, fruit, and vegetables from the farms about Santiago and Valparaíso. Other supplies are mainly from overseas. This transient population maintains financial, social, educational, and ecclesiastical relations with districts beyond the bounds of the northern provinces. It takes little cognizance of the other half of the inhabitants whose life is permanently tied up with the territories of the north. In fact, the two groups are located almost entirely in different zones, for the transients stick close to the coast or occupy the most forbidding sections of the desert—wherever minerals can be found.

The permanent population is of quite a different character. It is rooted to the land, is agricultural and stock-raising, and consists of farmers and descendants of farmers whose ancestors had tilled the soil in the same regions and tended flocks on the same scant pastures for many generations. It is probably the most firmly fixed population in the whole country. In some places the aboriginal element is strong and is descended from families who have been rooted to the soil here since the days of the Inca Empire or perhaps earlier times. Even where the white element predominates, the people are sprung from those who settled in these regions in early colonial days. There is little change of numbers or of families among them. Sections are known as the home of certain family groups, a small number of surnames recurring repeatedly in tax lists or other catalogues of residents.

This fixed agricultural and pastoral population, though relatively small in numbers, poor in possessions, widely disseminated in tiny clusters, and feeble in the part they play in the broader phases of the nation's life, cannot be entirely neglected in a consideration of agrarian matters. Their problems are unique, as are some of the systems of land tenure in use, the pattern of distribution of their usable lands, the conditions under which they live and work, and the relations of these things to their social institutions. A study of these settlements serves at least to show how little hope there is for any great extension of agricultural land in the northern provinces.

SETTLEMENTS IN THE TRANSVERSE VALLEYS

Agricultural settlement in the northern desert, dependent on water for irrigation, is distributed very unequally. At the southern border of the desert enough rain falls to form a trio of small rivers, each of which stretches a line of green across the arid slope between the Andes and the sea. The Elqui River, farthest south, irrigates a narrow band of fields along its course and supplies water for a string of little towns dependent on those fields (Fig. 52).

About 170 kilometers (*ca.* 106 miles) farther north the Huasco accounts for a similar thin line of settlements; while 120 kilometers beyond, the narrow valley bottom of the Copiapó shows another ribbon of fertile agricultural lands. Between each two of these streams lies an almost entirely uninhabited area, bare of all vegetation except a scattered growth of hardy xerophytic plants. Northward from the Valley of Copiapó stretches the most arid section of the desert. Here in this extratropical belt of high barometric pressure, there is so little precipitation, either on the lowlands or on the high Cordillera, that no stream is created of sufficient volume to cross the hundred miles of territory between the mountains and the coast. Only after traveling 650 kilometers northward beyond the Tropic of Capricorn does one find a stream, the Loa, that carries enough water to reach the sea. Here another thin line of settlement borders its banks, much interrupted, however, by the deep

Fig. 50—Northern Chile, 1:11,-300,000. (In scale, *for* 500 *read* 100.)

canyon in which the river flows in parts of its course and by salt in water or soil that makes cultivation impossible. Another stretch of 250 kilometers follows in which no water is found in sufficient quantity for agriculture and where the only settlements are about the nitrate deposits, dependent for all supplies on outside resources. From here northward several small streams—the Camiña, the Camarones, the Vitor, the Azapa, and the Lluta—afford limited supplies of water but enough to make possible a few diminutive settlements at favored points along their courses. Lying well within the tropics, these streams are fed by the scant summer rains which occur on the high Andes at this latitude, and by small snow fields about the higher peaks. The lowlands along the coast and back to the foot of the Andes receive no rain except in widely separated years when disturbed conditions along the Humboldt Current are associated with occasional heavy downpours. The wide intervening spaces between the desert streams from Taltal northward to Pisagua contain numerous nitrate oficinas but support no settlements themselves.

Piedmont Settlements Along the Andes

There is, however, another part of the northern provinces that offers conditions suitable for permanent human habitation: this is the westward slope of the Andes where numerous streamlets, rising high in the mountains, have cut deep canyons in their steep descent to the desert. Many of these canyons (*quebradas* they are called in Chile) contain patches of level land and sufficient water to support small settlements. The better of them support several little towns where they widen enough for small plots of tillable land; some of them are so narrow or so filled with sand that they offer no room for settlements except on the alluvial fans that spread out where the

streams debouch upon the desert. In all of these foothill towns stock raising supplements agriculture. A belt
of pasture land stretches along the flank of the mountains at about 8,000 feet (2,440 meters) elevation, where
clouds and rain bring enough moisture to support a scant
growth of grass. Along almost the whole front of the
Andes, in the thousand-kilometer extent from Copiapó
to the Peruvian border, there extends a fringe of these
agricultural villages. They lie from 4,000 to 8,000 feet
above the sea, separated from each other by spurs of the
mountains or by arid wastes and isolated from the rest
of the world by the desert in front and the almost impassable Andes in the rear. Calama, on the upper Loa
with 5,407 inhabitants (1930), is the largest of these
foothill villages. Most of them are far smaller, containing but a few hundred or a few score persons. However,
as there are several hundred such towns, the total population of the foothill fringe amounts, probably, to not fewer
than 50,000 or 60,000. Rather evenly spaced along the
slope of the Andes wherever a rivulet descends from the
mountains, these villages are connected by a main trail
that runs along the piedmont from one canyon mouth to
another. From some of the towns, also, mule paths extend
across the desert or connect with the nitrate railways,
while other trails lead up the more passable canyons to
high gaps in the crest of the Andes.[1]

The crops grown here—potatoes, quinoa, maize, beans,
and alfalfa—more nearly resemble those of the great tropical plateaus of the central Andes than those of central
Chile. In the lower oases at the edge of the desert or near
the mouths of the canyons, fruit also is grown for local
use or for the markets about the nitrate fields. The flocks,
too, are more representative of the highlands; llamas and
alpacas are raised, as well as cattle, goats, and sheep.
Both pastures and cultivated land suffer frequent shortage

[1] Bowman: Desert Trails of Atacama, 1924.

of water; indeed, an insufficient water supply constitutes the most serious problem imposed by natural conditions. Curiously enough, canyon and piedmont settlements alike occasionally suffer also from an excess of water, when sudden freshets sometimes sweep away fields and build new ones within a few hours.

LANDHOLDINGS IN THE TRANSVERSE VALLEYS

The type of landholding in the transverse valleys is different from that of the piedmont fringe. The former is European, the latter Indian. In the valleys most of the land is held by individuals, whether the plots are large or small—*haciendas, fundos,* or *chacras.* These are not unlike the individual holdings characteristic of central Chile, except that few, even of the largest, have inquilinos attached to the properties. Labor is supplied largely by free workers, hired by the day and not supported by rations from the farm. Thus the social organization is quite different from that which marks the estates of the central provinces. The landowners constitute no such aristocracy as that of the *hacendados* about the capital; nor do the laborers occupy the servile position characteristic of the "*roto*" in this latter region. A description of one of these northern valley farms will serve to give an idea of their general character.

The Hacienda Hornito lies in the bottom of the deep canyon in which the Copiapó River runs, about fifty kilometers upstream from the city of Copiapó. It stretches along the valley floor for twenty kilometers but has an average width of only one kilometer, a veritable shoestring farm, extremely difficult to supervise and costly to enclose, having 150 kilometers of fence. The administrator keeps several good saddle horses to be used alternately, and makes a trip upstream every morning to the upper part of the estate, and downstream in the afternoon. Proper inspection of the work compels him to spend most of the day in the saddle. All but a small section of the farm is irrigated, with 120 kilometers of its own canals leading from the river. At the time of my visit, however, only half of the 1,050 hectares (2,594 acres) were under irrigation, owing to a marked shortage of water in the whole valley, which required the strict application of a well-established system of *turno* (limitation *pro rata*) (Fig. 51).[2] Wherever the water can be carried one sees a lush growth of vegetation, but where irrigation ceases the desert immediately begins, the steep walls of the valley supporting almost no life except an occasional cactus or other drought-resisting plant. The larger part of the area is devoted to alfalfa, which is fed to a herd of several hundred milch cows; wheat, corn, and barley are also grown. No milk is sold; all is made into butter and cheese to be marketed in the nitrate fields and mines north of Copiapó.

The hacienda consists of four sections, formerly separate properties but now consolidated into one. The estate is divided into many fields by the meandering channel of the river and is further subdivided by railroad and roadway. Each field bears a separate name, given by the workmen, an arrangement which decidedly simplifies the directing of their labor.

Hornito constitutes a little community by itself. It belongs to an English mining company which bought it in 1826 to supply feed for animals used at the mines not far away. For many years the mines have been inactive, but the company still holds the farm, apparently hoping for the day when its produce will again be needed. There are some 150 persons living on the place, most of them

[2] *Ibid.*, pp. 119-128. The history of the water problem and the establishment of the *turno* is told in detail by Sayago, " Historia de Copiapó," 1874, pp. 254-269, who describes it as " la eterna cuestión de las aguas " (the eternal problem of water) and " el asunto capital de la vida del valle " (the matter of primary importance in the life of the valley).

FIG. 51—The Copiapó River at Hornito Hacienda. One finds it
hard to believe that such a small stream can supply so much land
with water as is the case in the Copiapó Valley, where this brook
is responsible for all the production of the valley farms.

Fig. 52

Fig. 53

Fig. 54

Fig. 52—The irrigated Elqui Valley above La Serena.

Fig. 53—The terraced valley of the middle Huasco, with irrigated haciendas occupying the better-watered lands.

Fig. 54—Alfalfa fields of the haciendas in the middle Huasco valley, with their herds of cattle being fattened to supply beef for mines and nitrate *oficinas*.

contracted as laborers but given house, wood, and a few other perquisites beyond the daily wage of from five to fifteen pesos. No land, however, is allowed them as " possessions "; none can be spared by the farm. Some of the tenants have been on the property for many years, some are newcomers. The employees here more nearly resemble the inquilinos of the central provinces than do those of most farms in the north, but their relations with the patrón are neither so close nor so fixed as in this latter region. The administrator, when I was there, was a Belgian with an English wife, both of kindly disposition to wayfarers—I can testify—as well as to their tenants. The government maintains a small school on the farm, and the manager and his wife take a keen interest in its success. The hacienda itself runs a general merchandise store; and in part the wages are paid in tokens (*fichas*), good in the community as well as on the estate. The system, fraught with possibilities of abuse, appears to work satisfactorily here.

Hornito normally supports about a thousand horned cattle, some two thousand sheep, and several hundred hogs. The administrator also manages an enormous highland pasture at the head of the valley—the rented Hacienda Jorquera, of perhaps a million hectares, where large numbers of stock can be driven for summer grazing.

There are a number of such large haciendas in the middle and upper Copiapó Valley. In fact, large holdings here have almost entirely shut out the small farms characteristic of similar sections along the Elqui and the Huasco. The cause of the difference seems to lie in the fact that the Valley of Copiapó, at the time of the Conquest, was granted to Spaniards in large blocks, the land of the entire valley being given to nine individuals.[3] Little but the Indian settlement of San Fernando, now an agricultural suburb of Copiapó city, was left to the natives. The numerous small

[3] Sayago: *op. cit.*, p. 244.

chacras of this village, each containing but a few acres, but intensively developed in fruit and vegetable gardens, seem to point to what the whole valley might produce and the large population it might support if it had not been entailed in a few great estates.

In the Huasco Valley there are not many such haciendas in the upper middle section, but almost every available foot of land is occupied by small holdings. In the far valley head, as in the corresponding part of all the northern valleys, on the high *vegas* where snow and cold make agriculture impossible, there exist several great summer pastures. Also, where the valley in its lower middle section crosses what corresponds to the longitudinal trough between the Andes and the Coast Range, large holdings have been created in relatively recent years. Here in the vicinity of Vallenar the river has left a series of terraces high above its flood plain (Fig. 53). Until the first decades of the nineteenth century these elevated flats formed part of the surrounding desert, only the valley floor itself and a little of the lower terraces being irrigated. In 1819 an earthquake did so much damage at Copiapó that many of the inhabitants removed to the Vallenar region. The presence of these newcomers increased the demands on agriculture. At about the same time there came a mining boom which created a still greater demand for food for man and for the animals employed in the mines. As a consequence, new canals were built and some of the terrace land was brought under irrigation. Further growth of the population in following years led to the construction of other canals and the expansion of irrigation onto the higher levels. As late as 1915 new canals were being built and additional land on the terraces was being brought under water. At the present time the wide terraces on the south side of the valley and some of the land on the north side are almost completely irrigated. This higher land is held in large estates and is devoted mainly to alfalfa growing. Here are located the beautiful haciendas of Buena Esperanza, Paona, La Florida, Quebrada Honda, El Telégrafo, La Centinela, and a number of others as extensive and well developed as many of those in central Chile.

The formation of these large haciendas with their great demand for water brought the entire valley of the Huasco face to face with a serious shortage, which resulted in much strife among the several communities. Huasco Bajo and Freirina far down toward the sea bitterly complained that, though their lands were on the valley floor, they were becoming parched for lack of water and that at times the inhabitants did not even have water to drink. Vallenar in turn, halfway up the valley, insisted she could not let a larger supply go past her fields. She protested against wasteful use of water in the many small farms of the upper valley. In years of large snowfall on the Andes there was usually no shortage. Not infrequently, however, by December or January, even if there had been the normal precipitation on the mountains, the snow was nearly all melted and the runoff was low; and this, combined with the higher evaporation and larger demands of the soil during the warmer months, resulted in a deficiency for irrigation and domestic use. Occasionally there was a series of years when strife over the water was forgotten because of the abundant flow in the stream. Again, a series of several dry years occasionally occurred. Finally, in 1859, a strict turno was established, by which fixed days and hours were assigned to canals in each section of the valley; a system of *celadores* (guards) and *zanjeros* (ditch runners) was organized, and a *juez de aguas* (water judge) was appointed, who was obliged to call a general assembly of all canal owners and make a periodical distribution of water. Though modified a number of times, the turno still exists and regulates the distribution of the precious fluid.[4]

It will be noted that little intensive production is carried on by the haciendas wherever located. Since the introduc-

[4] Morales: Historia del Huasco, 1896, pp. 185-200.

tion of mining machinery they have been given over mainly to the growing of alfalfa for pasturing beef cattle to supply mines and nitrate fields (Fig. 54.) Other crops are not commonly raised. In this the large farms contrast sharply with the many small holdings, particularly in the upper valleys and along the tiny streams farther north. There is a good market for both types of products, but these desert valleys are so admirably adapted to the production of fruits and vegetables, and the growing of these makes for so much more intensive use of the land and provides a living for so many more people that it seems unfortunate that they should not be put to this use. Morales voices the feeling of many residents of the north in maintaining that the large irrigated farms about Vallenar bring little benefit to the people of the valley. They support thousands of cattle, imported annually from the Argentine, but give little employment to the residents of the region. The cattle are all shipped out of the valley to other markets and their sale brings profit to the owners of the haciendas only.[5]

COLLECTIVE HOLDINGS

In the fringe of settlements that lie along the base of the mountains, as also in the upper reaches of the transverse valleys, the holdings are largely collective. They are of much the same character as the agrarian communities of the Andean plateaus and are still called *ayllus,* the term used to designate collective holdings of villages and kinship units during the Inca Empire and probably even before the founding of that dynasty.[6] The census styles these settlements *caseríos* and *aldeas,* but they are still termed " ayllus " by other Chilean writers. They differ from the agricultural villages of the central provinces mainly in being far older and in being fully organized social

[5] *Ibid.,* pp. 245-246.
[6] McBride: Agrarian Indian Communities of Highland Bolivia, 1921; Saavedra: El ayllu, 1913.

units. Many of them have probably been in existence since long before the founding of the republic and even before the Conquest.

The group of settlements about San Pedro de Atacama may be taken as typical of this region. There are some sixteen separate groups of inhabitants, varying in number from five to thirty or forty families, each group known as an ayllu. Each possesses a collective holding of a few hectares, the largest, that of Conde-Duque, having over 350 hectares under cultivation. The fields produce alfalfa mainly, since this locality is used as a resting place by herdsmen driving cattle over the Andes from the Argentine to Chile. Potatoes, quinoa, corn, and a little wheat and barley are also grown. The few fruit trees growing in the gardens require great care to keep them from freezing on winter nights, as the region lies at an elevation of nearly 2,500 meters above the sea. The *chañar* and the *algarrobo,* however, thrive well at this altitude, and their fruits contribute to the food supply of man and animal. Both trees, too, are of great value for their wood in an almost treeless land. This settlement, like many of the others on the piedmont belt, is very old ; it was in existence, apparently, with much of its present character when Almagro went by here on the first expedition to Chile (1536).[7]

The census for 1930 shows most of the inhabitants of this high foothill region as living in these settlements. The population in the District of Mamiña, east of Iquique, for example, consists of 720 persons, living in one aldea and six caseríos. The District of San Pedro de Atacama contains two aldeas and twenty-seven caseríos. Neither district shows a single fundo or hacienda, not even a one-house farm. Many other districts are of similar character. A few of the villages are mining centers rather than agricultural clusters, but most of them are distinctly farming communities, with stock-raising (horned cattle, sheep,

[7] Bertrand: Desierto de Atacama, 1865, pp. 266-272.

goats, llamas, and alpacas) as an adjunct to agriculture.[8] They hold their land in common, in the name of the village, and no member, not even the head man himself, is able to alienate the holdings.[9] In some of them the ancient custom of periodically reallotting individual plots probably survives, though detailed information on this point is not available. The practice is still common among some of the highland communities of Bolivia and Peru. The organization of the villages is largely independent of Chilean authority, as is the case among similar agrarian units in the neighboring plateaus. Hanson [10] reports that at least in two of the villages he visited (Toconce and Aiquina, near San Pedro de Atacama) the chief political officer (*alcalde*) is appointed by Chilean authorities in Calama, while Riso Patrón [11] states that this officer for Aiquina is elected annually by the people of the village. Both statements are probably true, since, if their organization still resembles that of the Indian villages in the Lake Titicaca region, the authorities of the republic are careful to name the person already approved by the inhabitants themselves.[12] In this, as in other respects, these foothill agrarian communities are much more like the holdings of Indians in Bolivia or Peru than like the typical forms of property in Chile.

SMALL INDIVIDUAL FARMING PROPERTIES

One other type of holding, characteristic of certain sections in the north remains to be described. This is the small individual farming property, most commonly devoted

[8] Hanson: Out-of-the-World Villages of Atacama, 1926, pp. 365-377.

[9] Boman: Antiquités de la région andine, 1908, Vol. 2, p. 434. " To the Indian inhabitant . . . . private property in land does not exist " (Bowman: *op. cit.*, p. 297). Both of these citations refer concretely to settlements on the Argentine side of the Andes, but the system of collective holdings seems equally common on the Chilean side.

[10] Hanson: *op. cit.*, p. 371.

[11] Riso Patrón: Diccionario jeográfico, 1924.

[12] Bandelier: The Islands of Titicaca and Koati, 1910.

to fruit-growing but producing also vegetables destined mainly for local consumption or for needs of the mines and nitrate fields. The valleys of the northern desert, favored with almost continuous sunshine, yield a quality of fruit probably unsurpassed in South America or elsewhere. Furthermore, climatic conditions are almost ideal for drying fruit, as bright sunshine and a dry atmosphere are all but constant. Peaches, figs, pears, and grapes of exquisite sweetness are grown in the narrow, sun-filled valleys and marketed through the ports at the mouths of the rivers. The Huasco raisins are famous along the entire west coast of South America. The peaches and figs are hardly less noted for their flavor. Nearly all of the fruit and vegetables are produced on small holdings. San Felix Commune, in the upper middle valley of the Huasco River in 1925 had 326 properties of less than five hectares each. They averaged less than a hectare and a half. The upper Elqui Valley in the communes of Vicuña and Paiguano had 978 such holdings averaging less than a hectare each.[13] There is no waste land on such properties: they are most intensively cultivated. Rows of great fig trees, some of them said to be a century old, alternate with peach and pear, while space between the trees is filled with vegetables, berries, or melons. The lower slopes of the bordering arid ridges are irrigated for a few feet above the valley floor, and here, too, the lush verdure meets the desert along a clearly traced line. The uppermost canal marks a sharp divide between the two extremes of vegetation.

Typical of such holdings are the little farms in Los Callejones at the mouth of the Huasco Valley. Across the valley from the port, on the north side of the almost dry channel of the river and on a small terrace that lies a few feet above the river bed, is situated this little settle-

[13] These figures must be taken with some reserve, since the statistics for 1925-1926 apparently do not distinguish between individual and collective holdings. However, in the regions here cited most if not all of the holdings are individual.

ment, consisting of some fifty families. Each family owns a small plot of land, from five to ten hectares in size. They irrigate their tiny farms from a canal, " La Cachina," which was built by co-operative effort over a hundred years ago and rebuilt on a high level some thirty-five years ago when the river, in freshet, swept away many of the fields below its former position and even threatened the canal itself. The settlement thus is an old one, apparently originating at the time the canal was constructed, after a great flood in 1833 had deposited extensive flats near the mouth of the river. A part of Huasco Bajo also grew up on similar alluvial deposits left by this freshet on the south side of the valley.[14] As would be expected, most of the families of Los Callejones are related, but there is no vestige of collective holdings. In fact, they seem to co-operate only in operating their canal and protecting its waters against encroachment of hacienda owners upstream. A school is maintained in the community, and the population is almost wholly literate; but there is no church, no public office of any kind, no police station. The farms in this settlement, like most of the small properties of these northern valleys, are devoted almost wholly to fruit and vegetable growing (Figs. 55 and 56). They have no grasslands and keep only the stock needed for labor— very little being used, since most of the work is done by hand. Their fruit can hardly be equalled elsewhere, in spite of the fact that many of their orchards and vineyards are very old and show relatively little care. The dried figs, dried peaches, raisins, strawberries, melons, pears, olives, and quinces produced are sent to the near-by port and thence to the mines and nitrate oficinas.

The people in this community are by no means prosperous, or were not when I saw them, though at that time they were just recovering from a severe earthquake which

[14] Morales: *op. cit.*, pp. 249-250.

FIG. 55

FIG. 56

FIG. 55—Produce of a small holding in Los Callejones, lower Huasco valley.
FIG. 56—Fruit trees and truck crops on small holdings in Los Callejones, lower Huasco valley.

Fig. 57

Fig. 58

Fig. 57—Lightly constructed dwelling in Los Callejones, probably built after the earthquake of 1928, with typical vine and fig tree characteristic of the Chilean countryman's home.

Fig. 58—Old fig orchards at Cármen Alto in the upper Huasco valley. Much of this land is held in small properties, intensively cultivated.

had damaged many of their houses, killed a number of the inhabitants, and left the population in a discouraged state of mind, (Fig. 57). The family in whose house I took dinner had lost two of their eight children in the earthquake. Their houses are small, modest, and some of them poorly constructed. Some, however, are equal to those of the artisan class or lower professional class in the cities. Few of them are as poor as the houses of the inquilinos on the haciendas. None of the people seem to be in actual poverty. They supplement the income of their little farms by occasional work on adjacent haciendas, by employment in mines, or by engaging in some business outside of the settlement. One of the men with whom I became acquainted was carrying on a thriving trade, driving a couple of small motor trucks far up the valley to the Cármen and Tránsito districts, there buying fruit and hauling it to the port of Huasco for shipment. Though he owned but ten hectares, he had every meter of it producing, and by the attention he gave to his orchard was obtaining results that would be a credit to any horticulturist. His home was modest but clean, orderly, and sanitary. He and his wife had received at least an elementary education, and his eldest daughter had been sent to Valparaíso to secure a high-school training. One can but contrast this family with that of a tenant on an hacienda in the central provinces.

In the upper middle section of the Huasco Valley one finds a similar type of settlement, as well as one resembling the agrarian communities of the piedmont fringe. About thirty-five kilometers above Vallenar the two main tributaries of the Huasco River unite; one, the Cármen, comes from far to the south, the other, the Tránsito, descends from the north. Both rise at the very crest of the Andes and derive their limited water supply mainly from snows that fall about their headstreams. Both flow through deep valleys, sharply flanked by bare ridges on whose slopes rain falls but infrequently. Both of these valleys have narrow strips of fertile land in their bottoms. They have been the home of skilful tillers of the soil for many centuries. The two valleys, however, have quite different characters. Both were the seat of ancient Indian communities, but at the time of the Conquest many Spaniards were given land in the Cármen Valley, which soon came to be known as the Valle de los Españoles (Fig. 58). Here grew up individual holdings, fundos both large and small. In the Tránsito Valley the Indian agrarian communities were left undisturbed to a great degree, and it came to be called the Valle de los Naturales. In the former a territorial judge acted as the authorized representative of the colonial government; in the latter, an Indian *cacique* continued in control and native social institutions prevailed. At the present time the names still persist, and the valleys show a marked difference in agricultural organization. The census of 1930 shows many fundos in Cármen Valley while the population of El Tránsito is made up almost entirely of caseríos. La Majada District, in the former, contains nineteen fundos, most of them one-house properties, and not a single village; while the Commune of El Tránsito has 24 caseríos, one aldea, and but four small independent fundos. One region has adopted the European agrarian unit, the other clings to its native American form of property.

RADICALISM IN THE NORTH

Enough has been said to show that, though northern Chile has little land to offer as an aid in solving the country's agrarian problem, it does, nevertheless, make an indirect contribution of no mean importance. The provinces of the north have an agrarian situation different from that of the central region. The régime of the hacienda is far less fixed upon it. There is no such clear stratification of society as in the central provinces. The social structure is simpler but more democratic. The landed aristocracy has had no such hold on the region as it has had about the capital. The laborer lives in no such servile state. It is no wonder, then, that the north has been restive under the oligarchical control of the center, that repeatedly subversive movements have had their inception in the north, that labor has acquired an independence there totally unknown in central Chile, and that the submissive " roto " who goes north for a few seasons of employment returns no longer submissive. The mines and nitrate works are largely responsible for this attitude of the laboring class, but so also is the agricultural population which has never known the subserviency of the inquilino. In the long, slow, disheartening struggle of the Chilean people for democracy, encouragement has frequently come from the north. The Mattas, the Gallo brothers, and the Lion of Tarapacá (as Alessandri is called, since he was elected senator from, though he is not native to, that province), represent that spirit of opposition to the central oligarchy characteristic of the north, and have also found their strongest support in that region. Radicalism (meaning opposition to the established order) has had its home in the northern provinces. Society, agricultural and industrial, in that part of the country has been free from the hacienda's dominance.

CONCLUSION

CHAPTER XVI

THE OUTLOOK FOR AGRARIAN REFORM

With the conditions portrayed in the preceding pages one would expect to find that the problem of landownership had long been acute in Chile. Such is not the case. Until recent years the country has been little disturbed in this respect. Her population has not been large nor has it increased rapidly; there has been no large immigration. The development of irrigation by the *haciendas* has gradually added new and very productive areas, while the timbered regions of the south, though offering discouraging difficulties to a people unaccustomed to a rainy climate and heavy forests, have provided a vent for the slowly increasing population. Nitrate and mining prosperity still further postponed the crisis, affording employment for many of those who became dissatisfied with their meager returns from the land. Furthermore, the rural laboring class, the group that has most severely felt the effects of the present system, has been virtually without means of making its needs known. Thus, until recent years, there has been little evidence of agrarian unrest.

RISE OF AGRARIAN UNREST

This situation has been gradually changing in the last twenty-five or thirty years. In common with her neighboring countries of South America, particularly Argentina, Brazil, and Peru, Chile has been experiencing a development of a strong movement of the laboring classes against the conservative landowners who have controlled the governments since the foundation of the republic. The point of saturation in population density has been approached in several of the central provinces. There has thus grown up a greater demand for land and land products. Domestic consumption of wheat, the principal agricultural crop, has increased to the point where little is now exported, though Chile formerly sent this commodity to Peru, Ecuador, and even to California. Barley is the only other distinctly agricultural product exported and that in very small quantities. Wheat and barley together constitute a bare three per cent of the nation's exports. As a consequence of this failure of production to keep pace with the increasing population, the agrarian problem for the first time in the history of Chile has become acute. The situation has been aggravated by the falling-off of employment in the nitrate fields and in the copper mines. Both of these great resources have failed as dependable economic bases for the national life. Chile is thus thrown back on its soil resources, and new need for land is being felt. Coupled with these economic factors is the changing social situation. The breaking down of the old patronal system as more and more of the *hacendados* and their families choose to live in the cities or abroad, leaving their properties and their *inquilinos* in the hands of hirelings, is creating a spirit of unrest throughout the rural districts. In addition, radical doctrines are reaching the laboring classes, penetrating even the haciendas. Much of the radical agitation is directed against the system of large landholdings, rightly regarded as the basis of inequality. The landless lower class is demanding a wider distribution of the nation's wealth, particularly its wealth in land. The nation as a whole is seeking a solution for this important problem in its various aspects, economic, social, and political—a solution that will bring her agricultural resources into more efficient use, will avert a threatened upheaval and the possible adoption of an extremist régime, and will be more in harmony with modern concepts of human equality—a solution, too, that will not completely destroy but will substantially modify the existing order. Mexico's and Russia's solution of a nearly identical problem is always in sight.

THE HACIENDA HAS OUTLIVED ITS PURPOSE

To the outside observer it would seem that the hacienda in Chile has largely outlived the purpose for which it was created. It came into existence as an instrument of conquest and served that purpose effectively. There is no longer need for such an agency. The conqueror has gradually blended with the conquered. Chile differs from some of the other republics of Spanish America in that her landless, socially and economically depressed, and politically voiceless class is virtually of the same blood as the landholding aristocracy. In the countries with a large Indian element caste is based on race as well as on economic and social position. But in Chile every inquilino on the haciendas and every workman in the cities, mines, or nitrate fields is a Chilean—as much so as the *patrón*. The two component races of the nation were so nearly equal numerically that the blending has almost wholly obliterated racial distinction. For four hundred years Spaniard and Indian have been intermarrying, and the result is a Chilean race with no marked ethnic cleavage. Except in the south the country contains no Indian language group, no aboriginal culture of consequence, no native economy. A few dances, some folklore, and some deep-seated traits of character are all that is left that is distinctly Indian. For a full century the " roto " has heard himself called not an Indian but a Chileno. He does not regard himself as racially distinct. The Conquest has succeeded to the extent that both of the original races have disappeared. An agency of conquest, such as the hacienda with its monopolization of the land by descendants from one of the original elements and its semifeudal organization based on the inferiority of the other, has been outgrown; if continued, it can but produce friction within the nation as now constituted of a virtually homogeneous population.

The system of large properties fitted naturally enough into the scheme of things for the two centuries or so in which the country was mainly a cattle land, when frontier conditions existed and society was organized on a semipastoral plan. This stage of development, however, has passed also. The need for great pastures has gone. Chile has become agricultural, and stock raising is but an adjunct of farming. As the broad ranches of eastern Texas gave way before the invasion of the smaller agricultural unit, and as the *estancias* of the Argentine and the *fazendas* of Brazil with their extensive methods of land utilization are yielding to the demands of intensive cultivation, so the hacienda, suitable for a cattleman's estate rather than for a crop farm, is feeling the pressure of present-day conditions in Chile. The large holdings, with their many untilled areas, now actually impede national economic development. The nation's lands are needed for more intensive production and to provide homes for the mass of the common people, essentially agriculturists but without land of their own.

RETARDING INFLUENCE OF THE HACIENDA

There is a social consideration that militates against the hacienda in its present dominant form. It is retarding the social and political development of the Chilean people. The marked economic inequality implied by such large holdings makes real democracy impossible. No country can hope to maintain genuine popular government when the bulk of the wealth is held by a small minority. If Chile is to be a democracy in anything but name she must have a far larger number of economically independent citizens who will take a proprietor's interest in public affairs. The hitherto slight influence of the small farmer in the south and the north must be augmented by that of a corresponding class in the center. The landless agricultural population (inquilinos, *medieros,* and itinerant laborers) must have land of their own if they are to be an asset rather than a dangerous liability to the republic. Left landless as they are at present, they can have little real interest in the established order; their lot will inevitably be cast with the elements of unrest. Equally important is it that many of the propertyless workmen of the cities, mines, and nitrate fields shall be anchored to the land with holdings (urban or rural) of their own— a thing to which they all aspire. Almost as necessary would it seem that many of the middle class should have an opportunity to take their places as proprietors and thus be freed from the dilemma of choosing between dependence upon rich relatives and sinking into the economic status of the " roto." The small farmers (at least the 48,000 with less than five hectares each) already established in agriculture, but with holdings too diminutive to provide a decent living for their families, also need an opportunity of acquiring properties large enough to give them higher standards of living, if they are to fulfill the promise of citizenship implied in their status as proprietors. Involved in this whole matter is the uncertainty of titles in the south, particularly among the small farmers. The country can ill afford to leave the problem of the *Propiedad Austral* unsettled. It has already seen the danger from the disillusioned homesteaders. That multitude of small holdings already created in the south, if given protection, should prove a bulwark of strength rather than a menace to the established social order, as it should also offer fine support to the cause of real democracy.

Revolution or Agrarian Reform?

A still more potent reason for agrarian reform in Chile is the mere matter of self-preservation. It seems no exaggeration to state that the established order is seriously menaced. The dominance of a small class of landed aristocracy has so long repressed the growth of democracy that the country is now more exposed to the dangers of a violent reaction than those nations, such as Argentina and Uruguay, in which the old feudal order has been gradually yielding. The situation is a serious one: the country lives in dread of a social upheaval. The working class constitutes the great mass of the population—probably a greater proportion than in almost any other country of the world. There is a more marked stratification than almost anywhere else. Few, even among the Latin American countries, have drawn such a sharp distinction between upper and lower class. The great group of the laboring class has been held in economic subjection far longer than has been possible in most parts of the world. The situation suggests the plight of Russia with its stubbornly maintained autocracy and its eventual far swing to the left, or, more strikingly, the pent-up forces of unrest in Mexico which finally plunged that nation into ten years of destructive revolution. It would seem that Chile can avoid what Mexico suffered and the fate of Russia only if her landowners are wise enough to help promote a modification of the present agrarian basis of society. Strongly repressive measures might still hold the populace in subjection, but not for long. If revolt is finally forced, the excesses in Mexico will pale in comparison. The Chilean " roto " (as every Chilean knows) would recognize no bounds to his violence, once the forces (material and moral) that have held him in check give way. It is doubtful if any leaders could hold him in control. For the sake of the hacienda-owning class itself, if for no other reason, the situation should not be allowed to reach such a stage. Timely agrarian reform probably would have saved Mexico ten years of civil war and would have left the hacendados with much of their former possessions. Moreover, any social order growing out of a complete overturn would probably be of extremely radical character. The inquilino, in common with the laboring class of the cities, the mines, and the nitrate grounds, has no property and virtually no experience as a landholder. He has developed no devotion to any land of his own. It would seem to be an easy step from his present landless condition into a concept of community ownership and a communistically organized society. It is in this direction that the country is drifting at present. No superficial reforms can long retard the movement. Only a fundamental modification of the hacienda-inquilino system seems capable of saving the country (and the hacendados themselves) from disaster and of establishing the nation upon a stable basis—only a reform that will bring about a wider distribution of Chile's one great source of dependable wealth, will make it possible for the laboring class to enjoy a larger measure of economic, social, and political independence, and will give the mass of its citizens a real interest in orderly government. To an outside observer agrarian reform seems inevitable. The statement already quoted [1] from one of Chile's own economists seems none too strong: " The Chilean landholders are face to face with the alternative of giving up a part of their lands voluntarily and without compensation, or losing them entirely." Recognition of this situation has brought many of Chile's leading men, even among the hacendados themselves, to advocate some kind of substantial agrarian reform; it led to the adoption of the provision in the Constitution of 1925 establishing the state's right to expropriate land on the basis of national necessity; it has influenced President Alessandri to urge the broader extension of the

[1] Page 277.

colonias agrícolas, by expropriation if necessary, and has brought a strong minority in Congress to support this far-reaching agrarian program.

The Problem of Redistributing the Land

How can agrarian reform be brought about in Chile? How can land be obtained to satisfy the demand of the landless that they be afforded the opportunity of becoming *propietarios?* How may the nation's resources in land be more equitably distributed, for the benefit not only of the present landless class but of the whole nation? How may the country be saved the sanguinary experiences of Russia and Mexico?

Land can be obtained in the desert north only in very limited amounts even with the expenditure of vast sums on irrigation projects; the frontier region of the south is already taken up, except for the restricted public domain and the small areas obtainable from Indian reservations; the far south offers little available agricultural acreage even when the extensive leases to sheepmen are withdrawn —and that little in a climate forbidding to most of the Chileans and to their customary crops. Neither the north nor the south can solve the problem. The center has un-used and poorly utilized land, but all in haciendas. Here if anywhere, however, must be found the land to satisfy the needs of the people. The nation's agrarian problem will require a redistribution of the land in this central area.

Can such a redistribution be brought about without great injustice to the present owners and without too greatly disturbing the existing social order? Will the members of the hacendado class themselves, still the dominant political element in the country, permit the adoption of measures tending in any manner toward a lessening of their dominance? Can the reform be accomplished (if at all) only by a violent revolution?

Opposition to Agrarian Reform

Unwilling to surrender that cherished "*privilegio de la cuna*" to which the upper-class Chilean has been accustomed; loath to yield their dominance in national affairs; unwilling to give up any part of their ancestral estates, for which, in the opinion of some, no pecuniary consideration could recompense them; and recognizing that land for the masses would put an end to the supply of cheap, subservient inquilino labor which they have enjoyed on their haciendas and would thus probably bring about still further modifications of the landholding system, a powerful group of the more conservative hacendados is attempting (1935) to block the present effort at land reform. They particularly oppose that feature of it which provides for possible expropriation, maintaining that this violates the basic principle of private property rights and threatens to undermine the economic foundation of the present social structure. Reports indicate that they are employing every possible stratagem in their opposition to such a program. In this campaign they are utilizing all the established agencies of the aristocracy. A conservative press reports developments in a way to favor its owners. The Church stands solidly behind established institutions.[2] Political organizations,

[2] During most of Chile's history the Church itself has figured as a great landholder. In former years, many of the best haciendas belonged to religious orders. The Jesuits in particular acquired extensive properties which they held and operated much as did the other Chilean hacendados. At the time of the expulsion of the entire Jesuit order from Spanish territory these properties were confiscated. Such holdings had been acquired by grants from the governors, by gifts from pious individuals in exchange for indulgences and masses, and by outright purchase. In spite of the precaution taken by the Spanish crown, which in its grants to individuals specified that land received in this fashion should never be alienated to any member of any religious organization, many of the best properties had found their way into possession of the Church. Most of this has now been brought back into private ownership, though there are still a number of haciendas belonging to religious orders in Chile. The Church forces continue to stand as an ally of the aristocratic landholders in most social, economic, or political questions. " La iglesia es el más sólido pedestal de la oligarquía y de la reacción " (The church is the strongest pillar of oligarchy and of reaction), protested one of the leaders of the Radical Party in a recent convention (*La Tribuna del Sur*, Nov. 24, 1934, p. 1). For descriptions of Jesuit possessions in Chile see Barros Arana: Riquezas de los antiguos Jesuitas de Chile, 1872; Vicuña Mackenna: Historia de Santiago, 1869, Vol. 2, pp. 155ff.

dominated almost wholly by the hacendados, forget their differences in face of a common danger. Class solidarity becomes more significant than political tenets. The Sociedad Nacional de Agricultura exerts its influence in the common cause. This element is prepared to resort to force if necessary. A powerful military organization (the Milicia Republicana) has been created with the avowed purpose of supporting existing institutions. This force enlists some 100,000 men and is said to be equipped with tanks, airplanes, hand grenades, and other armaments even superior to those of the regular national army. As the one point at which the present social structure is seriously threatened is in the land-tenure system, it appears that all such efforts are directed mainly, if not solely, against modification of that system. Thus one finds the people of Chile now sharply divided on this issue, largely irrespective of party lines except in so far as those lines represent social stratification. The intelligence of many among the nation's leaders, their ardent devotion to their native land, and their accustomed solicitude for the welfare of their dependents upon the haciendas may bring about a more general recognition of the precarious situation faced by the Chilean people and may lead them to put their country's interest above that of themselves or their social class. Here lies the nation's hope.

Orderly Reforms are Possible

It would seem that by orderly constitutional means a solution of the problem might be achieved. A far-reaching subdivision of the haciendas should be possible without injustice. There should be no need for actual expropriation—though the threat of its use may be necessary. The proposed plan for purchase and subdivision would seem to solve the difficulty. The many haciendas already on the market should supply the land required. The authority to expropriate need do little more than prevent an unreasonable advance in prices. If, in addition, a tax on unused agricultural land should be imposed, the voluntary subdivision now going on would be accelerated. The carrying-out of this plan, however, requires detailed legislation which up to the present it has been impossible to enact over the opposition of the conservative element. Should this opposition be too long maintained there is serious risk of a social upheaval.

Until recent decades there has been no great danger of this. The hacendado class has been so long accustomed to dominate the common people that many of them fail to recognize the changed conditions in the country. The growing social and political consciousness of the lower class, however, has created a new situation. Nominally recognized as citizens of the republic for a hundred years, but with no opportunity to exercise that right and with little economic basis for the development of independent self-respecting citizenhood, the so-called " roto " class of Chile and the lower middle class have reached the stage of frequent more or less violent protest and of constant unrest. Taking advantage of democratic forms of government that had long been little more than empty forms in an actual oligarchy, they have secured a slight participation in politics. There is little probability that they can be turned back or that they can be treated in the former manner, as if the country were still just " a great hacienda." Concessions will have to be made. The new situation will have to be recognized. That traditional relationship of " Master and Man " is fast disappearing; the social structure based on it seems doomed, as does also the system of land tenure that gave society and state their peculiar character.

The Lower-Class Chilean as a Farmer

It is often said that the lower-class Chilean is too irresponsible, too dissolute, too shiftless, to take proper advantage of a more favorable status in society. The measure of success attained by the small farmer in the difficult agriculture of the desert valleys in the north, the improved conditions among the holders of tiny properties in the center, and the stalwart pioneering of Chilean colonists in the south seem to disprove this assertion. As compared with other Latin-American laborers, the Chilean workman has no equal. In fact, it is Chile's claim (admitted by many foreign observers) that few countries of the world have better workers. The Chilean *huaso* and his fellow, the city "roto," possess an energy, a sturdy vigor, and an endurance that have made them famous in warfare, in athletic achievement, and in routine labor of farm, mine, or waterfront. They are enterprising, too, to a surprising degree, considering the almost total lack of incentive offered them by their position in life. The Chilean workman who wanders away from his native shores (as not a few of them do) is fully able to hold his own wherever he may be and to make his way in competition with men from any other part of the world. Usually handicapped by illiteracy and lack of training of any kind and too often, it is true, by a fondness for dissipation, he nevertheless adapts himself to new conditions with a readiness quite foreign to the more Indian element of the laboring population of Latin America. In his own country he takes to modern machinery, when given a chance, in a way decidedly different from that of the ultraconservative laborer of some neighboring lands and shows a sufficient degree of initiative in his daily tasks to warrant one in believing that as an independent farmer he would win a measure of success commensurate with that of small farmers in other lands. While largely unschooled in independent labor or management of property, he has carried a certain amount of responsibility in his own sphere of labor on the hacienda and, given a chance to become proprietor, generally makes good. He seems worthy of a higher status than he has inherited from the past. From the standpoint of the nation's future it would seem to the observer from abroad well worth while for Chile to make possible the development of this mass of " submen " (as Pinochet LeBrun not inaptly calls them), who are becoming a dangerous liability in their present status, into a great body of responsible, independent, self-respecting citizens.

CHANGE IS INEVITABLE

To one who has known the old Chile with its idyllic country estates, its simple patronal social order, its effective orderly government, and its substantial (though still limited) economic progress, the transformation that is coming about brings certain regrets. Much of the characteristic charm the country has offered to the foreign visitor is disappearing with the marked democratization that is taking place; much of it will be permanently destroyed. Such regrets, however, cannot blind one to the fact that the change is inevitable, that the Chile of the nineteenth century could not survive in the twentieth, and that its institutions were of the long ago. Altered racial, social, and economic conditions in Chile and in the world at large require a modification of the social organization. The passing of the dominance of the hacienda system, though fraught with hardship and turmoil, means progress toward a better and more united Chile. It means fuller utilization of natural resources, higher standards of living for the mass of the people, greater enlightenment over the nation as a whole, more genuine freedom, and more complete harmony among the several elements of the population.

BIBLIOGRAPHY

BIBLIOGRAPHY

Actas del Cabildo de Santiago, de 1541 a 1557, *and* de 1558 a 1577. *In* Colección de historiadores de Chile y de documentos relativos a la historia nacional, Vols. 1 and 17. Santiago de Chile, 1861 and 1898.

ACUÑA A., BENJAMÍN. Estudio agronómico del Departamento de Caupolicán. See "Government Department Publications" at end of Bibliography.

ACUÑA A., BENJAMÍN, and ARTURO MERINO E. Estudio agronómico del Departamento de San Fernando. See "Government Department Publications" at end of Bibliography.

Agricultor Chileno, El. Órgano de los intereses de la agricultura y de la industria. Began publication in January, 1927. Concepción, Chile.

Agricultura Austral, La. Órgano de la Sociedad Agrícola y Ganadera de Osorno. Began publication in June, 1928. Osorno, Chile.

Agronomía. Órgano de la Sociedad Agronómica de Chile. Began publication in 1911. Santiago de Chile.

AGUIRRE CERDA, PEDRO. El problema agrario. Paris, 1929.

AMUNÁTEGUI, MIGUEL LUIS. La crónica de 1810. Memoria histórica. Santiago de Chile, 1876.

AMUNÁTEGUI, MIGUEL LUIS. Descubrimiento i conquista de Chile. (2nd edit.) Santiago de Chile, 1885.

AMUNÁTEGUI, MIGUEL LUIS. Los precursores de la independencia de Chile. 3 vols. Santiago de Chile, 1909-1910.

AMUNÁTEGUI SOLAR, DOMINGO. Las encomiendas de indígenas en Chile. 2 vols. Santiago de Chile, 1909-1910.

AMUNÁTEGUI SOLAR, DOMINGO. Historia social de Chile. Santiago de Chile, 1932.

AMUNÁTEGUI SOLAR, DOMINGO. Mayorazgos i títulos de Castilla. 3 vols. Santiago de Chile, 1901-1904.

Anuario Estadístico . . . . Dirección General de Estadística. See "Government Department Publications" at end of Bibliography.

Archivo de la Capitanía Jeneral. *In the* Biblioteca Nacional, Santiago de Chile.

Archivo del Ministerio de lo Interior. *In the* Biblioteca Nacional, Santiago de Chile.

Archivo de la Real Audiencia. *In the* Biblioteca Nacional, Santiago de Chile.

ASTA-BURUAGA, FELIPE S. Diccionario geográfico de Chile. New York, 1876.

BANDELIER, ADOLF FRANCIS ALPHONSE. On the Distribution and Tenure of Lands, and the Customs with Respect to Inheritance Among the Ancient Mexicans. *Eleventh Annual Report, Peabody Museum of American Archaeology and Ethnology*, pp. 385-448. Salem, Massachusetts, 1878.

BARCLAY, WILLIAM SINGER. The Land of Magellan. London, 1926.

BARROS ARANA, DIEGO. Historia jeneral de Chile. 16 vols. Santiago de Chile, 1884-1902.

BARROS ARANA, DIEGO. Riquezas de los antiguos Jesuitas de Chile. Santiago de Chile, 1872.

BECKER, JERÓNIMO. La política española en las Indias (Rectificaciones históricas). Madrid, 1920.

BERANGER, CARLOS DE. Relación geográfica de la provincia de Chiloé. Santiago de Chile, 1893.

BERTRAND, ALEJANDRO. Memoria sobre la esploración a las cordilleras del Desierto de Atacama, *Anuario Hidrog. de la Marina de Chile*, Año 10, 1865, pp. 1-299, Santiago de Chile.

BILLINGHURST, GUILLERMO E. La irrigación en Tarapacá. Santiago de Chile, 1893.

Boletín del Ministerio de la Propiedad Austral. See "Government Department Publications" at end of Bibliography.

Boletín de los Servicios Agrícolas. See "Government Department Publications" at end of Bibliography.

Boletín de la Sociedad Agrícola del Norte. Monthly. Began publication in 1910. La Serena, Chile.

Boletín de la Sociedad Nacional de Agricultura. Began publication in 1869. Santiago de Chile.

BOMAN, ÉRIC. Antiquités de la région andine de la République Argentine et du Desert d'Atacama. 2 vols. Paris, 1908.

BOURNE, EDWARD GAYLORD. Spain in America, 1450-1580. (Vol. 3 of The American Nation: A History.) New York, 1921.

BOWMAN, ISAIAH. Desert Trails of Atacama. (*American Geographical Society Special Publication No. 5.*) New York, 1924.

CABERO, ALBERTO. Chile y los chilenos. Santiago de Chile, 1926.

Cabildos de Lima, Libro Primero, Segunda Parte, Apéndices. Lima, 1888.

Caja de Colonización Agrícola. For publications see "Government Department Publications" at end of Bibliography.

CAPPA, Padre RICARDO. Estudios críticos acerca de la dominación española en América. 20 vols. Madrid, 1899-1901.

CAVADA, FRANCISCO J. Chiloé y los chilotes, *Rev. Chil. de Hist. y Geogr.*, Vol. 3, 1912, pp. 362-463; Vol. 4, 1912, pp. 447-503; Vol. 5, 1913, pp. 389-472; Vol. 6, 1913, pp. 405-466; Vol. 7, 1913, pp. 452-474; Vol. 8, 1913, pp. 281-338; Vol. 9, 1914, pp. 246-287. Also published in book form with same title, Santiago de Chile, 1914.

X Censo de la Población (1930). See " Government Department Publications " at end of Bibliography.

CHILE: For all publications referred to, that begin with the word " CHILE," see " Government Department Publications " at end of Bibliography.

CLARO SOLAR, LUIS. Los canales de Los Andes. Santiago de Chile, 1920.

CLARO SOLAR, LUIS. El río Aconcagua: juicio sobre la distribución de sus aguas . . . . Santiago de Chile, 1917.

Colección de historiadores de Chile y de documentos relativos a la historia nacional. 45 vols. Santiago de Chile, 1861-1923.

COLLINGS, HARRY T. Chile's New Anti-Bolshevist Government, *Current History*, Vol. 26, 1927, pp. 108-109. New York.

Como deben esplotar sus cercos nuestros inquilinos. See " Government Department Publications " at end of Bibliography.

Constitución de la Propiedad Austral. See " Government Department Publications " at end of Bibliography.

Contrato de trabajo, El. See " Government Department Publications " at end of Bibliography.

COX, ISAAC JOSLIN. Chile. *In* Argentina, Brazil and Chile Since Independence. (A. Curtis Wilgus, Editor: Studies in Hispanic American Affairs, Vol. 3.) Washington, 1935.

CRUZ, ERNESTO DE LA (Edit.). Epistolario de don Bernardo O'Higgins. 2 vols. Santiago de Chile, 1916-1920.

DARWIN, CHARLES. The Voyage of the Beagle. (Harvard Classics.) New York, 1909.

DAWSON, THOMAS C. The South American Republics. New York, 1903-1904.

Departamento . . . etc. For publications see " Government Department Publications " at end of Bibliography.

Diario Oficial. See " Government Department Publications " at end of Bibliography.

Dirección . . . etc. For publications see " Government Department Publications " at end of Bibliography.

División territorial. See " Government Department Publications " at end of Bibliography.

DONOSO, RICARDO. Don Benjamín Vicuña Mackenna, su vida, sus escritos, y su tiempo, 1831-1886. Santiago de Chile, 1925.

DONOSO, RICARDO, and FANOR VELASCO. Historia de la constitución de la Propiedad Austral. Santiago de Chile, 1928.

DOUGLAS-IRVINE, HELEN. The Landholding System of Colonial Chile, *Hisp.-Amer. Hist. Rev.,* Vol. 8, 1928, pp. 449-495.

DROUILLY, MARTÍN, and PEDRO LUCIO CUADRA. Ensayo sobre el estado de la agricultura en Chile, redactado para el Congreso Agrícola de Paris en 1878. Santiago de Chile, 1878.

ECHEVERRÍA Y REYES, ANÍBAL. La agricultura en Antofagasta, *Rev. Chil. de Hist. y Geogr.,* Vol. 10, 1914, pp. 96-101.

EDWARDS, AGUSTÍN. Mi patria. London, 1928. (Also published in English under the title, My Native Land. London, 1928.)

EDWARDS, ALBERTO. Bosquejo histórico de los partidos políticos chilenos. Santiago de Chile, 1903.

EDWARDS, ALBERTO. La fronda aristocrática en Chile. Santiago de Chile, 1928.

EDWARDS, ALBERTO. El territorio de Aysén, *Rev. Chil. de Hist. y Geogr.,* Vol. 57, 1928, pp. 39-43.

ELLIOTT, G. F. SCOTT. Chile. New York, 1907.

ESPEJO, JUAN LUIS. Nobiliario de la antigua capitanía general de Chile. 2 vols. Santiago de Chile, 1917.

ESPINOZA, ENRIQUE. Diccionario geográfico de Chile. Santiago de Chile, 1903.

ESPINOZA, ENRIQUE. Geografía descriptiva de la República de Chile. Santiago de Chile, 1903.

Estadística Agrícola. See " Government Department Publications " at end of Bibliography.

Estudio . . . etc. See " Government Department Publications " at end of Bibliography.

ETCHEGAYÉN, HORACIO. Ensayo sobre irrigación de la Provincia de Atacama, *Rev. Chil. de Hist. y Geogr.,* Vol. 20, 1916, pp. 222-254; Vol. 21, 1917, pp. 229-251 ; Vol. 22, 1917, pp. 354-381.

EVANS, HENRY CLAY, JR. Chile and Its Relations with the United States. Durham, N. C., 1927.

FIGUEROA, VIRGILIO. Diccionario histórico, biográfico, y bibliográfico de Chile. Santiago de Chile, 1925-1931.

Folletos Nos. 1, 2, 3, Departamento de Tierras y Colonización. See " Government Department Publications " at end of Bibliography.

FUENTES RABE, ARTURO. Tierra del Fuego. Santiago de Chile, 1922.

FUENZALIDA GRANDÓN, ALEJANDRO. La evolución social de Chile, 1541-1816. Santiago de Chile, 1906.

GALDAMES, LUIS. El decenio de Montt. Santiago de Chile, 1904.

GALDAMES, LUIS. Los dos primeros años de la Constitución de 1833, *Rev. Chil. de Hist. y Geogr.,* Vol. 74, 1933, pp. 365-409.

GALDAMES, LUIS. Estudio de la historia de Chile. Santiago de Chile, 1923.

GALDAMES, LUIS. Historia de Chile, La evolución constitutional, 1810-1925. Santiago de Chile, 1925.

GALDAMES, LUIS. Jeografía económica de Chile. Santiago de Chile, 1911.

GAY, CLAUDIO. Historia física y política de Chile. 28 vols. and atlas, including section "Agricultura," 2 vols. Paris, 1862.

GONZÁLEZ DE AGÜERO, PEDRO. Descripción historial de la provincia y archipiélago de Chiloé. Madrid, 1791.

GRAHAM, MARÍA. Journal of a Residence in Chile. London, 1824.

GUERRA, J. GUILLERMO. Geografía de la Tierra del Fuego, Rev. Chil. de Hist. y Geogr., Vol. 44, 1922, pp. 164-182.

GUERRA, J. GUILLERMO. Origen y caída de la Constitución de 1833, Rev. Chil. de Hist. y Geogr., Vol. 74, 1933, pp. 346-364.

GUERRA, J. GUILLERMO. La soberanía chilena en las islas al sur del Canal Beagle. Santiago de Chile, 1917.

GUEVARA, TOMÁS. Chile pre-hispano. Santiago de Chile, 1929.

GUEVARA, TOMÁS. Historia de la civilización de la Araucanía. 8 vols. Santiago de Chile, 1898-1913.

GUEVARA, TOMÁS. Las últimas familias i costumbres araucanas. Santiago de Chile, 1913.

HANSON, EARL. Out-of-the-world Villages of Atacama, Geogr. Rev., Vol. 16, 1926, pp. 365-377.

HARING, CLARENCE H. Chilean Politics, 1920-1928, Hisp.-Amer. Hist. Rev., Vol. 11, 1931, pp. 1-26.

HERVEY, MAURICE H. Dark Days in Chile, An Account of the Revolution of 1891. London, 1891-1892.

Historiadores de Chile. See Colección de historiadores de Chile.

HOERLL, ALBERTO. Los alemanes en Chile. Santiago de Chile, 1910.

HOLDICH, Sir THOMAS H. The Countries of the King's Award. London, 1904.

HUNEEUS GANA, ANTONIO. La Constitución de 1833, Rev. Chil. de Hist. y Geogr., Vol. 74, 1933, pp. 231-345.

Informe presentado a la Misión Kemmerer. See Sociedad Nacional de Agricultura.

JARA, L., and M. MUIRHEAD. Chile en Sevilla. Santiago de Chile, 1929.

JEFFERSON, MARK. Rainfall of Chile. (American Geographical Society Research Series, No. 7.) New York, 1921.

JEFFERSON, MARK. Recent Colonization in Chile. (American Geographical Society Research Series, No. 6.) New York, 1921.

JONES, C. F. Commerce of South America. New York, 1928.

KAERGER, CARLOS. Landwirtschaft und Kolonization im Spanischen Amerika. Leipzig, 1901.

394   CHILE: LAND AND SOCIETY

KELLER, CARLOS. La agricultura chilena bajo la Colonia, *La Información,* Año 14, April, 1929, pp. 273-283. Santiago de Chile.

KELLER, CARLOS. La eterna crísis chilena. Santiago de Chile, 1931.

KELLER, CARLOS. The Social Evolution of the Chilean People, *Chile,* Vol. 5, 1928, pp. 151-155. New York.

KELLER, CARLOS. Un país al garete. Santiago de Chile, 1932.

KNOCHE, WALTER. Chile. Potsdam, 1931.

LATCHAM, RICARDO A. (hijo). La propiedad entre los indios del valle central de Chile, *La Lectura,* Año 1, July, 1922, pp. 17ff. Santiago de Chile.

LATCHAM, RICARDO E. La existencia de la propiedad en el antiguo imperio de los Incas, *Anales de la Univ. de Chile,* Santiago de Chile, 1923.

LATCHAM, RICARDO E. La organización social y las creencias religiosas de los antiguos araucanos. (Publicaciones del Museo de Etnología y Antropología de Chile, Vol. 3, 1924, pp. 254-268.) Santiago de Chile.

LEÓN, ANTONIO DE. Tratado de confirmaciones de encomiendas. Madrid, 1630.

Ley No. 4169 (also Nos. 4174, 4445, 4496, 4547). See "Government Department Publications" at end of Bibliography.

LILLO, JINÉS DE. Mensuras de tierras. Mss. dated 1603-1604, *in the* Archivo Municipal de Santiago de Chile.

LÓPEZ DE VELASCO, Fr. JUAN. Geografía y descripción universal de las Indias, recopilada por Juan López de Velasco, desde el año 1571 al año de 1574, publicada por primera vez en el Boletín de la Sociedad Geográfica de Madrid con adiciones e ilustraciones por don Justo Zaragoza. Madrid, 1894.

MACCHIAVELLO VARAS, SANTIAGO. Política económica nacional. 2 vols. (*Anales de la Universidad de Chile.*) Santiago de Chile, 1931.

MACKAY, JOHN. That Other America, New York, 1935.

MALDONADO, ROBERTO. Estudios geográficos e hidrográficos sobre Chiloé. Santiago de Chile, 1897.

MARIÑO DE LOVERA, PEDRO. Crónica del reino de Chile. *In* Colección de historiadores de Chile, Vol. 6. Santiago de Chile, 1865.

MARTNER, DANIEL. Estudio de política comercial chilena e historia económica nacional. 2 vols. Santiago de Chile, 1923.

MARTNER, DANIEL. Historia de Chile. Vol. 1: Historia económica. Santiago de Chile, 1929.

MATTHEI, ADOLFO. Landwirtschaft in Chile. Bielefeld und Leipzig, 1929.

McBRIDE, GEORGE McCUTCHEN. Agrarian Indian Communities of Highland Bolivia. (*American Geographical Society Research Series*, No. 5.) New York, 1921.

McBRIDE, GEORGE McCUTCHEN. Land Systems of Mexico. (*American Geographical Society Research Series*, No. 12.) New York, 1923.

MEDINA, JOSÉ TORIBIO. Colección de documentos inéditos para la historia de Chile desde el viaje de Magallanes hasta la batalla de Maipo, 1518-1818. 30 vols. Santiago de Chile, 1896.

Memoria del Ministerio de Fomento. See " Government Department Publications " at end of Bibliography.

MENADIER, JULIO. Estudio sobre las propiedades rústicas en Chile, *Bol. de la Soc. Nac. de Agric.*, Vol. 1, 1867, pp. 67-72; 93-97; 105-109.

Mercurio, El. Daily paper published in Santiago de Chile.

MIERS, JOHN. Travels in Chile and La Plata. 2 vols. London, 1826.

Ministerio . . . etc. For publications see " Government Department Publications " at end of Bibliography.

MONTESSUS DE BALLORE, FERNANDO DE. El valle longitudinal de Chile, *Rev. Chil. de Hist. y Geogr.*, Vol. 37, 1921, pp. 281-301.

MORALEDA Y MONTERO, JOSÉ DE. Memorias de viajes, *Anuario Hidrog. de la Marina de Chile*, Vol. 13, 1888. (Voyages of about 1795.)

MORALES, LUIS JOAQUÍN O. Historia del Huasco. Valparaíso, 1896.

MUTIZÁBAL, ARTURO, and JORGE SCHWARZENBERG. Monografía geográfica e histórica del Archipiélago de Chiloé. Concepción, Chile, 1926.

Nación, La. Daily paper published in Santiago de Chile.

Noticias Agrícolas. Periodical published in 1921.

Oficina Central de Estadística. For publications see " Government Department Publications " at end of Bibliography.

OLIVARES, BENJAMÍN. La subdivisión de la propiedad rural. (*La Agricultura Práctica*, Vol. 1, p. 515.) Santiago de Chile, 1912.

OPAZO GÁLVEZ, AUGUSTO. Como deben esplotar sus cercos nuestros inquilinos. See " Government Department Publications " at end of Bibliography.

OPAZO GÁLVEZ, ROBERTO. Desarrollo agrícola de los territorios situados al sur del río Bío-Bío. (*Sociedad Cooperativa y de Fomento Agrícola, Publicación No. 1*.) Temuco, Chile, 1920.

OPAZO MATURANA, GUSTAVO. Encomiendas del Corregimiento del Maule, *Rev. Chil. de Hist. y Geogr.*, Vol. 50, 1924, pp. 222-243.

OPAZO MATURANA, GUSTAVO. Las terratenencias del Corregimiento del Maule, *Rev. Chil. de Hist. y Geogr.*, Vol. 52, 1927, pp. 94-109.

OVALLE, ALONZO DE. Histórica relación del reyno de Chile. 2 vols. Rome, 1646. English edition: An Historical Relation of the Kingdom of Chile, *included in* A General Collection of the Best and Most Interesting Voyages and Travels in All Parts of the World. Edited by John Pinkerton. Vol. 14. London, 1813.

PALACIOS, NICOLÁS. Raza chilena. 2 vols. Santiago de Chile, 1918.

PÉREZ CANTO, JULIO. Chile. New York, 1912.

PÉREZ ROSALES, VICENTE. Ensayo sobre Chile. Santiago de Chile, 1859.

PÉREZ ROSALES, VICENTE. Recuerdos del pasado, 1814-1860. (Biblioteca de Escritores de Chile.) Santiago de Chile, 1910.

PINOCHET LEBRUN, TANCREDO. Inquilinos en la hacienda de Su Excelencia. Santiago de Chile, 1916.

PINOCHET LEBRUN, TANCREDO. Oligarquía y democracia. Santiago de Chile, 1917.

PLATT, ROBERT S. Items in the Chilean Pattern of Occupance. *Bull. of the Geogr. Soc. of Phila.*, Vol. 32, 1934, pp. 33-41.

POBLETE TRONCOSO, MOISÉS. El problema de la producción agrícola y la política agraria nacional. (*Seminario de Ciencias Económicas de la Universidad de Chile*, Vol. 1.) Santiago de Chile, 1919.

POBLETE TRONCOSO, MOISÉS. Quelques aspects de la politique agraire en Amérique Latine, *Rev. d'Amérique Latine*, Vol. 22, 1931, pp. 304-314.

POMAR, JOSÉ M. La concesión del Aisén y el valle Simpson, *Rev. Chil. de Hist. y Geogr.*, Vol. 45, 1923, pp. 329-368; Vol. 46, 1923, pp. 432-478; Vol. 48, 1923, pp. 160-200.

Primer congreso libre de agricultores de la República de Chile en 1875. Santiago de Chilé, 1876.

Resultados del X Censo. See *X Censo de la Población* in " Government Department Publications " at end of Bibliography.

Revista Agronómica. Santiago de Chile.

Revista Chilena de Historia y Geografía. Quarterly. Began publication in 1911. 75 volumes issued from 1911 to 1934. Santiago de Chile.

Revista de Tierras y Colonización. See " Government Department Publications " at end of Bibliography.

RISO PATRÓN, LUIS. Diccionario jeográfico de Chile. Santiago de Chile, 1924.

ROLDÁN, ALCIBÍADES. El centralismo de la Constitución de 1833, *Rev. Chil. de Hist. y Geogr.*, Vol. 74, 1933, pp. 410-416.

ROORBACH, G. B. How the Chemical Revolution changes Foreign Trade, *Chem. and Metallurgical Engineering*, Vol. 41, No. 2, 1934, pp. 78-80. New York.

ROSALES, Fr. DIEGO DE. Historia general de el reyno de Chile. 3 vols. Valparaíso, 1878.

RUDOLPH, W. E. The New Territorial Divisions of Chile, With Special Reference to Chiloé, *Geogr. Rev.*, Vol. 19, 1929, pp. 61-77.

RUÍZ ALDEA, PEDRO. Los araucanos y sus costumbres. Los Ángeles, Chile, 1868.

RUSCHENBERGER, WILLIAM S. W. Noticias de Chile, 1831-1832 por un Oficial de Marina de los EE. UU. de América. (Trans. by E. Hillman Haviland.) *Rev. Chil. de Hist. y Geogr.*, Vol. 67, 1931, pp. 130-148.

SAAVEDRA, BAUTISTA. El ayllu. Paris, 1913.

SALAS, JOSÉ H. Memoria sobre el servicio personal de los indíjenas y su abolición. Santiago de Chile, 1848.

SANTA CRUZ, JOAQUÍN. Crónica de la provincia de Colchagua, *Rev. Chil. de Hist. y Geogr.*, Vol. 52, 1927, pp. 159-178.

SANTA CRUZ, JOAQUÍN. Los indígenas del Norte de Chile antes de la conquista española, *Rev. Chil. de Hist. y Geogr.*, Vol. 7, 1913, pp. 38-88.

SAYAGO, CARLOS M. Historia de Copiapó. Copiapó, Chile, 1874.

SCHMIDTMEYER, PETER. Travels into Chile: Over the Andes, in the Years 1820 and 1821, With Some Sketches of the Productions and Agriculture, Mines and Metallurgy, Inhabitants, History and Other Features, of America, Particularly of Chile and Arauco. London, 1824.

SCHNEIDER, TEODORO. La agricultura en Chile. Santiago de Chile, 1904.

SCHWARZENBERG, JORGE, and ARTURO MUTIZÁBAL. Monografía geográfica e histórica del Archipiélago de Chiloé. Concepción, Chile, 1926.

SCOTT ELLIOTT, G. F. See ELLIOTT, G. F. SCOTT.

SHAW, PAUL VANORDEN. The Early Constitutions of Chile. New York, 1930.

SIMPSON, LESLEY BYRD. The Encomienda in New Spain. (*University of California Publications in History*, Vol. 19.) Berkeley, 1929.

Sinopsis Estadística. See " Government Department Publications " at end of Bibliography.

Sociedad Agrícola del Norte, Boletín de la. See *Boletín de la . . .*

Sociedad del Canal de Maipo. Antecedentes y documentos relativos a la apertura del Canal de San Carlos de Maipo y a la formación de la sociedad. Santiago de Chile, 1902.

Sociedad Esplotadora de Tierra del Fuego. Memoria presentada a la asamblea general ordinaria de accionistas, en Septiembre 21, 1928. Valparaíso, 1928.

Sociedad Esplotadora de Tierra del Fuego. Memoria presentada a la asamblea general ordinaria de accionistas, en Septiembre 26, 1929. Valparaíso, 1929.

Sociedad Nacional de Agricultura, Boletín de la. Began publication in 1869. Santiago de Chile.

Sociedad Nacional de Agricultura. Informe presentado a la Misión Kemmerer en Agosto, 1925, *Bol. de la Soc. Nac. de Agric.,* 1925, pp. 415-433. Santiago de Chile, 1926.

SOLORZANO PEREIRA, JUAN DE. De la política indiana. Antwerp, 1703.

SOTO ROJAS, SALVADOR. Apuntes para la historia agrícola de Chile, *La Agricultura Práctica,* 1915, pp. 178ff. Santiago de Chile.

STEFFEN, HANS. Westpatagonien. 2 vols. Berlin, 1919.

TESILLO, SANTIAGO DE. Guerra de Chile, causas de su duración, Advertencias para su fin, ejemplificado en el gobierno de Don Francisco Lazo de la Vega. Madrid, 1647. *Reprinted in* Colección de historiadores de Chile, Vol. 5. Santiago de Chile, 1865.

THAYER OJEDA, LUIS. Las antiguas ciudades de Chile. Santiago de Chile, 1911.

THAYER OJEDA, LUIS. Apuntes para historia económica y social durante el período de la conquista de Chile, 1540-1565, *Rev. Chil. de Hist. y Geogr.,* Vol. 34, 1920, pp. 174-222.

THAYER OJEDA, LUIS. Los conquistadores españoles. 3 vols. Santiago de Chile, 1913.

THAYER OJEDA, LUIS. Elementos étnicos que han intervenido en la población de Chile. Santiago de Chile, 1919.

THAYER OJEDA, TOMÁS. Santiago durante el siglo XVI. Santiago de Chile, 1905.

THOMSON, C. A. Chile's Struggle for National Recovery, *Foreign Policy Reports,* Vol. 9, 1934, No. 25, pp. 282-292. New York.

TORREALBA, A. La propiedad rural de la zona central de Chile. Santiago de Chile, 1917.

TORRES SALDAMANDO, ENRIQUE. Apuntes históricos sobre las encomiendas del Perú, Libro Primero de Cabildos de Lima, Segunda Parte, Apéndices, No. 2, pp. 93-158. Lima, 1888.

TORRES SALDAMANDO, ENRIQUE. Los títulos de Castilla en las familias de Chile. Santiago de Chile, 1894.

TRIBALDOS DE TOLEDO, LUIS. Vista jeneral de las continuadas guerras: difícil conquista del gran reino, provincias de Chile. (Written about 1634.) *In* Colección de historiadores de Chile, Vol. 4. Santiago de Chile, 1864.

Tribuna del Sur, La. Temuco, Chile.

UHLE, MAX. Los indios atacameños, *Rev. Chil. de Hist. y Geogr.,* Vol. 5, 1913, pp. 105-111.

VALENZUELA O., JUVENAL (Edit.). Álbum de informaciones agrícolas, 3 vols.: Zona Central de Chile; Zona Austral de Chile; Zona Norte de Chile. Santiago de Chile, 1925.

VALENZUELA, LIZARDO. El corregimiento de Colchagua, *Rev. Chil. de Hist. y Geogr.*, Vol. 63, 1929, pp. 173-204.

VARGAS, H. De la subdivisión de la propiedad. Santiago de Chile, 1926.

VELASCO, FANOR, and RICARDO DONOSO. Historia de la constitución de la Propiedad Austral. Santiago de Chile, 1928.

VENTURINO, AGUSTÍN. Sociología chilena. Barcelona, 1929.

VICUÑA MACKENNA, BENJAMÍN. La hacienda de San Isidro, *Bol. de Agric.*, Vol. 5, pp. 337-353.

VICUÑA MACKENNA, BENJAMÍN. Historia crítica y social de la ciudad de Santiago. 2 vols. Valparaíso, 1869.

VICUÑA MACKENNA, BENJAMÍN. Relaciones históricas. 2 vols. Santiago de Chile, 1877.

VICUÑA SUBERCASEAUX, BENJAMÍN. El socialismo revolucionario y la cuestión social en Europa y en Chile. Santiago de Chile, 1908.

WEBER, ALFREDO. Chiloé: su estado actual, su colonización, su porvenir (con un mapa que indica las colonias estrangeras y los terrenos colonizables). Santiago de Chile, 1903.

WILLIAMS, MARY W. The People and Politics of Latin America. Boston, 1930.

GOVERNMENT DEPARTMENT PUBLICATIONS

Anuario Estadístico de la República de Chile. Dirección General de Estadística. Vol. 7, Agricultura, 1923-1924. Santiago de Chile, 1925. *Ibid.*, 1925-1926. Santiago de Chile, 1926.

Boletín del Ministerio de la Propiedad Austral. Año 1. Santiago de Chile, 1930.

Boletín de los Servicios Agrícolas. Published quarterly. Dirección General de los Servicios Agrícolas. Santiago de Chile, 1925-1927.

X Censo de la Población (1930). Vols. 1 and 2. Vol. 2 entitled *Resultados del X Censo de la Población.* Dirección General de Estadística. Santiago de Chile, 1931.

Como deben esplotar sus cercos nuestros inquilinos, *by* Augusto Opazo Gálvez. Dirección General de los Servicios Agrícolas, *Boletín* No. 102. Santiago de Chile, 1923.

Constitución de la Propiedad Austral, Folletos Nos. 1 y 2. Dirección General de Tierras y Colonización. Santiago de Chile, 1926.

Contrato de trabajo, El. Recopilación completa de leyes, reglamentos y decretos vigentes. Santiago de Chile, 1927.

Diario Oficial de la República de Chile. Santiago de Chile.
División territorial de la República de Chile. Santiago de Chile, 1929.
Estadística agrícola. Dirección General de Estadística. Santiago de Chile, 1928.
Estudio agronómico del Departamento de Caupolicán, *by* Benjamín Acuña A. Ministerio de Fomento, Departmento de Agricultura, Servicio de Divulgación y Propaganda Agrícola, [*Publication*] *No. 166.* Santiago de Chile, 1929.
Estudio agronómico del Departamento de Ovalle. Ministerio de Fomento, Departamento de Agricultura, Servicio de Divulgación y Propaganda Agrícola, [*Publication*] *No. 156.* Santiago de Chile, 1928.
Estudio agronómico del Departamento de San Fernando, *by* Benjamín Acuña A. and Arturo Merino E. Ministerio de Fomento, Departamento de Agricultura, Servicio de Divulgación y Propaganda Agrícola, [*Publication*] *No. 152.* Santiago de Chile, 1928.
Estudio sobre el estado de la agricultura chilena. Ministerio de Fomento. Santiago de Chile, 1929.
Folletos Nos. 1, 2, 3. Ministerio de Fomento, Departamento de Tierras y Colonización. Santiago de Chile, 1928.
Ley No. 4169 y reglamento sobre división de comunidades y radicación de indígenas. Ministerio de Fomento, Departamento de Tierras y Colonización. Santiago de Chile, 1928.
Ley No. 4174, Impuesto a los bienes raices. Santiago de Chile, 1928.
Ley No. 4445, Legislación sobre regadío. Santiago de Chile, 1928.
Ley No. 4496, y su reglamento. Caja de Colonización Agrícola. Santiago de Chile, 1929.
Ley No. 4547, Sobre arrendamiento de terrenos magallánicos. Santiago de Chile, 1929.
Memoria del Ministerio de Fomento, 1928. Santiago de Chile, 1929.
Proyectos de reforma de la constitución política de la República de Chile. Santiago de Chile, 1925.
Resultados del X Censo de la Población. See *X Censo de la Población* supra.
Revista de Tierras y Colonización. Departamento de Tierras y Colonización. Santiago de Chile, 1928. (Apparently only one number issued, August 1, 1928.)
Sinopsis estadística de la República de Chile. Oficina Central de Estadística. Santiago de Chile, 1926.

INDEX

INDEX